Culture and Consensus

John Ruskin: The Argument of the Eye
Ruskin and Venice
New Approaches to Ruskin (ed.)
Under Siege: Literary Life in London 1939–45
In Anger: Culture in the Cold War 1945–60
Irreverence, Scurrility, Profanity, Vilification and Licentious Abuse:
  Monty Python – The Case Against
Footlights! A Hundred Years of Cambridge Comedy
Too Much: Art and Society in the Sixties 1960–75
The Heritage Industry: Britain in a Climate of Decline
Future Tense: A New Art for the Nineties

Robert Hewison

Culture and Consensus

England, art and politics
since 1940

Methuen

First published in Great Britain in 1995
by Methuen London
This revised edition published in 1997 by Methuen London
an imprint of Reed International Books Ltd
Michelin House, 81 Fulham Road, London SW3 6RB
and Auckland, Melbourne, Singapore and Toronto

A CIP catalogue record for this book
is available at the British Library
ISBN 0 413 71430 6

Phototypeset by Intype, London
Printed and bound in Great Britain
by Clays Ltd, St Ives plc

For Alexandra, Vita and Greta

Contents

Illustrations

1. *Annus Horribilis*: St George's Hall, Windsor, after the fire, November 1992.
2. Royal romance: Windsor Castle after being Gothickised by Wyatville.
3. Deep England: 'The South Downs', Army Bureau of Current Affairs wartime poster.
4. Blitzed Britain: still from Humphrey Jennings's film, *Family Portrait*.
5. New Britain: The Skylon and the Dome of Discovery on the South Bank, 1951.
6. Old Britain: a page from the Festival of Britain's South Bank exhibition guidebook.
7. New Elizabethanism: Cecil Beaton's official Coronation photograph of Queen Elizabeth II, 1953.
8. The Englishness of English architecture: the interior of Coventry Cathedral, 1962.
9. Swinging London: Pop goes the Union Jack.
10. *Nouvelle vague*: The painter Peter Phillips in Ken Russell's 'Pop Goes the Easel' for the BBC's *Monitor* 1962.
11. Cultural struggle: demonstration outside the American Embassy, Grosvenor Square, 1968.
12. Racial struggle: Notting Hill Gate Carnival, 1977.
13. Punk Britannia: Derek Jarman's film *Jubilee*, 1977.
14. Mutilated monarchy: Jamie Reid's record sleeve for the Sex Pistols' 'God Save the Queen', 1977.
15. Radical collage: Photomontage from *Temporary Hoarding*, August 1981.
16. Iron Britannia: Margaret Thatcher test-driving a Challenger Tank, 1988.

Acknowledgements

As a journalist and critic, I have had access to many of the personalities and more recent events referred to in this book, and I am very grateful to the people and institutions that have made this possible. I would like to thank in particular three people who gave me information specifically in relation to this study: Boris Ford, the Earl of Harewood, and David Mellor MP. I should also like to thank David Mills, editor of 'The Culture' section of the *Sunday Times*, who has enabled me to follow my enthusiasms while earning a living, as well as giving me an outlet for my ideas. Between 1988 and 1992 I also presented more than a hundred editions of the 'Issues' strand of *Third Ear* on BBC Radio Three, the majority of them produced by Julian Hale, and I would like to thank him and my other producers for the access to people and events which the programme gave me. I have also much enjoyed my work as a Visiting Professor in the School of Arts and Humanities at De Montfort University since 1993.

I would like to thank my friends Chris Orr, Chris Barlas and Paddy O'Sullivan for the fruitful and enjoyable discussions I have had with them, and my agent Michael Sissons for his advice and encouragement. To the publisher and editor of now no fewer than eight of my books, Geoffrey Strachan, I owe a very special debt indeed, for his commitment to what I can only call "real publishing" during a period that has seen the book business go through an upheaval as thorough as anything experienced by official cultural institutions. I would also like to thank Mary O'Donovan for her work in preparing text and illustrations for the press. Lastly and most sincerely, I thank my wife Erica for her patience and good humour during a parturition of excessive length.

Earlier versions of some sections of the book have appeared in *Enterprise and Heritage*, edited by J. Corner and Sylvia Harvey (Routledge, 1991); *Britten's Gloriana: Essays and Sources*, edited by Paul Banks for the Britten-Pears Library and Boydell Press (1993); *The Major Effect*, edited by Anthony Seldon and Dennis Kavanagh (Macmillan, 1994); *The Arts in the World Economy*, edited by Charles A. Riley (University of New England Press, 1994), and various editions of the *Sunday Times*. I would also like to acknowledge the stimulus of an annual invitation from Peter Catterall of the Institute of Contemporary British History to contribute an article on 'The Political Economy of the Arts' to the successive volumes of the ICBH's *Contemporary Britain* since it was launched in 1990.

The quotation from T. S. Eliot's 'Little Gidding' (p. 24) in his *Collected Poems 1909–1962* is by permission of the author's estate and Faber and Faber Ltd, as is the quotation from Philip Larkin's 'Going Going' (p. 10) in *High Windows* (1974).

The author and publishers would also like to thank the copyright holders for their kind permission to reproduce the illustrations in this book:

1 Camera Press London (ref. X 13175–1); 2 The Royal Collection/ Her Majesty the Queen; 3 Frank Newbould/The Trustees of the Imperial War Museum, London (ref. MH 13415); 4 H. Usill/British Film Institute (ref. 177885); 5 Central Office of Information; 6 Page from *The South Bank Exhibition: A Guide to the Story It Tells* by Ian Cox, HMSO, 1951; 7 Cecil Beaton/Camera Press London (ref. 00135954); 8 Keystone/Hulton Deutsch Collection Ltd (ref. 04112112); 9 Keystone/Hulton Deutsch Collection Ltd (ref. 04120003); 10 Monitor/BBC/Hulton Deutsch (ref. 01012265); 11 John Minihan/Evening Standard Collection/Hulton Deutsch Collection Ltd (ref. 02812495); 12 Colin Davey/Hulton Deutsch Collection Ltd (ref. 04112102); 13 Jean Marc Prouveur/British Film Institute (ref. 193077); 16 Patrick Piel/Frank Spooner Pictures London; 17 Anthony Andrews/Jeremy Irons/Diana Quick/Granada Television; 18 Adam Woolfitt/Robert Harding Picture Library (ref. 508/17792); 19 Robin Barton/Blueprint Magazine; 20 Hulton Deutsch Collection Ltd

Introduction

'Let it be no more said that States Encourage Arts,
for it is the Arts That Encourage States.'

William Blake

One of the many incentives to write this book was a conversation in
October 1991 with an official of the British Council. The Council –
Britain's cultural representative overseas – was, like every institution
with a liberal tradition of independence from government, undergoing
the uncomfortable process of adjustment to the ideology of "value for
money" that the Conservative administration had been forcing upon
it. The British Council officer, a senior policy-maker, said in essence
that the argument for the value of the arts was being allowed to go by
default. Governments, bureaucrats and ordinary people had the right
to ask why art was important, and more especially why it should be
financially supported. Yet the "intelligentsia" replied that the arts were
the arts, and no one had the right to question what artists were doing.
The argument that the work of artists serves a purpose, not in banal
material terms, but as part of the dialogue within and between nations,
and that the arts were the best means of introducing new ideas into a
society, was not being heard.

Instead, commercial arguments of the instrumental, "value for
money", job-creation-tourism-and-business-sponsorship kind were
allowed to fill the gap. Yet, the official argued, institutions like the
Treasury and the Foreign Office – as well as taxpayers, who might well
want to know the reasons for the National Theatre getting money that
would have been better spent on the National Health Service – were
prepared to listen, if a case were made.

One of the themes of this book is the argument that culture, and
cultural policy, have become increasingly important during the second
half of the twentieth century, and that they will be even more important
after the approaching millennium. This is not, however, for the economic reasons that have dominated public discussion since the early
eighties. Far from the arts being part of the social superstructure built

upon a base of economic activity, they form the frame upon which all other activities depend, for culture – of which the work of artists is the most easily identifiable manifestation – is the shaping, moral medium for all society's activities, including the economic. Hence the quotation from William Blake as the epigraph to this introduction.

Ultimately, I argue that the culture of an individual, group or nation is not merely an expression of personal, collective or national identity, it *is* that identity. It follows that a nation's culture is not a purely private matter nor a marginal public responsibility, but vital to national existence. As I argue in my final chapter, this has become generally recognised over the past half century – belatedly in Britain by the creation of the Department of National Heritage in 1992. Yet the "public culture" that has emerged is in many ways unsatisfactory. As the British Council officer pointed out, economic considerations have outweighed the more important social and moral responsibilities that those who make public policy bear.

I believe that the state has a responsibility to nurture and protect the work of artists, and that may well call for subsidy and the calculation of economic return, but governments are equally influential in terms of shaping cultural attitudes in other ways, through education, information and encouragement. Beyond the acknowledgement of the state's responsibility for the quality of a nation's cultural life, we need to develop a value system which not only asserts, but guarantees, the existence of a common interest in the health of the arts. For too long those for whom art is important have indeed allowed the defence of culture to go by default. Whereas what is plainly needed is a new argument for the arts.

Throughout Europe, and indeed most of the developed world, there is a crisis of identity – national, regional, local, personal – which artists, writers and performers are uniquely qualified to address. This is a political question, but only in the arts can these issues be confronted at the level at which they arise, at the level of the individual imagination, at the level where consciousness of being part of a society is formed. If we understand art in these terms – which by no means ignore its purely aesthetic value and its frequently oppositional relationship to the society within which it is generated – then the case for the arts begins to be made.

To understand how the present status and condition of the arts were arrived at in the British – or more specifically, English – context, it is necessary to go back to the point when a British government first took on a formal and general responsibility for the arts in January 1940. 1940 was a pivotal moment in British history, and it is not accidental that the decision to found the Council for the Encouragement of Music and the Arts was taken in that year. There are many examples of government cultural patronage that precede that date, from the foundation of the British Museum in 1753 to the formation of the British Broadcasting Corporation in 1927, but 1940 marks the beginning of the modern period in official British cultural policy.

Some readers may know that the beginning of the Second World War is the starting date for a trilogy of books I have already published: *Under Siege: Literary Life in London 1939–45*; *In Anger: Culture in the Cold War 1945–60*, and *Too Much: Art and Society in the Sixties 1960–75*. I have also published two further studies, *The Heritage Industry* and *Future Tense*, which, though differently focused, continue the account of the arts in Britain into the nineties. While the three surveys and the two more polemical books have obviously prepared the ground for a history of the period, however, this new book is in no way the compendium volume that digests the previous titles.

In my earlier survey of the years 1939 to 1975 I tried to cover as many art forms as I could manage. Here, I have deliberately chosen to concentrate more narrowly on a number of key cases in succeeding decades which serve as exemplars for my argument. While the institutional history of the Arts Council of Great Britain (which, ironically, ceased to exist as I was completing my work in 1994) is a constant thread, the examples I have chosen come from very different art forms. That one of the earliest of these is a grand opera, and one of the later, the moment of punk, says something about the shifting nature of cultural activity, and the critical approaches taken to it, over the past fifty years.

The principal method of the book is to analyse three areas: firstly, the theoretical definition of culture at a particular moment and how it has continued to change since the heydays of T. S. Eliot and F. R. Leavis; secondly, the extent to which these definitions were translated across the decades into institutional practices – for instance the creation of the BBC Third Programme in the forties – and thirdly, the relationship between these ideas and institutions and the creativity they encouraged or neglected. Between 1940 and today at least three generations have had their say in the cultural debate, and as the national situation has changed politically and economically, there has naturally been a shifting field of argument and practice.

The shape of the book is governed by this triple narrative on the development of intellectual, institutional and cultural history, but the narrative is both preceded and followed by two partially theoretical chapters. The first introduces my own theoretical approach; the last tries to draw some forward-looking conclusions. As the first chapter is in itself an introduction to what follows, I will only briefly summarise the argument here. The key concept is that of consensus: that is, the broad national political agreement that has kept Britain's social and economic institutions functioning throughout the shifts of power between Labour and Conservative governments since the war, once it had emerged in its particular modern form during the wartime National Coalition government of 1940 to 1945.

I draw a parallel between the distinctively British and empirical notion of "consensus" and the more theoretical concept, familiar across the Channel, of "hegemony". This is the means by which a state is governed by a ruling group or class which exercises power through a leadership based on compromises with, and concessions to, other interests and classes that are calculated to produce consent, without it being necessary to deploy the coercive powers which governments also have at their disposal.

The reality of all democratic government is that it is always a shifting balance of compromises both within the ruling group (be it a single party or a coalition) and between other political parties, economic interests and the various "estates" which influence public opinion. It follows that the consensus will always be partial and shifting. The shape of the national consensus is reflected in the results of periodic general elections, but it is in constant movement. British history since 1940 has seen several changes in the ruling consensus: a consensus in favour of revolutionary change led to the election of the Labour government in 1945, but this gave way to a more conservative and deferential consensus as pre-war social values were partially restored in the fifties. This in turn was gradually supplanted, from 1956 onwards, by a pro-gressive consensus demanding liberalisation and reform. By the seventies, however, when profound changes began to affect most of the developed world – economically, the shift to a post-industrial order, culturally, the shift from modernism to post-modernism – the broad post-war consensus began to break down entirely.

The result of the social and economic crises of the seventies was the election in 1979 of a Conservative government dedicated to halting Britain's economic decline, and determined to establish a new consensus around the ideas of economic individualism and enterprise. Paradoxically, the new Prime Minister, Margaret Thatcher, saw the very notion of consensus as an obstacle to progress, and through her policies undermined many of the civil institutions, such as the BBC, which had originally been developed to administer and create consensus. Three more Conservative election victories in a row were a measure of the extent to which the eighties saw a shift in the terms upon which Britain was governed; but the growth of the power of a centralising government has left the country in the hands of a hegemony prepared to use economic and legal coercion as well as seek consent. The dramatic increase in the number of non-government organisations nonetheless controlled by government appointees represents the alarming development of a parallel administration controlled by the party in power but outwith the democratic process.

The decline of consensus is one of the sources of the widespread dissatisfaction and anxiety that surfaced during the pivotal year of 1992, with which the book opens. It is a function of consensus to agree the terms in which a nation chooses to see itself. The breakdown of consensus leaves the nation with a weakened sense of its own identity, and therefore uncertain as to what the right course of action in any given situation should be. 1992 saw such a crisis, most specifically a crisis for the identity of the monarchy, which remains unresolved.

One of the reasons for the survival of the British monarchy into the late twentieth century has been that it supplies a convenient symbol of identity for a hybrid nation. It follows that a crisis in the monarchy is a crisis for national identity. The crisis is not only political and constitutional, it is profoundly cultural, for it is through such emblems as the Crown that the British make sense of the world, and of themselves.

A society's culture – which is an active process, not an inert collection of objects – supplies the medium for the interaction between the real and the imaginary, the historical and the mythical, the achieved and the desired, that constitutes the daily management of the social consensus. Culture shapes the context in which other social practices such as economic activity, politics and litigation take place. A country's culture is the means both of expressing national identity and maintaining – or challenging – political consensus.

This explains why the coupling in my title, *Culture and Consensus*, is followed by the triad *England, art and politics*. 'England', in this instance, stands for identity, and specifically English identity, for it is the English on this island, traditionally dominant in the national consensus, who now appear most uncertain about their identity and place in the world as the twentieth century closes.

Art and politics, together with ideas of Englishness, have mediated the relationship between British culture and consensus in the period under review. This book makes no predictions, but what does seem certain is that Britain is on the point of a change as significant as that of 1945, 1953, 1964 or 1979, if only because we are moving towards the fresh start symbolically presented by the year 2001. It is unlikely that, whatever the nature of the change, the transition will be smooth. The current crisis of national identity is one indication of the stresses that change brings, but a moment of crisis is also a moment of opportunity. In the field of cultural policy, it is an opportunity to examine critically what has been achieved in the more than fifty years since 1940, in order to prepare a fresh start. This book is intended as a contribution both to that process of examination, and to the argument that the arts have a value for society that places them at the top and not the bottom of the political agenda.

College House Cottage
January 1995
(revised, December 1996)

Note to the revised edition.
The publication of a paperback edition has allowed me to correct some errors, and substantially revise my final chapter to take into account developments that have taken place in the two years since the text was first completed. I am still convinced that Britain is at a point of change, but I have lost some of my optimism about the outcome of that change.

I

Dis-United Kingdom
Britain in the 1990s

'Friday 20 November 1992 was a day of high drama that will not be soon forgotten by the Queen, by Windsor or the nation. The Sovereign spent her forty-fifth wedding anniversary, in the fortieth year of her reign, working alongside her staff and subjects rescuing priceless treasures from her much-loved home as the ruinous flames licked the Castle and dense smoke billowed across the town and down the Thames Valley. The blaze became visible for miles around and the smell of burning hung in the air.'[1]

So begins an anonymous account of the fire that broke out in the north-east wing of Windsor Castle, destroying St George's Hall, the Grand Reception Room, the Private Chapel, the Crimson Drawing Room and the State Drawing Room (illustration 1). (More banally, the fire also damaged or destroyed fifty-eight staff bedrooms, eighteen bathrooms and twenty-six ancillary rooms, and affected the Great Kitchen.) Because the wing was undergoing improvements at the time many treasures had been removed, and others were got out undamaged. Only one painting was lost to the flames.

Nonetheless, this was a disaster for 'Britain's proud symbol of Royalty and national heritage', as the souvenir on sale at Windsor Castle records.[2] The symbolic significance of the event was recognised by witnesses of the fire interviewed on television, and by newspaper editorials in the following days. For the Queen, it was the latest blow to strike her during what she called, in a speech at the Guildhall in London four days later, her *Annus Horribilis*. This had begun with the divorce in April of her daughter Princess Anne, followed by the separation of her son, Prince Andrew, from the Duchess of York; the publication of a damaging biography of her daughter-in-law the Princess of Wales; topless pictures of the Duchess of York in the popular press; and public discontent about the Queen's exemption from income tax. As if the burning of one of her homes were not enough, on 9 December the Palace had to announce the formal separation of Prince Charles and the Princess of Wales. To cap it all, on 23 December the *Sun* published a leaked copy of the Queen's Christmas message.

In Britain what happens to Royalty touches everybody. Shortly before the fire at Windsor Castle, Andrew Morton, author of *Diana: Her True Story*, the book which had done so much to publicise the breakdown in the marriage of the future King and Queen of England, declared on the front page of the *Sunday Express*: 'The Royal Family as a model of exemplary family life has collapsed. Essentially, people in Britain are coming to terms with the collapse of this strand of ideology of the monarchy in the same way the Russians are coming to terms with the collapse of communism.'[3] But the *Annus Horribilis* of 1992 was not exclusively royal. The political editor of the *Sunday Times*, Michael Jones, quoted a (necessarily) anonymous government minister: 'We are losing our reference points. Everywhere you look, the country's institutions seem to be falling apart.'[4] It was a fair comment. The anticipated divorce of the Prince and Princess of Wales would have constitutional repercussions on the Church of England: the established national church but no longer the largest, let alone the majority church in the land, declining in numbers and wealth, and still divided within itself over the ordination of women, a decision finally taken in November 1992.

In the same year a number of successful appeals against conviction had shown the judiciary to be fallible and policemen corrupt. A politicised Civil Service was known to be willing to be "economical with the truth", and had lost its reputation for probity and commitment to the continuity of impartial administration regardless of the politicians of the day. The Bank of England had been called into question as a result of the scandalous collapse of the Bank of Credit and Commerce International, which went into liquidation in January 1992 as a result of the biggest banking fraud in history. The activities of Robert Maxwell, the newspaper owner and entrepreneur who had mysteriously drowned in November 1991, turned out to be a massive deception which had robbed the pension funds of the *Mirror* group. Lloyds of London appeared to be not much more than an incompetently managed gambling den run by untrustworthy croupiers who produced a loss of £1.5 billion in 1992, with further losses to follow.

Against the background of the longest economic recession since the thirties and what appeared to be a permanently postponed recovery, on the 'Black Wednesday' of 16 September 1992, international speculators forced Britain's withdrawal from the European Exchange Rate mechanism, producing a *de facto* devaluation in sterling of thirteen per cent. The economic insecurity which had begun with the "restructuring" of the manufacturing industry in the seventies and the establishment of long-term, mass unemployment in the eighties had spread to all levels of society with the collapse of the housing market and the rising rate of redundancies in management and the professions. Collectively, the fundamental assumptions upon which British institutions had operated since the Second World War no longer seemed to be valid; daily the pretences that sustained them were exposed. The fire at Windsor, caused by an incautiously placed electric lamp, seemed to be just one more indication of national incompetence. As Ian Jack commented in the *Independent on Sunday* while the embers of St George's Hall still smouldered: 'Nothing seems to work as it used to: government, trains, banks, courts, the economy, the monarchy. Now even a royal palace blazes in the night. Fate frowns down.'[5]

At times of stress and apparent national breakdown, it is a characteristic response to seek refuge and reassurance in the past. The Prime Minister, John Major, took this course when he announced at the 1993 Conservative Party conference: 'It is time to return to core values, time to get back to basics, to self-discipline and the law.' The anonymous memorialist of the Windsor fire could not fail to strike tiny echoes of the social solidarity of the Blitz. The Queen was described as 'working alongside her staff and subjects', while a large malachite urn, a gift from Tsar Nicholas I of Russia to Queen Victoria, which stood out among the ruins of the Grand Reception Room, seemed 'to have survived as a symbol of endurance amid the awesome destruction', an image evoking the survival of St Paul's under enemy fire.[6] Evocations of the past can also, however, serve to throw the present into an even gloomier light. Lord Goodman, former chairman of the Arts Council, a grand panjandrum at the nexus of cultural and political life from the fifties to the nineties, told an interviewer: 'You couldn't have been here during the war without developing an enormous respect for the British. They were at their very best when they were hardest tried. All that has, I'm sorry to say, evaporated. It's vanished. For instance, we have no leadership of any quality at the moment, political or moral.'[7]

Goodman's point was made when John Major's moralising 'Back to

Basics' campaign collapsed in ignominy in 1994 in the face of ministerial resignations over sexual misconduct, allegations of corruption in
local government and vicious in-fighting in the Conservative Party over
Britain's relations with the European Union. After 1993 proved a
further year of economic depression and political uncertainty, commentators both on the Left – Martin Jacques, former editor of *Marxism
Today* – and on the Right – Lord Rees-Mogg, former editor of *The
Times* – almost simultaneously detected signs of a national nervous
breakdown. Jacques blamed the country's anxiety on a lack of political
will to change and on 'the state of national depression. The latter
induces a mood of hopelessness, of can't do rather than can do.
National demoralisation is not so different in its effects from personal
depression. It leads to introversion, resignation and privatism.'[8] Rees-
Mogg concurred: 'We have to understand the public mood. If one were
dealing with an individual rather than a nation, the diagnosis would be
only too obvious. The British are showing the symptoms of clinical
depression. There is the feeling of futility, the feeling that no exertion
is worth making. There is the feeling of irritability: we are quick to turn
on each other . . . There is a lack of vitality, both in the Government and
in the nation itself.'[9]

What both Jacques and Rees-Mogg recognised was that their country
was going through a crisis of identity. Britain was not alone in suffering
problems of adjustment to a rapidly changing world. The art critic
Robert Hughes has made a similar point about the United States,
commenting on 'the profoundly unsettled state of American culture,
the crises of cultural identity that come with the dissolution of the
binary world held in place for forty years by the left and right jaws of
the Cold War's iron clamp'.[10] The causes of Britain's discontent were
internal as well as external, and the domestic crisis of the monarchy
was a crisis articulating that discontent. As the critic Marina Warner
argued in her 1994 *Reith Lectures*, 'the Queen symbolises the imaginary
personality of the nation'. That the monarchy's political function
appeared to be largely ceremonial only served to enhance its psychological authority: 'The monarchy's symbolic role in the country's sense
of identity has grown as its political power has withered.'[11] But the
Annus Horribilis of 1992 revealed a serious dysfunction between the
image of the emblematic mother of the nation and the real-life head of
an unhappy and wayward family. The symbolic order of the nation was
disturbed.

This was revealed by an unexpected response to the damage to Windsor Castle as 'Britain's proud symbol of Royalty and national heritage'. According to the memorialist, 'the hearts of the nation went out to the Sovereign',[12] but when the Secretary of State for National Heritage, Peter Brooke, announced even before the fires were out that the Government would bear the entire cost of the repairs – then put at sixty million pounds – the nation seemed reluctant to put its hand in its pocket. There was a general feeling of resentment that the Queen, believed to be the wealthiest woman in the world, and paying no tax, should make no contribution, and both Labour and Conservative Members of Parliament argued that the Queen should meet the bill. The trust fund opened by Brooke to receive donations from the public towards the cost of repairs raised only twenty-five thousand pounds in three months. Six days after the fire it was announced that the Queen would, from the following April, pay tax on her private income and pay for the public duties of all members of the Royal Family except Prince Philip and the Queen Mother, who would continue to be financed through the civil list. The Queen would, however, continue to receive until 2001 £7.9 million a year from the civil list, plus all the services provided by government departments such as the royal yacht, the Queen's flight and the royal train. In 1991 the total cost of the monarchy was put at fifty-seven million pounds a year; the Queen's private fortune was estimated at anything between £1.2 and £6.5 billion.

The issue of who should pay for the cost of the Windsor fire exposed confusion about the actual ownership of the emblems of national identity and heritage. Peter Brooke was technically right to tell the House of Commons that, unlike Balmoral and Sandringham which were the personal property of the Queen, Windsor Castle, 'a major state building, and a unique asset and attraction of our national heritage' and 'a world-famous symbol of this country', was a government responsibility, for an act of 1831 had made it so.[13] But it was also the Queen's 'home', and parts of it were decidedly off-limits, even to responsible officials of the government, such as English Heritage. One indirect cause of the fire was that, just as the Queen had been immune from taxation, the building, being Crown property, was immune from normal health and safety regulations. Fire prevention officers did not have the usual right of access, any more than the staff of English Heritage who had wanted to make surveys for conservation purposes while repair work was being carried out in the three years before the fire. (In 1992 the Royal Household had received £21.6 million from the Government for repairs and maintenance.) Windsor Castle was a Grade 1 listed building, but English Heritage, responsible for the listing, was not allowed to inspect it. How "national", then, was the national heritage?

As the loyal memorialist of the fire pointed out, 1992 was the fortieth anniversary of the Queen's accession to the throne on 6 February 1952, and she may have sensed that the anniversary might be an occasion which, if overemphasised, could prove counter-productive. A Buckingham Palace statement had asked that any public celebration in the manner of the 1977 Jubilee should be held back until her Golden Jubilee in 2002. A proposal for a commemorative fountain in Parliament Square was quietly squashed. The centre-piece of the anniversary, with which she co-operated (and over which she had total control), was the television documentary *Elizabeth R*. Significantly, this did not feature her family or private life. It was a return to regality, focused on the Sovereign herself, showing her as a *working* monarch – if not exactly the chief executive then the chairman of the firm, actively engaged in the enterprise of monarchy.

While British television had remained for the most part deferential, a key factor in the crisis of royal authority was the shift in attitude in the popular press, though less towards the Queen herself than to her family, including the couple who were expected to be King and Queen one day. This crisis had been a long time coming. As early as 1955 the journalist Malcolm Muggeridge had warned in the *New Statesman* that 'the Royal Family ought to be properly advised on how to prevent themselves and their lives becoming a sort of royal soap opera', which by the end of the eighties it had indeed become.[14] In 1982 the Queen asked newspaper editors to show restraint in their coverage of the Royal Family, but by 1993 Prince Charles and the Princess of Wales had become figures in a circulation war between the *Sun* and the *Daily Mirror*, while their respective households appeared to be conducting their own civil war over public popularity.

By revealing the private weaknesses of the actual Royal Family, the press, responding to the curiosity of their readers, were also eroding the pillars that supported the symbolic monarchy. For nearly two hundred years, the British had found their collective sense of identity through their attachment to what was both a real and a symbolic object, the Crown. Writing at a time when the Queen appeared content to allow the media to reinforce her allegorical power, the social critic Tom Nairn commented: 'Both the genesis of the contemporary monarchy and its apparently unstoppable popularity are quite clearly phenomena of *national* rather than merely social significance. They are elements in a drama of unresolved national identity.'[15] The Crown and the metaphor of the Royal Family have given a sense of belonging that obscures questions of equality, rights and the distribution of power. With the emblematic family in disarray, an unresolved national identity becomes unstable.

In theory, the damage done to the monarchy's symbolic status should not affect its constitutional position, but when describing that position, even the Government's official handbook, issued by the Central Office of Information, begins by using symbolism that would not have been out of place among the courtiers of Elizabeth I: 'The Queen personifies the State.' In law, the handbook continues, 'she is head of the executive, an integral part of the legislature, head of the judiciary, the commander-in-chief of all the armed forces of the Crown and the "supreme governor" of the established Church of England'.[16] In spite of the progressive limitation of the Crown's absolute power: 'The Queen still takes part in some important acts of government. These include summoning, proroguing . . . and dissolving Parliament; and giving Royal Assent to Bills passed by Parliament. The Queen also formally appoints many important office-holders, including government ministers, judges, officers in the armed forces, governors, British ambassadors and high commissioners and bishops of the Church of England. She is also involved in conferring peerages, knighthoods and other honours. One of the Queen's most important functions is appointing the Prime Minister.'[17] The monarch therefore still has a measure of real power. As is well known, the Queen sees Cabinet papers and intelligence reports, and keeps a close eye on public affairs.

This constitutional reality reinforces the monarchy's symbolic force. The existence of the monarchy defines the British not as citizens, but as subjects, and from that flow the socially binding British virtues of discipline and deference to authority – of which the corresponding vices are conformism, snobbery and obsession with class. These characteristics of a subject people have been reinforced by the failure of either the execution of Charles I in 1649 or the Glorious Revolution of 1688 to register as breaks in a continuous royal, and so national, descent from the Norman invasion in 1066. In the absence of a written constitution, the monarchy is the institution that binds a lattice-work of convention, common law and specific Acts of Parliament together. More subtly, but equally important, the monarchy is the keystone in the arch of the class system which supports the structure of British society. It therefore exercises powerful political, social and cultural force.

The symbolism of royalty extends from the presence of a Royal Mace lying between Her Majesty's Government and Her Majesty's Loyal Opposition on the table of the House of Commons when Parliament is in session, to the use of the prefix "Royal" to signify the "national" status of an institution. Absurdly, and redundantly, the National Theatre, founded in 1962, became the Royal National Theatre in 1988. The monarch is the guarantee of Britishness, at home and abroad. 'People come here for our "heritage", our arts, our fashion and our countryside,' the Marketing Director of the English Tourist Board told the *Observer*. 'Royalty is a branding device that pulls those attractions together.'[18]

This device has performed an important function, as Tom Nairn has argued, in obscuring the unresolved issue of national identity. The United Kingdom, the official handbook tells us, consists of England, Scotland, Wales and Northern Ireland and is referred to informally as Britain. Great Britain, however, is England, Scotland and Wales. It follows that inhabitants must have two national identities, as British, and as English or Scots or Welsh. (In Northern Ireland the position is more complicated.) The Scots and Welsh, as members of smaller countries gradually absorbed into the United Kingdom – though allowed a measure of separateness through language, customs and institutions – have had their difference from the English to reinforce their own sense of national, as opposed to British, identity. Until recently, the dominant nation, the English, did not have to worry. As Anthony Barnett wrote in the context of the Falklands War: 'Most English will be puzzled if not confounded by the question of identity. For them it is not a dual affiliation: they are both English and British, the latter is really the global expression of the former and completely "natural" to it. The more their Englishness comes into question, however, as it did with the *English* riots of 1981, the more many will welcome an assertion of their Great Britishness. The Falklands episode may not be the last of such demonstrations, even if it remains the clearest.'[19] Even Great Britishness, however, has been thrown into question by ever closer ties with the European Union, causing political difficulties for the Conservative government and provoking the anxieties revealed in John Major's promise at the 1992 Conservative Party conference: 'I will never, come hell or high water, let our distinctive British identity be lost in a Federal Europe.'

Britishness was thus to be negatively defined. It appears that the less conscious a group or nation is of having an identity, or of needing to protect it, the more secure it is in that identity. Since 1945, however, the British have become more and more conscious of their loss of status, and the insecurity of their identity. The English have felt this most acutely, and have therefore clung most tightly to the Union and to the monarchy that is the guarantee of the Union. But an empty space has opened up which demands to be filled by a secure sense of Englishness. One reason for this is the disappearance of an even greater union, which dissolved the issue of what it was to be English into a greater whole, the British Empire. The Empire not only exported the problem of Englishness by projecting it on to an imperial frame that covered one fifth of the globe, the opportunities of Empire also provided a compensatory worldwide context for the Welsh and Scots. It was Empire that provided the positive images that mere Englishness lacked – lacked, because they were unnecessary. But with the ending of Empire, there has been little to replace them except imperial echoes.

In a recent study of twentieth-century English writers, *Literary Englands*, David Gervais has pointed to the lack of such positive images. He traces an English literary tradition that has been at best elegiac since the Great War, though a pastoral nostalgia goes back farther than that. England is an 'absence' and writers 'fall back on their regional identity for lack of a clear national one'.[20] Gervais has worried whether there is an 'English' mainstream literary tradition at all: 'Viewed sceptically, the tradition from Hardy through Thomas to Larkin and his heirs begins to seem like a progressive retreat or exile from some lost England.'[21] In fact, England was only lost because it was absorbed into the rhetoric of Empire, which received a powerful boost from the political demands of the Second World War. In wartime films English national identity can be seen to have been constructed around a quasi-imperial community of deference, with young English upper-class officers leading Welsh-Scots-Irish-Yorkshire-Cockney-White Dominion platoons, or commanding similarly crewed bombers, ships and submarines. The non-military rhetoric of Empire was constructed around "the family", the extended Imperial Family of Queen Victoria that shrank after the Great War to a nuclear family, the Royal Family of the House of Windsor.

But though in the Second World War Britain was saved by her Empire, she forfeited that Empire as the price of survival. The Americans had not fought the Second World War to preserve the British Empire, any more than had the Russians, and Britain could no longer hold on to it. Britain was effectively bankrupt in 1945, and along with the Empire, other emblems of power and success went too: the fiscal power of sterling was effectively halved by the devaluation of 1947, industrial and technological supremacy was challenged by the Americans, and soon afterwards by countries Britain had helped to defeat. Finally, in 1956, Britain's military and diplomatic power was humiliated at Suez. By 1972 it is not surprising that a conservative nationalist like Philip Larkin should write the poem (commissioned by the Department of the Environment) 'Going, Going':

> For the first time I feel somehow
> That it isn't going to last,
>
> That before I snuff it, the whole
> Boiling will be bricked in
> Except for the tourist parts – [22]

The attempts to shore up a sense of national identity (British/English, rather than Irish, Welsh or Scots), once it had become threatened by the possibility of invasion in 1940, is one of the themes of this book. As was argued earlier, with the loss of Empire, monarchy has become an even more important source of symbolic reassurance. But the void that appears to be opening up at the centre of English cultural identity is matched by an emptiness at the heart of the Royal Family. On a visit to Madame Tussauds early in 1993 Marina Warner noticed that the waxwork figures of the Royal Family had been rearranged, so that Prince Charles and Diana now stood apart. The Royals, she wrote, were 'suffering the consequences of mythological breakdown'.[23]

One way of expressing and reconfirming national identity is precisely through myth. Myth may at first be dismissed because it is taken to mean the opposite of truth. In fact, myths are simple ways of conveying complex truths, and it does not matter whether they are true or false, so long as they are believed. The cultural critic Donald Horne has put it well:

> I take "myth" to mean a belief held in common by a large group of people that gives events and actions a particular meaning. It is a particularly sharp form of "reality"-making. It covers a lot of ground, as it were, in a short space. And it is particularly effective in "legitimations" of power because a "myth" can appear to explain and justify power with high voltage clarity. . . . "Myths" have the magic quality of transforming complex affairs into simple but crystal-clear "realities" that explain and justify how things are now, or how we would like them to be. Whether altogether false, or partly true, they have the transforming effect of hiding actual contradictions, confusions and inadequacies. When we speak of "myths" we are not dealing with little things, but with the ways we simplify or deny the great contradictions of society.[24]

Myth can be about a presence, or an absence, so that paradoxically the myth of a lost England has contributed to ideas of English identity. Myths sustain people, but as Horne points out, they also serve to legitimate institutions. The myth of continuity, legitimacy and authority that sustains the British monarchy is a classic mixture of the actual and the magical, the true and the believed. For all that the Queen does not govern the country on a day-to-day basis she is the head of state, the apex of political power and, it has been argued, her authority is enhanced by her actual distance from mundane government. The best way to describe how that kind of authority operates is in terms of a leadership which brings coherence to all the different, sometimes competing, sources of power in the state: in other words, it operates as a form of *hegemony*.

The term has been in existence since the Greeks. In the twentieth century it has been most closely associated with the writings of Antonio Gramsci (1891–1937), a founder member of the Italian Communist Party who did most of his thinking in Mussolini's gaols. Gramsci developed a theory, recorded in his somewhat fragmentary prison notebooks, which argued that the dominant group in society exercised its power by leadership and consent, rather than command and coercion. To secure consent, it was necessary for the dominant group to make concessions to other groups or classes in society, though always stopping short of giving up their fundamental economic power.

This position of leadership, which could be held by any group in society so long as it achieved the right balance of consent and economic control, Gramsci termed hegemony. Contemporary Western society being in constant movement as a result of the restless drive of capitalism, the balance of interests which maintains a hegemony is also shifting, and requires constant adjustment: 'The life of the state is conceived of as a continuous process of formation and superseding of unstable equilibria (on the juridical plane) between the interests of the fundamental group and those of subordinate groups – equilibria in which the interests of the dominant group prevail, but only up to a certain point.'[25] Hegemony, Gramsci further wrote, is achieved through 'a certain compromise equilibrium' between the leaders and the led.[26]

This was a much more subtle understanding of the relationship between the economic base of all societies and their individual social superstructures than the mechanical "economism" of Marxists who assumed a direct and automatic link between economic causes and political effects, reducing all arguments to economic ones. Gramsci importantly also drew on non-Marxist sources to argue for the significance of moral and cultural factors in the functioning of society. To achieve and maintain hegemony, it was essential to recognise 'the cultural fact, of cultural activity, of a cultural front as necessary alongside the merely economic and political ones'.[27] It was the function of intellectuals both to secure 'the "spontaneous" consent given by the great masses of the population to the general direction imposed on social life by the dominant fundamental group' within 'private', civil society, and to administer the coercive power of the public, political state.[28]

As the chapters that follow will show, Gramsci's ideas began to filter into British political thinking during the sixties, firstly through articles by Tom Nairn and Perry Anderson in the *New Left Review*, becoming much more accessible when the collection *Selections from Prison Notebooks* was published in English in 1971.[29] During the seventies Stuart Hall, director of Birmingham University's Centre for Contemporary Cultural Studies, applied Gramsci's ideas to the post-war situation in Britain, with particular emphasis on the role of cultural factors in maintaining, and on occasion challenging, the prevailing hegemony. In the eighties Andrew Gamble was among those who used the concept of an economic, political and cultural hegemony to analyse contemporary political history. A successful hegemony, Gamble has written, 'requires the economic dominance of a successful regime of accumulation to be combined with the winning of political, moral and intellectual leadership in civil society'.[30]

As George Orwell wrote in 1940, 'the English are not intellectual. They have a horror of abstract thought,' and it is fair to say that "hegemony" is still a specialised term.[31] Yet it is possible to see how across history the English monarchy has maintained its power (and wealth) by a series of concessions and adjustments that have gradually transferred its powers to an elected government. What it has lost in the public, political realm it has gained in what Gramsci called the private, civil realm, so that its symbolic power and importance have actually increased. While Gramsci was interested in promoting a proletarian revolution by achieving a working-class hegemony, he saw that his theory applied to all forms of government; so it has proved in the post-war period as successive Labour and Conservative governments have sought to establish and maintain their leadership through democratic consent.

In the British context, there is a word which offers a more familiar alternative to hegemony: "consensus". By maintaining a consensus of agreement on some key issues, opposing political parties have been able to adjust the equilibrium of power without provoking so much resistance that assent was withdrawn. In keeping with the empiricist slant of British thought, the concept took a practical form in the shape of the wartime and post-war policy agreements between Conservative and Labour parties and was a familiar feature of the political landscape long before it became the subject of academic theory. "Consensus" was given prominence by the publication of Paul Addison's account of wartime politics, *The Road to 1945*, in 1975, which argued that whereas there had been a general agreement between the parties in the twenties to do as little as possible, 'the new consensus of the war years was positive and purposeful. Naturally the parties displayed differences of emphasis, and they still disagreed strongly on the question of nationalisation. At the hustings the rhetorical debate between state socialism and laissez-faire capitalism was renewed with acrimony. In practice, the Conservative and Labour leaders had by-passed most of it in favour of "pragmatic" reform in a mixed economy.'[32]

For a country to be governable at all, there must be a degree of mutual consent by both the governors and the governed to abide by its laws, and Britain with its long history of gradual rather than bloody revolutions can be said to have been governed by a form of consensus since William and Mary. However, the marked continuity of policy between rival parties in the immediate post-war period implies a consensus of a stricter kind, and brings it much closer to Gramsci's notion of a 'compromise equilibrium'. In February 1954 the *Economist* invented the word 'Butskellism' to describe the continuity between the economic policies of the previous Labour Chancellor, Hugh Gaitskell, and the Conservative R. A. Butler.[33] The participation of the trades unions in managing the economy from 1940 to the seventies is an example of a concession made to a subordinate group in the interests of maintaining economic power. As Gamble has written: 'The establishment of a durable hegemony requires the emergence of a *consensus* [italics added] both on the desirable shape of the society and the policy priorities of the government. True hegemony comes about when there is no longer serious conflict over the fundamentals of social organisation.'[34]

Addison's comment on the 'pragmatic' agreement between Labour and Conservative which ignored the rhetoric of the hustings also points to another important link between consensus and hegemony. As Dennis Kavanagh and Peter Morris argue in their study, *Consensus Politics From Attlee to Major*: 'Consensus politics are inextricably linked with policy-making as an élite process (carried out by senior ministers, civil servants, producer interest groups and communicators) and with the existence of a government that possesses authority.'[35] Hegemony is the means by which those in the dominant group sustain their authority, and that authority is maintained by precisely the people that Kavanagh and Morris describe. They do so by control of the coercive power of the state (through the army, the police and the judiciary) but also by managing popular consent to the continuation of their authority. In a country without a written constitution, such as the United Kingdom, hegemony *is* the constitution, and consensus its popular expression.

As was established earlier, consensus is not the same as full agreement: party politics will continue and there will always be areas of society – in Northern Ireland for instance – where consensus is absent. The political historian Ben Pimlott has questioned whether the post-war consensus ever existed, such was the degree of political conflict between the parties throughout the whole period, but it is not necessary to have complete accord to maintain a working consensus.[36] It is a confluence, not a conformity of agreement, and within broad limits, a national consensus will remain fluid as social and economic forces dynamically interact. Being partial, it can also break down, as was the case during precisely the period when both hegemony and consensus were being theorised in the seventies. The "compromise equilibrium" can lose its balance, and imperfect hegemonies are more likely to be encountered than perfect ones. This can be just as well. A consensus may be, as Addison has written of the wartime consensus, 'positive and purposeful', but it can equally be negative and undirected. Without the movement that produces shifts and adjustments to the consensus, dynamism gives way to stasis. Consensus can produce social harmony, but it can also hold the creative forces of society in check.

Consensus in Britain has tended to be conservative, and it is not difficult to see why. As an old country, which experienced religious reformation, civil war, constitutional change and industrial revolution early in its history, Britain – notwithstanding the execution of Charles I and the deposition of James II – adjusted to these upheavals without the eradication of a single class or dominant group. Gradualism, by which things change without appearing to do so, has been the character-istic British approach, and has left both the monarchy and the aristoc-racy constitutionally and economically intact. The tradition of "one nation" Conservatism, which seeks to temper the social depredations of capitalism, predates the Industrial Revolution. Andrew Gamble has argued: 'The success of the British state in avoiding both internal overthrow and external defeat has ensured that most of the national myths are Tory myths, and most of the rituals and institutions of the state are Tory rituals and institutions . . . This makes the national cul-ture a Tory culture.'[37] The monarchy is justified on the grounds of its ancient tradition *and* its contemporary usefulness; its preservation is common sense but, as Gramsci pointed out, one of the ways that a hegemony is maintained is to make its particular distribution of power appear natural and normal.[38] The claim in a Conservative Political Centre's pamphlet, 'The Right Approach', in 1976 that 'the facts of life invariably turn out to be Tory' is a classic example of ascribing to a particular point of view the authority of common sense.[39]

The most useful way to manufacture "common sense" – that is, a general acceptance that certain concepts or courses of action are right and natural – is through a society's culture, through the ideas, images, and values which are embodied in its rituals and its historical memory – in its mythology. Culture puts the flesh on the bones of national identity, and a sense of national identity is one of the pre-requisites of political consensus. As the sociologist Anthony Smith has written: 'The most salient political function of national identity is its legitimation of common legal rights and duties of legal institutions, which define the peculiar values and character of the nation and reflect the age-old customs and mores of the people. The appeal to national identity has become the main legitimation for social order and solidarity today.'[40] A secure national identity supports a successful hegemony: that hegemony reinforces national identity.

As Gramsci pointed out, society has both a public and political realm, and a private and social one. Similarly, national identity has both a political expression, through government, and a social expression, through culture. Both aspects are closely interrelated, but culture is important precisely because it does not appear to be directly connected with politics, in the same way that the authority of the modern British monarchy is supposed to derive from its *not* having political power. But just as there are competing interests in society seeking to shift the equilibrium on the political plane, so they are seeking to shift the equilibrium on the cultural. As Stuart Hall has written: 'The dominant culture represents itself as *the* culture. It tries to define and contain all other cultures within its inclusive range. *Its* views of the world, unless challenged, will stand as the most natural, all-embracing, universal culture. Other cultural configurations will not only be subordinate to this dominant order: they will enter into struggle with it, seek to modify, negotiate, resist or even overthrow its reign – its *hegemony*.'[41]

For the dominant group, culture will become a means of authority, and a source of authority for those who attach themselves to its values. It will be an expression of political authority, the basis of critical authority and an emblem of social aspiration. Control of the resources that support cultural activity will in itself be a form of authority. The intelligentsia will be employed in servicing and policing culture. It has the crucial task of disseminating it to those beyond the immediate group in power, for one way of maintaining consent is to ensure that the culture of the dominant class is not enjoyed exclusively by that class, but that its values permeate the whole of society. Thus the culture of the dominant class becomes identified with the culture of society as a whole. In the twentieth century Britain has developed institutions to ensure this, as will be shown. The decision to establish a 'national curriculum' in schools is an attempt to reassert a particular view of national identity through a prescribed history and literature. The manipulation of the idea of a 'national heritage' performs a similar function in reuniting contemporary Britain with a particular version of its past and reconciling it to that past.

It is not surprising, then, that the very concept of culture has become dauntingly associated with ideas of authority. Examined more closely, it is the field in which the struggle for authority takes place. As Stuart Hall has argued: 'It is crucial to replace the notion of "culture" with the more concrete, historical concept of "cultures": a redefinition which brings out more clearly the fact that cultures always stand in relations of domination – and subordination – to one another, are always, in some sense, in struggle with one another.'[42] This struggle between dominant cultures and sub-cultures will be expressed in cultural terms, but not necessarily in terms that the dominant culture will recognise. Dick Hebdige has argued: 'The challenge to hegemony which sub-cultures represent is not issued directly by them. Rather it is expressed obliquely, in style.'[43] Within this force field of daily contestation the shifting equilibrium is found. It follows that culture in its broadest sense, though expressed through objects, images and utterances, cannot be an object in itself. It is the process, the channel of transmission for the ideas, dreams and values which are given form by the specific media of the arts.

Within a cat's cradle of dynamic forces, between the counterbalances of solid and fluid, chaos and order, inner and outer, dark and light, physical and spiritual, national and emotional, abstract and concrete, idealist and realist, male and female, the symbolic elements that constitute the particularities of a culture are shaped. This process can equally be described as the emergence of myth, suspended as it is between objective truth and subjective belief. One of the most important myths is the myth of national identity, which is constructed, replicated and reshaped by the sense-making procedures of culture.

The relationship between national identity and political consensus turns out to be, not a simple dialogue, but a musical triad, in which the third element is culture. When culture, consensus and identity form a harmony, a successful hegemony can be established. More often than not, this complex equilibrium of forces is only partially established. At times of crisis, there is only dissonance. A truly exclusive study of any one of these elements will fail, because it will ignore the other forces that interact with it and shape it. That is why a study of culture must also look at politics, and why politics are better understood if cultural factors are taken into account. In the nineteenth century, English literature flourished as a consequence of the dialectic between politics and culture; literary criticism became a form of social criticism, with its own moral standpoint and values, which became attached to the subject they discussed. John Ruskin (1819–1900) saw no conflict or contradiction in discussing art, morality and politics at the same time, as his monthly public letters addressed to the 'working-men of England', *Fors Clavigera*, showed. When the proponents of "cultural studies", whose development as a field of academic inquiry is another theme in this book, introduced an explicit (as opposed to implicit) political dimension into cultural criticism in the sixties and seventies, they were doing nothing new.

The subject of contestation, within culture, but also more importantly between culture, consensus and national identity, is that of values. What are the values that a society wishes to express? Does it even have any control or volition in the matter of values? The evidence suggests that it does, for values are one more of the dynamic forces that are active in the social process. As Anthony Smith has written: 'If a nation, however modern, is to survive in this modern world, it must do so at two levels: the socio-political and the cultural-psychological. What, after all, is the *raison d'être* of any *nation* (as opposed to state), if it is not also the cultivation of its unique (or allegedly unique) culture values?'[44] Values, however, turn out to be contingent. They vary in relation to the equilibrium of forces within a society, although the dominant group will seek to reinforce its position by asserting the absolute nature of the values it holds. That all values are, ultimately, relative, does not however make them valueless, for they have a key role within the dynamic of society.

The enduring problem for the cultural historian is that he or she is not in the supposedly neutral position of an anthropologist observing from a distance the customs of a tribe, but is caught up in the web of cultural values that is the object of study. As one of the founding fathers of British – not English, for he was border-Welsh – cultural studies, Raymond Williams warned: 'No community, no culture, can ever be fully conscious of itself, ever fully know itself.'[45]

One of the ironies of the fire at Windsor was that the Castle, like the House of Windsor, was a pastiche. The place was real enough, and had been there since William the Conqueror but, just like the monarchy it housed, which had changed its name from Saxe-Coburg-Gotha as late as 1917, its appearance was largely a nineteenth-century creation. At the end of the twentieth century, the issue became whether everything should be restored as it was supposed to have been, or whether this 'symbol of royalty and national heritage' might not be modernised in some way. In the symbolic "magical" realm of national identity, the manner in which a royal palace is restored could also convey something about the state of the nation, just as its near-destruction had done.

In 1824, following Britain's triumph in the Napoleonic wars, Parliament voted £150,000 for the restoration of Windsor Castle, to provide a suitable setting for the reception of crowned heads and foreign statesmen. The modern equivalent would be the Queen Elizabeth II Conference Centre in Westminster. After a competition, George IV and his commissioners employed Jeffry Wyatt (who embellished his own name at the same time as the Castle by medievalising it to Wyatville) to make radical alterations. The grand banqueting hall, St George's Hall, was reconstructed in 1832 out of two earlier rooms, a royal chapel and a state reception room, which in turn had been remodelled for Charles II between 1675 and 1684 out of the original St George's Hall created for Edward III in 1363. The Waterloo Chamber was designed to celebrate a British (and Prussian) victory over the French. Overall, Wyatville gave the Castle a more chivalric and romantic appearance, in line with the nineteenth-century taste for medievalism. As the architectural historian Mark Girouard has explained: 'All windows were gothicised, crenellations and machicolations replaced plain battlements or flat parapets, bay and oriel windows were protruded, towers were heightened; and overall rose the dominating silhouette of the Round Tower, raised by an extra thirty-three feet (illustration 2).'[46] The Brunswick Tower, whose flaming outline in November 1992 made an ironic contrast to images of the dome of St Paul's untouched amid the smoke and flames of the Blitz in 1940, was a Wyatville confection. As with modern building projects such as the British Library, there was a severe cost overrun, and building continued into the reign of Queen Victoria.

Immediately after the fire in 1992 a debate started about how repairs should be carried out, alongside the debate about how they should be paid for. The editor of the *Architects' Journal*, Stephen Greenberg, argued that the country 'should not be refaking what are fakes anyway. Instead we should add another layer to an unfolding history in order to express the art and spirit of our times.'[47] The Royal Institute of British Architects (RIBA) proposed a competition to find a new solution to the question of rebuilding, and held a seminar and exhibition in 1993. The magazine *Country Life* ran its own competition; Mark Girouard invited celebrity architects and designers to submit ideas for inclusion in his book on the Castle. It appeared, however, that a decision to restore St George's Hall to its previous appearance had been taken in principle before consultations with the RIBA, English Heritage and the Royal Fine Art Commission (RFAC) had been completed. At a meeting chaired by the Duke of Edinburgh on 22 April 1993 the chairman of the RFAC – and royal courtier – Lord St John of Fawsley (the former Conservative Arts Minister Norman St John-Stevas) concurred with English Heritage that Wyatville's work should be restored. This was not the view of the other commissioners of the RFAC, who later argued in May that full restoration would be wrong.

The final conclusion was a compromise: to restore St George's Hall as far as possible in the original style, to upgrade the kitchens for banquets and rebuild with modern materials within the Brunswick Tower. On 29 April 1993 it was announced that the work would be a blend of 'restoration and redesign', with 'the best of contemporary design and craftsmanship' in destroyed parts such as the Private Chapel. At the same time it was announced that in order for the Queen to implement her decision to contribute substantially to the cost of rebuilding, Buckingham Palace would be opened to the public for the first time, at a charge of eight pounds a head from August to September (when the Queen would not be in residence) for the next five years. It was calculated that this, plus the new charge to enter the precincts of Windsor Castle, would meet seventy per cent of the costs of the repairs, now put at thirty-five million pounds.

The Queen was almost certainly in a position to meet all the costs from her private fortune, but instead the public, while relieved of the charge as taxpayers, would pay for the repairs through royalty's greater commercial participation in the heritage industry of which it was already the 'branding device'. As a further move towards public "ownership", in April 1993 the seven thousand oil paintings and more than five hundred thousand prints and drawings in the Royal Collection were placed in the control of the newly created Royal Collection Trust, chaired by Prince Charles, with the intention of putting more of the collection on public display. Royal Collection Enterprises Ltd, the "trading arm" of the monarchy, in its first year received £4.8 million from charging admission to royal residences, but only £2.2 million was passed on to the restoration of Windsor Castle.

The announcement that the Castle would be treated to a mixture of restoration and redesign was ambiguous. In June the possibility of a radical new treatment of St George's Hall was foreclosed when an architect expert in restoration was appointed, and it became known that the Hall, along with the Grand Reception Room, and the Crimson and Green Drawing Rooms, would be restored to what it had been. There would be no public competition. Selected architects would be invited to submit "contemporary" designs for the remainder. In June 1994 it was announced that a committee chaired by the Duke of Edinburgh, and including Prince Charles, the Lord Chamberlain, Lord St John of Fawsley, Jocelyn Stevens, chairman of English Heritage, and Frank Duffy, president of the RIBA, had chosen the Sidell Gibson Partnership to produce new designs. Sidell Gibson's most celebrated building project was opposite the National Gallery in Trafalgar Square, a new office and shopping complex within a reproduction of the building's original frontage. For Windsor Castle, they produced a pastiche of Wyatville's pastiche. The Royal Household said the reconstruction represented the best of twentieth-century architecture. The architects said there was nothing of the 1990s about it. Not for the first time, the monarchy had decided to modernise while not appearing to do so, employing experts in the creation of a false façade.

Whatever the final outcome of the restoration, it would appear that an opportunity to make a fresh start had been lost. Immediately after the fire *The Times* commented: 'Just as old forests can renew themselves by fire, so can old castles.'[48] But the question was whether an old country could do the same. Moments of crisis are also moments of transition, and therefore also of opportunity. Such was the situation in 1940. There is much to be learned from the adaptations, and refusals to adapt, that have taken place in Britain since then.

II

Deep England

Britain in the 1940s

On 9 April 1946, the House of Commons gathered to hear the new
Labour government's Chancellor of the Exchequer, Hugh Dalton,
introduce his second budget. Dalton's exaltation at being the first
socialist Chancellor to have the authority of a large majority elevated
his final words, in a passage that rose above the mundane practicalities
of abolishing Excess Profits Tax and introducing free school milk:

> We still have a great wealth and variety of natural scenery in this land. The
> best that remains should surely become the heritage, not of a few private
> owners, but of all our people and, above all, of the young and the fit, who
> shall have increased opportunities of health and happiness, companionship
> and recreation, in beautiful places. Yes, there is still a wonderful, incompar-
> able beauty in Britain, in the sunshine on the hills, the mists adrift the
> moors, the wind on the downs, the deep peace of the woodlands, the wash
> of the waves against the white unconquerable cliffs which Hitler never scaled.
> There is beauty and history in all these places.[1]

Budget speeches are not customarily the place for the affirmation of
national myths, but the Chancellor's rhetoric reveals an almost mystical
relationship with the landscape. In keeping with the still-visionary
atmosphere of the times, Dalton's budget created a new instrument for
the protection of the countryside, a National Land Fund to be used to
acquire sites of "beauty and history" as a memorial to those who had
died defending their country in the war so recently ended.

As with many of the good intentions of 1945, the National Land
Fund was to have an unhappy history. Yet in the aftermath of a world
war, and sensing himself on the threshold of a new era of social justice
and peaceful reconstruction, Dalton felt justified in using one of the
most powerful emblems of national identity – the English landscape –
as a link between the dead and the living. There was a great deal more

to this national myth than the white cliffs of Dover and echoes of Vera Lynn.

Dalton was celebrating "Deep England", an image of the national heartland constructed as much out of folk memories, poetry and cultural associations as actuality. The social historian Angus Calder uses the phrase in his account of the mythology of the 1940–41 Blitz to summon up the image of a green and pleasant land that 'stretched from Hardy's Wessex to Tennyson's Lincolnshire, from Kipling's Sussex to Elgar's Worcestershire'.[2] This imagined pastoral landscape served as contrast to, and compensation for, all the destruction and stress of war. Somewhere among its bright fields and bosky shades nestled the nation's soul.

Deep England became a resonant theme in wartime propaganda, but the Ministry of Information had no need to invent it (illustration 3). It was rooted in the national consciousness: Calder's Victorians and Edwardians were themselves drawing on a pastoral myth that went back beyond the Industrial Revolution and even the Enclosures. Britain's extreme isolation during the early part of the war reinforced a picturesque idea of the landscape that had been shared in the thirties by conservative landowners, socialist ramblers and communist members of the Clarion Cycling Club alike – even if the ultimate ownership of the view was in dispute.

The circumstances of war encouraged a neo-romanticism among British artists that was already burgeoning before the war began: Deep England was also John Piper's Derbyshire, Paul Nash's Oxfordshire, Graham Sutherland and John Craxton's Pembrokeshire, Benjamin Britten's East Anglia. The painters' vision derived from William Blake and Samuel Palmer, a mystical sense of the numinous in the landscape that corresponded to a personal, religious inscape. Religion flourished in the emotional intensity of wartime; Anglicanism was an aspect of Deep England that appealed to neo-romantics like the great memorialist of parish churches, John Piper. A strand of native mysticism found its correspondence in surrealism, the last contemporary continental influence to be felt in Britain before the isolation of 1940. Surrealism sanctioned the celebration of the magical and the irrational, besides rediscovering both landscape and figure as subjects for imaginative transformation. For Henry Moore, landscape and figure, monument and matriachal archetype, became virtually one.

In the work of artists like Ceri Richards and David Jones the myths of Deep England reached back beyond Blake to Arthurian legends and a Celtic past that was yet present, a timeless monarchical Albion. The film-maker Humphrey Jennings tapped the same emotional springs; Michael Powell and Emeric Pressburger's film *A Canterbury Tale* (1944) offered a pastoral poem to the Kent countryside that drew on the country's first national poet to collapse past and present in 'a semi-religious, mythical landscape'.[3] The fusion of past and present had already been achieved by T. S. Eliot in his *Four Quartets* (1935–42). An American by birth, Eliot, like Henry James, had a particularly intense vision of his adopted country. While the 'Sea Interludes' from Britten's opera *Peter Grimes* (1945) evoke the atmosphere of Eliot's third quartet, 'The Dry Salvages', 'Little Gidding', the setting for Eliot's fourth, suggests the subject of a drawing by John Piper. Eliot places the poem in a perfect site for England at its deepest, the chapel built by a small seventeenth-century Anglican community that fell victim to the depredations of the English Civil War, and which seemed all the more precious for being once more endangered by the modern war that Eliot evokes in the quartet. At Little Gidding, past and present are bound together in a single visionary moment:

> So, while the light fails
> On a winter's afternoon, in a secluded chapel
> History is now and England.[4]

The landscape myth at the heart of Deep England, reinforced by wartime propaganda that gave painters and writers commissions, privileges and exemptions which turned them briefly into official artists, was so powerful that Dalton could not fail to be touched by it, even if he had not himself been a rambler and a friend of the National Trust. Its institutional expression in a National Land Fund would indeed be a 'memorial which many would think finer than any work of art in stone or bronze'.[5] The myth was fundamental to the British sense of national identity, and as such was a source of reassurance at a moment when it was needed even more urgently than in wartime itself. Deep England embodied a nostalgia for the certainties of an older order and older ways that had been put into question by the war and its aftermath. As Kenneth Morgan put it in his history, *The People's Peace* (1990): 'Amidst the very euphoria of victory in 1945, the nation offered not a triumph of the will but a suspicion of change and the paralysis of doubt.'[6]

That doubt was the result of changes brought about by the violence of war. Ironically, the uncertainties of the Blitz had served to create a new sense of national identity, a shift of attitudes made possible by the social solidarity produced by common dangers (illustration 4). Fifty years on, and in more fragmented times, the myth of the Blitz can still exercise such a pull that it is tempting to dismiss it as no more than that, a myth with no correspondence to reality. Yet the contemporary record and the long-term changes that resulted point to a shared experience, at its most powerful at the moment of greatest danger between 1940 and 1941, that shifted national consciousness. Social and political divisions remained but, to quote the verdict of the historian Peter Hennessy, after May 1940 wartime Britain was 'a more politically united nation than at any other time in the twentieth century'.[7] It was not only united (literally so, for in 1940 Labour and Liberal politicians joined a coalition government under Churchill), but it was also prepared for change.

This was the key theme in George Orwell's study, written during the Blitz and published in 1941, a time when Russia was still an ally of Germany, and America a friendly neutral, which specifically addressed the question of English identity. *The Lion and the Unicorn: Socialism and the English Genius* was the first of a series of 'Searchlight Books' co-edited by Orwell and the journalist and social scientist T. R. Fyvel, intended to define a set of political as opposed to purely military war aims. Orwell, an eyewitness of the Blitz, confirms the reality of that moment of national solidarity. To him, the summer and autumn of 1940 revealed the essential security of English identity, what he called 'the soundness and homogeneity of England'.[8] True to his social origins, Orwell makes no apology for eliding British identity into Englishness, and is not embarrassed to link that security of identity to patriotism. Patriotism takes different forms in different classes but it is the binding thread: 'The English sense of national unity has never disintegrated, because patriotism is finally stronger than class-hatred.'[9]

It was this same security of identity which allowed the hypocrisy, snobbery, insularity and philistinism of English life to continue: the English are not gifted artistically, although – and here Orwell unconsciously invokes the pastoral tradition – they love flowers. Nor are they intellectual, having a horror of abstract thought. But there is a self-confidence that explains why 'in moments of supreme crisis the whole nation can suddenly draw together, and act upon a species of instinct, really a code of conduct which is understood by almost everybody, though never formulated'.[10] This sense of common purpose led Orwell famously to describe England as 'a family': 'It has its private language and its common memories, and at the approach of an enemy it closes its ranks. A family with the wrong members in control – that, perhaps, is as near as one can come to describing England in a phrase.'[11]

The circumstances of wartime, however, had meant that the family had decided it wished to alter its domestic arrangements: 'This war, unless we are defeated, will wipe out most of the existing class privileges. There are every day fewer people who wish them to continue.'[12] Already in 1941 Orwell was seeking to build on what he believed had been the potentially revolutionary situation of 1940 to propose a socialist blueprint for the post-war period. Orwell's subjective impression that people were indeed turning against the privileges of the old order was independently confirmed by the public-opinion gatherers of the social monitors Mass Observation, who in January 1941 discovered that 'less class distinctions', 'more state control' and 'educational reforms' were the leading changes people expected as post-war trends.[13] The point was, as one of the fortnightly educational pamphlets distributed to the armed forces by the Army Bureau of Current Affairs put it in October 1942: 'We are fighting not to win, but to win *something*, and the more we clear our minds here and now about the world we want after the war, the more likely we are to attain it.'[14]

This 'something' was to emerge as the welfare state, based on the principles of the Beveridge Report published in December 1942. Even the historian Correlli Barnett, who has concluded that the decision of the wartime coalition to concentrate its forward planning on social welfare rather than technological and industrial revolution was a further cause of Britain's long-term decline, admits that the 'New Jerusalem' he despises was earnestly desired by most people in the population, and not just by the ' "enlightened" Establishment' and the Left.[15] While Sir William Beveridge was still preparing his report, the Minister responsible for planning post-war reconstruction asked the Ministry of Information's Home Intelligence department to prepare a report on public attitudes. It was discovered that people were not thinking much about the future, but that a return to pre-war mass unemployment was a universal worry. The priorities among those who were looking to the future were first of all that there should be 'work at a living wage for everyone who is capable of doing it' and secondly, that 'private profit must cease to be the major incentive to work; everyone must work primarily for the good of the community'. There should be financial security for all unable to work, decent homes at reasonable cost, and the same education available to all.[16]

These desires were translated into proposals as a result of the assumptions made by Beveridge about what would be needed to defeat the menacing giants waiting on the road to post-war recovery: Want, Disease, Ignorance, Squalor and Idleness. Beveridge's original brief in May 1941 had been to sort out the confused and inadequate system of pre-war social insurance, but for Beveridge 'a revolutionary moment in the world's history is a time for revolutions, not for patching'.[17] Accordingly, he proposed a comprehensive system of social welfare, based on other, crucial assumptions: that there would be full employment, child allowances and a free national health service. The report, for all its dry statistics, became a 635,000-copy best-seller. It was also a threat to the unity of the coalition. Implementation of the report was left till peacetime, but the debate in the House of Commons in February 1943 made it plain that while Labour was totally committed, Conservatives were deeply sceptical.

The Beveridge Report marked a turning point in the social history of the war, just as Hitler's attack on Russia and the entry of the United States into the conflict were military turning points. It seized on what both the socialist Orwell and the liberal technocrat Beveridge had recognised as the revolutionary aspects of 1940 and turned the feeling of "never again" into a positive commitment to the future. The Ministry of Information's Home Intelligence unit reported that the plan had been 'welcomed with almost universal approval by people of all shades of opinion and by all sections of the community' and that it was seen as 'the first real attempt to put into practice the talk about the new world'.[18] As Correlli Barnett records, by 1944 'the 1940–41 vision of New Jerusalem was fast becoming the new political consensus'.[19] This was not the socialist programme outlined in *The Lion and the Unicorn*, but it was a plan for social reform that formed the basis of the Labour victory in July 1945. It is important to remember that, in spite of the doubts of Conservative members of the wartime coalition from Churchill downwards, the foundations of the post-war settlement were laid in wartime, in terms of a commitment to full employment and a national health service in White Papers of 1944, to educational reform in the Butler Education Act of the same year, in the Family Allowances Act of June 1945 and plans to improve social security and to give priority to building houses. This shift shows that consensus, like the distribution of political and economic power to which it consents – what Orwell described as 'the subtle network of compromises, by which the nation keeps itself in its familiar shape' – is indeed a moving equilibrium.[20] As the political historian Paul Addison writes: 'The growth of consensus in the realm of government was not in contradiction to the popular swing to the left. Both represented a loss of initiative by the Conservatives in home affairs, and a repudiation of the record of the National government of 1931–40.'[21]

It was that swing which had placed the nation's financial resources at Hugh Dalton's disposal in his second budget in 1946, but the certainties of 1940 and 1941 were inevitably to wane amid the uncertainties of peace, solidarity was to dissolve as perils faded, and reality acquire its halo of myth. The danger was that a moment of potential, which had indeed led to change, would become a touchstone for backward reference, an emotional lever that could be pulled by politicians of both Left and Right, as active memory hardened into generalised "heritage". As Angus Calder points out: 'The war, and the mythical events of 1940, would become subjects for historical nostalgia on the Left as well as on the Right – perhaps more than on the Right – but the effect of the Myth would be conservative. For the Left it would encapsulate a moment of retrenchment as a moment of rebirth; a moment of ideological conservatism as a moment of revolution. Because the Blitz was held to have had near revolutionary consequences, to have somehow produced a "welfare state", the Myth would divert attention from the continuing need for radical change in British society. The Left would think that in 1940 it had captured History. In fact, it had been captured by it.'[22]

The thinking behind Dalton's Land Fund showed these contradictory thrusts. The scheme was reassuringly conservative and conservationist, an appeal to the values of "beauty and history" through its preservation of the choicest sites of Deep England. But at the same time these places were to be brought into common ownership, and their acquisition was to be financed in a revolutionary way. Fifty million pounds from the sale of surplus military equipment was set aside to establish a fund for the purchase of real estate to help create the then projected National Parks, or to be handed on to the National Trust. Its principal function would be to reactivate a rarely used clause in the 1910 Finance Act which allowed the Inland Revenue to accept property in lieu of death duties. In future, when land was accepted instead of cash, the Fund would reimburse the government for the tax forgone.

Imaginative though it was in conception, the National Land Fund was to be ineffective in practice. Had the principle of an independent, self-financing cultural institution been applied more creatively, Dalton's "peace dividend" of 1946 might have been the foundation of a system that freed the finance of cultural activity – conservation *and* creativity – from the capricious pressures of annual funding through government budgets. The originality of the idea was recognised by the chairman of the Trustees of the National Gallery, Lord Robbins, who called it 'one of the few forward-looking and imaginative acts of Government in this century in relation to general culture'.[23] Sadly, political and economic factors worked against the Fund, as will be seen, and a great opportunity was lost.

By contrast, the Royal Charter granted to the Arts Council of Great Britain in 1946 was to have a determining influence on the shape of culture in post-war Britain. Because the 1945 Labour government took financial responsibility for the Arts Council, so accepting for the first time the contemporary and performing arts alongside museums and art galleries as a permanent national responsibility, the Arts Council tends to be seen as part of the post-war settlement, as a minor aspect of the welfare state that did indeed fulfil wartime demands for full social security, free higher education and a National Health Service. But the Arts Council was hardly a Labour, and certainly not a socialist, creation. It had grown out of an ad hoc wartime institution, the Council for the Encouragement of Music and the Arts. The decision to perpetuate this organisation as the Arts Council of Great Britain was one of last announcements of the caretaker Conservative administration, left to run the country after Labour's withdrawal from the wartime coalition prior to the election of July 1945. Like the principles of the Beveridge Report, like the Butler Education Act of 1944, it was something that the new government had inherited from the wartime consensus. Like the Butler Education Act, it was to prove a force for cultural conservatism.

This had not been the case when the Council for the Encouragement of Music and the Arts was set up during the extraordinary months of

1940. True, the circumstances of its creation were in the best tradition of political expediency and the old boy network, but there was vision as well. In December 1939, with virtually all forms of cultural activity other than going to the pub blacked out, with amateur organisations at a standstill and nearly all professional artists and performers out of work, the secretary of the independent educational charity the Pilgrim Trust, Dr Thomas Jones, arranged a meeting between the president of the Board of Education, Lord De La Warr, and the chairman of the Pilgrim Trust, Lord Macmillan. Jones was a passionate advocate of adult education who had run the Pilgrim Trust since it was established with money from the American Harkness Foundation in 1930. During the pre-war depression Jones had helped to send art exhibitions and music and drama organisers (who would now be called *animateurs*) to distressed areas, including Jones's native Wales. The Board of Education was concerned about the effect of the wartime emergency on voluntary organisations involved in adult education, and De La Warr had approached the Treasury about finding additional funds, only to be told to try the Pilgrim Trust first. The Board of Education's view was that, in wartime, it was essential 'to show publicly and unmistakably that the Government cares about the cultural life of the country'.[24]

De La Warr's approach to the Pilgrim Trust was certain of a sympathetic hearing, for its chairman Lord Macmillan was also a member of the government, in charge of the recently established Ministry of Information, responsible for monitoring morale, and for propaganda and censorship. At a period when morale was low – especially at the Ministry of Information – Macmillan could see the advantages of reviving cultural activity, as could his cabinet colleagues. In his capacity as chairman of the Pilgrim Trust Macmillan offered twenty-five thousand pounds to set up a Committee for the Encouragement of Music and Arts, on the understanding that the government might be ready to offer a similar sum. On 19 January 1940 the Committee, which was to adopt the grander-sounding title of "Council" when, after a decent interval, the Treasury had been persuaded to put up a matching twenty-five thousand pounds, met officially for the first time. For the Chamberlain government, CEMA, as it quickly became known, was not only a solution to the problem of what to do about the arts in wartime, it was also a solution to the problem of what to do about Lord Macmillan, for he had not been a success as Minister for Information. Macmillan became chairman of CEMA, though in the opinion of CEMA's first secretary, he was 'quite useless'.[25]

Although this was the first time the government had taken substantial responsibility for the performing arts (sharing it initially with a voluntary body) it was by no means the first time that the state had acted as patron of the nation's cultural life. The British Museum had been created by Act of Parliament (and funded by a national lottery) in 1753. As the British Museum's collections grew, they also divided, so that the creation of the National Gallery followed in 1824, the National Portrait Gallery in 1856 and the Tate Gallery in 1896. The science collections moved to South Kensington in 1883. The Victoria and Albert Museum was founded in 1852. The British Library, housed within the British Museum, only acquired separate institutional status in 1974. By 1988 there were eighteen "national" museums, governed by their own boards of trustees, but funded directly by the State through government departments. In 1931 the Standing Commission on Museums and Galleries had been set up to advise the government on museums policy as a whole, although it did not acquire any grant-giving responsibilities until 1963, and was given a Royal Charter as the Museums and Galleries Commission in 1987.

In one respect CEMA was not even the first in the field in the contemporary arts. In 1933 the government had established the British Film Institute to bolster, albeit indirectly, the British cinema industry against the heavy competition from Hollywood, by working as an educational resource that would promote the development of public appreciation of the art of film. In 1934, in response to the growing propaganda battle with Germany and Italy that preceded the Second World War, the British Council was established by Royal Charter to promote wider knowledge overseas of Britain, its people and its institutions, and the contemporary arts became part of the publicity for "the British way of life".

The most significant act of pre-war cultural policy, however, had been the decision to create the British Broadcasting Corporation in 1927. The BBC's Royal Charter in effect nationalised what had been a private monopoly of broadcasting in Britain, granted by the government to the British Broadcasting Company in 1922. The licence permitting households to receive wireless broadcasts was sold by the government through the Post Office, and the money was then passed on to the BBC. This means of financial control was reinforced by the government's power under the charter (which had to be renewed periodically) to appoint the board of governors of the BBC, who in turn appointed its director-general and all its staff. In addition, the government had reserve powers to direct the BBC to do whatever it wished, but the day-to-day convention was that, within parameters that were rarely described because they were so rarely tested, the BBC was an independent institution.

This relationship between the State and the institutions which it has not only created, but also finances, has become known as "the arm's-length principle". Although the principle was not codified in relation to cultural policy until the seventies, it had long operated as a practical means of distancing politicians and government servants from the activities they wished to promote. The length of the arm, and the extent to which it controlled the operations at its end, was a constant source of speculation and debate, as will be seen, but technically the term was legal parlance for a transaction between two parties in which neither one controls the other. When Lord Redcliffe-Maud published the results of his independent investigation into the funding of the arts for the Gulbenkian Foundation in 1976, he traced the device back to H. A. L. Fisher, who as president of the Board of Education in 1919 established the University Grants Committee: 'An unelected body of university men, appointed by the Chancellor of the Exchequer, on whose advice the government of the day asked Parliament each year to vote money for distribution, without strings, to each university. This system has survived, with modifications, for more than fifty years.'[26] His report brought the term into popular use in relation to the Arts Council: 'By self-denying ordinance the politicians leave the Council free to spend as it thinks fit. No minister needs to reply to questions in Parliament about the beneficiaries – or about unsuccessful applicants for an Arts Council grant. A convention has been established over the years that in arts patronage neither the politician nor the bureaucrat knows best.'[27]

Redcliffe-Maud concluded that it would be madness to abolish the Arts Council or abandon the arm's-length principle, but a convention that rests on the holder of power not wielding the power that is possessed is always open to question. Indeed, the arm's-length principle was only codified after the questioning had begun. After serving on the Arts Council from 1975 to 1978, the cultural critic Raymond Williams decided that in no way was the supposed protective distance from government of intermediate bodies such as the Council genuine: 'The true social process of such bodies as the Arts Council is one of administered consensus by co-option.'[28] Williams's experience gave rise to wider conclusions about the nature of British society:

> It would be naïve to discuss the principles and problems of intermediate bodies without paying some attention to the character of the British State and its ruling class. Indeed, it can be argued that intermediate bodies of the kind we have known were made possible by this character. The British State has been able to delegate some of its official functions to a whole complex of semi-official or nominally independent bodies because it has been able to rely on an unusually compact and organic ruling class. Thus it can give Lord X or Lady Y both public money and apparent freedom of decision in some confidence, subject to normal procedures of report and accounting, that they will act as if they were indeed state officials.[29]

History has shown that Williams was right.

In the disputatious times of the seventies Williams was making a practical application of Gramsci's theory of hegemony. In the self-disciplined consensus of wartime such questions did not arise. In 1940 there were further, more practical issues that were left unaddressed. On 6 March 1940 the Council for the Encouragement of Music and the Arts made a formal request to the Treasury for financial assistance. The terms of this memorandum established the fundamental confusion of purpose that was to bedevil the public funding of the arts in Britain.

While the first clause of the memorandum committed CEMA to the 'preservation in wartime of the highest standards in the arts of music, drama and painting' and the second referred to the 'widespread provision of opportunities for hearing good music and the enjoyment of the arts generally', these essentially aristocratic, though benign, intentions are at odds with the democratic sentiments of the clauses that follow. Here cultural activity is treated as something done by, rather than for, people, 'the encouragement of music-making and play-acting by the people themselves'. Temporarily unemployed professional artists were to draw incidental benefit from this: 'Through the above activities, the rendering of indirect assistance to professional singers and players who may be suffering from a wartime lack of demand for their work.'[30] Following the practice that Dr Jones had encouraged with funds in the thirties, unemployed professional artists would be given jobs as *animateurs* to stimulate local drama and music-making in rural areas and small towns that would be more than usually deprived in wartime.

The confusion which stems from CEMA's founding terms of reference has been fourfold. The most obvious source of conflict, since it involves the distribution of money, is between the financial claims of the professional artist and the amateur. The second is between the interests of the artist, of whatever status, and the audience for the work. The third lies in the problem of defining what constitutes 'the highest standards' in the arts. The fourth, and most important, distinction is the difference between a view of culture that, following the definition offered by Matthew Arnold in 1869, sees it as 'a pursuit of our total perfection by means of getting to know, on all the matters which most concern us, the best which has been thought and said in the world', and that other view which sees culture as the common expression of a people, where values emerge from below, and are not imposed from above.[31] In outline, these are the practical and theoretical issues which shaped all public policies, both positive and negative, towards the arts in democratic countries in the latter half of the twentieth century. As we shall see, the definition of the word "culture" was to be the fundamental issue in the post-war critical debate.

Such theoretical issues were not at the forefront of people's minds in the stressful days of 1940, but their practical effects were felt. CEMA's first secretary was a civil servant, Mary Glasgow, who had been seconded from the Board of Education to the Ministry of Information. In her account of the early years of CEMA she wrote that the driving force was Dr Jones, who saw the organisation's work as an extension of the 'social service' of pre-war Pilgrim Trust activities: 'Of the two purposes proclaimed, helping artists and serving audiences, there is no doubt that the second was uppermost in his mind. There was a built-in conflict between the claims of art and those of social service, and in the lifetime of CEMA, it was never fully resolved.'[32]

Although by 1945 this conflict had been almost entirely resolved in favour of art and the professional artist, an assumed obligation to act as a form of social service has always exerted a contrary pull against the Council's responsibility for "standards", and the consensus among policy-makers has shifted accordingly. The conflict was to resurface in the battles between the Arts Council and "community artists" in the early seventies and was to influence policies towards ethnic and other minorities in the eighties. CEMA, while still struggling to work out its internal contradictions, had to deal with another perennial cultural conundrum: the distinction between "the arts" and "entertainment". The problem became institutionalised in the competition and friction between CEMA and another wartime creation, the Entertainments National Service Association.

ENSA had been set up as a voluntary association in 1938 by the theatrical producer Basil Dean, who had foreseen that there would be a need for troop entertainments, just as there had been during the First World War. Both ENSA's administrators and its performers were closely connected with the commercial theatre (there being very little of any other kind) and ENSA rightly saw no shame in presenting itself as show business in battledress. Its principal audience was military, and by 1944 its budget of £2.2 million was more than twelve times that of CEMA. After Dunkirk its mandate had been extended from troop shows to entertaining the large numbers of civilian war workers in government factories, where CEMA – which had pioneered concerts in air raid shelters and rest centres – was already operating. ENSA provided entertainment mainly in the form of concert parties and variety shows, but it also sponsored major orchestral concerts (one hundred and sixty in 1943) and presented plays in productions loaned by commercial managements. By the end of 1943, when it was also operating abroad, ENSA was presenting hundreds of dramatic performances a week. CEMA, criticised by many, including the coalition Minister of Labour Ernest Bevin, as too highbrow, resented ENSA's intrusions on its assumed territory, while ENSA resented the implication that it pandered to lowbrow taste. Here too was a future cultural issue. While the 'music travellers' of CEMA, who in the first six months of 1940 managed to establish thirty-seven amateur orchestral groups and two hundred and forty-four choral groups, represent one view of people's art, ENSA's entertainers embodied another popular culture.

ENSA was wound up in 1945, but there were still those who had hoped from the beginning that the recognition of a responsibility to culture – high or low – which wartime had forced on a largely reluctant state would not be forgotten with the coming of peace. In August 1940 the novelist and playwright J. B. Priestley, whose broadcasts have themselves become part of wartime mythology, devoted a Sunday evening 'postscript' after the nine o'clock news to describing ENSA's factory concerts. The moral of his encouraging homily was a vision of future cultural reconciliation:

Let us, by all means, have four young women in green silk playing 'Oh, Johnny, Oh Johnny', but at the same time, let's have the great symphony orchestras pealing out the noblest music, night after night, not for a fortunate and privileged few, but for all the people who long for such music. Let's have comedians in the canteens, but at the same time let's have productions of great plays in our theatres, so that the people who work may also laugh, and weep and wonder. We must all have a glimpse, while we labour or fight, of those glorious worlds of the imagination.[33]

Priestley's passionate sincerity is another testament to the emotions of 1940, and such broadcasts may well have contributed to the Labour victory of 1945. Conservatives, notably Churchill, regarded him as too radical, and had his postscripts taken off the air in 1941. But CEMA was some distance from realising Priestley's vision. As the organisation became more securely established, the internal contradictions of policy became more painful. Mary Glasgow recorded:

An actual conflict developed between what may be called the amateur and the professional point of view. According to the professional attitude, all performances should, if possible, be self-supporting and it was assumed that there was something wrong with entertainment, or at least its method of presentation, if it persistently ran at a loss. The amateur attitude, on the other hand, may be described as the missionary approach, which demanded music, plays, and exhibitions for all who wanted them, regardless of the total numbers who attended, of their ability to pay or of the final appearance of the balance sheet.[34]

Again, this was to be a familiar debate in the next fifty years.

CEMA's problems were compounded by the policy adopted by the Carnegie Trust, which had an interest in promoting music. Initially it had agreed to work alongside the Pilgrim Trust in helping CEMA, but then decided to act independently and much of the work of encouraging amateur music-making fell to the Carnegie Trust. CEMA's amateur-drama organisers ceased work by the end of 1941, and by 1944 its music travellers had been turned into regional administrative officers. The "amateur" faction on the Council, led by Dr Jones and the composer Vaughan Williams, gradually gave way to those, like Sir Kenneth Clark, who saw the arts as an essentially professional activity and CEMA's duty as the maintenance of standards. Clark, a future chairman of the Arts Council, epitomised the tastes of the mandarin aesthete, passionate about art and artists, less passionate about people. As director of the National Gallery, Clark helped Dame Myra Hess institute the celebrated wartime lunchtime recitals in the gallery, emptied of its pictures to prevent their destruction by bombs. He was a key figure in the War Artists Advisory Committee which secured commissions for artists to record both the military and domestic life of the nation at war. This public patronage was matched by the personal help which his private fortune allowed him to give to Henry Moore and Graham Sutherland, among others.

The exigencies of wartime drew CEMA inexorably into supporting professional artists and performers. Very early in 1940 CEMA organised twenty concerts by the London Symphony Orchestra and the London Philharmonic in industrial districts around London, which saved the orchestras from probable disbandment. The Ministry of Labour recognised employment by CEMA as a form of National Service, and therefore as a professional activity as far as war work was concerned. Thus when the composer Benjamin Britten and his lover, the singer Peter Pears, returned from America in 1942 and were registered as conscientious objectors, the recitals they gave for CEMA were accepted as appropriate war work. There were, as Mary Glasgow pointed out, professional artists who identified themselves with the 'missionary approach', notably the Old Vic theatre company led by Tyrone Guthrie, which had a long tradition of missionary zeal inherited from its founder Lilian Bayliss. When the Old Vic theatre was shut down by bomb damage in the autumn of 1940, CEMA funded tours by the company to Lancashire and the mining areas of South Wales, and then supported them when they temporarily established a base in Burnley, Lancashire.

The turning point in the battle between professional and amateur came in March 1942 when the Pilgrim Trust, possibly because the commitment to amateur work was already weakening, decided to withdraw its funding from CEMA, having given it a total of £62,500. Not only did this mean that CEMA became entirely a government responsibility, but the 'useless' Lord Macmillan and his 'missionary' vice-chairman Dr Jones had to resign, since the Trust need no longer be represented. The choice of Macmillan's successor turned out to be one of the most important decisions in the history of British government policy towards the arts.

In practice, cultural activity is a matter of taste, and taste is an expression of personality. There can have been few more powerful personalities than the economist John Maynard Keynes. Born in 1883, brilliant, bisexual, he had spent his life at the heart of that artistic nexus, "Bloomsbury": from his membership of the exclusive intellectual society of the Apostles at Cambridge before the First World War, to his liaison with the painter Duncan Grant, his teaching at King's College, Cambridge, and the house in Gordon Square, Bloomsbury, where he lived after his marriage to the former Diaghilev dancer Lydia Lopokova in 1925. A Treasury adviser in the Great War, he bought a key collection of Impressionist pictures for the nation while attending the Versailles peace conference in 1919, and throughout his life was a collector of books and works of art. In 1941 he became a trustee of the National Gallery. He founded the London Artists Association in 1930 as a means of supporting young artists, and was treasurer of the Carmago Society, a short-lived attempt in the thirties to fund contemporary ballet. He was the founder and principal financier of the Arts Theatre in Cambridge, which opened in 1936. In 1940 he returned as an unpaid adviser to the Treasury, and though he had no formal duties, other than as a governor of the Bank of England, he was closely involved in wartime economic policy, and was a key figure in the negotiations with the United States over the Bretton Woods financial agreement of 1944. Like Sir William Beveridge, he was a liberal technocrat. To achieve the full employment that was one of the founding assumptions of Beveridge's welfare state, a post-war government would have to rely on Keynes's theories about economic pump-priming and demand management. Keynes advised the Labour government until his death in 1946. Hugh Dalton, who had been his pupil at Cambridge, described him as his 'most trusted counsellor at the Treasury'.[35]

Given the stress of wartime on such a high-powered figure (especially one already suffering from heart disease), it is surprising that Keynes agreed to take on the chairmanship of CEMA, but he was self-confident, even arrogant. Sir Kenneth Clark welcomed his appointment: 'He was not a man for wandering minstrels and amateur theatricals. He believed in excellence.'[36] But even Clark had reservations: 'Although I admired his brilliance, I thought he displayed it too unsparingly. . . . Although a kind man, I have seen him humiliate people in a cruel way.'[37] One of those who suffered under Keynes at CEMA was the associate drama director, Charles Landstone, who as a professional drama administrator thought Keynes was the amateur: 'He loved glamour, he loved success, and he was not impervious to flattery.'[38] Mary Glasgow, though devoted to Keynes, acknowledged his weaknesses:

'Just as his own favourites were apt to get special treatment, so he was, in the nature of things, suspicious of some of the activities he inherited from the original CEMA.'[39]

Part of this suspicion was derived from an early clash with CEMA in May 1940, when Keynes had tried to get CEMA to support a tour by the actor-manager Donald Wolfit that would end with a season in London. Keynes was critical of CEMA's policy of directly setting up and managing theatre tours, and argued that it would be better simply to offer an established company a guarantee against loss which, if the production were a success, would save money. CEMA, in missionary mood, replied that it did not finance "commercial" companies, and that it was not planning to support work in London. Keynes would not take no for an answer, especially when he learned shortly afterwards about CEMA's help to the Old Vic company. He therefore offered to provide a guarantee against loss for Wolfit through the Arts Theatre in Cambridge, if CEMA found the rest. CEMA agreed, and the tour went ahead.

Keynes was officially offered the chairmanship of CEMA in December 1941 by the new president of the Board of Education, R. A. Butler, a Cambridge colleague whose father-in-law, the art patron Samuel Courtauld, was a friend of Keynes. Keynes protested that he had 'only limited sympathy' with the principles on which CEMA had been run because he thought "welfare" was being developed at the expense of "standards", but accepted the chairmanship, along with the offer of a peerage.[40] Keynes became chairman on 1 April 1942, and the government, now sole sponsor, raised CEMA's grant-in-aid to one hundred thousand pounds for the new financial year.

Keynes's administrative dispositions and artistic preferences laid the foundations of the post-war Arts Council, which he was planning as early as 1943, under the grander and nationally defining title, the Royal Council for the Arts. Keynes extended CEMA's responsibility to include opera and ballet, and set up three advisory panels, for music, art and drama, serviced by a salaried director for each. In keeping with British bureaucratic tradition, the unit of decision-making was the committee (however much a committee might be dominated by an individual like Keynes). It was also in the bureaucratic tradition to fund organisations and institutions, rather than individual artists. The nine members of the Council met only five or six times a year, leaving day-to-day decisions to the panels, which were given executive power. Keynes intended to chair the meetings of all the panels, but his government work made this difficult, and they were chaired by council members: the principal of the Royal College of Music, Sir Stanley Marchant, for music; Sir Kenneth Clark for art; and the drama critic and wartime editor of the *Observer*, Ivor Brown, for drama. Eleven regional offices were established, corresponding to the geographical areas covered for Civil Defence: ten in England and one in Scotland. A twelfth, for Wales, was added in 1944. In November 1942 CEMA moved out of the accommodation provided by the Board of Education in Kingsway to offices at the smarter address of 9 Belgrave Square.

Not only did Keynes see to it that in future subsidy would be concentrated on professional organisations, he also reversed CEMA's policy of not funding work in London. As his critics saw it, Keynes ensured that the future Arts Council would be both élitist, and metropolitan in bias. According to Charles Landstone, the Council 'under the influence of Keynes – and that influence persisted for a long time after his death – was always more interested in "glamour", than in the solid "backroom" groundwork'.[41] Landstone's view of Keynes was conditioned by the Council's lack of appreciation of his own work organising CEMA tours to factory hostels during the war, and his post-war efforts to revive provincial repertory theatres. He writes of the hostel tours that the Council 'always approached them with the happy glow of an aristocratic lady going slumming'.[42]

Keynes continued to support the work of the Old Vic, and brought the Sadler's Wells opera and ballet companies (also creations of Lilian Bayliss) into association with CEMA, but he was offended by Guthrie's decision to return to London from Burnley in 1942 without consulting him, and he was constantly critical of the Old Vic company. As an economist, Keynes was happier with the not-for-profit theatre companies set up by commercial managements after Entertainment Tax was raised to one third of gross receipts in 1941. It was possible to gain exemption from the tax by achieving charitable, non-profit-distributing status on the grounds that the company had an educational purpose. CEMA could not grant the exemption, but the phrase 'in association with CEMA' (even if the Council gave the company no funds) was a useful seal of approval. The first of these companies was Tennent Plays, set up by the leading West End producer Binkie Beaumont in 1941 to manage a tour of *Macbeth* staring John Gielgud that became the centre of a London repertory season. Wartime appetite for the arts was such that not-for-profit companies became very profitable. Some money went to CEMA, but commercial managements found a way of extracting profits from their charitable subsidiaries by charging a large management fee.

Only in the field of art did Keynes receive something of a check to his policies, and that was partly due to the influence of a personality who was to be as significant in the Arts Council's history as Keynes himself, W. E. Williams. In 1935, as the young secretary of the British Institute for Adult Education, Williams had launched a series of travelling exhibitions as 'Art for the People', which Dr Jones had funded from 1936. Williams became a protégé of Jones's, and was at the meeting that set up CEMA in 1939. CEMA took 'Art for the People' under its wing, and Williams remained on the Council when he became director of the Army Bureau of Current Affairs in September 1941. ABCA carried over the principles of adult education into military life, by producing pamphlets on issues in current affairs for use by platoon officers during the compulsory training session devoted to discussion (illustration 3). (Williams wrote the article for the *Current Affairs* pamphlet quoted on p. 26.) ABCA, like Priestley and his broadcasts, have become part of the demonology of the Right that is used to explain the defeat of the Conservatives in 1945. Churchill unsuccessfully tried to have ABCA wound up in 1942, and the bureau's pamphlet on the Beveridge Report was withdrawn from circulation.

Williams proved adept at dealing with the more blimpish aspects of the military. Although offered the equivalent rank of a brigadier, he never wore a uniform. While running ABCA and keeping a close watch on affairs at CEMA, Williams continued to serve as a key editorial adviser to the publisher Allan Lane, who had founded one of the most significant (and commercially successful) instruments for popular education, Penguin Books, in 1935. Lane's biographer, and Williams's colleague at Penguin, J. E. Morpurgo, drew this character sketch:

William Emrys Williams was a Welshman to every letter of his unmistakably Welsh name; even if he did come from Manchester. The rich rhythms of his Welsh voice, cunningly modulated by a controlled stammer, freed him from the suspicion of patronising the audience that hung over so many of the Oxonian and metropolitan popular educators of that era. He was mercurial, as eager to make friends as he was quick to find enemies, and his earnest political opinions, like his devout concern for public understanding, was tempered by commercial shrewdness. . . . Although his career had been so studiously dedicated to the earnest and generally left-of-centre adult education movement, his enthusiasm for the political, social and economic theorising that was the staple diet of that movement did not match his zest for the arts. He also shared with the Lanes . . . an unfettered capacity for hedonism.[43]

Williams made a useful ally in Sir Kenneth Clark, but he made an enemy of Keynes. According to Williams: 'There was, alas, in this great scholar and art connoisseur a streak of donnish superiority and a singular ignorance of ordinary people.'[44] Keynes disapproved of the use of lecturers to guide people round CEMA's 'Art for the People' shows, and when Williams joined ABCA Keynes considered 'a gradual winding-up of our relations' with him.[45] In 1943 Keynes halved CEMA's grant of ten thousand pounds for the exhibitions, although with Clark's help Williams got two and a half thousand of this reinstated. Keynes kept further grants down, and CEMA began to mount its own touring shows, including an early celebration of Moore, Sutherland and Piper. Williams, never one to remove his finger from a pie, stayed on the Council.

In April 1944 the government's grant to CEMA rose to £175,000, and with R. A. Butler's active support, Keynes pressed on with his post-war plans. On 30 January 1945 he chaired a full-scale Council debate on the future, at which it was decided that CEMA (which had no precise legal status) should seek incorporation under a Royal Charter, with a council of sixteen members, an executive committee, separate committees for Scotland and Wales and advisory panels for some art forms. Clark is credited with suggesting the title 'The Arts Council of Great Britain', and the first meeting of this new body was held in February 1945. At this meeting Keynes won an important constitutional point, by insisting that the panels should have a purely advisory function. The reason for this change from his earlier position was that experience – particularly with the troublesome drama panel – had taught that the chairman (himself) could not closely control the doings of all the panel. The effect was that the Arts Council was always to give the appearance of consulting the experts in the respective art forms – and most of the time this consultation was genuine – but the real power of decision lay with the members of the Council and their executive officers.

The announcement that CEMA was to become the Arts Council of Great Britain was made in the House of Commons on 12 June 1945 by Sir John Anderson, Chancellor of the Exchequer since 1943. Anderson had been Keynes's patron at the Treasury and was, like Keynes, a Liberal, but he was an administrator *par excellence* and sat as an independent MP. The Arts Council's first grant, for 1945–6, was to be raised to £235,000, but Keynes had not succeeded in remaining under the protection of the Board of Education, and in future, the ministry responsible would be the Treasury. This shift away from a "spending" ministry to the keeper of the purse-strings was to be a problem for the Arts Council until it returned to the patronage of Education in the sixties.

The Arts Council's Royal Charter was granted on 9 August 1946. Its purpose was described as:

> developing a greater knowledge, understanding and practice of the fine arts exclusively, and in particular to increase the accessibility of the fine arts to the public throughout Our Realm, and to improve the standard of execution of the fine arts and to advise and co-operate with Our Government Departments, local authorities and other bodies on any matters concerned directly or indirectly with those objects.[46]

The Royal Charter of 1946 was a less contradictory document than CEMA's memorandum to the Treasury in 1940, but it did not have as strong an emphasis on standards and professionalism as Keynes would have liked and it still presented aims which, without adequate funding to achieve them, would prove contradictory in practice. On the one hand, the Arts Council was enjoined to increase knowledge and improve access to the arts, but the commitment to 'standards of execution' implied a belief in professionalism that could only be achieved at the expense of the more "missionary" intentions. The phrase 'the fine arts exclusively' could be – and was – read as a narrow definition of culture that excluded both the amateur and the popular. Keynes would not have disagreed with this reading, but in fact he had inserted the phrase in the hope of obtaining rate relief on Arts Council buildings, the practice of 'the fine arts exclusively' being a theoretical qualification for such relief from local taxation under the Scientific Societies Act of 1843. In the event the relief was not forthcoming. The phrase was dropped when the Arts Council's charter was renewed in 1967.

Sadly, Keynes died at Easter 1946 so he never saw the finished Charter for the institution he had done so much to shape. His last public appearance was at the Royal Gala to reopen the Royal Opera House, Covent Garden. During the war the building had been a Mecca dancehall, but the lease was taken over by the music publishers Boosey and Hawkes, who in turn let the building to the newly formed Covent Garden Trust. The first chairman of the Trust was Keynes himself, and funds came from the Arts Council, thus establishing a long and intimate link between the two organisations. The establishment of a national opera house was the first step towards the formation of national performing companies that Keynes saw as an essential part of post-war culture. For better or worse, the financial needs of Covent Garden, housing as it would both an opera company and a ballet company with attendant orchestra, were to be a constant pressure on the Arts Council in the years ahead.

Apart from the connection with the Opera House, Keynes's legacy to the Arts Council was the text of a broadcast he made for the BBC in July 1945, in which he set out the 'policy and hopes' of the Arts Council. He began by remarking how 'English' the process of its creation had been: 'I do not believe it is yet realised what an important thing has happened. State patronage of the arts has crept in. It has happened in a very English, informal unostentatious way – half-baked if you like. A semi-independent body is provided with modest funds.'[47] Keynes's words betray a similarly English search for consensual compromise. He publicly rejected the metropolitan bias that was already part of the Arts Council's thinking. He talked about decentralising cultural life by co-operating with local authorities and persuading them and the government to put some of the limited resources for reconstruction into facilities for the arts. He had in mind the saving of the Bristol Old Vic, which CEMA had reopened as a playhouse in 1943. He was also discreetly echoing the Labour Party's 1945 manifesto: 'By provision of concert halls, modern libraries, theatres and suitable centres, we desire to assure our people full access to the great heritage of culture in this nation.'[48] But towards the end of his broadcast Keynes produced a tangled knot of assertions:

> Nothing can be more damaging than the excessive prestige of metropolitan standards and fashions. Let every part of Merry England be merry in its own way. Death to Hollywood. But it is also our business to make London a great artistic metropolis, a place to visit and to wonder at.[49]

The rival claims of London and the regions parallel the contradictions in the Royal Charter. Within that tension the phrase 'Merry England' suggests that Keynes had a patronising view of what he imagined to be popular culture, while the 'Hollywood' he damns represents the commercial culture that the majority of people in reality enjoyed. This was at a time when the cinema had a regular audience in Britain of thirty million. Keynes's broadcast introduces key themes in post-war cultural policies and politics: anti-Americanism and the promotion of a conservative image of English identity.

Only someone like Keynes could have managed the transition from an ad hoc wartime committee to a brave new institution. His commitment to the arts was genuine, his standing was high in the arts establishment, and his close contact with government, especially the Board of Education and the Treasury, gave him the ear of the decision-makers. Indeed the formation of the Arts Council could be described as a reward for his services as economic strategist to the nation. Yet, as another economist with a close interest in the arts, Sir Alan Peacock, the chairman of the Scottish Arts Council from 1986 to 1992, has pointed out: 'Keynes's view on the role of the body which he largely created was never adopted by the Arts Council of Great Britain.'[50] Keynes hoped that once a network of suitable buildings had been established across the country, "pump-priming" by the Arts Council would persuade the public of the virtue of spending their money on the arts, and so the need for subsidy would wither away. Instead, the Arts Council, according to Peacock, 'has always perceived its role as the perpetual funder of arts institutions which would never by themselves be able to raise all their funds from the box office and private sponsorship'.[51] Keynes may have formed the Arts Council in his preferred image, but the institution then took on its own life.

The 1945 Labour government, busy with larger and more pressing issues, seems to have been content to accept the fledgling Arts Council as it stood. The Treasury's still modest grant-in-aid almost trebled between 1945–6 and 1950–51, when it reached £675,000, but this generosity was somewhat tempered by the government's choice of successor to Keynes. Kenneth Clark had resigned as Director of the National Gallery in 1945, and as a founder member of CEMA and active supporter of the Royal Opera House, anticipated taking over the empty chair at the Arts Council. He was considerably put out when an obscure former Warden of the Drapers' Company, Sir Ernest Pooley, was appointed instead. Clark recorded in his memoirs that Pooley, 'having no interest in the arts . . . could be relied on not to press their claims too strongly'.[52]

The Labour government's most important legislation, as far as the arts were concerned, came in the 1948 Local Government Act, which allowed local authorities, other than county and parish councils, to levy up to the equivalent of a sixpenny rate for the support of the arts. (County councils did not gain this power until 1963, when authorities were also allowed to support ventures outside their administrative boundaries, an important benefit for Regional Arts Associations.) Local government arts expenditure (as opposed to spending on libraries) was, and has remained, discretionary rather than mandatory, and did not qualify for contributory support from central government as part of its subvention to local authority budgets. In 1948 up to fifty million pounds could have been spent by local authorities on the arts, but it never was. Local authority support was patchy, varying from the generous to the non-existent, and was always hard to quantify. Nonetheless, it became an increasingly important part of the arts economy and increased substantially during the seventies, so that by the beginning of the nineties local authority expenditure on arts, museums and libraries exceeded that of central government, £750 million as opposed to £607 million in 1988–9.

This development was made possible by the 1948 Act, which also cancelled the clauses of the 1925 Public Health Act which expressly forbade local authorities to put on plays, variety or film shows. In 1949 the government at last acceded to a campaign launched in 1906 (with support from Winston Churchill) for Britain to have a national theatre; one million pounds was set aside for its construction, and a foundation stone was laid in 1951 (though it was subsequently moved). The National Theatre company took over the Old Vic in 1963, but construction of a new building on the South Bank did not begin until 1969 and it was not officially opened until 1976, an indication of the sense of cultural urgency felt by both Labour and Conservative governments.

The post-war Labour government's cultural policies were not limited to the arts. The Town and Country Planning Act of 1947 and the creation of the National Parks laid down important guidelines for the future of the landscape and the built environment, creating "green belts" around cities and extending the protection of specifically listed buildings that had been introduced in 1944. Sadly, the Labour government's most imaginative stroke, the National Land Fund, fell victim to political and economic circumstances. In the event, no land was acquired through the Fund for the new National Parks, and although the National Trust and the Youth Hostels Association were beneficiaries, the Fund was under-used. One reason for this was that Dalton set up no separate arm's-length organisation to administer it, so that the money remained with the Treasury, safely invested in government bonds. When Dalton was forced to resign as Chancellor in 1947 following a breach of Parliamentary etiquette, he was no longer in a position to promote its use. Other parts of Dalton's own 1946 budget were a positive discouragement to the use of the Fund. Not only did he maintain punitively high rates of income tax, but while ending death duties on very small inheritances, he increased duty on large ones from ten per cent to seventy-five per cent. Tax rates at that level only encouraged the practice of making probate valuations (on which the tax would be paid) well below true market value. Since land was acquired by the Fund only at its probate value, owners preferred to settle their tax bills by selling land at its much higher market price, once probate had been granted, rather than passing it to the Fund. (Dalton was also responsible for abolishing surtax relief on donations to charities which – as was even more the case in the United States – had been one of the ways in which the rich had patronised the arts.)

Between 1947 and 1957 average expenditure by the National Land Fund was less than two hundred thousand pounds a year, and although the Conservative government that succeeded Labour in 1951 extended its application to works of art, by 1957 the Fund had grown in idleness to nearly £60 million, producing an investment income of £1.4 million a year. (In 1957 the Arts Council's grant-in-aid was just under £1 million.) In that year, short of money, and showing a strangely careless attitude to the future of the nation's heritage, the Conservative government decided arbitrarily to reduce the Fund to £10 million (in effect pocketing the rest), so that it became almost a dead letter. In 1980 the Fund provided the capital base for the National Heritage Memorial Fund (see pp. 266–7). The word 'Memorial' was added as an afterthought, when Dalton's original intentions were dimly recalled.

The fundamental problem for the Labour government of 1945 was that the reforming zeal and sense of community engendered by the war proved difficult to sustain in peace. In July 1947 the editor of *Horizon*, Cyril Connolly, who had launched his literary magazine in 1940 on the wave of passionate concern about the future of the arts in wartime, spoke for many when he described his disillusion: 'The fact remains that a Socialist government, besides doing practically nothing to help artists and writers . . . has also quite failed to stir up either intellect or imagination.'[53] Artists and intellectuals were themselves suffering a negative reaction to the coming of peace, and retreating into private concerns, but arts administrators were also disappointed to find that the new public, avid for the arts that had been discovered in wartime, was evaporating. Charles Landstone recalled: 'At the end of the war, all of us thought that all that remained to be done was to provide new buildings and new theatres for this vast new audience. But unfortunately, an extraordinary thing happened. The audience dispersed from their hostels, their rest camps and their war centres and, in a flash, appeared to have left their interest behind them.'[54]

It did not occur to Landstone that the institution created to build on that wartime enthusiasm might itself be responsible for allowing it to disperse. However critical he was of Keynes, he did not go so far as to suggest that the Arts Council had been wrongly constituted. Yet the institutional framework that had been devised in 1945 missed opportunities that had existed in 1940 to define the arts so as to embrace a wider range of activities and to include a broader definition of the audience for them. It might even have encouraged those audiences to become active, rather than passive, in their participation. As one of the institutions to emerge from the "revolutionary" consensus of 1940, and with the powerful weapons of cultural possibility and opportunity to hand, the Arts Council was in a position to maintain the momentum of change that had brought it into being. But it did not do so, falling back on older definitions of culture and conservative habits of thought. The Labour government, which, as Raymond Williams has pointed out, did little to encourage specifically socialist cultural organisations such as the documentary film movement, only belatedly accepted the importance of cultural activity when planning began in earnest for the Festival of Britain in 1947 (as the next chapter shows).[55] Even then it preferred to work at arm's length through institutions such as the Council of Industrial Design and the Arts Council which, born out of a wartime consensus, were more at ease administering the one that succeeded it.

Behind the question of how to manage the now accepted responsibility for the arts lay the issue of how a national culture should be defined and in whose interests it should be managed. That question in turn depended upon what the new conception of Britain's identity should be. In the face of the uncertainties of peace, it was by no means clear that the 'soundness and homogeneity' that Orwell had detected in 1940 would be sustained, or that the consensus for change would not become a consensus for continuity and, ultimately, retreat.

III

New Britain

Britain in the early 1950s

On 12 November 1947 Hugh Dalton found himself making another budget speech, but in a far less exalted mood than that of eighteen months before. This was a short, emergency budget, setting higher taxes and sharply reducing purchasing power. It was necessary because of the series of disasters that had overtaken the Labour government that year, beginning in January with the worst winter for a century, and culminating with a sterling crisis that threatened to bankrupt the country. As he spoke, Dalton was unaware that personal political disaster was overtaking him. On his way into the Commons he had had a few words about the contents of his speech with a lobby correspondent on a London evening paper, the *Star*, which was able to publish a report before Dalton had finished speaking. Dalton was technically guilty of a budget leak, and he was obliged to resign. He was replaced by Sir Stafford Cripps, with whose name "the age of austerity" of the late forties is indissolubly linked.

The crises of 1947 brought home the difficulties that Britain's post-war economy faced, and the failure of the Labour government to move very far towards the New Jerusalem hoped for in 1945. The bulk of the legislation that created the post-war settlement was in place: the National Health Service, national insurance and nationalisation of transport, coal and steel, but there had indeed been a failure 'to stir up either intellect or imagination', as Connolly had complained.[1] Labour's leaders were exhausted and several of them were ill, while their constituents began to lose patience with the narrow life that the economic sacrifices of socialism appeared to impose. The novelist J. G. Ballard has vividly described his return to England from a Japanese internment camp to find the middle classes 'seething with a sort of repressed rage at the world around them'.[2] Abroad, the country's dependence on American aid was underlined, while British power was confronted by a new threat, the possibility of war with Russia. The retreat from Empire began with the granting of independence to India and Pakistan in 1947, but there was no clear way forward at home.

In future, the welfare state settlement was to be "consolidated" rather than completed. Proud as they were of their defeat of Germany, the British people could no longer celebrate their country as the workshop and entrepôt of the world, nor were the national characteristics of endurance and mutual co-operation manifested in wartime so easily discovered in peace. While the Labour government suffered a crisis of confidence from which it never recovered, Britain as a whole faced a wider crisis of national identity.

It was precisely at this moment that plans began positively to be laid for a celebration that would attempt both to reassert the British sense of national identity, and to modernise it: the Festival of Britain. But the difficulty facing anyone who wished to stimulate the nation's intellect and imagination was that those who might be expected to do so – artists, authors, poets, composers, critics, in short, the intelligentsia, by and large shared Connolly's disillusion, and had either simply abandoned their wartime political commitments, or moved positively to the Right. The 'strategic retreat of the Left' had begun as early as 1943, and the high ground once held by the Left was now occupied by Christians and conservatives with no ardour for the collectivism of the Welfare State.[3]

Christians and conservatives – who are often the same people – share a pessimistic view of the fallen nature of man and of civilisation. There can be few more pessimistic statements than this, of T. S. Eliot's, published in 1948, a year after what Dalton called Labour's '*Annus Horrendus*'.[4]

> We can assert with some confidence that our own period is one of decline; that the standards of culture are lower than they were fifty years ago; and that the evidences of this decline are visible in every department of human activity. I see no reason why the decay of culture should not proceed much further, and why we may not even anticipate a period, of some duration, of which it is possible to say that it will have *no* culture.[5]

According to his biographer Peter Ackroyd, Eliot enjoyed 'almost shamanistic authority' in the post-war period, as poet, publisher and cultural commentator.[6] In 1928, shortly after he had resolved his own problems of identity by being baptised into the Church of England and exchanging American for British nationality, Eliot described his point of view as 'classicist in literature, royalist in politics, and anglo-catholic in religion'.[7] These values became fundamental to his writings on culture, most importantly *The Idea of a Christian Society* (1939) and *Notes Towards the Definition of Culture*, published in 1948.

Notes Towards the Definition of Culture is a scrappy little book, assembled from essays and broadcasts that went back to 1943, but it made an impression, partly because of Eliot's authority – further added to in 1948 by the award of both the Nobel Prize for Literature and the Order of Merit – and partly because it was so hostile to the direction European culture appeared to be taking. In the era of the foundation of UNESCO as well as of the Arts Council, the arts had become a matter of state concern: 'We observe nowadays that "culture" attracts the attention of men of politics: not that politicians are always "men of culture", but that "culture" is recognised both as an instrument of policy, and as something socially desirable which it is the business of the State to promote.'[8]

Accordingly, Eliot set out to enquire what the word might mean, answering: 'A "culture" is conceived as the creation of the society as a whole: being, from another aspect, that which makes it a society.'[9] Earlier he had made the astute comment that 'boiled cabbage cut into sections, beetroot in vinegar, nineteenth-century Gothic churches and the music of Elgar' could all be considered as culture in so far as they revealed the characteristic activities and interests of a people.[10] But Eliot did not develop this anthropological idea of culture as a collective creation embracing more than the high arts. There were two other meanings attached to the idea of culture, that of the culture of an individual, and the culture of a group or class. Eliot believed that while culture might spread throughout society, it became more concentrated the higher it rose through the classes, until it was distilled by élites. It was this purer, literally "high" culture which interested him. The anthropological application of the idea of culture to the whole of society, as something – as his list suggests – autonomous, organic and contradictory, was cited to oppose the notion that culture, as part of the Welfare State, could be planned.

Eliot's model of culture conjures up a mental picture of a cultural landscape dominated by a high ridge of artistic achievement, towering above a middle-ground of average endeavour, which then falls away to the lowlands of popular pursuits. These lower reaches of recreation were menaced by invaders from across the sea: the bearers of crass American entertainment. "Culture" – with a capital "C" – was what it had been even before Matthew Arnold's day, not just the alternative to Anarchy, but a defence against the corruptions of industrialisation and mass society that threatened to blot out all sweetness and light. All classes in society might have some share in the values of this Culture, but the preservation of these values was the specific responsibility of the élites which occupied the high ground.

The welfare state was a threat to Culture because of 'the dogma of equal opportunity' and the potential changes that could be brought about through state control of education.[11] The peaks of high art were menaced by 'levelling'. Not noticing, it seems, that the Butler Education Act of 1944 itself preserved an educational hierarchy with its social division between grammar schools, secondary moderns and technical schools, Eliot feared the consequences of equal opportunity: 'There is no doubt that in our headlong rush to educate everybody, we are lowering our standards . . . [we are] destroying our ancient edifices to make ready the ground upon which the barbarian nomads of the future will encamp in their mechanised caravans.'[12] The true purpose of education was 'to preserve the class and to select the élite'.[13] The élite would preserve Culture – and Culture would preserve the élite.

Eliot was by no means the only one to hold this view. In 1949 the Student Christian Movement Press published Sir Walter Moberley's *The Crisis in the University*, the product of a conference of forty committed Christian university lecturers which argued that 'the present situation of the British universities resembles that of the British nation'.[14] Moberley, who was in a position of considerable influence as chairman of the University Grants Committee, concluded: 'For Western civilisation at least, and notably for Great Britain, reconstruction is to be achieved, not by abandoning our tradition but by rediscovering and reinvigorating it.'[15]

"Tradition" was the touchstone of cultural conservatism – the point at issue was precisely how that tradition was to be defined. It is for that reason that Eliot's book was dismissed in the pages of F. R. Leavis's critical quarterly *Scrutiny* for failing 'to arouse any interest in those who are actively engaged in the study of society'.[16] Although *Scrutiny* itself ceased publication in 1953, Leavis and his followers were to continue to be enormously influential. They shared Eliot's pessimistic view of society, his sense of loss of order and certainty, his concern about the institutionalisation of culture and, like Eliot, fiercely upheld the values of a minority culture over against those of a mass civilisation. The difference lay in the stricter definition of a tradition based on English literature, as opposed to Eliot's more catholic and cosmopolitan taste, and in their belief in the value of a university-based, critical clerisy, over against Eliot's metropolitan élite.

In essence, Eliot and Leavis fell on either side of a cultural divide that can be traced back to the English Civil War. Both are authentic traditions, but while Eliot reflected an aristocratic, High Anglican taste Leavis was fundamentally a puritan. The difference might be described in terms of a cavalier pleasure in poetry, over against a reforming commitment to prose. Though Leavis had championed the Eliot of *The Waste Land* (1922), Leavis and Eliot were to shape two different cultural traditions. While Eliot appealed to metropolitan upper-class conservatives, Leavis, though no less conservative himself, was an inspiration to lower-middle-class provincial radicals, heirs of the Methodist dissenters who had been excluded from Oxford and Cambridge until the final repeal of the Test Acts in 1871. Teaching in Cambridge, but at odds with his own university, Leavis warred against the London institutions, especially the literary journals and the quality press, which did not come up to his high standards or promote his views. The non-conformist radicalism which had prompted Leavis to found *Scrutiny* in 1932 had become bitter by the time this comment was published in the final issue in 1953: 'The BBC, the British Council and the related institutions are manifestations of the same modern developments as those which issued in the welfare state.'[17]

While the conditions of post-war Britain could do nothing to bring back the lost, ideal organic society that peopled the landscapes of both Eliot and Leavis's imaginations, it is difficult to see why the welfare state, as it turned out in practice, should be thought such a menace. The 'ancient edifices' of the public schools were untouched, and the theoretical opening of higher education to all by the provision of state scholarships did nothing to weaken the privileged positions of Oxford and Cambridge. If anything, it strengthened them, by allowing them to recruit more widely into the élite.

The one significant cultural institution apart from the Arts Council which was created at this period, the BBC's Third Programme, followed Eliot's cultural model precisely. William Haley, the BBC's director-

general responsible for bringing it into being, saw the Light, Home
and Third Programmes as a cultural pyramid up which the aspiring
listener could climb towards an Arnoldian sweetness and light.
Launched in September 1946, and initially broadcasting only from
6 p.m. to midnight, 'the Third' broadcast classical music, plays, documentary features and talks, with speech and music in roughly equal
proportions, though music subsequently came to predominate. It
turned out to be listened to by about one per cent of the BBC's total
audience. Echoes of the debates within CEMA can be heard in the
description of the Third's policy by its first head, George Barnes:

> There are those who dislike being "talked at", who demand "performance"
> and nothing else, who find popular exposition often condescending and
> often irritating – highbrows is the name given to them by their opponents.
> On the other side are those who want things to be explained; believing that
> the generally cultivated person no longer exists; who have, like horses, to be
> led to water or, like the Prom' audiences, want their programmes to have
> notes. Compromise on this issue antagonises all. We shall therefore provide
> the programme, and not the notes. There will be few "hearing aids" for
> listeners to the Third Programme.[18]

Rather than adopt the "missionary" approach of someone like Dr
Thomas Jones, Barnes, himself a scion of Bloomsbury, preferred the
patrician attitude of Keynes. When the Third had its broadcasting
hours reduced in 1957 because of a need to cut costs coupled with the
no-longer defensible smallness of the audience, Eliot became vice-
president of the Third Programme Defence Society and took part in a
protest delegation to the governors of the BBC.

Where attitudes to culture were not explicitly conservative, they were
Fabian. The Fabian Society had served as a "think tank" for the Labour
Party ever since Sidney and Beatrice Webb had helped to create the
party's constitution during the First World War. True to the Webbs'
reformist principles, Fabians held that it was the duty of those in
possession of culture to lead those who were not gently towards the
light. What they failed to appreciate was that "culture" was valued
precisely for its minority appeal, and its status would be altered by its
wider availability. More than half the Labour MPs in the 1945 parliament were members of the Fabian Society; the dominant professions
were lawyers, teachers, managers and technocrats.

The Fabian attitude obscured other possibilities for cultural change.
Two wartime institutions which had contributed to popular culture and

popular education, ENSA and the Army Bureau of Current Affairs, were allowed to lapse. W. E. Williams commented later: 'If ABCA had *really* won the election for the Labour Party why were they in such haste to wind it up?'[19] While the Arts Council continued the policies of J. M. Keynes, pulling out of direct management of the arts in favour of subsidising existing institutions, and favouring the metropolis at the expense of the regions, state sponsorship of the documentary film movement, which had flourished during the war, was gradually withdrawn. University extension lecturing and the Workers' Educational Association were still resources for popular education, but having accepted the Arts Council's definition of the arts, the 1945 government noticeably failed to encourage any specifically socialist forms of popular culture, though mass entertainments like sport and cinema-going flourished.

Even those like J. B. Priestley, who supported Labour's approach to the arts, were not satisfied with the results. In his 1947 Fabian Society lecture *The Arts Under Socialism* he grumbled: 'I declare, without hesitation, as one still bleeding from the battle, that every bit of art we manage to achieve is almost a miracle. Artists of every kind are faced with a nightmare obstacle race, and this is not simply because of the transition from a wartime to a peacetime economy, and production, in a half-ruined world, for this we can all understand; but it is also because there are too many people in authority here who fail to appreciate the importance of art to a society like ours.'[20]

There was a further reason for the caution of the Left and the intellectual dominance of the Right in post-war cultural discussions: the hardening of the Cold War. While "good" culture was recruited in the cause of the West – the American Central Intelligence Agency's funding of the European Congress for Cultural Freedom, which in turn funded the London-based magazine *Encounter*, launched in 1953, is a case in point – communist intellectuals in Britain were marginalised, their jobs jeopardised and their views ignored. Ex-communists who did not explicitly break with their past (as virtually a whole generation did) found themselves in a difficult position. Raymond Williams, whose small volume *Reading and Criticism*, published in 1950, is notable for its fulsome acknowledgement to Leavis, has described 'the pain and confusion of a younger generation for whom communism had not been a god but who were trying to reject Stalinism and to sustain, under heavy attack, an indigenous socialism'.[21]

For the moment, the most influential voice in literary criticism was that of F. R. Leavis (notwithstanding the work of literary journalists like Cyril Connolly, Raymond Mortimer and V. S. Pritchett); while the debate about the definition of culture was dominated by T. S. Eliot, as Raymond Williams was to acknowledge in his pioneering study, *Culture and Society*, in 1958: 'The next step, in thinking of these matters, must be in a different direction, for Eliot has closed almost all existing roads.'[22] The direction taken by Williams was eventually to lead him to a late-twentieth-century Marxism, but there was to be a further decade of Cold War before that way became clear. In the thirties Leavis's radicalism had appeared to run in parallel with Marxist criticism of industrial society, but he rejected the solutions offered by Marxism, on the grounds that these were no more than a continuation of the destruction of organic cultural life that modern capitalism had begun. Eliot's position in the thirties was much further to the Right. The cultural conservatism of both men was reinforced by the conditions of the Cold War.

The crisis of confidence within the Labour government in 1947 was so severe that there was an attempted Cabinet coup against the Prime Minister. Attlee survived, while one of the chief plotters, Herbert Morrison, lost influence, though not his seat in the Cabinet as Lord President. Morrison was one of the chief exponents of the consolidation that emerged in 1948.[23] He was concerned about the middle-class floating voters – especially in his London constituency – who would be put off by further nationalisation measures and who wanted some relief from austerity. Underemployed in government in the autumn of 1947, Morrison took up the cause of the Festival of Britain, something that would both appeal to the middle classes, and soften the prevailing atmosphere of harsh austerity.

It is not unusual for governments to organise great expositions or other public spectacles as a way of demonstrating recovery after a period of national danger and stress. The French did it after the Revolution and the Terror that followed, and again after the débâcle of the Franco-Prussian War in 1870. The Americans did so after the Civil War. The idea of marking the centenary of the Great Exhibition of 1851 had first been mooted as early as 1943. The message of national recovery was explicit in the terms of reference of the Ramsden Committee, set up in 1945 to consider a 'Universal International Exposition' in Hyde Park, that would 'demonstrate to the world the recovery of the United Kingdom from the effects of war in the moral, cultural, spiritual and material fields'.[24]

By the time the decision to go ahead was taken in 1947, the idea had been whittled down to a national, rather than international, exhibition, but it remained for Herbert Morrison, who became the government minister responsible, 'a great symbol of national regeneration'.[25] Morrison described the Festival site as 'new Britain springing from the battered fabric of the old'.[26]

The Festival was planned by a special directorate, under the control of a Festival Council operating at arm's length from the government. The Festival Council worked closely with the Science Council and the newly created Council of Industrial Design, which helped select the exhibits, while the accompanying arts events were made the responsibility of the Arts Council. Morrison was aware of the potential political benefits to Labour of the event (and Attlee delayed calling the 1951 election until it was over), but he was scrupulous in excluding direct party political propaganda. This did not stop the Conservative opposition making party political points against the alleged extravagance of the Festival at a time of extreme material shortages, but Churchill's criticisms were muted by the choice of his former Chief of Staff, Lord Ismay, as chairman of the Festival Council. Opposition was further muted when the King and Queen became patrons of the Festival in 1950. The most consistent opposition came from Beaverbrook's *Evening Standard* and *Daily Express*. The *Express* was at least being consistent. When the first Treasury grant to CEMA was announced in 1940 it had thundered: "The government gives fifty thousand pounds to help wartime culture. What madness is this? There is no such thing as culture in wartime."[27]

The political climate in which the Festival was created was recalled by Sir Hugh Casson, the South Bank's director of architecture, in 1991: 'Churchill, like the rest of the Tory Party, was against the Festival which they (quite rightly) believed was the advanced guard of socialism. The hard-line Labourites were not enthusiastic either, believing it to be the usual charade of Hampstead wets teaching the working classes how to have fun. (Right again).'[28]

With a final budget of eleven million pounds, after one million was cut to meet the financial emergency created by the outbreak of the Korean War in 1950, the Festival made a genuine attempt to be a celebration for the whole of Britain. It consisted not only of the South Bank exhibition, but the Pleasure Gardens in Battersea, architecture in Poplar, science at South Kensington, industrial power in Glasgow, farming in Belfast, a travelling exhibition, and a Festival ship, the converted aircraft carrier *Campania*. There were also a great many local celebrations, encouraged, but not financially supported, by the Festival Council. The Arts Council organised a special season of exhibitions, music and drama in London, and gave extra help to local arts festivals, some of which, like the Edinburgh International Festival and Aldeburgh, were already in existence, while others were specially mounted for 1951. With 2,700 broadcasts covering every aspect of the Festival, the BBC did its best to create a sense of communal celebration.

The message of the Festival was not just that Britain had recovered from the war, but that she could look to a bright, dynamic future. That was certainly the impression given to visitors to the South Bank exhibition, yet the lasting imagery of the Dome of Discovery and the Skylon (illustration 5), the struts and wires, the abstract 'atomic' designs and the fabric patterns derived from crystals, suggests that the Festival of Britain was more forward-looking than it really was. The theme was 'the Land and the People',[29] comfortably democratic words from the lexicon of wartime propaganda that created a space within which to explore the way a nation had shaped its environment and been shaped by it. The modernist architecture was a lightweight framework for yet another exploration of Deep England. The emphasis was on 'the arts of peace',[30] with imperial echoes sounding only in the celebration of British explorers in the Dome of Discovery. Aware of Britain's indebtedness to the United States, the government had no wish to lay undue emphasis on Empire.

The optimistic, technological vision promoted on the South Bank was at odds with the neo-romanticism associated with the prevailing ideas of Land and People. The site was too cramped for any imposing architectural master plan; the artists brought in to provide murals and sculptures, among them Graham Sutherland, Henry Moore, John Piper, Edward Bawden and John Minton, tended to add a biomorphic or vegetable overlay which softened the designers' abstractions. Ernest Race's 'Antelope' chair, a special feature of the Festival, is a Piper pen drawing in steel rod, its very name biological, its character playful. Even for designers, the echoes of 1851 justified recourse to Victorian lettering and decorative motifs that had been so frowned on by the modernists of the thirties. While promoting "contemporary" architecture and product design, the Festival also nurtured the Victorian revival promoted by John Betjeman in the *Architectural Review.*

The Festival took place at a moment of interregnum in visual taste, with Paris no longer pre-eminent and New York not yet a magnet. Both artists and designers saw their commissions as opportunities to explore the idea of "Englishness", notably in the Lion and Unicorn pavilion dedicated to the British character (illustration 6). The British Lion alone had served as a symbol for the British Empire Exhibition in 1924, but in 1951 imperial ardour was tempered by domestic whimsy. The commentary written by the poet Laurie Lee explains that the pairing of the Lion and Unicorn 'serves to symbolise two of the main qualities of the national character: on the one hand, realism and strength, on the other fantasy, independence and imagination'.[31] The display featured the growth of the English language, the 'instinct for liberty' and love of the countryside. Lee comments: 'There is something deeply revealing, too, about the British view of nature as it has been expressed in landscape painting from the time of Gainsborough and Constable until the present day.'[32] Lee reassures the overseas visitor that if he left the pavilion 'still not much the wiser about the British national character, it might console him to know that British people are themselves very much in the dark about it'.[33]

The pavilion became something of an in-house project for teachers and students of the Royal College of Art, which under its rector Robin Darwin was establishing its dominance as an art and design school.[34] The coy confusions of the English picturesque, barely under control in the pavilion's 'eccentrics' corner', ran riot in the Battersea Pleasure Gardens. There John Piper and Osbert Lancaster's Grand Vista, and Rowland Emmett's Far Tottering and Oyster Creek Railway, offered a comic alternative to the modernist styling favoured by the Council of Industrial Design. The nation's attitude to science and technology was better reflected in the 1951 Ealing comedy *The Man in the White Suit.* At first the genial protagonist, played by Alec Guinness, is greeted as a 'knight in shining armour' for inventing an everlasting fibre, but mill-workers and owners combine against him when the consequences of this invention are realised. The film's final verdict comes from an old woman: 'Why can't you scientists leave things alone?'[35]

The celebration of national identity – which was sufficiently self-conscious to suggest an uncertainty about the durability of that identity

– was highlighted as the Festival's theme in the sermon given by Archbishop Fisher at the opening service of dedication: 'The chief and governing purpose of the Festival is to declare our belief in the British way of life. . . . It is good at a time like the present so to strengthen, and in part to recover our hold on all that is best in our national life.'[36] The parenthetical 'and in part to recover' shows that hold was not as secure as people would wish.

The 'dangers and anxieties'[37] besetting Britain which the chairman of the Arts Council, Sir Ernest Pooley, hinted at in his introduction to the Council's report covering the Festival were real enough. The long-term economic crisis since 1947 had been compounded by the need for a massive rearmament programme following the outbreak of the Korean War in June 1950. The conflict brought with it the very real threat of a Third World War involving atomic weapons. The need to pay for rearmament caused the Labour government, which lost ground in the 1950 general election, to abrogate the principle of a completely free National Health Service, provoking resignations which weakened it in the run-up to the election of October 1951. All in all, the Festival of Britain did not take place in the warm political and economic climate it had been planned for: it also rained a great deal in the summer of 1951.

Yet the Festival was undoubtedly a popular success. Herbert Morrison had wanted 'to see the people happy. I want to hear the people sing.'[38] By all accounts the break from austerity was welcomed, as pleasure became officially licensed once more. There were over two thousand spontaneous and unsponsored Festival events in towns and villages up and down the country, and eighteen million visitors to Festival sites. The Festival was mounted in a remarkably short time, in the face of considerable difficulties. It had had to be an exercise in *planning*: that keyword of the post-war period, inherited from the experience of wartime. The masterminds were young architects and designers, while most of the people actually working on the Festival had seen war service. These military and design skills met in the complex art of logistics that on opening day at the South Bank had the painters and cleaners leaving by the exit just as the first visitors entered by the turnstiles. The Festival's service of dedication ended with the hymn 'Jerusalem': in retrospect the Festival was one little bit of the welfare state that worked.

Yet if the Festival of Britain was a particular manifestation of post-war culture, that culture must be seen for what it was. In 1963 Michael Frayn published a penetrating essay on the Festival which argued that it was not the beginning of anything, but rather the end of a period when a certain social group had held sway. These were 'the radical middle classes – the do-gooders; the readers of the *News Chronicle*, the *Guardian*, and the *Observer*; the signers of petitions; the backbone of the BBC. In short, the Herbivores or gentle ruminants.'[39] The tone of the Festival, wrote Frayn, was 'philanthropic, kindly, whimsical, cosy, optimistic, middlebrow, deeply instinct with the Herbivorous philosophy so shortly doomed to eclipse'.[40] That eclipse was to be brought about by the Carnivores, 'the upper and middle classes who believe that if God had not wished them to prey on all smaller and weaker creatures without scruple, he would not have made them as they are'.[41] Frayn was writing of the 1950s; the Carnivores were to rule the earth with even greater ferocity in later decades.

Frayn's point was that, although the Festival celebrated 'the Land and the People', the people, for the most part, and certainly the working class, had little say in how they were celebrated. In so far as the Festival had any socialist colouring, it was socialism of a distinctly Fabian kind. The design historian Reyner Banham described the Festival as being run by 'kindly ex-officers and gentlemen'[42] and the principal beneficiaries of the State's patronage were not so much the individual artists who received commissions, as the institutions through which Festival funds were channelled. This was especially true of the Arts Council, given direct responsibility for the cultural programme, and an extra four hundred thousand pounds by the Treasury. This show of confidence in the Arts Council seems in turn to have given the Council confidence to go beyond its then fairly hesitant practice of giving small subsidies and guarantees against loss, and to commission work for the first time, notably Benjamin Britten's opera *Billy Budd*. Unfortunately, the opera was not given its première until 1 December 1951, by which time the Festival was effectively over. Not only over, but as some would have it, dead and buried.

The somewhat wistful, Herbivore spirit of the Festival can be sensed from Humphrey Jennings's documentary film, *Family Portrait*, commissioned by John Grierson of the Festival Committee for the promotion of the forthcoming Festival and completed in 1950, just before Jennings's accidental death. Subtitled 'a film on the theme of the Festival of Britain', *Family Portrait* shows nothing of the Festival itself, other than Abram Games's festival logo, a modernised head of Britannia poised on a red, white and blue star.[43] Jennings's script – no voice is heard other than that of the narrator Michael Goodliffe – was written, appropriately, in the first person plural. It begins: 'Perhaps because we in Britain live on a group of small islands, we like to think of ourselves as a family. And of course with the unspoken affection and outspoken words that families have. And so the Festival of Britain is a kind of family reunion. So let us take a look at ourselves, to let the young and the old, the past and the future, meet and discuss. To pat ourselves on the back, to give thanks that we still are a family, to voice our hopes and fears, our faith for our children.'[44]

Jennings wanted to show that technological creativity offered a future, but the past dominates his words and images. A photograph of blitzed houses quickly appears in the "family album" that frames the film (illustration 4). He begins at the white cliffs of Dover and the ruins of a wartime radar station; the dome of St Paul's, that icon of wartime survival, makes its appearance during the film, without comment on the soundtrack. The film is soon in Deep England, celebrating the variety of the landscape and the diversity of its people: 'Remember Kipling? "Where the Long Man of Wilmington stands naked to the shires"?' The hope is for a reconciliation between nature and science so that the scientist will 'accept the richness and subtlety of nature, not as error to be corrected but as part of the truth to be understood'.

Britain is celebrated for its inventors and explorers, but even the running theme of the invention of radar evokes the past: 'The Elizabethan journey ended with the Battle of Britain.' The emphasis is on industrial continuity: coalmining and iron-forging led naturally to the construction of the de Havilland Comet. The social costs of the Industrial Revolution are acknowledged as 'rifts in the family we are still having to repair', and the urban landscape is presented in images of smoky terraces and cobbled streets, to the sound of a brass band. Londoners are either massed ranks of hatted and mackintoshed commuters, or cockney caricatures, downing pints as a barrel-organ plays.

Continuity, reconciliation and consensus underlie the theme of the celebration of pageantry and constitutional progress (set to Elgar's 'Pomp and Circumstance'): 'We were lucky to learn the trick of voluntary discipline, of dining with the opposition' which has led this island, 'small and varied and restrained' (image of a rose garden) to export its democratic values to the 'vast and violent areas of the globe' (a ship's bow thrusts through the waves). Yet the celebration of imperialism is muted by the recognition that 'times have changed' and that now Britain is 'too small, too crowded, to stand alone'. The solution offered follows conventional British post-war foreign policy: closer links with Europe, but in the context of Britain's role of mediator with the rest of the world.

Throughout the film, the quiet authority of Michael Goodliffe's voice with its official, received pronunciation, advocating planning and compromise, is matched by the recurring image of a mace. The film closes on the pageantry of the Mace of the House of Commons, the monarchical guarantee of constitutional democracy, borne in procession, as the narrator asks what values Britain can return to the world that has made it rich: 'Perhaps the very things that make the family, the pattern, possible. Tolerance, courage, faith, the will to be disciplined and free, together' (illustration 6).

Family Portrait is not complacent, but the stress on continuity and conciliation, like Archbishop Fisher's Festival sermon, suggests that the values that are being celebrated are less secure than Jennings would wish. His ruling image of the family recalls George Orwell's description of Britain in *The Lion and the Unicorn* as 'a family with the wrong members in control'.[45] The film-maker Lindsay Anderson, while admiring Jennings's work, believed it demonstrated 'only too sadly how the traditionalist spirit was unable to adjust itself to the changed circumstances of Britain after the war. By the time Jennings made *Family Portrait* . . . the "family" could only be a sentimental fiction, inhabiting a Britain dedicated to the status quo.'[46] Anderson took particular exception to the penultimate sequence in the film as 'a preposterous procession of ancient and bewigged dignitaries. The Past is no longer an inspiration: it is a refuge.'[47]

Anderson is right, yet in that image of authority Jennings, whether he was conscious of it or not, captured a reassuring deference to tradition that was to be triumphantly reasserted in an even greater celebration of national identity in 1953.

The Festival of Britain officially ended when the South Bank exhibition closed on 30 September 1951. The Labour administration folded soon afterwards, when Parliament was dissolved on 5 October. There is debate as to what extent the victorious Conservative administration acted with deliberate vindictiveness towards the Festival. There had been discussion of the possibility of a second season in 1952, but the buildings were temporary structures, and part of the site was needed for further work on the Festival Hall. The new Minister of Works, David Eccles, quickly ordered the clearance of the site around the Festival Hall, with the exception of the Riverside Restaurant, the Tele-kinema (which became the National Film Theatre) and the walk along the new Embankment. The rest of the site remained empty until 1961, and in the nineties part of it was still what most of it became – a car park. 'I am unwilling to become the caretaker of empty and deteriorating structures,' Eccles declared in 1952, adding that he wanted the site cleared so as to be available for use as a garden in time for the Coronation.[48]

The death of King George VI in February 1952 gave rise, in June 1953, to celebrations that cost over one million pounds, which for one week makes the expenditure on the whole Festival year relatively modest. But then, in spite – or because of – the manipulation that royal occasions have always been susceptible to, coronations touch deep roots in the national subconscious. For most of the twentieth century, the British monarchy *was* British identity. The Royal Family was a microcosmic ideal version of Jennings's national 'family'. The fact that the House of Windsor had adopted that name only in 1917, in order to purge the Crown of its German origins, troubled almost no one, nor did the fact that most of the rituals and traditions of the Crown were of nineteenth- and early twentieth-century invention. Just as *Family Portrait* moved constantly between past and present, the anachronistic costumes of royal rituals, a mish-mash of medieval, Tudor, Jacobean, Georgian and modern dress, suggested that the monarchy existed in an eternal present, in and out of time.

The Crown also drew strength from the (unwritten) constitutional arrangements that placed it unquestionably at the pinnacle of the social hierarchy but gave it the appearance of standing to one side of the messy business of government itself. The monarch was a symbol, but even in Queen Victoria's time, when she had insisted on continuing to wear her widow's weeds rather than robes of state, the untouchable icon co-existed with an apparant ordinariness, of which the idea of "the Royal Family" (an invention of George V, who made the first Christmas broadcast in 1932) is the abiding expression. The conflict between the symbolic role and human needs of the monarch had been worked through, if not resolved, by the abdication crisis of 1937, while the identification of Crown and people had been sealed by the conduct of George VI and Queen Elizabeth during the Second World War.

In his study *The Enchanted Glass* (1978) Tom Nairn characterised the monarchy as 'the lay religion of modern Britain'.[49] Certainly the Crown has inspired an enormous amount of devotional literature and, as Nairn points out, very little serious study: 'Such attention as it has got consists mainly of acts of worship rather than examination.'[50] The editorial in the June 1953 number of the *Twentieth Century* (a serious journal, heir to the reviews of the Victorian era, which folded in 1972, well before the millennium) illustrates the point: 'Devotion to our Sovereign is not an intellectual concept that it is easy to discuss, but it corresponds exactly to the basic emotions on which families are built, and on which any living community must be built.'[51]

Yet, as the self-invention of the House of Windsor shows, the mythical identity of monarchy depends on constant adaptation and renewal. The Festival of Britain was one attempt at national renewal, the arrival of a new sovereign on the throne provided an even better opportunity for another, as the *Twentieth Century* recognised: 'The quick common sense of the Queen, and the shrewd modernity of the Duke of Edinburgh have already begun to help the nation in its formidable task of trans-forming itself to take a new place in a new world.'[52]

What was needed was a new version of the national myth, and it was supplied by the youth and name of the monarch herself. The socialists' "New Britain" had hardly had time to establish itself when it was replaced by the "New Elizabethan Age". "New Elizabethanism" can be traced back to the cultural nationalism of the Second World War, when Britain faced the threat of a sea-borne invasion, just as it had from the Spanish Armada. The conservative critic A. L. Rowse was predicting a New Elizabethan Age in the *Evening Standard* as early as June 1942. It was an obvious tag for the new times that reassuringly linked them back to the past. The *Daily Express*, scourge of the Festival, was quick to celebrate the arrival of the New Elizabethan Age. This renewal also implied a break with the immediate past of the post-war years, just as the return of Winston Churchill as Prime Minister sug-gested a return to wartime solidarity. In 1953 the popular journalist Philip Gibbs published a survey of British youth, *The New Elizabethans*, which contained this revealing rhapsody:

Our poets loved the song of the cuckoo heralding the summer – and all the flowers of an English spring and the drowsy days of summer with the ripple of a streamlet nearby, and the song of the lark rising high, and the love song of the nightingale in the dusk of starlit nights and the peace and delight of English fields. They would grieve that so much of English beauty is being defaced and destroyed by the ugliness of sprawling cities, the blight of factories, the utter wantonness of those who grab and invade our heritage of beauty when often they might spare it – these Borough councils and governmental tyrants who do not care a jot for any loveliness of our countryside.[53]

The state – meaning the welfare state – is the bureaucratic and industrial enemy of the sweet pastoral of Deep England to which British notions of heritage are so firmly attached. On Coronation Day the poet laureate, John Masefield, published in *The Times* 'A Prayer for a Beginning Reign' which covertly pleaded for release from governmental tyrants, hoping:

That she may re-establish standards shaken,
Set the enfettered spirit free.[54]

The most modernising aspect of the Coronation itself was the recognition of the importance of the mass media, especially television. Although the Coronation Commission set up under Prince Philip in April 1952 had initially resisted televising the ceremony – Churchill for one had warned that the intrusion of television would destroy the mystique of monarchy, a prescient comment – these arguments were outweighed by the need to make the Coronation a dramatic national spectacle. The government minister responsible, David Eccles, said: 'My job is to set the stage and build a theatre inside Westminster Abbey.'[55] In the event, the cameras were made to turn away from the most sacred part of the ritual, the anointing. A similar compromise between pomp and modernity is a feature of Cecil Beaton's official Coronation photograph, which shows the Queen in full regalia, against a backdrop of the interior of Westminster Abbey, projected on a screen (illustration 7). The different planes of foreground and background create an unsettling dynamic, so that Westminster Abbey appears to be falling backward, while the Queen on her chair is tilting forwards. Significantly, the spectator's eyeline is not respectfully looking up to the monarch, but is on the same level, or even slightly above her.

2 June 1953 marks a watershed in the history of broadcasting, for 20.5 million people, fifty-six per cent of the adult population, watched the ceremony on television; 11.7 million, thirty-two per cent of the

adult population, listened on the radio. The coverage of the Coronation also meant a boom for newspapers, with the *Daily Mirror* increasing its readership by fifty per cent. Following the example of the Festival of Britain, there were many spontaneous local events and celebrations, from tree plantings to pageants. As though to give everyone a share in the official feasting, in Coronation week rationing was relaxed, and everyone was allocated an extra pound of sugar and four ounces of margarine.

The Coronation did receive serious attention from two sociologists, Edward Shils (an American) and Michael Young, who published their findings in the *Sociological Review* for December 1953. It was clear to them that the popularity of the event was more than simply the product of commercialism, hysteria or the desire for a national binge. In an interpretation that took seriously the concept of a "lay religion" that Tom Nairn intended only satirically, they argued that such cynical explanations 'overlook the element of communion with the sacred'.[56] The 'theatre' of the Coronation was 'the ceremonial occasion for the affirmation of values by which the society lives'.[57]

On the eve of Coronation day, they noted, there was 'an air of gravity accompanied by a profound release from anxiety' as the celebrations became an affirmation of family and community ties.[58] Shils and Young were themselves swept up in the celebration of national myths of solidarity and resistance: 'Something like this kind of spirit has been manifested before – during the Blitz, the Fuel Crisis of 1947, the London smog of 1952, even during the Watson–Bailey stand in the Lord's Test or Lock's final overs at the Oval.'[59] Even sociologists, it seems, can recapture the Dunkirk spirit. But the evocation of the Blitz was important – especially to Shils, who was to develop this theme further in 1955 – for it was the touchstone of national unity. Just as many British intellectuals 'who in the twenties and thirties had been as alienated and cantankerous as any, returned to the national fold during the war', so the Coronation was a mark of 'the assimilation of the working class into the moral consensus of British society'.[60]

The notion of consensus was to be a key theme of the fifties, but Shils and Young's idea of national assimilation was rightly challenged in the *Sociological Review* by Norman Birnbaum (another American, a refugee from McCarthyism), who argued that the working class remained a very distinct and excluded caste: 'The very absence of shared values in Great Britain accounts for some of the attention paid to the Coronation.'[61] The celebrations were merely a holiday from disunity.

It is possible to reconcile these views, for as the American historian Ilse Hayden has argued in *Symbol and Privilege: The Ritual Context of British Royalty* (1987), the powerful symbolism of the Coronation secured assent to hierarchy: 'The Coronation did indeed confirm the moral values of British society, but these values were the solidarity of the upper class, the exclusion of the lower ones, the importance of social distance, the unequal distribution of social honour, and the domination of society by an hereditary élite.'[62] Shils and Young were certainly aware of the political subtext to the event that confirmed the consensus of the fifties: 'It appears the popularity of the Conservative administration was at least temporarily increased by the Coronation, and at the time much newspaper speculation centred on the question whether Mr Churchill would use the advantage to win a large majority for his Party in a General Election.'[63]

Although on a much smaller scale than that of the Festival of Britain, the Coronation celebrations included a cultural programme. The Queen and Prince Philip attended the première of Tyrone Guthrie's production of Shakespeare's *Henry VIII* at the Old Vic, the first royal appearance at a première since the reign of Edward VII. The Arts Council mounted exhibitions of Gainsborough, Graham Sutherland and John Piper, and spent seven hundred and fifty pounds on music commissions, among them William Walton's march 'Orb and Sceptre'. With Arts Council support the London County Council presented a series of Royal Philharmonic concerts at the Festival Hall featuring British composers. But the most significant event – both in terms of its context and the issues of patronage and identity that it raised – was Britten's opera *Gloriana*. The House of Windsor has not been known for its enthusiasm for the arts. It was unfortunate that this occasion was to be, in the words of one of those most closely involved, 'one of the great disasters of operatic history'.[64]

Shortly after the opera's gala performance in the presence of the Queen six days after the Coronation, the composer Vaughan Williams wrote a letter to *The Times*, asserting that 'for the first time in history the Sovereign has commanded an opera by a composer from these islands for a great occasion'.[65] But although the opera has been seen as a rare case of not just state, but royal patronage, its origins are more complex, and its status less certain.

That a cousin of the Queen, Lord Harewood, should be not only a passionate admirer of the work of Benjamin Britten but also on the staff of the Royal Opera House, Covent Garden, is an accident of history. But Britten stood out among British composers, even more than his contemporary Michael Tippett. In 1945 *Peter Grimes* had been greeted as the start of a British operatic renaissance, and Britten and George Lloyd shared official opera commissions for the Festival of Britain. As Lord Harewood has recorded in his autobiography, the idea for a Coronation opera was the result of a conversation about national musical identity between Britten, Peter Pears and himself, while he and his wife were on a skiing holiday with them at Gargallen, early in 1952:

> What was "national" expression in opera, we asked ourselves: what were the "national" operas of different countries? . . . 'For the Italians undoubtedly Aida,' said Ben. 'It's the perfect expression of every kind of Italian nationalist feeling, national pride – but where's the English equivalent?' 'Well, you'd better write one.' The next three or four hours were spent discussing a period – the Merrie England of the Tudors or Elizabethans? and a subject – Henry VIII? too obvious and an unattractive hero. Queen Elizabeth? Highly appropriate! What about a national opera in time for next year's Coronation?[66]

The problem, of course, was that an opera would take time to write, and Britten had a number of other projects and commitments, including concerts with Pears that Pears, for one, was reluctant to drop. It was this, rather than a desire for prestige, that led Britten to suggest that 'his Coronation opera was made in some way official, not quite commanded but at least accepted as part of the celebrations'.[67] Britten did not seek a royal commission, and there was no question of money changing hands, but if he was to clear his desk in order to be able to write the work in time, he needed a royal reason for doing so. Pears was not pleased.

Lord Harewood, who suggested using Lytton Strachey's *Elizabeth and Essex: A Tragic History* (1928) as a basis for the libretto, was able to arrange royal approval for the project. The Queen was his cousin, and so was her private secretary, Sir Alan Lascelles, who gave Harewood an enthusiastic reception when he discussed the idea informally with him. Harewood then put his proposal in a letter which was shown to the Queen, and permission was given for the project to go ahead in

May 1952, on the understanding that it would be in assocation with the Coronation, rather than a direct commission. The title page reads: 'This work is dedicated by gracious permission to Her Majesty Queen Elizabeth II in honour of whose Coronation it was composed.'[68] The principal sign of royal approval came on 1 June 1953, when Britten was made a Companion of Honour in the Coronation honours list.

The question of national musical identity was of importance to more than just Britten and Harewood. Covent Garden had reopened in 1946 with David Webster as general administrator, an appointment secured by Sir Kenneth Clark who, with J. M. Keynes, was instrumental in ensuring full Arts Council support for an all-year-round programme of opera and ballet. Keynes's plans for financing Covent Garden were dealt a severe blow in Dalton's 1946 budget, which abolished surtax relief for covenanted charitable donations. Keynes's successor as chairman of the Covent Garden Trust was Sir John Anderson, who accepted the appointment chiefly to please his socially ambitious wife. Anderson knew little about opera, but as a former Chancellor was able to extract from the Treasury assurances about continued financial support from the government. While the ballet company under Ninette de Valois, which had transferred from Sadler's Wells, prospered, opera productions at Covent Garden were much criticised in the early years. The policy was to perform in English, which limited the choice of singers severely, and it became a regular practice to have mixed-language productions, with perhaps the tenor singing in German and the bass in English. The prospect of an opera in English, by a leading English composer, was therefore especially significant. Webster assured Britten that if the Treasury was not forthcoming, the money for the production would be found by the Opera House. In the event there was an additional grant of fifteen thousand pounds from the Arts Council for Covent Garden's Coronation season, which also featured a new production of Strauss's *Elektra*, conducted by Erich Kleiber. *Gloriana* was to be given its première at a gala in the presence of the Queen and Prince Philip, produced by Basil Coleman, conducted by John Pritchard, and designed by John Piper, with Joan Cross as Elizabeth and Peter Pears as Essex. The libretto was to be prepared by William Plomer, with whom Britten had been considering other musical projects, although this was to be his first full-length opera.

Britten was too serious an artist to sacrifice his creative imperatives to courtly prudence. There had already been controversy about his decidedly unfestive *Billy Budd*, an all-male opera whose discreet homosexual subtext appears to be the reason why it was not performed, as originally intended, at Sadler's Wells. The homosexual theme was deeply hidden in what might be read as a cold-war allegory: the rules of war and the menace of revolution demand unbending conformity to public discipline, though at great personal cost. At a period when homosexual acts were criminal offences, strict outward conformity was a requirement for public figures who had homosexual private lives. The conflict between private desires and public responsibility surfaced once more in *Gloriana*.

Britten was clear that cod-Elizabethan pastiche alone would not be appropriate to the New Elizabethanism the Coronation was intended to encourage. He wrote to William Plomer that he wanted 'lovely pageantry'[69] but it is to his credit that he was intending to create more than that. He told Lord Harewood: 'It's got to be serious. I don't want to do just folk dances and village green stuff.'[70]

Although the only censorship imposed was the Lord Chamberlain's insistence, as the royal official responsible for licensing the performance of all new theatrical works, that a chamber-pot should not appear in a London street scene, the choice of a book by Lytton Strachey, debunker of eminent Victorians, as the basis of the libretto might have sounded a warning. While the Elizabethan period gave an opportunity for the reworking of Tudor music (and the setting gave John Piper the opportunity to create a Tudor décor), the pageantry was undercut by the essentially tragic nature of the story. William Plomer summarised its theme: 'Queen Elizabeth, a solitary and ageing monarch, undiminished in majesty, power, statesmanship, and understanding, sees in an outstanding young nobleman a hope for both the future of the country and of herself.'[71] The Queen is made to appear foolish, however, in her attraction to Essex, while Essex fails her, turns against her, and is finally executed on her orders. In its closing moments the opera abandons all pretence of naturalism, and Elizabeth abandons music for speech, as the shades of her own death close about her.

With hindsight, it seems that Britten may have been equating the difficult decisions facing Queen Elizabeth I with the difficult decisions facing the country as it sought refreshment in the youth of Queen Elizabeth II. But this interpretation was not available to (and would not have been understood by) the audience at Covent Garden at the opera's gala première. Lord Harewood recalled: 'It never occurred to me that it would be other than a salutation on the part of the arts to their sovereign.'[72] The people who might be said to represent the arts had not been invited to the gala; instead the house was filled with dignitaries unprepared for a piece of new music. Lord Drogheda, who was to become chairman of the Royal Opera House in 1958, described the evening:

> Long remembered it was, but as a fiasco. The music was not remotely difficult to music-lovers, but much of the audience were not in the habit of attending opera at all. *Gloriana* was quite long, the evening was warm, the intervals seemed endless, stick-up collars grew limp, and well before the end a restlessness set in. "Boriana" was on everyone's lips. Most distressing was that in one scene the elderly Queen Elizabeth I removed her wig from her head and was revealed as almost bald: and this was taken, for no good reason at all, as being in bad taste.[73]

What little enthusiasm there was in the house was further muted by the white gloves worn by the audience, which muffled their polite applause. The professional critics were inevitably influenced by the atmosphere of boredom, distaste and embarrassment around them. Had Britten simply provided 'lovely pageantry', he might have got away with it, indeed he might have caught some of the more reactionary aspects of the New Elizabethanism of the time. William Plomer's recollections of that disastrous first night make the point: 'Were these chatterers interested in anything beyond a plenteous twinkling of tiaras and recognisable wearers of stars and ribbons in the auditorium? Did they perhaps expect some kind of loud and rumbustious amalgam of *Land of Hope and Glory* and *Merrie England,* with catchy tunes and deafening choruses to reproduce the vulgar and blatant patriotism of the Boer War period? If so, they didn't get it.'[74]

What they did get was something altogether more thoughtful, and possibly more prescient about the problems that Britain, diminished in majesty, power and statesmanship, would face in the coming years. The *Gloriana* story demonstrates the sense of blockage in public cultural life. It certainly blocked Britten's career, and there was an envious backlash against the favour he had been enjoying. In spite of singing the part of Essex, Peter Pears had never been enthusiastic about the project, and he urged a further retreat into the more private world that he and Britten were creating for themselves in Aldeburgh. Britten did not write another large-scale opera for seventeen years, and then it was for television. *Gloriana* was subsequently revived, notably to celebrate

Britain's joining the Common Market, but no commercial recording was made until after Britten's death. However limited the actual extent of royal patronage, the reception of the piece cannot have encouraged the Royal Household, which was reported not to have liked the opera, to favour the arts in future. The music critic David Cairns has argued that the fiasco helped to discourage public patronage in general: 'The particular nastiness of the *Gloriana* episode lay in the unholy alliance that was forged between traditional British philistinism, in one of its most reactionary periods, and forces within the musical profession activated by prejudices of a scarcely superior kind. In opposing state-subsidised opera, and Britten as the pampered symbol of it, traditional British philistinism was only acting according to its sad lights.'[75]

While the Coronation was successful, at least in the short term, in papering over any 'rifts in the family', it had an even less modernising effect on the British sense of identity than the Festival of Britain. Indeed, it served to reinforce what Lindsay Anderson has described as the dedication to the status quo. And while it set a ruling tone for the rest of the decade, it too marked an end as much as a beginning. The Queen was the first monarch to take the title 'Head of the Commonwealth' and as the overseas contingents marched through the rain on Coronation day, the parade marked a fitting close to the era of Empire, just as the Festival of Britain had brought down the curtain on the aspirations of 1945. With the old domestic order symbolically renewed, the country settled into comfortable patterns of hierarchy and deference under a Conservative government led by Winston Churchill. The social structure was modelled on an ideal of organic unity symbolised by the country house. This uniquely British focal point of social and economic power, as Nigel Dennis pointed out in his satirical novel *Cards of Identity* (1955), had long been felt to be 'a heart and centre of the national identity'.[76] During the war country houses great and small appeared to be facing extinction, but in the fifties they began to flourish again, under private ownership, or under the patrician protection of the National Trust, while their imaginary counterparts became a frequent setting for popular novels and plays (illustration 17).

This restored, deferential consensus depended on common agreement that, as in the social and economic relationships sustaining the micro-society of the country estate, each sector of society had its place and was secure in it. The aristocracy continued to follow a modified form of service at court by gracing the boards of public and private institutions, while following their traditional country pursuits. The upper-middle classes ran the country in co-operation with middle-class professionals, of whom the intelligentsia formed a subsection. Shopkeepers, managers, trades union officials and engineers maintained the economy, while the almost entirely urban working class supplied their labour in exchange for the security in which to lead a life grounded on the family, clubs and trades unions, with sport and other forms of mass entertainment as principal recreation.

As was suggested in Chapter I, consensus implies a confluence, but not a uniformity of agreement. At all times there will be individuals and groups significantly at odds with prevailing opinion, and in a position to influence it. Paradoxically, the capacity of the consensus to absorb change ensures its survival. Thus the British myth could be comfortably sustained at a time of rising affluence and full employment, and the Conservative administration that ran the country until 1964 did not disturb the post-war welfare settlement created by the Attlee government. Full employment and state welfare were popular policies; it had accepted since 1940 that trades unions had a part to play in the economic management of industry, and the unions were willing to co-operate so long as their legal immunities were not interfered with. There was another side to the evident desire to draw together: from 1948 onwards the world had begun to divide into two armed camps as the United States and the Soviet Union settled into the opening phases of nearly forty years of cold war. Anxiety at the prospect of nuclear destruction found its counterpart in fear of communist subversion, enforcing a political conformity on the Labour Party and the Trades Union movement that supported the status quo.

Without insisting on uniformity, consensus encourages conformity, and even myths must be managed if the hegemony of power backed by consent is to be maintained. In empirical fashion the British state had evolved an unofficial institution to administer the consensus. It is no coincidence that halfway through the decade, in 1955, a number of independent but concurring explanations were offered to account for the existence of an institution variously described as 'the intellectual aristocracy', 'the Establishment' or simply, 'the Great and the Good'.

The historian Noel Annan's essay 'The Intellectual Aristocracy' set out to explain the rise to power during the nineteenth century of an administrative class which replaced the traditional aristocracy in government without ever challenging it socially. Born to service in the Church and the State, the members of this new class spread out from the reformed universities of Oxford and Cambridge into the new professions, especially the reformed Civil Service. Philanthropic and reforming themselves, and coming from a group of families with a strong propensity to intermarry, they became the new intelligentsia. Yet, as Annan pointed out: 'The English intelligentsia, wedded to gradual reform of accepted institutions and able to move between the worlds of speculation and government, was stable.'[77] Annan's argument was supported by comparison with Russia at the same period. There the disaffected, unestablished middle-class intellectuals (who coined the term 'intelligentsia') led opposition to the Tsar, whereas in Britain intellectuals were a counter-revolutionary force. Annan did not make this point, but it is during the 1860s, as the intellectual aristocracy achieved its formation, that thinkers like John Ruskin and Matthew Arnold (Ruskin, an Oxford-educated Evangelical, risen from the merchant class; Arnold a schools inspector, son of a reforming public-school headmaster) were appealing to the newly enfranchised but culturally dispossessed working class to integrate with society through the ideal of an organic culture.

The result of this evolution, Annan wrote, was 'the paradox of an intelligentsia which appears to conform rather than rebel against the rest of society'.[78] Annan was producing a powerful version of the consensus myth, consciously embracing the whole of (English) society, to describe the unofficial institution that emerges: 'Here is an aristocracy, secure, established and, like the rest of English society, accustomed to responsible and judicious utterance and sceptical of iconoclastic speculation.'[79] The security of this institution continued into the fifties and beyond. While the multiplication of organisations requiring their services meant that members of the founding families were spread thin over English intellectual life, their gradualist and co-optive values had been adopted throughout the administrative class. 'Here at any rate,' Annan triumphantly concluded his essay, 'seems to be an aristocracy that shows no sign of expiring.'[80]

As a celebrant of the Coronation's powers to produce consensus, not surprisingly Edward Shils also drew attention to the conforming nature of British intellectuals in an article for *Encounter* in April 1955. The contemporary consensus was well to the fore:

Who criticises Britain now in any fundamental sense, except for a few communists and a few Bevanite irreconcilables? There are complaints here and there and on many specific issues, but – in the main – scarcely anyone in Great Britain seems any longer to feel that there is anything fundamentally wrong. On the contrary, Great Britain on the whole, and especially in comparison with other countries, seems to the British intellectual of the mid-1950s to be fundamentally all right and even much more than that. Never before has an intellectual class found its society and its culture so much to its satisfaction.[81]

What, Shils asked, could have 'produced this extraordinary state of collective self-satisfaction'?[82]

The answer drew on the argument Shils had used in 1953, that the alienation of the British intelligentsia in the thirties had been an aberration, and that the war, in offering its members employment as intellectuals, had begun a process of reconciliation that was now complete, secured by the creation of such institutions as the BBC Third Programme, the Arts Council and the British Council. Quite independently of Noel Annan, he produced an account of the consensus myth based on similar ideas of aristocracy. It was 'the vindication of the culture associated with the aristocracy and gentry, and its restoration to pre-eminence among the guiding stars of the intellectuals. It is a change which is not confined to the intellectuals. All English society has undergone this process of submission to the moral and cultural – but not the political or economic – ascendancy of the aristocracy and gentry.'[83]

Such submission prevailed into the eighties, when Margaret Thatcher's utilitarian radicalism severely disturbed the comfortable consensual complacency of the intellectual aristocracy. Professor Martin Kemp, who felt this wind of change as it blew through the board of trustees of the Victoria and Albert Museum in 1988, has written: 'Trustee Boards have probably always been cosy establishment clubs, capable of drawing in potentially rebellious minds and cosseting them in the warm glow of corrupting self-importance which ensures that one of "us" becomes one of "them". It is heady stuff for a humble academic to be in cahoots with knighted captains of industry, minor Royals and major aristocrats.'[84] According to Shils, as the intellectual aristocracy advanced, what he labelled bourgeois culture, the culture of the dissenting, provincial middle class, was in retreat before the 'London–Oxford–Cambridge Axis'.[85] There is a loud echo here of the Eliot versus Leavis debate about the social role and location of élites.

Annan and Shils were not the only social anatomists at work in 1955. A third analysis of the power of this aristocratic formation came in an article for the *Spectator* by the conservative columnist Henry Fairlie. It was his article that brought the term "the Establishment" into common currency. Ironically, Fairlie used the term to attack what he described, for he was angered by the way the traitors Burgess and Maclean had managed to escape to Russia as a result of warnings from friends in the Establishment:

> By the "Establishment" I do not mean only the centres of official power ...
> but rather the whole matrix of official and social relations within which
> power is exercised. The exercise of power in Britain (more specifically, in
> England) cannot be understood unless it is recognised that it is exercised
> socially. Anyone who has at any point been close to the exercise of power
> will know what I mean when I say that the "Establishment" can be seen at
> work in the activities of not only the Prime Minister, the Archbishop of
> Canterbury and the Earl Marshal, but much lesser mortals as the chairman
> of the Arts Council, the director-general of the BBC, and even the editor of
> the *Times Literary Supplement*.[86]

Fairlie rightly stressed the informal, subtle way in which the Establishment worked, though the family connections described by Annan and the institutional links pointed to by Shils reveal the essential outline of its network. Yet no writer at the time seems to have been aware that there was also an official institution which corresponded to the unofficial structure they described.

As with so many aspects of contemporary British life, its origins lay in the emergencies of wartime. Thanks to the secretive habits of British administration, its existence was not fully revealed until Peter Hennessy published his research report for the Policy Studies Institute in 1986, *The Great and the Good: An Inquiry into the British Establishment*.[87] The origins of the coining 'the Great and the Good', Hennessy wrote, are lost in the mists of time, but the official existence of the institution it describes – the class of persons thought suitable for the forty thousand voluntary and part-time public appointments to be kept filled, from royal commissions to museum trusteeships – can be traced to the Ministry of Labour's register of eighty thousand people whose brains might be useful in wartime, and to a similar list kept by the Treasury. These became the basis of the post-war Central List, administered first in the Treasury and then by the Civil Service Department, until its existence was more publicly acknowledged in 1975, when it became known as the Public Appointments Unit. This unit still functions, and since 1980 it has been possible to nominate oneself for inclusion in the list of some five thousand names.

The ideal candidates for such a list have always been civil servants themselves, heirs to the intellectual aristocracy, well placed on the London–Oxford–Cambridge axis, mandarin officials trained to serve whatever government is in power, and, with the longer perspective of the career administrator, naturally inclined to seek consensus. The Arts Council and its major clients formed part of natural territory of the Great and the Good: the intimate connections between the Royal Opera House, the Arts Council and its sponsoring ministry, the Treasury, were vital to Covent Garden's survival in the immediate post-war period, as the memoirs of Lord Drogheda, a wartime Treasury official who later became chairman of Covent Garden, reveal.[88]

The interlocking post-war careers of W. E. Williams and Sir Kenneth Clark afford a case history in the operation of the institution. Clark, as we saw in Chapter II, had been disappointed when not he, but the obscure Sir Ernest Pooley had succeeded J. M. Keynes as chairman of the Arts Council, and he resigned from the Council in 1947. Pooley's one significant action at the Council was to set himself to get rid of his secretary-general, Mary Glasgow, who had been faithfully preserving the policies set by Keynes. The timing of Glasgow's resignation in 1951 was highly convenient, to say the least, for W. E. Williams. Williams, like Clark a founder member of CEMA and to some extent his protégé, had remained as a Council member after Clark resigned. As a Welsh-man, educated at Manchester University and with his background in adult education, Williams was not by birth a member of the Great and the Good, and his wartime career as director of the Army Bureau of Current Affairs showed that he was not afraid of upsetting the military and political establishment. But in the next ten years he transformed himself into one of the most powerful cultural mandarins in the country.

In the immediate post-war period Williams served as director of the Bureau of Current Affairs – a lesser, peacetime equivalent of ABCA sponsored by the Carnegie Trust – while cultivating his contacts through journalism and committee work, including the Arts Council. But the Carnegie Trust decided not to continue funding the Bureau of Current Affairs and in 1950 Williams faced the prospect of a new decade without a significant position, other than as an adviser to Penguin Books. It was just at this moment that Mary Glasgow gave up her post at the Arts Council. After all the prospective candidates for the secretary-generalship were deemed unsuitable, the Council decided to offer W. E. Williams the job.

Williams, the first of three secretary-generals who were former Council members, ran the Arts Council from 1951 until 1963, becoming in J. E. Morpurgo's phrase 'the arch-manipulator of patronage' and making full use of the advantage his length of tenure gave him over politicians and artists alike.[89] From 1951 onwards there was a new sprightliness and confidence about the Arts Council's annual reports, but the policies they described show how far the Council had moved from its original mission towards administering a safe metropolitan cultural consensus. 'The Arts Council of Great Britain is an instrument of State patronage,' declared Williams, a situation that had been made abundantly clear by the Festival of Britain.[90] But while defending the unprofitability of the sort of work it supported, and the need for public subsidy, Williams argued that it could only be carried out in the larger concentrations of population.

The dilemma facing the Arts Council, as always, was 'Raise or Spread?'[91]: 'Might it not be better to accept the realistic fact that the living theatre of good quality cannot be widely accessible and to concentrate our resources upon establishing a few more shrines like Stratford and the Bristol Old Vic?' Williams's answer to his own question was: ' "Few, but roses" – including, of course, regional roses.'[92] But the regional roses became fewer as the Council's regional offices were wound up and the Council withdrew from directly managing regional theatres and theatre tours. Only Arts Council exhibitions (Williams's original interest) survived as directly managed activities. A financial crisis in 1952 which wiped out the Council's small reserves encouraged Williams's regional retrenchment. In his 1952 report Williams wrote: 'It seems wiser that the Arts Council should now concentrate its limited resources on the maintenance and enhancement of standards. If an emphasis must be placed somewhere in that motto of "Raise and Spread" it seems wiser and more realistic to concentrate on Raise.'[93] Until the sixties the Arts Council held to a purely "reactive" policy, responding as it saw fit to requests for funds, but taking no major initiatives of its own.

Williams concentrated not only on consolidating the position of the Arts Council within the Establishment, but on consolidating his own power. Thus, when his former patron Kenneth Clark returned in 1953 to take over the chairmanship from Sir Ernest Pooley, he found himself sidelined by Williams. He was allowed no secretary of his own, and permitted to see only such correspondence as the secretary-general saw fit. It is no wonder that Clark felt bored and wasted at the Arts Council: 'I cannot say that the Arts Council prospered under my chairmanship, or that I enjoyed my spell of office.'[94] The cautious policy it had adopted found its rationale in a chronic shortage of money under the Conservative government, but the Council seems to have done little to justify being given more: 'Our meetings often had that negative and despondent character which has now spread to every branch of a bankrupt country,'[95] he recorded in 1977.

Eighteen months after becoming chairman of the Arts Council, Clark took on the additional, and far more challenging, job as first chairman of the newly formed Independent Television Authority, where his talents as a communicator were put to proper use. He owned no television set at the time, and was discreetly booed at the Athenaeum for accepting the job of overseeing the launch of a commercial challenge to the BBC, but his resistance to the crasser political and commercial pressures brought to bear on him by the independent companies meant that his status among the Great and the Good was to rise even higher.

The question that remains is what kind of culture W. E. Williams (knighted in 1955) and Kenneth Clark (knighted in 1938, made a life peer in 1969) were called upon to administer. Shils characterised the aristocratic values embraced by the British intelligentsia as 'moderate, unspecialised and unobsessed, civil, restrained, diversified, and personally refined' – a description that could well have been applied to the public persona of Lord Clark.[96] It was certainly a more educated and unprejudiced culture than that of the playwright Terence Rattigan's imaginary Aunt Edna, a 'hopeless lowbrow' who 'does know what she likes', and whose conventional tastes dominated the commercial theatre.[97] Shils was prepared to argue, almost to the point of absurdity, that its governing characteristics added up to a distinctly English identity. Its features are worth quoting at length:

> Continental holidays, the connoisseurship of wine and food, the knowledge of wild flowers and birds, acquaintance with the writings of Jane Austen, a knowing indulgence for the worthies of the English past, an appreciation of "more leisurely epochs", doing one's job dutifully and reliably, the cultivation of personal relations – these are the elements in the ethos of the newly

emerging British intellectual class. It is around an ethos of this sort that nowadays the new attachment to Great Britain is formed.[98]

Though Shils warned that this was a culture of exclusion, and therefore limited, he argued that Britain's decline as a world power had served to enhance these values, even if his own words call their positive qualities into question: 'The feeling of being without an empire, a feeling of being bereft of something, a feeling of loss, enhanced the sense of national identity. . . . Little Englanders could feel more comfortable in such a country and could love it more easily.'[99]

It was left to another foreigner, though one, like Shils, who had adopted many of the values of his host country, to make the connection between national and cultural identity and apply it, not just to the post-war intelligentsia, but to the whole of its history. It was again in 1955 that, from that most Establishment of platforms, the annual lectures founded by the BBC in honour of their first director-general, Lord Reith, that Nikolaus Pevsner propounded his ideas about the Englishness of English Art.[100]

Pevsner, who died as Sir Nikolaus Pevsner in 1983, was a member of a remarkable generation of middle-European refugees who began to arrive in Britain in the mid-thirties, and who were to have a powerful cultural influence on their adopted country. Among them were Sir Ernst Gombrich, Sir Claus Moser, Sir Isaiah Berlin, Sir Karl Popper, Hans Eysenck, Melanie Klein, and an important group of publishers, Bela Horovitz, founder of the Phaidon Press; Walter Neurath, founder of Thames and Hudson; and Lord Weidenfeld, of Weidenfeld and Nicolson. Released from the internment that had rounded up alien friend and foe alike in 1940, Pevsner became assistant editor of the *Architectural Review* and editor of the King Penguin list for Allen Lane. In 1946 he persuaded Lane to begin the monumental series *The Buildings of England* which, by the time his county-by-county survey was finished in 1974, had become a British institution in its own right.

Unlike his colleague at the *Architectural Review*, John Betjeman, Pevsner was a modernist. As an outsider he was well placed to contribute to the debate about Englishness that had become a significant theme since Orwell's wartime writings, and which had become more urgent with the loss of Empire. As a refugee from fascism, he was in a position to appreciate the characteristic moderation of British attitudes.

He had been collecting the materials for his 1955 Reith Lectures since the thirties, and first used them while teaching at Birkbeck College in 1941 and 1942. In a phrase that recalls the theme of 'the land and the people' of the Festival of Britain, he called them 'an essay in the geography of art'.[101] And while seeking to define the essence of English identity (not the Scots or Welsh, who are hardly mentioned) he was also discreetly trying to modernise it. His description of Englishness was also partly prescription, for he projected back onto his listeners an identity that they could recognise, and which was reinforced by their institutions, notably his host, the BBC. His efforts sum up many of the themes of the previous chapters of this book.

Pevsner was quick to point out that national character was not constant across the centuries, and in dialectical manner structured his examples around polarities: Celt versus Norman, Hogarth versus Reynolds, Blake versus Constable and, by implication, the progressive features of modernism versus regressive neo-romanticism. The management of such polarities, he argued, resulted in illogicality, a lack of doctrinaire attitudes, moderation and compromise: ' "Every case on its own merit" is one of the greatest blessings of English civilisation,' was Pevsner's version of the consensus myth.[102] But even as he celebrated the moderation from which he had himself benefited, Pevsner drew significant political conclusions from it: 'Revolutions in England are unbloody, like that of 1688 and that of the last twenty years. Everything changes, but names, formulas, the outer, demonstrative signs do not change. There are two causes for this, both equally English. One is reasonableness. . . . The other is conservatism.'[103] Pevsner noted that Americans and Germans considered contemporary Britain's conservatism dangerously close to inertia. Like Orwell, he did not consider intellectual abstraction or systematic thought a national characteristic. The esteemed illogicality of the English led to a distinct lack of follow-through, a failing which he significantly (though discreetly) linked to the 1945 revolution: 'This will not surprise any of those who start their definition of Englishness from present-day or at least recent cultural experience. The distaste of the English for carrying a thought or a system of thought to its logical extreme is too familiar to need comment.'[104] If conservatism meant a hostility to experiment, reasonableness meant a lack of fanaticism in following it through. The ruling spirit of English culture and identity, Pevsner might have argued, is that of the Herbivore. 'Reasonableness is primarily a middle-class ideal and so much in English art and English culture in general, and at all levels, is so eminently reasonable.'[105]

Yet the rationality of English middle-class culture (and even the eighteenth-century aristocracy, Pevsner argued, were essentially middle-class) has its polarity in fantasy, a trait descending from the Celts. Pevsner stressed what he termed the linear, 'anti-corporeal or disembodied' nature of English art.[106] The line is traced from medieval manuscripts through Decorated architecture to Blake, and discovered even in the empirical art of observation of Constable, while dissolving entirely in the fantasies of Turner. Assisted by the wet and misty climate, atmospheric landscape painting was the great English contribution to European Romanticism.

Pevsner's passages on the English landscape tradition strayed towards the pastoral shades of Deep England. For him, the synthesis and summation of the English polarities of fantasy and rationality was the Picturesque, the planned informality of landscape gardening and town planning that survived the energetic brutality of the Victorian era before returning in the creation of garden suburbs, and even the layout of the South Bank for the Festival of Britain. In contemporary architecture, the tradition of 'each case on its merit' had found its expression in functionalism.

In his praise for contemporary British town planning and architecture, which in the age of the New Town schemes he fondly believed had a great future, Pevsner was following his own modernising agenda. Even he, however, could not avoid pointing out the constraints on creativity in the English national character. On the one hand there was moderation, reasonableness, rationalism, observation and conservatism; on the other imagination, fantasy, irrationalism. Disembodiment, the most significant formal quality in English art, can attach itself to both groupings, but is more closely related to the second. Aspects of the first group branched out into such categories as understatement, self-discipline, a practical approach to each individual case. They also may turn anti-aesthetic and prevent self-realisation by means of art. Self-discipline may prevent that single-minded enthusiasm or fanaticism indispensable for the highest achievements in art. The practical approach may neglect art altogether.[107]

In spite of his enthusiasm for Henry Moore, who as a sculptor was the exception who proved the rule about the disembodied nature of English art, Pevsner saw little prospect of major artistic developments.

He took refuge in the argument that 'the spirit of the age' was incompatible with 'the spirit of England': 'Art in her leaders is violent today, it breaks up more than it yet reassembles.'[108] Yet Pevsner, for all of his reservations about Victorian architecture, regretted the way that a vivacity, an energy, a commercial and technological inventiveness had gone out of the English character since the nineteenth century. England distrusted individuals, and was now governed by committees. His penultimate sentence warned against the very consensus that the reconciliation of polarities in the English character had set out to achieve: 'the danger of timidity and inertia and of the unquestioning faith in the majority vote'.[109]

The Englishness of English Art was not entirely the celebration its title suggests, but Pevsner's analysis was accurate, and it described an identity for which many people in Britain, including the intelligentsia, had evidently settled. The building which best conveyed the artistic character of this identity was one that was still under construction when Pevsner mentioned it in his Reith Lectures, the new Coventry Cathedral (illustration 8). For Pevsner, Basil Spence's design reconciled Celtic fantasy and magic with the neo-classical discipline of Edwin Lutyens. But the building synthesises more than that. Standing beside the blackened ruins of the Gothic cathedral destroyed in the Coventry blitz, the building literally replicates Herbert Morrison's vision of a new Britain springing from the battered fabric of the old, and Spence consciously conceived it as a bridge between history and the future. He had been the architect of the Glasgow exhibition for the Festival of Britain; the high nave of the cathedral recalls, with its etiolated pillars, wooden panels and engraved glass, a permanent version of the South Bank's temporary constructions. Commissioned in the Festival year, 1951, its ground plan, designed for a modernised Anglican liturgy, is a reminder of the need to devise a twentieth-century religious ceremony for the Coronation. As with other aspirations of post-war Britain, there was not enough money to fulfil Spence's original scheme.

Almost inevitably, the artists employed to embellish Spence's prestressed concrete included Graham Sutherland and John Piper. (As a war artist, Piper had drawn the old cathedral in ruins in 1940.) A commission to the sculptor Jacob Epstein provoked an unpleasant anti-Semitic response among Coventry city worthies. The music commissioned to mark its formal opening in 1962 was Benjamin Britten's

War Requiem. It is no wonder that the building has been described as a 'seamless triumph of Neo-Romantic Art'.[110] It is also why, at this distance in time, the building looks more dated than the Gothic ruins around it.

While aspects of the consensus created around the ritual and reality of the Coronation lingered on until the eighties, the artificial spirit of New Elizabethanism quickly evaporated. Shils noted in his essay for *Encounter*: 'The New Elizabethans who were conjured up in aspiration two years ago as the carriers of British tradition have petered out into thin air.'[111] Pevsner could detect no signs of 'the so-called new Elizabethan age'.[112] Speaking retrospectively, Lord Harewood thought the spirit had been genuine: 'We felt we were on the crest of everything going right, with a young Queen looking to the future, not looking back. The feel of it was very real, but in the end it lacked substance.'[113] Lurking behind the complacency of Shils's essay was that 'feeling of being without an empire, a feeling of being bereft of something, a feeling of loss'.[114] That bereavement was reinforced by the disastrous military expedition to Suez in the autumn of 1956, which turned the last whispers of New Elizabethanism into what the young playwright John Osborne called 'the Brave New-nothing-very-much-thankyou'.[115]

Even within the Establishment there were people who recognised that a vitality had gone out of English life as the post-war consensus had entered in. The mandarin hero of C. P. Snow's sequence of novels *Strangers and Brothers* (1940–70), Lewis Eliot, like his creator a member of the Great and the Good long habituated to the London–Oxford–Cambridge axis, comments in the 1956 novel, *Homecomings*: 'English society had become more rigid, not less, since our youth. Its forms were crystallising under our eyes into an elaborate and codified Byzantinism, decent enough, tolerable to live in, but not blown through by the winds of scepticism or individual protest or sense of outrage which were our native air.'[116] Yet Pevsner's polarities hold true. Scepticism, protest and a sense of outrage were already in the air. The Suez crisis of 1956, when the Labour Opposition opposed Britain's going to war, was the first major challenge to the political consensus. In 1957 Lord Altrincham brought down opprobrium on his head for voicing mild criticism of the Royal Family by suggesting a modernisation of the royal household. In 1958 the first attempt by the Right to break up the post-war Keynesian economic consensus ended with the resignation of the Chancellor of the Exchequer, Peter Thorneycroft, along with his

Treasury team of Enoch Powell and Nigel Bush. A new generation of novelists, poets and playwrights were beginning to challenge the metropolitan and Oxbridge establishment, while a rising group of self-consciously provincial intellectuals were beginning to make a more critical assessment of the nation's cultural life.

IV

The Uses of Culture
Britain in the later 1950s

The article by Edward Shils for *Encounter* on the British intelligentsia took the consensual complacency of the mid-fifties almost to the point of parody, but it did sound one note of warning. Describing the distinction between an aristocratic, metropolitan high culture and that of a dissenting, provincial bourgeoisie, Shils detected 'the vestigial but persisting traces of the barrier between the Two Nations within the intellectual class – the Nation of London, Cambridge, Oxford, of the higher civil service, of the genteel and sophisticated; and the Nation of the provinces, of petit-bourgeois and upper-working-class origin, of bourgeois environment, studious, diligent and specialised'.[1] The consensus was not quite as homogeneous and complete as the rest of his article suggested.

Shils's 'brilliant' essay was taken up by the sociologist A. H. Halsey when he addressed the question of 'British Universities and Intellectual Life' for the *Universities Quarterly* in 1958.[2] For Halsey, the difference between the ancient foundations of Oxbridge and the provincial universities, founded chiefly during the period of industrialisation by dissenters excluded from Oxford and Cambridge by the religious conformity imposed by the Test Acts, was such that a fault line ran through British higher education, bridged only by the fact that provincial fathers produced metropolitan sons given access to the Establishment by the gatekeepers of Oxbridge. Oxbridge's emphasis on the values of a generalist education had kept the liberal arts in being, but at the expense of technology and applied science, whereas the provincial universities were more specialised and technocratic. Even in the humanities their principal object was the training of schoolteachers. The consequence was that an 'arts don' at a provincial university 'will often have a sense of failure through the very fact of being there rather than in an Oxbridge college'.[3] In Halsey's view, in spite of post-war change the British class system was as powerful as ever, indeed: 'Oxbridge has never had a firmer grasp on its position at the apex of British educational life.'⁴ While the expansion of educational opportunity offered the chance of a 'revolutionary democratisation', the dominance of the London–Oxford–Cambridge axis meant there was 'grave danger that this revolution will leave the British universities more socially stratified than ever before'.⁵ But no sooner had a conservative hegemony been reasserted than the power structure of class, and the institutions which gave it cultural expression, began to be challenged by new elements shaped by the post-war settlement.

English cultural life in the fifties tends to be remembered in terms of the new novelists, the new poets, and above all the dramatists, who seemed to challenge the culture of deference that had been reconstituted in the early part of that decade. No account of the period can ignore them, but there was another group of dissidents whose eventual influence was even greater than that of the more celebrated writers and poets of the period. Well before the so-called Angry Young Men appeared on the scene in 1956, there was evidence of a tension developing between intellectual adherents to what might be crudely distinguished as "metropolitan" and "provincial" values. The opposing terms were more metaphorical than strictly descriptive, and did not depend on an individual's precise location or education, for the tension was also produced by differences of generation and class. Representatives of the metropolitan cultural élite – what had come to be known during the fifties as "the Establishment" – began to detect a resentment of the privileges and power they were assumed to enjoy. The poet Stephen Spender, a survivor of the pre-war Auden generation who became literary editor of the "metropolitan" magazine *Encounter*, noted in the magazine's second issue, published in December 1953: 'There are a good many signs in literary England today of what might be called a rebellion of the Lower Middlebrows. . . . It is an uprising against the intellectual trends of Oxford, Cambridge and London, and the influence on literary figures of Paris and Berlin.'⁶ The rebellion, he wrote, was led by university teachers, many from redbrick universities, and according to Spender the source of their criticism was a 'new provincial puritanism'⁷. A similar disdain for these upstarts was expressed in the pages of the aptly named *London Magazine*, launched under the editorship of the doyen of metropolitan literary life, John Lehmann, in February 1954.

The specific example Stephen Spender had in mind was that of John Wain, who as it happened was a don at Oxford. During his brief editorship of a literary radio programme, *New Soundings*, in 1953 Wain had criticised the old guard, and introduced a new generation of poets and writers, among them Kingsley Amis, Philip Larkin and Donald Davie. Spender's article is an oblique comment on the literary squabble that followed, but he had detected a trend that seemed to be confirmed when John Wain published his first novel, *Hurry on Down*, in October 1953 and Kingsley Amis published his first, *Lucky Jim*, in January 1954. The Oxford-educated Amis was teaching at University College Swansea, and had written a comic novel about a provincial lecturer whose chief butt was the values attributed to the metropolitan élite. "Academic" joined "provincial" as one of the code words for the arrival of a new generation of writers that was coming to maturity with the meritocratic advantages of the welfare state.

Lucky Jim, Amis was to protest, 'is a man in a book, not a "generation" '.[8] The discussion provoked by the novel, however, did provide a useful metaphor for the generational and class warfare that was beginning to break out as the new writers like Wain and Amis established a metropolitan bridgehead in the literary pages of the *Spectator*. Amis's work also appeared in the poetry anthology *New Lines*, edited by Robert Conquest in 1956, which, including as it did the work of John Wain, Philip Larkin, Donald Davie, John Holloway, Elizabeth Jennings, and Thom Gunn, established that the new "Movement" in poetry that the literary editors of the *Spectator* had been vigorously promoting since 1953 really did exist. The appearance of these "academic" poets with their anti-modernist return to strict forms was overshadowed in 1956, however, by the simultaneous bursting on to the scene of the so-called Angry Young Men, with the publication of Colin Wilson's immediately successful study *The Outsider* and the production of John Osborne's less immediately well received, but much more significant, play *Look Back in Anger*.

The tag "Angry Young Man" fixed the myth of the fifties, and Osborne's play was to have a permanent effect on British theatre. Its provincial setting and class politics were to be practical forms of cultural critique, as was the work of Joan Littlewood's Theatre Workshop at the Theatre Royal, Stratford East. But the Angry Young Man became a victim of his own success, and though the myth reached a far wider public through the popular press and television, attempts to make "anger" into a coherent movement were shown to be fruitless, as the mutually contradictory voices, gathered together by the editor Tom Maschler for his prose anthology *Declaration* in 1957, demonstrated. Kingsley Amis conspicuously refused to take part. But while a common thread between the rising "provincial" poets and writers was their individualism – a belief in the self rather than the community that was to emerge later as strongly Conservative convictions – they shared a principled distaste for, and a less honourable social envy of, the upper-class literary metropolitan mandarins who with their Europhile and modernist tastes had dominated culture since the mid-thirties.

It is not difficult to detect the influence of F. R. Leavis in shaping this attitude, and Spender had been quick to point to it in his *Encounter* article. In 1956 a young provincial don, working on his first novel, set in a redbrick university, summed up the situation as 'The Rise of the Provincials', in an article for the American *Antioch Review*. Declaring himself a disciple of Leavis, Malcolm Bradbury claimed to share with others 'the moral sphere which he defines; they are people who have been brought up in lower-middle-class households where this kind of non-conformist strenuousness is to be found, where moral issues are pressing. It has only been in fairly recent years that the children of these homes have been able to obtain a university education and even achieve to eminence in the world of letters and the groves of academe.'[9]

Bradbury argued that Leavis's influence had in fact increased since the demise of his magazine *Scrutiny* in 1953, and that it was the source of a new tone in the literary scene: 'A new provincialism in the better sense of the word, a stringency not at all urbane, beating out the meaning of good taste on its own pulse.'[10] Bradbury was right, both about Leavis's influence and its spread by the force of his personality and that of his disciples. The launch of a new review, the *Critical Quarterly*, in 1959 was intended to fill the gap that *Scrutiny* had left. But while the Lucky Jims and Angry Young Men were getting all the attention, there was another group of "provincial puritans" much closer in spirit to Leavis who, independently of one another, were quietly working on cultural critiques of far greater long-term significance.

There can hardly be a more provincial form of academic life than that of the peripatetic tutors for the Workers' Educational Association. Even as academics they had a satellite existence attached to the extra-mural departments of universities. The WEA had been founded in 1903; it was a product of the tradition of working-class self-education begun by the Mechanics' Institutes that made a link with the missionary impulse of the Victorian university extension teaching movement. In that spirit, members of a WEA class were not looking for university degrees or professional qualifications (although evening classes and short courses run by the WEA were a recognised route for would-be full-time trades union officials); they were employed people, or their wives, who genuinely wished to widen their education for its own sake. The WEA was a democratic, self-governing, voluntary body, with a federal structure that divided the country into districts served by full- and part-time tutors appointed by the extra-mural departments of associated universities. The WEA supplied the organisation and recruitment, the universities guaranteed the academic quality of what was taught. WEA tutors were, in a sense, the people that Mrs Leavis had called for in *Fiction and the Reading Public* in 1932: 'A picked few who would go out into the world equipped for the work of forming and organising a conscious minority.'[11] The WEA offered a variety of courses, but the key teaching form was a three-year course of weekly evening classes during the winter months with a tutor to lecture, lead discussions and comment on written work. Not being tied to a university syllabus, tutors and students had a freer hand in devising their own courses, offered mainly in politics, international relations, economics, history, psychology, music, arts and literature, and some science, though there were also courses on Public Speaking and 'How To Be A Good Housewife'.[12]

Funded by grants from the Ministry of Education, which relaxed its academic requirements for adult education in 1945, the WEA expanded rapidly after the Second World War, hoping to build on the appetites created by the Army Education Corps and the Army Bureau of Current Affairs. Here was another attempt to secure the quiet social revolution of wartime. Membership of the WEA was at its highest in 1947, with forty-five thousand members. The number of full-time tutors rose from forty-three in 1945 to a peak of two hundred and thirty-six in 1951, which was also the peak year for the core tutorial classes, but then the first post-war Conservative government cut grants and the number of courses and enrolments fell back. They were to pick up again later in the decade but, by then, at least some of the original missionary impetus of the organisation had been lost.

The socialist traditions of the WEA naturally attracted the more radical and committed teachers who saw education as having a greater purpose than the manufacture of degrees. Among those who became tutors after the war were the ex-soldiers Richard Hoggart, Raymond Williams and E. P. Thompson, the founding fathers of what was to become known as British Cultural Studies, and key figures in the formation of the New Left. Stuart Hall, a Rhodes scholar from Jamaica at Oxford, continued and significantly developed their ideas, and took part in the work of the WEA. It was adult education, so different from the often claustrophobic world of provincial university life satirised by Kingsley Amis in *Lucky Jim* and Malcolm Bradbury in *Eating People is Wrong* (1959), that encouraged a new approach to the function of – indeed the very meaning of – culture in society.

The Workers' Educational Association supplied the stimulating context in which this approach developed, but part of that stimulus came from the difficulties and controversies that racked the WEA itself. In addition to financial cuts, in the early fifties the WEA suffered a crisis of identity and purpose. To begin with, there was the historic ideological split with the National Council of Labour Colleges, who fiercely guarded their independent working-class tradition, rejecting links with universities and receiving no government aid. But with growing affluence, the question arose as to whether there still was a truly working-class tradition to preserve. 'The real worker is often a rare bird in WEA classes nowadays,' wrote Richard Hoggart in 1952.[13] By 1956 only fifteen per cent of WEA students were classed as manual workers, and most of these were on the increasingly popular shorter courses aimed at trades unionists. This raised the question of what the WEA was for, when it could be argued that education was now a universal provision for all classes.

One problem was that, as with public libraries, and indeed other aspects of the welfare state, an institution originally intended primarily to benefit the working class was rapidly taken over by middle-class people who saw adult education as an extension of their leisure. J. F. C. Harrison, a member of the extra-mural department at Leeds, observed: 'The problems of the WEA in the fifties are part of the wider dilemma of the Left. . . . The full-employment welfare state has created for men and movements of the Left new fundamental problems. Hence the drive for rethinking the socialist goals of the Labour Party, the confusion of the trades unions and the prevelant bewilderment and frustration in many voluntary organisations with a humanitarian or philanthropic ancestry.'[14]

The more radical tutors saw the WEA as a means of continuing the 1945 revolution, by empowering those who in spite of change had nonetheless been deprived of their educational rights, but they had to face the criticism of the National Council of Labour Colleges that they were merely giving individual workers a ladder to climb out of their own class. The image of the ladder troubled Raymond Williams, as can be seen in *Culture and Society*.[15]

The WEA adjusted to the changed circumstances of the fifties by, on the one hand, catering more and more for middle-class further education and cultural recreation, and on the other by providing vocational training for trades union officials and other administrators needed by the institutions of the Welfare State. Tutorial classes went into decline. The staff of the WEA were divided over which direction to take. In 1961 Raymond Williams identified three groups: the 'Old Humanists', who believed, like Eliot, that the values of education could only be spread so far before being diluted; the 'Industrial Trainers', who wished to fit people to society as it was; and a group to whom Williams was closest, the 'Public Educators', who saw 'the process of society as itself a process of education'.[16]

The debate about the WEA's social purpose was conducted at two levels. One was about "standards", as the university side of the partnership increasingly insisted on written work and achievement in academic terms. The second was more sinister, for the WEA was also split by what Williams described as 'a sharp local form of the Cold War'.[17] Educated communists like E. P. Thompson had found a natural home in the WEA. The Oxford Extra-Mural Delegacy for which Raymond Williams began to work in 1946 had as its secretary a well-known communist, Thomas Hodgkin, and nearly a third of its thirty full-time tutors were Party members or sympathisers. Williams had joined the Communist Party as an undergraduate at Cambridge in 1939, but had allowed his membership to lapse when on active service in 1941. As the Cold War got under way several Oxford WEA tutors were purged or, like Hodgkin, decided to resign. Williams stayed, though he did not like the situation. It was 'a politically dangerous time'.[18]

The official arena for this conflict was the debate about standards launched by the powerful figure of Sydney Raybould, head of the department of extra-mural studies at the University of Leeds. In Williams's terms an "Old Humanist", Raybould was a passionate believer in what he called 'the Movement'. He was against the trend towards shorter courses, and wanted university academic standards to apply but, backed by one of his tutors, Roy Shaw, he also questioned whether members of the Communist Party could be sufficiently neutral to be good tutors. (Though he continued to employ the communist E. P. Thompson on his staff.)

Gradually, the radical, pioneering ideals of a working-class movement were eroded. Williams recalled the veteran socialist and WEA tutor G. D. H. Cole saying at a meeting of the Oxford Delegacy: 'I am damned well not interested in adult education, I am interested in workers' education.' Williams commented: 'That was the conflict. He was a minority voice and he lost.'[19] By 1960 the Raybould line on standards had overcome the opposition, and universities were increasingly taking direct control of extra-mural teaching. The WEA was absorbed into the general system of adult further education to the extent that by 1992 Hoggart could write: 'The Workers' Educational Association is now on the fringe of a fringe.'[20] Yet it was in the evening classes of the WEA that the foundations of cultural studies were laid.

In 1952 Hoggart had written: 'Our present training fits mainly the worker who has torn up his class roots, and is on his way to join the rootless intelligentsia.'[21] The comment might well apply to WEA tutors themselves. For Hoggart, born into the urban working class in Leeds; for Williams, born into the rural working class in Wales; and for E. P. Thompson, the son of a Methodist missionary in India, engagement with the WEA was an extension of their own experiences as they had been shaped first by university education and then by membership of the officer class during the war. But extra-mural teaching meant that they were not completely absorbed into the educational establishment. As Stuart Hall has pointed out: 'We thus came from a tradition entirely marginal to the centres of English academic life and our engagement in the questions of cultural change – how to understand them, how to describe them, what their impact and consequences were to be socially – were first reckoned with within the dirty outside world.'[22]

For Williams, the tutors of the WEA formed the natural constituency for the short-lived magazines *Politics and Letters* and *The Critic*, which he edited with Wolf Mankowitz and Clifford Collins in 1947 and 1948 as an attempt to 'unite radical Left politics with Leavisite literary criticism'. His first book, *Reading and Criticism* (1950), grew out of his classes.[23] But as their nightly tutorials in different towns and cities across England built up what Hoggart has described as 'a sense of the many and major injustices in the lives of working people and so a deep suspicion of the power of class in Britain', their independent positions encouraged them to question the culture that supported that system, from outside the conventional academic boundaries.[24] Away from the literary gang warfare in London, these provincial, dissenting academics – Williams in Hastings, Hoggart in Hull, Thompson in Halifax – spent the early fifties developing a new form of cultural criticism whose history conventionally begins with the publication of Hoggart's *The Uses of Literacy* in 1957 and Williams's *Culture and Society* in 1958. But as Williams said in 1983, speaking in honour of a former WEA colleague (and former communist), Tony McLean:

> When I moved into internal University Teaching, when at about the same time Richard Hoggart did the same, we started teaching in ways that had been absolutely familiar in Extra-Mural and WEA classes, relating history to art and literature, including contemporary culture, and suddenly so strange was this to the Universities that they said, 'My God, here is a new subject called Cultural Studies.' Tony McLean was one of the best of them, teaching Cultural Studies for years before the announcement of the birth of this new subject. . . . That shift of perspective about the teaching of arts and literature and their relation to history and contemporary society began in Adult Education, it didn't happen anywhere else.[25]

The prefaces and acknowledgements to the key early texts of all three men bear this out. In the 1980 edition of *The Making of the English Working Class*, E. P. Thompson wrote that he was puzzled to know how the book actually got written between 1959 and 1962, for he was also heavily engaged in the New Left, the Campaign for Nuclear Disarmament – and his classes for the WEA: 'Discussion in these classes, as well as practical political activity of several kinds, undoubtedly prompted me to see the problems of political consciousness and organisation in certain ways.'[26] In his concluding chapter he quoted William Cobbett: 'I always say that I have derived from the people . . . ten times the light that I have communicated to them.'[27] Compare this with Raymond Williams: 'I have learnt as much as I have taught.'[28] Cobbett described his relationship with his audience in a vivid image: 'It is the flint and the steel meeting that brings forth the fire.' E. P. Thompson commented: 'How moving is this insight into the dialectical nature of the very process by which his own ideas were formed!'[29] Thompson was moved, because he recognised the process as one that he was himself engaged in.

It would be wrong, however, to assume that at this stage the development of cultural studies was a conscious movement, or that its potential for subverting the literary canon in which its pioneers were raised was realised. Thompson fiercely rebutted later attempts to link him historically with the positions of Hoggart and Williams in the early fifties. The puritan tradition had radical antecedents, but also a respect for the values of the past as embodied in great literature. As a Marxist historian, Thompson was seeking to revive the radical aspects of the tradition, but Williams did not question the nature of the canon until the seventies, and the anti-Marxist Hoggart, who in 1992 described himself as 'irreducibly Arnoldian and Leavisite', fundamentally accepted it.[30]

Hoggart began to write his study of working-class life in Leeds in 1952, the same year that Williams began to turn his exploration of a British tradition of cultural criticism in WEA classes into a book. But although they were aware of each other's contributions to the on-going debate about adult education, they did not meet each other until after their books were published, in 1959. There are differences in their attitudes that can be traced in the nuances of the "cold war" in the WEA and their participation in that debate. The most striking similarity is their very isolation, which both subsequently stressed. Members of the post-war Communist Party were much preoccupied with the internal debates that culminated in the purges and resignations following Khrushchev's secret denunciation of Stalin in April 1956. Because Williams had not rejoined the Party on his return to Cambridge after war service, it was not until after 1956 that he began to form links with now ex-Communists like E. P. Thompson. All three were raising families on modest salaries; Hoggart's memoirs suggest that life in Hull – the town where Philip Larkin settled as a university librarian – was decent, honest, and deeply dull.

Both Hoggart and Williams acknowledged the influence of, but were anxious to distinguish themselves from, the looming figures of T. S.

Eliot and F. R. Leavis. Eliot's conservatism was easier to reject, but Williams first used 'Culture and Society' as a course title in 1948, under the impetus of *Notes Towards the Definition of Culture*: 'I first started to look at the idea of culture in an adult education class, and it is very significant that the writers I discussed then were Eliot, Leavis, Clive Bell and Matthew Arnold. They were all I knew.'[31] Hoggart too rejected Eliot's conservatism, but found *Notes Towards the Definition of Culture* 'the hardest book I knew, from that side of the cultural debate, to rebut'.[32]

The direct line stems from F. R. and Q. D. Leavis. F. R. Leavis had contributed to Williams's *Politics and Letters* (as did George Orwell); the title *Culture and Society* is an echo of Leavis and Denys Thompson's seminal *Culture and Environment* (1933). In 1958 Williams wrote that he had been 'deeply impressed' by Leavis's diagnosis, 'deeply enough for my ultimate rejection of it to be a personal crisis lasting several years'.[33] Both Williams and Hoggart developed exercises in close reading in their classes. Hoggart's *The Uses of Literacy* was an acknowledged continuation of Mrs Leavis's project in *Fiction and the Reading Public*. As Stuart Hall – who met Williams at Oxford and discussed drafts of *Culture and Society* with him – has acknowledged, nearly all those who entered the field of cultural studies were formed in the Leavisite mould: 'As his neophytes, albeit in a critical sense, we took our distance from his educational programme and from his conservative cultural values. But our respect for the other aspect of his project came from the fact that no other place could be found within the humanities that took these questions seriously.'[34]

Hoggart attributed his failure to get a job at Cambridge after the war to this Leavisite seriousness, but he won the approval of Sydney Raybould, 'chiefly because I too was a puritan in these matters'.[35] The term that had been pejoratively applied by Stephen Spender in his article for *Encounter* was an echo of Mrs Leavis's identification in *Fiction and the Reading Public* of a 'puritan tradition' in English literature as the now polluted well-spring of a healthy common culture. Her chapter on 'The Puritan Conscience' concluded: 'If for the Bible and *Pilgrim's Progress* are substituted the *News of the World* and the *Sunday Express* it will be evident that popular taste is likely to be in some danger.'[36] Working with the original title *The Abuses of Literacy*, Hoggart tested her thesis by exploring contemporary working-class culture, based on his own experience of life in Leeds. The analytical part of the study was written first, but it became necessary for him to place this in some context, and so the more literary and evocative first section was added. The book was closer to literary reportage than sociology – it included material from an abandoned novel – and owed a debt to George Orwell and even, in the excursion to Scarborough, J. B. Priestley. Like Williams's *Culture and Society*, Hoggart's was a specifically English enquiry, with a grainy texture of concrete experience created by the semi-autobiographical material.

These studies were a questioning of national identity and an attempt at its redefinition in terms of the communitarian values of the working class as opposed to the individualism, tempered by notions of "service", of the bourgeoisie. In the field of history – it should be noted that he also taught English Literature for the WEA and that his first book combined literary criticism and history in a study of William Morris – E. P. Thompson's *The Making of the English Working Class*, published in 1963, similarly showed how between 1780 and 1832 political reaction on the one hand and industrialisation on the other had helped to shape an industrial working class, but that this was by no means a passive process: 'The working class did not rise like the sun at an appointed time. It was present at its own making.'[37] What Thompson was later to call 'history from below'[38] meant the treatment of working people as more than data for statistics, victims of *laissez-faire* economics or as occasional individual organisers and pioneers. They were members of a community of interests sharing a process of social and cultural formation in which they were active agents, not mere products of economic change. Thompson and Williams were to disagree as to whether this constituted a 'whole way of life' or, as Thompson would have it, 'a whole way of *struggle*'.[39] Thompson's book ended with a discussion of the contribution of William Cobbett and Robert Owen (among others) to the formation of working-class consciousness. Williams's *Culture and Society* (to which Thompson refers) began by contrasting Edmund Burke and William Cobbett, Robert Southey and Robert Owen.

Industrialisation, with its contribution to the changing meaning of the word "culture", formed the context, not just of these books by Thompson, Williams and Hoggart, but the whole tradition of British cultural criticism. As Williams demonstrated, the response of intellectuals to industrialisation had been largely negative, and the opposition between culture and mass society posited by Matthew Arnold in *Culture and Anarchy* in 1869 was still a conventional assumption in the fifties. Hoggart's fear of 'a world of monstrous and swirling undifferentiation' was Arnold's, though in Arnold's case the fear was produced by the prospect of mass democracy, and in Hoggart's by the mass market.[40] The working class, Hoggart argued, had a distinctive, all-pervading culture, as formal as any attributed to the upper class, and it was his achievement to make this culture the serious subject of study. But this drive to define what truly constituted working-class culture was produced by the knowledge that its values were in danger: 'We are moving towards the creation of a mass culture ... the remnants of what was at least in part an urban culture "of the people" are being destroyed ... the new mass culture is in some important ways less healthy than the often crude culture it is replacing.'[41]

The enemies of this way of life were the popular press, radio, cinema and, increasingly, television. There was more than an innate puritanism to Hoggart's argument: 'We are a democracy whose working people are exchanging their birthright for a mass of pin-ups.'[42] There was the Leavisite emphasis on the moral connection between reading, language and "life". As Q. D. Leavis put it: 'It is only by acquiring access to good poetry, great drama, and the best novels, the forms of art that, since they achieve their effects through language, most readily improve the quality of living, that the atmosphere in which we live may be oxygenated.'[43] The effect of mass communications and commercial interests was, as Hoggart the WEA lecturer well knew, to reduce all expression to the lowest common denominator, the limited vision of 'the little man': 'Complex – that it, searching or taxing – literature must therefore be discounted; good writing cannot be popular today, and popular writing cannot genuinely explore experience.'[44]

The means to resist the abuses of literacy lay with 'the earnest minority' who sought education through the WEA, or the virtuous aspects of the mass media such as the Third Programme and Penguin books; it lay with the uprooted and anxious scholarship boy and above all, as Raymond Williams was also to argue, with the institutions and the self-generated culture and customs of the working class itself.

Yet although Hoggart could write that 'for all ages such a life can have a peculiarly gripping wholeness', he was writing about a world that was rapidly disappearing.[45] Working-class life as described by Hoggart was settled and fixed, with no foreign travel other than during military service, and very little domestic travel, because of the lack of private transport. The likeliest change was that of place of work, not of address. Hoggart was drawing on his pre-war childhood to evoke the solidarity of a world where 'life centres on the groups of known streets, on their complex and active group life'.[46] But by the time his book was published such streets were being demolished in their hundreds, as they and the heavy industries that had led to their creation began to undergo post-war economic transformation. It was no coincidence that Granada Television should launch the mythopoeic soap opera *Coronation Street* in 1960.

It is one of the limitations of *The Uses of Literacy* that it seeks to establish working-class culture as another form of consensus with, as Hoggart admitted, its own neutralising pressure to conform. It becomes, not a way of adapting to change, but of resisting it. To the moral dangers of the mass media and entertainment, Hoggart added that of 'progressivism' which 'assists living for the present by disowning the past; but the present is enjoyed only because, and so long as, it is the present, the latest and not the out-of-date past; so, as each new "present" comes along, the others are discarded. "Progressivism" holds out an infinite perspective of increasingly "good times" – technicolor TV, all-smelling, all-touching, all-tasting TV. "Progressivism" usually starts as a "progressivism" of things, but cannot stay there; it ineluctably spreads beyond things, by dubious analogies.'[47]

Progress and change are by no means identical, but Hoggart's Leavis-ite cultural conservatism severely limited the possibilities of what he was trying to do. It was one thing to take working-class culture seriously, but another to apply Leavisite principles largely to condemn it as it was. Raymond Williams drew attention to this problem in a review of *The Uses of Literacy*, pointing out the danger of equating working-class culture with 'the mass commercial culture which has increasingly dominated in our century. Richard Hoggart's book has been read in this way, and not altogether without justification.'[48]

By contrast, it was a key point of Williams's argument in *Culture and Society* that 'nearly all theoretical discussions of art since the Industrial Revolution have been crippled by the assumed opposition between art and the actual organisation of society'.[49] Williams here used the word "art" rather than "culture", but it was his case that culture was a great deal more than the narrow definition that was customarily applied. There was an implicit criticism of Leavis when he wrote: 'Great litera-ture is indeed enriching, liberating, and refining, but man is always and everywhere more than a reader, has indeed to be a great deal else before he can even become an adequate reader.'[50] The experience of fifteen years as a WEA tutor is clearly behind this statement. *Culture and Society* was an attempt, through an examination of the use of the term since it was brought into common currency by Burke and Cobbett, to reintegrate the reforming, morally valuable idea of culture with that of culture as 'a whole way of life' in the modern industrial world.

Yet although Williams recognised the dangers of *opposing* culture and society, the essentially conservative tradition with which he was working meant that, like Hoggart, he continued to reproduce the myth of the fall from grace of a once organic culture, corrupted by industrialism. In the British tradition that Williams analyses, the ideal was a culture that was "natural" and expressive, but also ordered and harmonious in its internal structures and class relations – in fact, a form of consensus. But attached to this organic approach there was also an élitism – only the cultured few could maintain the ideal – and a pessimism, for the organic society was either destroyed by, or grievously under threat from, social and economic forces, so that the "moment" of this society and its culture was always in the past. *The Uses of Literacy* was firmly in this tradition.

Williams recognised the difficulty of a nostalgia for the security (and authority) of an idealised past. He wrote of Leavis: 'If there is one thing certain about "the organic community", it is that it has always gone.'[51] But almost in the same breath he referred to the rural community of his childhood in the thirties. When he wrote of D. H. Lawrence's 'rich experience of a working-class family' he was also drawing on his own.[52] The ideal of a 'common culture' that Williams discussed in his conclusion brings together 'at once the idea of natural growth and that of its tending'.[53] The difference was that the tending would be by common democratic consent, rather than at the whim of élitist or mass commercial pressures. Yet, sincere socialists as they were, both Williams and Hoggart essentially transferred the conservative organic myth on to the culture and institutions of the working class, institutions that were under threat from 'progressivism' (Hoggart) and 'Americanism' (Williams).

It was, however, understandable that they should perpetuate the myth of an organic society. As Williams pointed out, such imagined societies existed only in the past. But that was because actual society was subject to constant change. From the seventeenth century onwards traditional ways of life had been breaking up under the pressure of industrialisation, and that was equally true in the fifties, when the urban working class that Hoggart describes was beginning to experience both voluntary and involuntary mobility. Hoggart's description of the 'peculiarly gripping wholeness' of working-class life contrasts with the violence and disturbance that ran through Alan Sillitoe's novel *Saturday Night and Sunday Morning*, published a year after Hoggart's study.

Some of Richard Hoggart's most vituperative comments in *The Uses of Literacy* were reserved for the young, who submitted to the 'shiny barbarism' represented by an imported American mythology of 'the teenage "gang" fond of jive and boogie-woogie but still healthy and open-faced, informally dressed in crew-neck sweaters and slacks, full of gaiety and drive, the reverse of everything dusty and drab'.[54] In Hoggart's eyes, Britain's 'Jukebox Boys' were anything but healthy and open-faced: 'Most of them have jobs which require no personal outgoing, which are not intrinsically interesting, which encourage no sense of personal value, of being a maker. The job is to be done day by day, and after that the rest is amusement, is pleasure; there is time to spare and some money in the pocket . . . they have no responsibilities, and little sense of responsibilities, to themselves or to others.'[55] Hoggart might have been describing the life of Alan Sillitoe's protagonist, Arthur Seaton.

While many of the novelists and playwrights who gave impetus to the "new realism" of the fifties were university educated (John Osborne and John Braine were exceptions), Sillitoe's background was authentically working class. His experience of pre-war Nottingham was as firsthand as Hoggart's Leeds. He was distanced from his material, not by higher education and war service, but by exile in Majorca where he moved in 1952 after eighteen months' convalescence from TB following national service in the ranks of the RAF. The novel has similarities with, as well as differences from, Hoggart's account: there is a celebration of the feeling of community, and even fleetingly a sense of the loss of a more organic way of life, represented by Seaton's grandfather's forge. There are hints of nostalgia for the Blitz. As with Hoggart, there is hostility to television. The community Sillitoe described was 'the solid bloc of anarchist Labour in the street' who have little respect for institutions of any kind, including trades unions.[56] Drinking, fighting and womanising are his hero's principal pleasures as an antidote to the grinding tedium of piecework in a factory. But the effect of full employment was recognised and there is an appreciation of the changes that it implies. There was awareness of the new territory created by the council estate where Seaton's girlfriend lives, one of the estates which have supplanted his grandfather's rural forge and its self-sufficiency, 'long ago destroyed to make room for advancing armies of new pink houses'.[57] Seaton's prospective mother-in-law's house on the estate is not presented as a bourgeois ideal, but is especially squalid. Sillitoe briefly introduces the strange, disruptive figure of an Indian migrant worker, a harbinger of the changes that immigration was to have on the texture of urban working-class life and on the British image of themselves. There were serious racial disturbances in Nottingham and the slums of Notting Hill Gate in 1958.

The governing emotion for the hero is a sense of unease. The violent beating he receives as a result of his affairs with two married sisters leads Seaton to the realisation of the uncertainty of his existence: 'He felt a lack of security. No place existed in all the world that could be called safe, and he knew for the first time in his life that there had never been such a thing as safety, and never would be, the difference being that now he knew it as a fact, whereas before it was a natural unconscious state.'[58] This is more than his immediate sense of danger, it is to do with the violent struggle for existence, the noise of the factory, the physicality of the pleasures of drink and sex. Where Hoggart presented working-class life as fixed and static – and took almost no account of the world of work – Sillitoe's hero struggles to resist the effects of change, while being carried along by them.

Ironically, Alan Sillitoe's novel was itself a beneficiary of the cultural shift that was taking place. The emergence of a new realism that signalled a move away from the patrician concerns of country-house novels and plays made it easier for a working-class novelist to be published, but it was not until the novel was made into a film and sold as a mass-market paperback that it became well known. The stage success of *Look Back in Anger* had enabled John Osborne and the director Tony Richardson to form Woodfall Films, which released *Saturday Night and Sunday Morning*, directed by Karel Reisz and starring Albert Finney, in 1960. Richardson, Reisz and Lindsay Anderson were largely responsible for the brief British cinematic New Wave at the beginning of the sixties that had its roots in the Free Cinema movement of 1956. The paperback of Sillitoe's novel sold one million copies in a year, following the publicity generated by the film, although censorship imposed significant modifications to the violence and anarchy of the original novel.

The "Angry Young Man", of whom the new realism was taken to be an expression, was a creation of the mass media, as Harry Ritchie's study *Success Stories* (1988) has shown, but the label served as a symbol of change. Even Hoggart could be associated by reviewers with this mythical figure.[59] As with Sillitoe, it was not until *The Uses of Literacy* was published as a Pelican paperback by Allen Lane in 1958 that the book began to have wide impact. Penguins and Pelicans were benign aspects of the mass media, but Hoggart's negative reaction to popular commercial culture and particularly television was another sign of the anxiety that had been felt about the direction which popular culture, particularly for young people, had been taking ever since the film *Rock Around the Clock* had been greeted with such enthusiasm by the young and horror by the old in 1956. Teachers felt especially threatened, and the National Union of Teachers held a special conference on 'Popular Culture and Personal Responsibility' in 1960 whose almost despairing papers were published as *Discrimination and Popular Culture* in 1964.

Like it or not, growing affluence was bringing change and people were taking advantage of it. Hoggart acknowledged that in many parts of life mass production had brought good, and he was forced to admit: 'These things are enjoyed by the very people whom one believes to be adversely affected by them.'[60] Economic change was bringing cultural change, and the old theories of culture were no longer adequate.

The problem began with the way culture was defined. Criticising F. R. Leavis's excessively narrow concentration on the moral value of literature, Raymond Williams wrote: 'The difficulty about the idea of culture is that we are continually forced to extend it, until it becomes almost identical with our whole common life. When this is realised, the problems to which, since Coleridge, we have addressed ourselves are in fact transformed. If we are to meet them honestly, we have to face very fine and very difficult adjustments. The assumption of a minority, followed by its definition in one's own terms, seems in practice to be a way of stopping short of this transformation of the problems, and of our own consequent adjustments.'[61] By the time Williams came to write the introduction to *Culture and Society* he had realised that his book was only the beginning of the evolution of a new general theory of culture that treated it as the study of complex relations within a whole way of life: 'We need also, in these terms, to examine the idea of an expanding culture, and its detailed processes. For we live in an expanding culture, yet we spend much of our energy regretting the fact, rather than seeking to understand its nature and conditions.'[62] By calling for a new way of defining (and evaluating) this expanding culture, Williams hoped to set a new agenda that reflected Britain's changed circumstances at the end of the fifties.

Britain's political, economic and military weakness had been forcibly demonstrated by the débâcle of the Suez invasion in October 1956, when American opposition forced Britain and France to make a hasty diplomatic and military retreat, leaving the West morally thwarted in the face of the brutal Russian suppression of the Hungarian uprising that same month. Although these events can be seen to have focused, rather than inspired, the "anger" of 1956, they were nonetheless the catalyst for a significant realignment on the British Left, one that was to have a permanent effect on the debate about the nature of culture.

Until 1956 the circumstances of the Cold War had isolated the small but important group of intellectuals who were members of the Communist Party from the rest of the British Left, which in turn responded with a guarded conformity to its own version of the party line, fearing the taint of fellow-travelling. The Hungarian uprising had a devastating impact on the British Communist Party's membership, already disturbed by reports of Khrushchev's attacks on Stalin in his speech at the twentieth Party Congress that February. E. P. Thompson and a fellow WEA lecturer, John Saville, members of the Party's historians' group, had started a cyclostyled magazine, the *Reasoner*, in July 1956 in order to promote Party debate, but with the Hungarian uprising the debate got out of hand as far as the Party bureaucracy was concerned, and Saville and Thompson were expelled from the Party for calling for Russian withdrawal from Hungary. According to Saville and Thompson, 'the Communist movement was in a shambles of intellectual disgrace and moral collapse'.[63] In 1957 the Party lost a fifth of its membership, some seven thousand people, through resignations and expulsions. Freed from Party discipline, in the summer of 1957 Saville and Thompson launched a 'journal of socialist humanism', the *New Reasoner*, which sought to establish a British radical tradition stemming from Tom Mann and William Morris.

Almost simultaneously a younger group of former Communist Party sympathisers who had run a university magazine, *Oxford Left*, launched the *Universities and Left Review*, edited by Raphael Samuel, Stuart Hall, Gabriel Pearson and Charles Taylor.

The injection of fresh thinking from a newly independent, radical Left had a stimulating effect on the orthodox Labour movement, which had settled into its own consensus about the impossibility of general economic, military or political change. But the break in the intellectual log jam also coincided with a much bigger political change, the launch of the Campaign for Nuclear Disarmament and the first Aldermaston march at Easter 1958.

CND was a genuinely new form of politics, founded on moral rather than party principle, which, as a single-issue campaign, could attract support all the way from the Liberal Party to the most revolutionary Trotskyite. It had the appearance of a mass movement, and the theatre of its marches and demonstrations, with their jazz bands and cheerful air of carnival, was immensely attractive to young people. The roots of the sixties underground can be traced to the proto-free festivals that the Easter marches represented. The existence of CND gave impetus to what rapidly became known as the New Left, and while the *New Reasoner* continued the traditions of an orthodox intellectual journal, *Universities and Left Review*, with its fashionable layout, gritty photographs and accessible mixture of political and cultural commentary, achieved a creditable circulation of eight thousand copies an issue.

The purpose of the New Left was always, and fundamentally, political: to use the energy released by the collapse of the Communist Party monolith and the appearance of CND to breathe new life into socialism and, if possible, capture the Labour Party. In retrospect, E. P. Thompson argued that it was the political impetus of the New Left that focused the cultural critique: 'What brought that jumble-sale of theoretical elements together in the first New Left was not a moment of culture at all, but a common sense of political crisis. It was the *politics* of that moment which directed all of us, from different traditions, to certain common problems, which included those of class, of popular culture and communications.'[64] But equally the cultural critique gave a new inflection to the political debate. As Stuart Hall commented in 1960: 'Politics, too narrowly conceived, has been the main cause of the decline of socialism in this country, and one of the reasons for the disaffection from socialist ideas of young people in particular.'[65] A greater awareness of cultural change might encourage political change and the New Left recognised that politics, too, should be seen as part of a 'whole way of life'. As Raymond Williams put it to Richard Hoggart in a recorded conversation: 'To understand this society, we have to look at its culture, even for political answers.'[66]

Here was a positive focus for the diffuse sensations of "anger". The New Left was the answer to Lindsay Anderson's call in his contribution to *Declaration* for 'a new intelligentsia'.[67] Raymond Williams's personal isolation came to an end as he took part in New Left meetings and went on CND marches: 'There was a general sense of trying to gather together a whole generation which the experience of the Cold War decade had disrupted.'[68] The first editorial of *Universities and Left Review* declared: 'The narrow gap left by the Marxism of the thirties in British intellectual life is now an open, gaping void,' and set out to fill it with the creation of the first of nearly forty New Left discussion clubs that sprang up across the country.[69] E. P. Thompson called in the same issue for 'books, pamphlets and journals: discussion groups and forums: poems and novels: a reawakened student movement: and cultural activities (like the old Unity theatres movement) which do not mope about the debasement of standards but begin to hit back. If we set such a movement of ideas afoot, with the élan of the thirties but with more maturity, we may find the mass commercial media are something of a dragon.'[70] New Left discussions sometimes made way for skiffle sessions, and the ground floor of the magazine's headquarters at 7 Carlisle Street in Soho became the Partisan café, advertised as 'A coffee house for the left. An anti-espresso bar.'[71]

The purpose of this exciting but exhausting ferment was, as *Universities and Left Review* editorialised: 'To draw together the discussion and research of many people in different fields in the common theme of culture and community. This theme has not existed as a subject for discussion, debate and propaganda, in its own right, for many years. We have come to it ourselves only in the course of trying to push past the limits of specialised problems, in the attempt to find some vantage point from which to make a deep criticism, not merely of some institutions, but of a whole culture – a way of life, under capitalism.'[72] Stuart Hall argued: 'The political intellectual is concerned with the institutional life of the society: the creative artist with the attitudes, the manners, the moral and emotional life which the individual consummates within that social framework. It seems to me that the beginning of a common socialist humanism is the realisation that these are not two distinct areas of interest, but the complementary parts of complex, common experience.'[73]

This became in effect Hall's editorial policy when it was decided at the end of 1959 that the forces of the *New Reasoner* and *Universities and Left Review* should merge to launch the *New Left Review*. The first number in January 1960 included a recorded conversation between Richard Hoggart and Raymond Williams, extracts from Arnold Wesker's play *The Kitchen*, and reviews of John Arden's play *Serjeant Musgrave's Dance* and Vladimir Nabokov's novel *Lolita*. But a discussion of the new vogue for pop music was almost entirely negative about the 'unbearable ugliness ... wrung from saxophones and guitars' while betraying an intellectual taste for jazz.[74] The answer to the review's rhetorical question, 'Is it true that when you scratch a New Leftist you reveal an old puritan?' appeared to be, yes.[75]

Beyond an enthusiasm for the new wave in British theatre and cinema, the cultural critique was slow to develop, although a submission to the Pilkington Committee on the future of broadcasting did argue: 'All forms of expression have their own validity and all are deserving of serious appreciation. Whether we are considering cool jazz or a classical symphony, Elizabethan drama or a television thriller, the important thing is not to categorise them in the pejorative sense but to determine whether they are good or bad of their own kind.'[76] This pluralism was progressive but as yet, however, no critical methodology had been developed that would satisfactorily relate the political and cultural aspects of 'a whole way of life'.

The obvious philosophical starting point was Marxism, but the weakness of the British tradition and the lasting inhibitions caused by the Cold War meant that people were slow, possibly even reluctant, to begin a Marxist analysis. A decade and half later the critic Terry Eagleton could still write of Continental Marxism: 'To intervene from England is almost automatically to disenfranchise oneself from debate. It is to feel acutely bereft of a tradition, as a tolerated house-guest of Europe, a precocious but parasitic alien.'[77] During the fifties, the painter and writer John Berger was one of the few to argue from an explicitly Marxist position, in his art reviews for the *New Statesman*.

In spite – or because of – his former Communist sympathies, Raymond Williams gave a highly sceptical account of Marxist cultural theory in *Culture and Society*, arguing for a more complex model than the crudely determinist theory that posited a mechanical relationship between society's economic base and its cultural superstructure. His 1958 essay 'Culture is Ordinary' was an attempt to clarify where he stood between the competing traditions of Leavis and Marx, and at least admitted the basis for a materialist analysis: 'A culture is a whole way of life, and the arts are part of a social organisation which economic change clearly radically affects.'[78]

Williams's next book, *The Long Revolution* (1961), was far less coherent than *Culture and Society*, as Williams struggled to find a language that would cope with the theoretical complexity of the study of culture as a whole way of life, rather than the narrow seam of literary criticism to which Leavisism had trained him. The book was also less well received because it was harder to grasp, and because it was more overtly political. The 'long revolution' of his title was the process by which people gradually won control over their own lives, as Williams put it, the 'struggle towards a culture recognisable as common'.[79] Writing at a time of decolonisation and emergent liberation movements, Williams was describing what he called 'a cultural revolution' by which societies and classes liberated themselves from the domination of others.[80] The process, which was at a very early stage, involved developments in democracy, industry, education and the technology of communication (the subject also of a separate study, *Communications*, published in 1962), all of which contributed to the *'structure of feeling'* [italics his] which constituted the specific culture of any one period.[81] At this stage Williams had not met the work of the French–Romanian Marxist Lucien Goldmann, whose idea of *'structures mentales'* helped him to develop a more grounded Marxist approach after 1968. Stuart Hall has argued that *The Long Revolution*, rather than *Culture and Society*, marks a decisive shift in the British approach to cultural studies. By writing an account of the English tradition of critical thinking about the adversarial relationship between culture and society, he was helping to bring it to a close, whereas *The Long Revolution* was a new beginning, an attempt to develop a theoretical approach within an empirical framework: 'It shifted the whole ground of debate from a literary–moral to an anthropological definition of culture.'[82]

Ironically, the perceived need for a more rigorous Marxist approach was one of the causes of the sudden collapse of the promising New Left movement. The alliance of cultural and political analysis reached

1. *Annus Horribilis*:
St George's Hall, Windsor, after the fire,
November 1992.

2. Royal romance: Windsor Castle
after being Gothickised by Wyatville.

3. Deep England:
'The South Downs',
Army Bureau of Current Affairs wartime poster.

4. Blitzed Britain:
still from Humphrey Jennings's film,
Family Portrait.

9. Swinging London:
Pop goes the Union Jack.

The Uses of Culture **111**

its apogee in 1960 with the publication of *Out of Apathy*, a collection of essays edited by E. P. Thompson that was intended as the first of a series of New Left Books to complement the *Review*. The book was addressed to the new intelligentsia, notably in Thompson's essay 'Outside the Whale', a reply to Orwell's 1940 essay 'Inside the Whale' which, Thompson argued, reads as 'an apology for quietism' that was picked up, along with *Animal Farm* and *1984*, and amplified by the conditions of the Cold War.[83] The philosopher Alasdair MacIntyre similarly argued that contemporary intellectuals were guilty of a *trahison des clercs* by accepting Karl Popper's anti-Marxist general theory that there could be no such thing as a general theory which did not lead to totalitarianism, thereby voluntarily giving up their freedom to change their ideas. For Thompson, for whom the historical rediscovery of popular radicalism was a means of countering the contemporary conservative hegemony, the challenge to the consensus of the fifties was 'the politics of anti-politics' of CND.[84]

CND proved, however, to be the New Left's undoing. As a campaign with a single issue, it could not develop into a political movement in its own right, and was therefore at the mercy of the politics of political parties, in this case, the Labour Party. Labour's third consecutive electoral defeat in 1959 helped to create the conditions by which a number of trades unions, hostile to the retreat from nationalisation proposed by the party's leader, Hugh Gaitskell (a retreat partly prompted by the unpopularity of nationalisation with the electorate), became sympathetic to the cause of CND and forced the passage of a motion in favour of unilateral disarmament at the Party conference in 1960. But Gaitskell reversed the position in 1961: CND split between liberals and pacifists on the one hand, and the believers in more direct action on the other, who formed the Committee of 100.

Political frustration combined with purely practical problems to weaken the movement. In spite of its critical success, the *New Left Review* was under-capitalised, with an unnecessarily large editorial board and an overworked inner cadre who were equally busy in running the magazine and the Left Clubs, and arguing their case in CND and the Labour Party. At the end of 1961 Stuart Hall, who had been at the centre of things since 1956, decided to give up the editorship, and a 'restructuring' was announced that gave the editorship to a team of four, while E. P. Thompson took over chairmanship of a smaller board from John Saville. New Left Books went into cold storage. One of the new editors was a former editor of the radical *New University* magazine, an Eton-educated Oxford graduate with considerable private means, Perry Anderson. After one issue Anderson became the sole editor, and at the beginning of 1963 he also became the owner. All the former board members, including Thompson, resigned or were removed, while Anderson began gradually to recast the review as a rigorously theoretical journal interested in continental Marxism and third-world liberation. The New Left Clubs, along with CND, went into decline. By November 1963 Thompson was able to write: 'The movement which once claimed to be "The New Left" . . . has now, in this country, dispersed itself both organisationally and (to some extent) intellectually. We failed to implement our original purpose, or even sustain what cultural apparatus we had.'[85]

The decline of the New Left coincided with the foundation of an institution specifically created to address questions of 'cultural apparatus', the Birmingham Centre for Contemporary Cultural Studies. Both Hoggart and Williams had become widely recognised for their publications. In 1959 Hoggart left Hull to become a senior lecturer in the English Department at Leicester University. In 1961 Williams accepted the offer of a university lecturership at Cambridge and became a fellow of Jesus College, relieved to give up work for the now changed Workers' Educational Association. In 1961 Hoggart was offered a chair in English at Birmingham University, a post he took up in 1962, on the understanding that he would be able to create a new post-graduate centre for contemporary cultural studies.

Hoggart was given his centre, which opened in 1964, but he had to face the hostility of both the English and Sociology departments, who viewed this hybrid with deep suspicion. Hoggart also had to find his own funds, which he did by means of a seven-year covenant from Allen Lane, his publisher at Penguin Books (a decision encouraged by Lane's adviser W. E. Williams), and lesser sums from Chatto and Windus and the *Observer*. Specific projects were funded by grants from the Rowntree Trust. Hoggart was able to appoint a research fellow and, recognising their mutual interest in popular art while acknowledging their differences – 'He was a Marxist and I a centre socialist'[86] – gave the job to Stuart Hall, who had been teaching film and media studies at Chelsea College of Science.

The Centre for Contemporary Cultural Studies led an embattled existence within Birmingham University, emblematised by their precarious housing in temporary accommodation, yet Stuart Hall has made the point that the establishment of the centre was a withdrawal from the more direct engagement of the period 1956–62. It was a place 'to which we *retreated* when that conversation in the open world could no longer be continued: it was politics by other means'.[87] Although the subject matter was clear, the approach was still tentative, as Hoggart's inaugural lecture at Birmingham demonstrated. While warning that 'perhaps no one should engage in the work who is not, in a certain sense, himself in love with popular art', he showed a careful deference to the Leavisite traditions of the English department he was joining.[88] The approach would be 'roughly' one third historical and philosophical, one third sociological, and 'the third – which will be the most important – is the literary critical'.[89] But when it came to shaping these elements into a coherent discipline, Hoggart freely admitted: 'We have as yet hardly begun to get any of the terms in the debate straight.'[90]

The Birmingham Centre for Contemporary Cultural Studies was to develop into an important source of new ideas about popular culture and a hotbed of what became known as "theory", but at the beginning of the sixties the New Left was hamstrung by two essentially conservative critical traditions. Not only was the very idea of culture indissolubly linked to the conservative tradition that stemmed from Matthew Arnold, but thinkers like Williams, Hoggart and Hall had been trained in its methodological habits as well. The heirs of F. R. Leavis, they made critical evaluations in terms of some notionally absolute (and ideologically value-free) standard. This standard was that of the "high culture" that appeared to be threatened by the corrupting influence of the mass media. Attempts to understand "popular art" (a consciously less pejorative term than "mass entertainment") were confused by the difficulty of distinguishing between discriminations based on aesthetic grounds and distinctions that had their ultimate justification in issues of power and class. Judgements of value were clouded by the social and political differences between the art enjoyed by a privileged minority and that by a wider community.

The critic Alan Sinfield has pointed out that 'the idea that high culture transcends material conditions, such as class, has a good socialist lineage', especially when British culture could be seen as a means of resistance to American capitalist culture.[91] 'These attitudes I call "left-culturalism". They were quite compatible with the approach of

Matthew Arnold and F. R. Leavis, which in schools and colleges were helping to ratify class mobility by entangling it with the acquisition of a superior culture.'[92] An early example of such 'Left-culturalism' was Arnold Wesker's Centre 42, the most practical experiment, other than the discussion clubs and the magazine itself, in the creation of a cultural apparatus.

In 1960 Wesker persuaded the film and television technicians' union ACTT to sponsor a successful resolution (number 42) at the annual Trades Unions Conference which called on the unions to recognise their responsibility towards the arts. At the same time he assembled a group of writers and artists to mount a series of people's festivals, seven of which were held in different parts of the country in 1962. There followed a pause, as Wesker sought an appropriate building, which turned out to be a decaying engine-turning shed in Camden, the Round House. The pause developed into a permanent hiatus as the need to rescue and restore the building absorbed all other energies.

Wesker's experiment failed, thanks to the inertia of the TUC, the hostility of the Arts Council and the suspicions of the Labour Party establishment once it got into power, but what is significant is that Wesker, while taking an obviously political initiative in trying to involve trades unions in the arts, was not seeking to change or relocate the arts themselves. He did not accept that there was, in this sense, such a thing as "working-class culture" and he did not believe that the arts were exclusively class based. The artists he mentioned in his campaigning articles were W. H. Auden, Benjamin Britten, Joan Littlewood and himself. His vision of Centre 42 was: 'A cultural hub which, by its approach and work, will destroy the mystique and snobbery associated with the arts. A place where artists are in control of their own means of expression and their own channels of distribution, where the highest standards of professional work will be maintained in an atmosphere of informality; where the artist is brought into closer contact with his audience enabling the public to see that artistic activity is a natural part of their daily lives.'[93] But when the Round House later became a focus for the artistic activity and riotous informality of the underground, Wesker despaired, and in 1970 Centre 42 was wound up.

Raymond Williams had foreseen the problems in simply trying to spread the values of pre-existing culture to more people in 1958: 'We should not seek to extend a ready-made culture to the benighted masses. We should accept, frankly, that if we extend our culture we shall change it: some that is offered will be rejected, other parts will be radically criticised.'[94] The truth was that culture itself was changing, as film and television, pop music and the pulp press made more and more impact on 'a whole way of life' that was itself changing in response to a greater affluence, that made the moral austerity of the forties appear unnecessary. The dilemma of the New Left was encapsulated in a book published in 1964 and aimed primarily at teachers in secondary schools, *The Popular Arts*, written jointly by Stuart Hall and Paddy Whannel, a contributor to *New Left Review* and an education officer at the British Film Institute.

After paying fulsome tributes to Hoggart and Williams, the authors explained:

> The struggle between what is good and worthwhile and what is shoddy and debased is not a struggle *against* the modern forms of communication, but a conflict *within* these media. Our concern is with the difficulty which most of us experience in distinguishing the one from the other, particularly when we are dealing with the new media, new means of expression, in a new, and often confusing social and cultural situation. This book attempts to develop a critical method for handling these problems of value and evaluation in the media.[95]

The authors rejected Leavis's pessimistic conservatism, but did not deny that ethical questions were involved in judging popular art: 'The moral statements made by art are made in aesthetic terms; that is to say they are embodied in the manner of presentation. To discover the moral meanings in art and entertainment we must first respond to them in their own terms.'[96] While attempting to do so in the test cases that make up the bulk of the book, Hall and Whannel still made the automatic coupling 'good work/high culture', as in: 'The new media are significant means for transmitting good work, "high culture", to wider audiences.'[97] In spite of recognising the new cultural conditions that existed, *The Popular Arts* could not bring itself to accept that such conditions might be capable of creating a new art. A puritan approach prevailed: 'The typical "art" of the mass media today is not a continuity from, but a *corruption of*, popular art.'[98]

Although the New Left did not achieve the 'real break-through' that Stuart Hall had claimed in his first editorial for *New Left Review*, by the early sixties there was a sense of changed circumstances as the new novelists, poets and dramatists became accepted, and a new theatre, in particular, began to flourish.[99] Osborne's *Look Back in Anger* gave a voice to the pent-up frustrations of a post-war generation who lacked the puritan seriousness of the forties, and who felt stifled by the conformity of the fifties. The theatre critic Kenneth Tynan had recognised Jimmy Porter as his contemporary: 'The Porters of our time deplore the tyranny of "good taste" and refuse to accept "emotional" as a term of abuse; they are classless, and they are also leaderless. Mr Osborne is their first spokesman in the London theatre.'[100]

While the purists of the New Left remained largely contemptuous of the mainstream, the generational and class tensions that had been evident among the liberal intelligentsia during the first half of the decade became less marked as the metropolitan establishment absorbed the new arrivals. If not 'Left-culturalism' then a "liberal-culturalism" that welcomed a more popular approach to the arts, became the ruling ideal. As early as February 1957 there was a symbolic move away from the promotion of "high" culture when the BBC, in response to financial pressures and the fall in radio audiences caused by the expansion of television, decided to cut back the hours of the Third Programme, and try to achieve a wider audience for this expensive minority channel. In spite of the protests of T. S. Eliot, Michael Tippett, Vaughan Williams, Laurence Olivier and other members of the newly created Sound Broadcasting Society (successor to the Third Programme Defence Society) the changes went ahead in September. Network Three was launched, with the Third restricted to evening broadcasts. Whereas in the first ten years of its existence half of the Third's output had been speech, an increase in music diluted its "missionary" character as an all-round, high cultural medium. The pressure on the BBC to respond to the needs of a general audience meant that the Third's version of Eliot's cultural élitism gradually had to be abandoned. Kate Whitehead has commented in her history of the channel:

> Reith's public service was founded on the concept of promoting a unified and educated democracy; a programme devoted to a cultural élite could only reinforce received ideas about high culture being the preserve of the highly privileged, and thus the audience for "high culture" never expanded. In fact the Third programme was riven by a series of incompatibilities, contradictions and paradoxes, which had to lead to its eventual fragmentation and demise.[101]

The Third Programme became Radio Three in 1967.

The key point about the minor literary revolution of the fifties was that it had been in one sense a counter-revolution, a revolt against modernism and the obligation to be stylistically avant-garde. The shift in literature was in subject matter, a return to realism that allowed the rising generation to dismiss the stylistic inventions of their elders as élitist. (There had been a parallel return to realism in painting in the early fifties, but the influence of American abstract expressionism from 1956 onwards restored style, and not content, as the recognition sign of the avant-garde.) Kingsley Amis could argue (on the Third Programme): 'The adventurous path is the one that leads away from experiment.'[102] Realism ensured a large middlebrow audience and, both for stylistic and political reasons, was the ruling mode for the new British cinema and television drama as it developed in the sixties.

The provincial–academic versus metropolitan–mandarin debate that opened the decade was in the end less about the nature of culture, than about access to the levers of cultural power, and as Amis emblematically moved from the former status to the latter (he moved from Swansea to Cambridge in 1961 and gave up teaching altogether in 1963) the conflict was partially resolved by the expansion of opportunities in broadcasting, journalism and education. The foundation of the University of Sussex in 1961 was followed by a further six new universities whose bright new architecture symbolised their modish distinction from the older redbrick institutions outside the Oxford–Cambridge–London axis. The market for "quality" newspapers, where the arts and literature were seriously discussed, expanded. The *Sunday Telegraph* was launched in 1961 and the *Sunday Times* published the first colour supplement in 1962. It was a sign of the times that a weekly journal addressing the interests of the new professionals in social work, administration, planning and higher education, and taking a lively interest in cultural issues, appropriately called *New Society*, could be successfully launched that same year.

'Left-culturalism', in alliance with the mainstream, had two significant victories during this period, one against traditional conservatism, the other against the new forces of commercialism. In 1959 a new and more liberal Obscene Publications Act had become law, but the limits to this liberalisation were put to the test in October 1960 when Penguin Books were prosecuted for publishing an unexpurgated edition of D. H. Lawrence's *Lady Chatterley's Lover*. An army of expert witnesses – a cultural equivalent to the broad coalition of CND, from bishops to young students – was drawn up in the novel's defence, and both Richard

Hoggart and Raymond Williams were prominent in the witness box. It became clear that Penguin's crime was not so much publishing sexually explicit language and descriptions, but making them available in a mass-market paperback rather than an expensive and exclusive edition. The explicit class assumptions of the prosecuting counsel, who asked the jury if they would wish their wives or servants to read the book, were shown to be thoroughly out of date, and Penguin won their case.

The cultural coalition that had defended *Lady Chatterley* was less successful in prosecuting commercial television before the Pilkington Committee, although the principles of public-service broadcasting were upheld. Much of the moral panic about the spread of a mass, commercial culture had focused on the new Independent Television network, which had begun broadcasting in 1955. The ascendancy of Carnivore over Herbivore can be seen in the shift of official opinion between 1951, when a committee chaired by Sir William Beveridge, architect of the welfare state, decided against commercial television in favour of continuing the BBC's monopoly, and 1954 when ITV won parliamentary approval. In 1960, with the BBC's charter due for renewal and pressure mounting for the opening of a third television channel, it was decided to set up a Royal Commission on Broadcasting, under the chairmanship of an industrialist, Sir Harry Pilkington. Richard Hoggart became a member of the committee, and was widely credited with influencing the shape of the report when it was published in 1962. This was partly because he made a convenient target for the storm of protest from the popular newspapers (with financial interests in the television companies) when the activities of the commercial companies were sternly criticised: 'The disquiet about television is mainly attributable to independent television and largely to its entertainment programmes.'[103]

Although independent television was forced to improve its news coverage and moderate some of its advertising practices, the Pilkington Committee's chief recommendation – the separation of programme-making from the sale of advertising – was not accepted. The BBC, under its new director-general Hugh Carleton-Greene, was found to be generally satisfactory, and was awarded the third channel, BBC2, which opened in 1964. As a questioning of the cultural influence of television in general, the Pilkington Report came to two important conclusions. One was that "entertainment" was not the problem, but trivialisation, which could happen at any level. The second was that to conceive of mass audiences at all was patronising and arrogant. (As Raymond Williams had written: 'There are in fact no masses, only ways of seeing people as masses.'[104]) "Giving the public what it wants" was almost always an underestimation of any individual's taste, and a reinforcement of social and cultural stratification.

In view of the Arts Council's contribution to this process, a striking omission from the cultural debates of the New Left at this period was any discussion of its role and influence. Raymond Williams, for instance, did not mention it in his outline proposals for greater institutional protection of culture from the depredations of commerce in his concluding chapter to *The Long Revolution*. In his view, post-war cultural policy had been no more than a defensive holding operation, while the market steadily increased its influence over all but a small sector of what was regarded as most valuable. This was better than nothing, but unlikely to produce change. Certainly, the Arts Council of the fifties, notwithstanding its financial help to the Royal Court, had done much to preserve a patrician culture, and very little to widen access to the arts. The attitude of the Council's secretary-general, W. E. Williams, seems at best to have been one of narrow ambitions for the arts. As a later secretary-general, Sir Roy Shaw, has commented, Williams's earlier reputation as a democratiser and populariser of knowledge appeared to have been forgotten. Williams 'seemed to leave his educational zeal behind him when he took up the post. I found no record of his trying to encourage the Council to take up the educational responsibilities implied in its charter.' Shaw pointed out that Williams's response to Wesker's proposals for Centre 42 was an article in the *Daily Telegraph* titled 'Art is for a Minority' – a (mythical) classless minority from stockbrokers to stokers that enjoyed equal access to the arts.[105] Those who had known Williams in the war years felt that his grand life and powerful position had rather corrupted him.[106] According to Lord Goodman, Williams's successor, Nigel Abercrombie, an austere former academic seconded from the Admiralty, was appointed 'to instal proper notions of discipline and control in the ranks of Bohemia'.[107]

Williams's justification for adopting the policies of regional retrenchment and limited "response" described in the previous chapter was the smallness of the funds at his disposal, although these had doubled over ten years to £1,745,000 by 1961. *Art in the Red* was Williams's vivid title for the Council's annual report for 1956–7; *The Struggle for*

Survival that for 1958–9. Surveying the Council's position in 1956, he wrote: 'The Arts Council believes, then, that the first claim upon its attention and assistance is that of maintaining in London and the larger cities effective power-houses of opera, music and drama; for unless these quality institutions can be maintained the arts are bound to decline into mediocrity.'[108] At this point the Council had few clients: Covent Garden, Sadler's Wells and the Old Vic were absorbing half of the Council's funds between them. Williams's final report before his retirement in 1963 was more optimistically titled *A Brighter Prospect*, but he continued to assert: 'High values in the arts can only be maintained on a restricted scale.'[109] Williams evidently shared the New Left's fear of cultural decadence brought on by commercialisation, but this did not prevent him enjoying his power and prestige. When Kenneth Clark was succeeded as chairman in 1960 by the Conservative politician Lord Cottesloe, Williams found his new chairman too interventionist, telling him: 'You are the admiral; I am the captain. Now please get off my bridge.'[110]

The continuing consensus between the political parties on maintaining the welfare state meant that arts policies were mainly expressed in terms of rival bids at elections. In 1959 the Labour Party produced *Leisure for Living*, promising greater provision for the arts, but asserting that this should not be a party-political matter. The Conservatives replied with *The Challenge of Leisure* which firmly accepted the need for state support for the arts, and urged a marked increase in the Arts Council grant overall, with the Royal Opera House's allocation negotiated as a separate item, and a significant increase for theatre. Such an increase became in any event necessary, for the long campaign to establish a National Theatre at last began to bear fruit. While the foundation stone for a National Theatre building had been laid on the South Bank in 1951, funds were at last released in 1962, and Sir Laurence Olivier was appointed artistic director of a National Theatre company that took up residence in the Old Vic Theatre in 1963. The Royal Shakespeare Company, meanwhile, which Peter Hall had formed from the company he had built up at the Shakespeare Memorial Theatre in Stratford, had begun London seasons at the Aldwych in 1960, and while it had been self-sufficient at Stratford, it too was hungry for Arts Council funds to support the expansion of its activities. The government decided that from the financial year 1963–4 the Arts Council's grant-in-aid should be planned on a triennial basis with increases of at least ten per cent a year. The 1964 Library and Museums Act redefined the duties of public libraries in terms of a "comprehensive service", which meant that fiction as well as non-fiction had to be freely available.

At the general election in October 1964 Labour won power under Harold Wilson, with a small majority. Writing in September, Perry Anderson commented in the *New Left Review*: 'The Labour Party at present has no official programme of any seriousness in the field of culture and communications. Wilson's speeches make no reference to them.'[111] Yet he shrewdly observed that the contrasting examples from the United States (the Kennedy administration's self-glamorisation through association with the arts – Kennedy's so-called "Camelot") and France (where General de Gaulle's policy of major cultural investment under André Malraux generated a modernised version of '*la gloire*'), and the lessons learnt from the Attlee government's glum association with austerity, meant that a British version of the French and American models was likely to emerge 'worthier, duller, and more *bien-pensant* no doubt – but in essence the same'.[112]

This was to prove the case. Wilson decided to shift responsibility for the arts away from the Treasury to the Department of Education and Science, partly to accommodate the energetic personality of Jennie Lee, widow of Aneurin Bevan, whom Harold Wilson chose to become Britain's first official Minister for the Arts, albeit as a junior minister in the DES. Lord Goodman has recorded: 'Although Harold Wilson was in artistic matters a Philistine, he was better than the later Philistines, since he recognised that the ambit of British culture could not be controlled by his own personal predilections, and he responded with speed and generosity to applications from Jennie Lee for better support for the arts.'[113] In February 1965 Lee published the first ever government White Paper on cultural funding, *A Policy for the Arts*.

The White Paper had a threefold purpose. The first was to acknowledge that government funding had 'hitherto been on a relatively modest scale and has grown up in response to spasmodic pressures rather than as a result of a coherent plan. The same picture emerges locally.'[114] The second was to announce increased funding and new initiatives to help younger individual artists, and for the first time to provide the Arts Council with capital funds to spend on building projects with the creation of a Housing the Arts Fund. The third was tentatively to acknowledge that there had been a shift in the way culture was defined and the uses to which it was put: 'Diffusion of culture is now so much a part of life that there is no point at which it stops. Advertisements, buildings, books, motor-cars, radio and television, magazines, records, all can carry a cultural aspect and affect our lives for good or ill as a species of "amenity".'[115] The White Paper welcomed the development of a network of Regional Arts Associations as a balance to metropolitan culture, but it still sought an adjustment between cultural forms, preserving a hierarchy of value even while questioning that it existed: 'It is partly a question of bridging the gap between what have come to be called the "higher" forms of entertainment and the traditional sources – the brass band, the amateur concert party, the entertainer, the music hall and pop group – and to challenge the fact that a gap exists. In the world of jazz the process has already happened; highbrow and lowbrow have met.'[116]

This was not the radical document that the New Left hoped for, it was another example of the "Wilsonism" that was so disenchanting to the young radicals who were moving towards the confrontational attitudes of 1968. Raymond Williams has recorded that he had no contact whatsoever with the Labour establishment during their period of office. Arnold Wesker's experience of that establishment was profoundly unhappy. Nonetheless the emphasis on the importance of cultural issues by the New Left must be given some credit for turning the government's mind to cultural policy.

A Policy for the Arts ushered in a new and expansive period for official support for the arts, coming as it did at a time of renewed cultural confidence (built on the new radicalism of 1956) and apparent economic improvement. But if a society was to be understood by looking at its culture – as Hoggart and Williams would have it, even to find political answers – then the debate about that culture had only just begun. Having challenged the privileged guardians of the old hierarchy of the arts, the provincial puritans of the fifties would have to come to terms with the metropolitan hedonists of the sixties.

V

A Swinging Meritocracy
Britain in the 1960s

In the spring of 1992 Richard Hoggart published the final volume of
his autobiographical trilogy, *Life and Times*. In an article for *The Times*
he lamented the seismic shifts in language and cultural values that had
taken place since the late fifties. He referred in particular to events that
in the last chapter were accounted as victories for the 'Left-culturalism'
of those years:

> The *Lady Chatterley's Lover* trial showed in relief a deeply divided society;
> but both sides sought the same moral high ground. The Pilkington Report's
> discussion of the purposes of public-service broadcasting came from a com-
> mittee whose members, though they had little in common socially and
> politically, invoked an agreed language of judgment; there was a sort of
> consensus.[1]

Hoggart's consensus, however, was not the deferential consensus
described in Chapter III. From 1956 onwards the rising generation
associated with the Angry Young Men and the New Left had challenged
the social compact confirmed by the Coronation and, in the form of
'Left-culturalism' had at least partially succeeded, as the turning point
of the *Chatterley* trial on a question of class had demonstrated. Hoggart's consensus is the progressive consensus which sought to supplant
it, which deployed the rhetoric of meritocracy and technological modernisation, and which found its political expression in the Labour
administration of Harold Wilson from 1964 to 1970.

The transition was neither smooth nor complete. In 1959 in a lecture
at Cambridge on 'The Two Cultures and the Scientific Revolution',
the novelist C. P. Snow revived a theme he had first broached in an
article for the *New Statesman* in 1956: the growing conflict between
the worlds of a pessimistic literary culture and an optimistic scientific
one. In the thirties Snow had done scientific research at Cambridge,

publishing his first novel in 1932, before becoming a temporary civil servant responsible for recruiting scientists for war work. After the war his reputation as a novelist had grown, and he felt well qualified to comment on what he saw as a worrying divide: 'literary intellectuals at one pole – at the other scientists'.[2] Snow offered as representative polarities T. S. Eliot and the atomic scientist Ernest Rutherford. He regarded this polarisation and mutual incomprehension as a loss, with both sides impoverished – scientists by their ignorance of traditional culture, literary intellectuals by their belief that their culture was the only possible one. The divide was a problem for the whole of the West, but more acute in Britain because of the degree of educational specialisation, and it was hardening into antagonism as science forged ahead. It was therefore essential to rethink an educational system that produced such a narrowly trained, tiny élite.

Snow highlighted the conservatism of the British cultural tradition: 'Intellectuals, in particular literary intellectuals, are natural Luddites.'[3] In an argument that was to be repeated by Correlli Barnett in the eighties, he warned that the British were trained for administration, not wealth creation, that engineers and technologists were sadly neglected. British 'aesthetic revulsion' at industrialisation had led to a fatal ignorance of the scientific and technological needs of the twentieth century, even among "pure" scientists.[4] He foresaw economic and social decline as a consequence of the bias of British education. The solution to world poverty was a scientific revolution, but only through a reformed educational system could the necessary new scientists be trained 'not only in scientific but in human terms'.[5]

The lecture, which articulated a genuine and general concern, was very well received, for its title made a convenient frame for a debate that still continues. Snow's simplified vision chimed with the modernising rhetoric of Harold Wilson's speeches about the "white heat" of technology, and when Wilson became Prime Minister in 1964 Snow was made a life peer and a junior minister in Wilson's new Ministry for Technology. But first Snow had had to endure a vicious attack in another Cambridge lecture, F. R. Leavis's Richmond Lecture at Downing College in 1962: 'Two Cultures? The Significance of C. P. Snow'.

Snow represented everything that Leavis hated: a successful popular novelist, promoted by the British Council, and a member of the Athenaeum who symbolised the Cambridge academic establishment, as opposed to the 'essential Cambridge in spite of Cambridge' that Leavis and *Scrutiny* represented.[6] Before he addressed Snow's argument, Snow's personality and reputation had first to be demolished: 'Not only is he not a genius; he is as intellectually undistinguished as it is possible to be.'[7] As 'a novelist he doesn't exist; he doesn't even begin to exist'.[8] In his lecture, Snow had mistaken the *haute culture* of the 'modish literary world' for a genuine traditional culture.[9] Snow's version of the literary intellectual was 'the enemy of art and life'.[10] His ignorance meant he misunderstood the response to industrialisation of those, from John Ruskin to D. H. Lawrence, who knew the distinction 'between wealth and well-being'.[11]

Leavis's contemptuous fury caused him unintentionally to reveal the reason why he had never developed the explicitly political social critique that his radicalism appeared to point his towards: his insistence on the individual as the only source of moral judgement. Quoting Lawrence's maxim, 'Nothing matters but life', Leavis likewise insisted 'on the truth that only in living individuals is life there, and individual lives cannot be aggregated or equated or dealt with quantitatively in any way'.[12] Snow's collectivist hopes for the social benefits of technology were therefore a chimera.

Leavis's lecture caused as much stir as had Snow's, though both men were producing caricatured versions of the positions they were attacking. Snow and Leavis were arguing past each other; they certainly never debated with each other, and Snow forbore to reply until 1970, when he developed an idea he had already hinted at, that there was a third culture, a culture of the social sciences that might synthesise the other two. Both men were partially right, Snow was right to be concerned about the prospects of long-term economic decline, and Leavis foresaw the dangers in coming structural change: 'The advance of science and technology means a human future of change so rapid and of such kinds, of tests and challenges so unprecedented, of decisions and possible non-decisions so momentous and insidious in their consequences, that mankind – this is surely clear – will need to be in full possession of its intelligent humanity,' a humanity which Leavis characteristically, if imprecisely, defined as 'something with the livingness of the deepest vital instinct'.[13]

Both Snow and Leavis seemed to detect the deep shift that was taking place as the tectonic plates of the world economic system began to move so as to undermine the old industrial order and the social structures built upon it. In the same year that the Pilkington Report reached its consensus on the future of broadcasting, Anthony Sampson published the first edition of what was to become a series of surveys under the title *Anatomy of Britain*. In it Sampson noted not confident agreement, but 'a loss of dynamic and purpose, and a general bewilderment . . . both at the top and the bottom of Britain today'.[14] Having woken from her economic sleep, 'Britain is becoming *visually* aware of living in a state of perpetual and perilous change'.[15] Anatomising Britain was a growth industry at this period, precisely because of the features that Sampson noted, features that pointed to the disruption of the previous sustaining consensus. As George Orwell's former co-editor of the wartime Searchlight Books, T. R. Fyvel, noted in 1968: 'In the turmoil of British society there has been an unusual loss of almost every kind of social authority.'[16]

Such comments register the shift in national consciousness from the conservatism of the fifties towards a much more dynamic self-image in the sixties. That image was in part wish-fulfilment, but the conditions of economic, social and international change that rendered the deferential consensus of the fifties unstable called for just such an image, one which would adjust to the erosion of traditional class hierarchy. This change gave Fyvel the theme for his book *Intellectuals Today*. 'The affluent society's forces of demolition are steadily, corrodingly at work and . . . bourgeois values are fast being knocked down, out-dated and satirised.'[17]

Fyvel continued the line of argument that had been put forward by Edward Shils in 1956, that British intellectuals enjoyed a harmonious relationship with the institutions of the state. His book describes the emergence of a new integrated meritocratic and technocratic intelligentsia who showed no signs of rebellion because of the career possibilities that were available to them and the professionalisation of the intellectual class. Fyvel believed that the chapter of irritation and protest between 1956 and 1962 was now closed: 'In Britain more than across the Channel there is therefore awareness of a recent period of rebelliousness now dwindling.'[18]

The year 1968 did not turn out to be the best one in which to make that case, but certainly Britain had never had an autonomous, antagonistic intelligentsia on the Continental model. Because of the narrow social base of higher education, intellectuals were essentially members of the administrative class, and such radicalism as that class had felt during the war was stifled by the Cold War that followed. The

New Left had sought to keep that radicalism alive and build upon it but most of its sympathisers were absorbed by the expanding academic and social agencies or by broadcasting and journalism. Williams, Hoggart, Thompson and Hall were all to become professors; ironically, private means secured Anderson's independence as owner and editor in chief of the *New Left Review*. Generally, it made more sense to speak in terms of a meritocracy than a separate intelligentsia; new recruits were absorbed into an expanding administrative class. Fyvel noted shrewdly: 'I have found it interesting to watch the transformation of Oxford and Cambridge from institutions for the confirmation of special status (as they were in my time) to institutions for its acquisition.'[19]

The meritocratic products of post-war higher education were needed to administer the expanding field of communications, from the BBC to the burgeoning advertising industry. Just as Britain began to be described as an affluent or consumer society, communications in the form of television, radio, newspapers and magazines became increasingly objects of consumption, in that they absorbed an important part of people's expanding disposable income and their greater leisure. As such, they symbolised and amplified the sense of living in a consumer society, governed by mass communications, and so contributed to the notion that Britain was undergoing 'perpetual and perilous' change, where former conceptions of authority and social value were being challenged. As registers of social change, the media were primary subjects for the expanding field of cultural studies.

The shift to a more progressive consensus both resulted from the changes in the mass media, and changed the nature of the mass media themselves. The BBC was particularly successful in adapting to the new mood. Hugh Carleton-Greene's period as director-general from 1960 to 1969 was one of remarkable cultural and political self-confidence for the institution, which began with its successful appearance before the Pilkington Committee, and ended only when a Labour Prime Minister imposed a Conservative chairman, Lord Hill, in September 1967 with the intention of bringing the BBC closer to the government's heel. Greene had seized the opportunity, as he put it, 'to open windows and dissipate the ivory-tower stuffiness which still clung to some parts of the BBC'.[20] He was particularly successful in comedy with shows like *Till Death Us Do Part* and drama, where between 1963 and 1970 the single plays broadcast as *The Wednesday Play* regularly projected a discomforting image of society and even, in the case of *Cathy Come Home*, first broadcast in 1966, produced political change on the issue of homelessness. Greene's belief in the ventilation of ideas encouraged the BBC's current affairs department in 1962 to experiment with the contemporary vogue for satire with an entirely new genre of programme, *That Was The Week That Was*.

The "satire-boom", signalled by the success of a 1960 Edinburgh Festival revue, *Beyond the Fringe* (which ran in the West End, with several changes of cast from the original Jonathan Miller, Alan Bennett, Peter Cook and Dudley Moore, from 1961 to 1966), the launch of the Establishment Club and the magazine *Private Eye* in 1961, showed that deference was out of fashion. The public-school and Oxbridge origins of most of the satirists, however, and the indulgent attitude of most of the satirised (as Prime Minister, Harold Macmillan expressly forbade any action being taken against his caricature in *Beyond the Fringe*) shows that there was still a degree of consensus that licensed such jesting. *That Was The Week That Was* was dropped by the BBC in 1964 on the grounds that there was to be a general election, but Greene was also prudently removing a possible source of political irritation ahead of the discussion of the renewal of the BBC's charter in that year.

The political establishment did far more damage to itself than any satirist could inflict when the Minister for War John Profumo was forced to resign in 1963 after lying to the House of Commons about his affair with Christine Keeler. Macmillan resigned later that year, and his successor Alec Douglas-Home, who renounced his peerage in order to become Prime Minister, proved no match in the media against Labour's new leader, Harold Wilson. There followed a significant break in post-war political history when Labour won the 1964 election, albeit by a majority of only four seats.

Much of Wilson's success lay in harnessing the rhetoric, if not the reality, of progress. His speeches about the "white-heat" of the scientific revolution appealed to the rising meritocracy of post-war graduates who hoped to see the long-heralded modernisation of their society take place. The importance of Wilson's skill as a television performer showed the increasing significance of the medium, indeed his hostility to the BBC was a back-handed compliment to Hugh Carleton-Greene for developing its social and cultural potential so successfully. The one lasting memorial to the Wilson years is the Open University, which broke with the older patterns of higher and adult further education by using television to create an electronic campus. As the Open University acquired academic confidence, its staff were able to develop new approaches in the field of cultural studies.

Television, and the awareness of change transmitted by television, was of interest to more than just canny politicians. It was central to the debate about cultural value and identity that the growing power of mass communications had provoked. As the new discipline of cultural studies pioneered by Hoggart and Williams developed, analysis of the media became a central focus. Whereas in America media analysts in the fifties had sought to show that television was a benign, or at least neutral influence, British attitudes were shaped by an intellectual tradition shared by Marxists and liberals that went back to the nineteenth century, when the argument that a "mass society" was replacing a previously organic society had been first developed. Essentially, television as a mass medium was seen as a threat to traditional literary culture which placed such emphasis on individual discriminations.

In *Understanding Media* (1964), the most talked-about book on the subject, the Canadian critic Marshall McLuhan argued that the effect of television was to reshape the linear and hierarchical culture formed under the influence of print into a single, all-inclusive and instantaneous web of communication that eliminated both hierarchy and distance. Such a culture (which foreshadows the "counter-culture" of the later sixties) substituted instant, mass effect for the critical distance of literary evaluation. This was anathema to those reared in the Leavisite tradition, as can be seen in the National Union of Teachers' decision to hold their conference on 'Popular Culture and Personal Responsibility' in 1960. Denys Thompson, Leavis's collaborator on *Culture and Environment* (1933), edited the Pelican paperback that resulted from the conference, arguing, 'Our national culture is being replaced by a synthetic substance that exists only in the media.'[21] In his essay on 'Mass Communications' for the final volume of the strongly Leavisite Pelican Guide to English Literature, *The Modern Age* (1961), Richard Hoggart blamed the very structure of the mass media for their corrupting influence: 'The disinclination to suggest real choice, individual decision, which is to be found in the mass media is not simply the product of a commercial desire to keep the customers happy. It is within the grain of *mass* communications.'[22]

Raymond Williams followed up his discussion of the media in *The*

Long Revolution with *Communications* in 1962, partly as a result of his contribution to the NUT conference in 1960, and drawing on the approach he had taken in his WEA classes. He took a more sympathetic view of the potential of the media, arguing for the primary importance of communications in promoting change, in that 'society is a form of communication'.[23] The media therefore needed their own critical analysis, so that the way that forms of communication and their related institutions imposed their own models on society could be traced. Williams developed this analysis in two further revised editions of the book as the situation changed between 1962 and 1976, and wrote television criticism for the *Listener* between 1968 and 1972. His experience of American television while teaching at Stanford University in 1973 led him to a further revision of his views in *Television: Technology and Cultural Form* (1974) which examined the relationship between the technology of television and its distinctive formal codes, thus following the general trend in the analysis of television towards looking at the *way* it transmitted its messages as opposed to the actual messages themselves.

Essentially, however, what became known as "media studies" were rooted in a deep suspicion of the media, because of their powerful influence on social values and their capacity to transmit and reinforce capitalist ideology. As Stuart Hall put it at the 1960 NUT conference: 'There is bound to be a very sharp conflict between the task of education and the role of the media, which are still closely linked to securing profit and to the advertising industry.'[24] The Marxist tradition was even more hostile to the mass media than the Leavisite. In *The Dialectic of Enlightenment* (originally published in German in 1947) Theodor Adorno and Max Horkheimer chose the phrase 'culture industry' to describe 'mass culture', and treated it as something essentially hostile to both "high" and "popular" culture. Adorno's position was:

> The culture industry intentionally integrates its consumers from above. To the detriment of both it forces together the spheres of high and low art. . . . The seriousness of high art is destroyed in speculation about its efficacy; the seriousness of the lower perishes with the civilisational constraints imposed on the rebellious resistance inherent within it as long as social control was not yet total.[25]

A third member of the "Frankfurt School" of Marxist cultural critics, Herbert Marcuse, took a similar line:

If mass communications blend together harmoniously, and often unnotice-ably, art, politics, religion, and philosophy with commercials, they bring these realms of culture to their common denominator – the commodity form. The music of the soul it also the music of salesmanship. Exchange value, not truth value counts.[26]

Adorno, Marcuse and other members of the Frankfurt School were driven into exile by Hitler's manipulation of mass psychology through the radio, press and cinema. Adorno's dislike of the mass media was reinforced by his experience of American commercial radio, television and popular music during his exile there from 1938 until his return to Frankfurt after the war. Marcuse however became an American citizen in 1940. His argument in an influential text for the sixties counter-culture, *One-Dimensional Man* (1964), that technological change had created a system of domination which negated the old dialectic of classes and the possibilities of opposition and therefore change, was strikingly backed by reference to the American mass media: 'Perhaps the most telling evidence can be obtained by simply looking at television or listening to the AM radio for one consecutive hour for a couple of days, not shutting off the commercials, and now and then switching the station.'[27]

In Britain, philosophical objections to the influence of the mass media were also significantly coloured by anti-Americanism, a reflection of the resentment felt at Britain's relative decline after the war. As Peter Hennessy has pointed out: 'Britain, as the price of survival, became in effect an economic subsidiary of the United States for the duration of the war and for many years afterwards.'[28] The glamour of Hollywood and the frequent appearance of American television programmes on British screens were constant reminders of the changed position. In 1951 the National Cultural Committee of the Communist Party of Great Britain tried to make political capital out of this with a conference on 'The American Threat to British Culture', and in 1952 followed up with a similarly angled conference on 'Britain's Cultural Heritage'.[29] Leavis warned in 1962: 'The vision of our imminent tomorrow is today's America: the energy, the triumphant technology, the produc-tivity, the high standard of living and the life-impoverishment.'[30] Richard Hoggart deprecated American influences throughout *The Uses of Literacy*; in *Communications* Williams wrote that the very worst of the mass media 'is American in origin. At certain levels, we are culturally an American colony. . . . To go pseudo-American is a way out of the

English complex of class and culture, but of course it solves nothing; it merely ritualises the emptiness and despair.'[31]

Anti-Americanism was a grudging admission of just how successful, at a popular level, American commercial culture was, and how seductive were the objects of its conspicuous consumption. There was a sense of limitless possibility about the American way of life that was not felt in Europe, and especially in Britain. This expansiveness was cleverly exploited for purposes of Cold War propaganda by the United States Information Service – covertly assisted by the CIA – with its promotion of American contemporary art abroad. The British may not have liked their economic dependence on America – and in 1961 Britain made a move towards recognising its changed economic circumstances by applying to join the Common Market, only to be rebuffed by General de Gaulle's veto in 1963 – but for a younger post-war generation especially, American culture could be popular in Europe precisely because it wasn't European. President Kennedy's "Camelot" projected an appealing image of change. The attractions of America became increasingly ambiguous during the sixties as the Vietnam War rose to its height. On the one hand America was the monstrous Golem of technological might, on the other it supplied the model for the protests against it, in terms of political action by young people, and their use of popular culture to that end.

Popular culture, which in the second half of the twentieth century was bound to use the mass media as its vehicle, became the testing ground for new arguments about the nature and purposes of culture as a whole. The purpose was twofold: the first was to establish that culture was itself a political issue, and secondly, to seek to understand the break-up of an earlier cultural tradition (as Hoggart had done in *The Uses of Literacy*) by studying the new forms of cultural activity and consumption as they emerged.

The argument, as ever, was between those who held that culture was an ideal, a standard of excellence and therefore a restricted category, and those who simply saw culture as descriptive, as 'a whole way of life', even when they sometimes regretted the way that life was led. But at the beginning of the sixties the whole high/low debate was turned on its head when fine artists went to mass culture for inspiration, and transmuted popular culture into Pop Art. This high cultural development acutely demonstrates the way an older cultural tradition was breaking up under the impact of new conditions, specifically, those created by the existence of the mass media. In the face of the views of Eliot and Leavis, and even Hoggart and Williams, the principles of Pop Art were truly radical, for they were a response to structural shifts in the nature of society produced by economic change. As the art critic Lawrence Alloway, one of the principal theorists of Pop Art, put it: 'Acceptance of the mass media entails a shift in the notion of what culture is.'[32]

The period between the public recognition of Pop Art at the beginning of the sixties as a disruptive novelty and its official acceptance into the high art canon with a retrospective at the recently opened Hayward Gallery in 1969 (sponsored by Times Newspapers) was shaped by a whole series of developments which challenged the previous order, which shifted opinions and expectations, but which fell far short of the hopes for revolutionary change that were raised. The Arts Council's 1969 exhibition, one of the most important collective statements of the Pop Art aesthetic, was a conscious attempt at *re*-definition, taking the title *Pop Art Redefined*.

The British co-curator of this Anglo-American show, John Russell, chose to present Pop in terms that echo the mythology of the Angry Young Men:

> Pop was a resistance movement: a classless commando which was directed against the Establishment in general and the Art Establishment in particular. It was against the old-style museum-man, the old-style critic, the old-style dealer and the old-style collector. . . . Pop in England was, as I have indicated, a facet of the class struggle, real or imagined. . . . It was for the present, and even more for the future: it was not for the past, and saw nothing to regret in the changes which had come about in England since 1945.[33]

This was as much the rhetoric of the fifties "New Brutalism" in architecture advocated by such critics as Reyner Banham as it was specifically the language of Pop. In 1956 the neo-romantic John Minton, a tutor at the Royal College, had denounced the work of a group of his students, Richard Smith, Robyn Denny and William Green, who had been experimenting with a mixture of American action painting and French *art brut*, as the work of disillusioned Angry Young Men.[34] But even though, as Alloway was to put it in 1962, one of the motives for Pop was 'to reduce the idealism and snobbery of English aesthetics and art criticism', it was not a negative movement.[35] Unlike the theorists of the New Left, the promoters of Pop were positively pro-American. At the time of the Hayward Gallery show Rayner Banham felt it necessary to remind people 'how salutory a corrective to the sloppy provincialism of most London art of ten years ago US design could be. The gusto and professionalism of wide-screen movies or Detroit car-styling was a constant reproach to the Moore-ish yokelry of British sculpture or the affected Piperish gloom of British painting.'[36]

The term Pop, coined by Lawrence Alloway, was originally applied, not to art at all, but to the American artefacts that were to become the principal source of Pop Art imagery: 'I used the term, and also "Pop Culture", to refer to the products of the mass media, not to works of art that draw upon popular culture.'[37] By 1958, for Alloway, Pop Art 'was a friendly way of saying mass media'.[38] The focus for this enthusiasm for things American was the series of meetings at the Institute of Contemporary Arts of the so-called Independent Group, the first of which was convened in 1952 by Reyner Banham. Alloway and John McHale resumed these meetings in 1954–5 on the theme of popular culture. The group also included the architects Alison and Peter Smithson, the photographer Nigel Henderson, the sculptors Eduardo Paolozzi and William Turnbull and the art critic Toni del Renzio. Alloway later recalled:

> The area of contact was mass-produced urban culture: movies, advertising, science fiction, Pop music. We felt none of the dislike of commercial culture standard among most intellectuals, but accepted it as a fact, discussed it in detail, and consumed it enthusiastically. One result of our discussion was to take Pop culture out of the realm of "escapism", "sheer entertainment", "relaxation", and to treat it with the seriousness of art. These interests put us in opposition both to the supporters of indigenous folk art and to anti-American opinion in Britain.[39]

As a new term, "Pop" first surfaced publicly in the catalogue of the *This is Tomorrow* exhibition at the Whitechapel Gallery in 1956, for which the artist Richard Hamilton had created a collage whose title – as well as the commodities chosen – was an ironic celebration of consumerism: *Just What Is It That Makes Today's Homes So Different, So Appealing? This is Tomorrow* displayed installations, not art, and it was only after the exhibition that Hamilton wrote a letter to the Smithsons that speculated as to what Pop Art might be: 'Popular (designed for a mass audience)/ Transient (short-term solution)/ Expendable (easily forgotten)/ Low cost/ Mass produced/ Young (aimed at youth)/ Witty/ Sexy/ Gimmicky/ Glamorous/ Big business.'[40] Hamilton pointed out later: 'At the time the letter was written there was no such thing as "Pop Art" as we now know it.'[41] Those artists who were exploring the area, like Hamilton and Paolozzi, were interested in its aesthetic possibilities as subject matter for fine art. Alloway and Paolozzi liked to go to watch first-run monster movies at the London Pavilion: 'It was our assumption that what we felt at, say, *Tarantula*, was as serious and interesting and worthwhile as our other aesthetic feelings. What happened was that these emotionally charged images from the mass media dramatically reduced aesthetic distance.'[42] The sheer scale of American abstract painting, as enveloping as Cinerama, encouraged British artists to experiment with size, as revealed by the 'Situation' group exhibition in 1960.

As experimentation with the painterly possibilities of Pop increased, it became more and more apparent that the growing power of the mass media was forcing a new definition of culture. In 1958 Alloway contributed an article to *Architectural Design* whose illustrations, citing Elvis Presley, post-war Westerns, Vista Vision, Cinemascope, horror comics, pulp magazines, fashion photographs, strip cartoons and science fiction, were laid out not unlike an early Paolozzi collage, but the word 'Pop' only appeared once. Alloway asserted: 'The élite, accustomed to set aesthetic standards, has found that it no longer possesses the power to dominate all aspects of art.'[43] His conclusions drew on the mass-media debate of the fifties, and that redescription of culture as 'a whole way of life' that Raymond Williams had urged:

> The definition of culture is changing as a result of the pressure of the great audience, which is no longer new but experienced in the consumption of its arts. Therefore it is no longer sufficient to define culture solely as something that a minority guards for the few and the future (though such art is uniquely valuable and as precious as ever). Our definition of culture is being stretched beyond the fine art limits imposed on it by Renaissance theory, and refers now, increasingly, to the whole complex of human activities. Within this definition, rejection of the mass-produced arts is not, as critics think, a defence of culture but an attack on it.[44]

This was the crucial difference between the Pop theorists and the Hoggart school, in whose minds there still lurked that pyramidal image of culture that Eliot had defended. In 1959 another article by Alloway suggested a new model: 'The Long Front of Culture'.

Instead of reserving the word for the highest artefacts and the noblest thoughts of history's top ten, it needs to be used more widely as a description of "what a society does". Then, unique oil paintings and highly personal poems as well as mass-distributed films and group-aimed magazines can be placed within a continuum rather than frozen in layers in a pyramid. (This permissive approach to culture is the reverse of critics like T. S. Eliot and his American followers, Allen Tate, John Crowe Ransom, who have never doubted the essentially aristocratic nature of culture.)[45]

Alloway was careful to stress that this model did not mean there was cultural uniformity, indeed the monolithic mass audience was a fiction. But it was the industrialised, rather than hand-crafted arts that offered the most consumer choice. The model was highly appropriate to the developing idea that Britain was becoming a "classless" society, and conformed to market-research-based sociology such as Mark Abrams's *The Teenage Consumer* (1959), which argued that in an age of general prosperity class hierarchies were less important, and that an American-style youth market was developing. Abrams believed that generational, rather than class divisions were to be more significant in the future.

One of the long-term effects of this cultural definition was that once the new electronic-based arts, indeed commercial culture as a whole, were included and set in a context of consumption, the high arts began to be seen as having an economic context, and it would not be a long step from there to see them as having an economic role. In this sense, the term "cultural industry" acquired a benign meaning, rather than the pejorative one applied by Adorno. It also meant that governments and local authorities had to begin to develop policies to manage this aspect of the arts as they acquired a new significance within urban and political life.

The immediate impact of Pop theory, however, was to create a climate in which a new generation of painters could find acceptance, and one in which their connection with, rather than alienation from, society was noted. Richard Hamilton wrote in 1961: 'Pop-Fine-Art is a profession of approbation of mass culture.'[46] John Russell stressed the point in 1969: 'Pop is not, as many people have supposed, a satirical art: it is an affirmative art, and affection plays a great part in it. . . . A healing art, therefore: a dis-alienating, non-discriminatory art: one that binds people together instead of setting them one against the other.'[47]

The artists who began to supply the art that matched the theory were closely associated with the Royal College of Art, beginning with a group who graduated in the later fifties, including Robyn Denny, Richard Smith and Roger Coleman, who were interested in fusing the iconography of popular culture with current developments in abstraction. Peter Blake, a figurative painter drawn to specifically British popular art, served as a bridge with the succeeding generation who made a strong impact in the 'Young Contemporaries' exhibitions of 1961 and 1962. These included Derek Boshier, Patrick Caulfield, David Hockney, Barrie Bates, Allen Jones, R. B. Kitaj, Peter Phillips and Norman Toynton. John Russell summed up the collective achievement of these artists in terms of national identity: 'What came out of the college between 1959 and 1962 was a contribution to the idea of an England at last recovered from the lethargy of the immediate post-war period.'[48]

National identity was of interest to the painters themselves, in that for all of their enjoyment of American artefacts, they were resistant to the more aggressive American cultural imperialism of the latter half of the fifties. In 1960 Alan Bowness, then teaching at the Courtauld Institute, was one of those responsible for buying works for the Arts Council's collection. He visited the Royal College of Art's painting school early in 1960, in order to see David Hockney, from whom he had already bought, on the Arts Council's behalf, an abstract work, *November*. He saw that Hockney and his colleagues 'were bent upon developing a new kind of painting in reaction to the American-influenced abstraction that had swept through the British art colleges in the late 1950s. In their first year these painters were not popular with the college authorities – indeed, Allen Jones was asked to leave – but by the end of the three-year course everyone was convinced.'[49] Bowness was able to exchange Hockney's *November* for the more typical *We Two Boys Together Clinging*. In 1962 the Tate bought Hockney's *The First Marriage*.

1962 was the "moment" of British Pop and, coincidentally, the year that the potential of American Pop, which had a different pedigree closely allied to abstract expressionism, was recognised by New York dealers. Hockey was awarded the Royal College's Gold Medal for painting; the Grabowski Gallery held the first group show devoted to Pop. Thanks to Pop Art's exploitation of the graphic qualities of the mass media, there was a spontaneous alliance between the artists and their source, and the mass media played its part in promoting Pop. In February Hockney was featured in *Queen* magazine and Peter Blake appeared in the first issue of the *Sunday Times* colour magazine.

Blake also took part in a documentary by Ken Russell, 'Pop Goes the Easel', for the BBC arts programme *Monitor* along with Pauline Boty, Derek Boshier and Peter Phillips (illustration 10). Russell's film self-consciously played with contemporary film styles, including a Karel Reisz or Lindsay Anderson-style fairground scene, and an elaborate parody of the *nouvelle vague*. Its most telling image was of a clockwork space robot bearing an American flag marching into and knocking down a toy monkey carrying the Union Jack. The programme's editor, the avuncular Huw Wheldon, who had moved into television as a result of his work as press officer for the Festival of Britain, introduced the film with barely concealed disdain as he was forced to refer to such contemporary dance crazes as 'the twist'. The world of these young painters, he explained was 'a world which you can dismiss if you feel so inclined as being tawdry and second-rate, but a world all the same in which everyone to some degree lives whether they like it or not'.[50]

Huw Wheldon's attitude shows that the critical success was not total. Lawrence Alloway, who had helped select the 1961 'Young Contemporaries', but whose strongest allegiance was to the Robyn Denny–Richard Smith 'Situation' group, was disappointed by the 1962 'Young Contemporaries' because of the lack of formal control that they displayed. (In 1960 Alloway resigned as programme director of the Institute of Contemporary Arts and in 1962 finally left Britain to take up a post at the Guggenheim Museum in New York.) One of the fiercest attacks came from Herbert Read, the chairman of the institution which had incubated Pop Art. In *The Origins of Form in Art* (1965) Read dismissed the 'antics' of Pop and its claim to be art: 'Until we can halt these processes of destruction and standardisation, of materialism and mass communication, art will always be subject to the threat of disintegration. The genuine arts of today are engaged in a heroic struggle against mediocrity and mass values, and if they lose, then art, in any meaningful sense, is dead.'[51]

Read, the champion of the British avant-garde of the thirties, was less happy with that of the sixties. But the notion of an avant-garde was part of the traditional model for the arts. The 'long front of culture' was a challenge to that conception, as the art critic Edward Lucie-Smith wrote after a visit to New York in 1962:

The success of Pop put in question all the attitudes which had previously been held to modern art. In particular, it dealt a damaging blow to the concept of the avant-garde, a fact already acknowledged by many Americans. As the word implies, it was the function of the old avant-garde – that of 1905 to 1925 – to march in the forefront, to point the direction in which art was to go. Pop art points nowhere. It exists beside, not in front of. The new extremists live in a kind of symbiotic relationship with the coarsest and most vulgar elements of mass culture. It is for this reason, precisely, that the term "underground" has acquired such a wide currency in New York. The "underground" has replaced the avant-garde, but it is indeed something quite different.[52]

Edward Lucie-Smith's comment suggests that even as Pop was success-fully replacing one definition of culture with another, the consequences of that shift were to lead to a further change – one that would challenge the material base of "art" altogether. The "death of the avant-garde" was to be one of the harbingers of post-modernism.

Pop Art, for all of its effect on cultural perceptions, remained a "high art" practice. Yet the early years of Pop confirm Stuart Hall and Paddy Whannel's argument in *The Popular Arts* (1964): 'New art forms fre-quently arise when profound modifications are taking place in social life and in the "structure of feeling" in the society. Often this change is first recorded in popular work.'[53] In this case, Pop Art supplied a useful means for understanding the exciting change in national mood that was taking place.

The new mood was one of individualism, personal liberation and, in comparison with the fifties, hedonism. The progressive consensus saw to it that the sixties were a decade of liberalisation in the personal and cultural sphere, beginning with the Obscene Publications Act of 1959 and the legalisation of gambling in 1960, and followed by the abolition of the death penalty in 1965; homosexual law reform and easier abor-tion in 1967; the abolition of the Lord Chamberlain's censorship of the theatre in 1968; and the Divorce Act of 1969. There were attempts by police and local magistrates to uphold literary and artistic censorship in the wake of the revised Obscene Publications Act in 1960, and the pirate radio stations were silenced by the Marine Broadcasting (Offences) Act of 1967, but censorship eased until the end of the decade, when it proved useful as a means of dispersing the underground press.

Following the Labour government's *A Policy for the Arts* in 1965, the Arts Council's grant-in-aid was significantly increased, by forty-five per cent for 1966–7 and twenty-six per cent in 1967–8, so that it rose to £7,200,000 in that year. In 1967 the Council's Charter was renewed and revised, its purposes expressed more simply: 'To develop and improve the knowledge, understanding and practice of the arts' and 'to increase the accessibility of the arts to the public throughout Great Britain.'[54] The membership of the Council was increased to twenty, and separate councils were established for Scotland and Wales, although technically they were to remain sub-committees of the Arts Council of Great Britain until there was further constitutional change in 1994. The Great and the Good continued to hold sway. In 1970 the American sociologist John Harris concluded that there were 'strikingly few differences' in the social background of Labour and Conservative appointees to the Council – except that Labour tended to appoint more from the top twenty public schools. Almost none were working-class in origin, only two were below the age of forty, and only a quarter of the sixty-eight appointees surveyed had earned their living as artists.[55] In 1965 Kenneth Clark's successor, the Conservative politician Lord Cottesloe, was succeeded by the solicitor Arnold Goodman, who had acted for several prominent members of the Labour Party and who had become an unofficial adviser to Harold Wilson. He had known Aneurin Bevan well and had a close friendship with his widow, Jennie Lee, the first Minister for the Arts. Goodman had first made his mark in the arts by preparing the Royal Charter of 1956 which brought together Sadler's Wells Ballet, Covent Garden, Sadler's Wells Theatre Ballet and Sadler's Wells Ballet School as the Royal Ballet, and he was to enjoy a long career as a fixer in the arts world. He was engaged on an investigation into what the Council believed was an excess of orchestral provision in London when he became chairman of the Arts Council and shortly afterwards was made a life peer. In 1966 he also became a member of the British Council, and served as deputy chairman from 1976 until 1991. Goodman, in his own words, 'gravitated to almost every unpaid chairmanship in England at one time or another'.[56]

Goodman and Lee, with the support of both Roy Jenkins as Chancellor of the Exchequer and Wilson as Prime Minister, set about expanding the activities and staff of the Council, which moved to fresh premises at 105 Piccadilly. To do so they had to overcome the reluctance of the civil servants in the Department of Education and Science, and of their surrogate, the then Secretary-General, Nigel Abercrombie, who had once described the Council in an annual report as less a sugar-daddy than a nanny to the arts.[57] The partnership between Lee and Goodman was such that they were able to circumvent the difficulties put in their way. Goodman's memoirs have described Sunday evening suppers with Lee at which he was able to dictate the Minister's replies to the civil service criticisms he encountered, which went as far as their altering the Council's financial estimates. Within the limits of Goodman's liberal, but not radical tastes, the Arts Council became a generous patron:

> We travelled to the extreme limits. Sometimes we went over the edge of what to me and many others appeared to be sensible, since only by going over the edge could we cover the total area. I took the view, unrepentantly, that some wastage of public money was unavoidable to achieve an ecumenical approach that would give confidence to the whole art world. The wastage was trivial in terms of percentages, but it meant that on the whole almost any artistic experience short of dementia had a chance of receiving some encouragement within our walls, and the effect was healthy and buoyant in relation to artists of real quality. They approved immensely because they sensed that the old canons of restrictive censorship and repression were being reduced to a minimum. This had an importance in itself, coinciding as it did with the general libertarianism of the period, and did much good in fomenting an atmosphere of artistic freedom.[58]

This attitude was confirmed by Jennie Lee. She told the *Sunday Times*: 'My function is merely a permissive one. I keep repeating that like a gramophone record . . . permissive, permissive, permissive. I want simply to make living room for artists to work in.'[59]

The expansion in the Arts Council's activity was most significant in the field of housing the arts. From 1957 onwards local authorities had begun to create – or induce developers to create – new theatres, galleries and auditoria as part of the extensive redevelopment schemes that radically altered the centre of virtually every major town in Britain. In 1965 the Arts Council was empowered for the first time to give capital grants to encourage local authorities and developers to build arts facilities. In co-operation with the Greater London Council (which took over from the London County Council in 1963) the South Bank saw the building of the Queen Elizabeth Hall and the Purcell Room as further concert auditoria in addition to the Royal Festival Hall, and the Hayward Gallery, which was directly managed by the Arts Council as a temporary exhibition space and the store for the Council's expanding art collection. In 1969 work at last began on the construction of a new building for the National Theatre. Between 1965 and 1971 the

Arts Council put a total of £2,750,000 into one hundred and twenty-four building projects across the country. It was also during this period that plans were laid to build a separate British Library, although the orginal scheme to build south of the British Museum in Bloomsbury was blocked by planning difficulties in 1967. The decision to build was to have a long-term effect on the national arts budget.

The expansion in capital and revenue funding for the arts was as nothing in comparison with the increased expenditure on higher education. The Robbins Report of 1963 led to the creation of six new universities and the upgrading of ten colleges of advanced technology to university status. In 1966 the Plan for Polytechnics created thirty new polytechnics by merging existing local-authority institutions into larger units. The increase in student numbers in higher education, from four per cent of school leavers in 1960 to sixteen per cent in 1975, although not great in comparison with Continental or American standards, diluted the pool of recruits to the "intellectual aristocracy" into something closer to the "technical intelligentsia" that T. R. Fyvel described in 1968. The strain on resources and facilities during the early years of expansion was one of the sources of the new rebelliousness that Fyvel had not anticipated would erupt in that year.

Educational and cultural expansion, rising affluence, low inflation and full employment all helped Labour to make significant gains in the general election of March 1966. In the following month a team of reporters from America's *Time* magazine published the results of their findings about the new Britain in a famous article, strap-lined 'London: The Swinging City', which both codified and amplified the defining myth of the mid-sixties.

The flow of envy between Britain and America appeared to have gone into reverse. The article described London as 'a city steeped in tradition, seized by change, liberated by affluence. . . . In a decade dominated by youth, London has burst into bloom. It swings; it is the scene.'[60] From the evidence of the expansion in the arts and the increase in general consumption, the reporters concluded that a bloodless revolution was replacing the Tory–Liberal Establishment: 'In their stead is rising a new and surprising leadership community; economists, professors, actors, photographers, singers, admen, TV executives and writers – a swinging meritocracy.'[61] Richard Hoggart was quoted directly in support of the idea that 'a new group of people is emerging into society, creating a kind of classlessness and a verve which has not been seen before'.[62]

The classlessness of what was in fact a narrow metropolitan élite was questionable, even at the time, but there is no doubting the verve with which the British as a whole accepted their offered new identity. The Union Jack was no longer the proud flag fluttering on cinema screens as the night's performance ended with the national anthem. Instead it became an ironic emblem of Pop Art decoration on shopping bags, or was tailored into pop musicians' jackets – or worse (illustration 9).

The high-gloss culture of consumption produced a curious parody of itself, a perverse inversion of its commodity values, a mirror image signalled by the prepositions and prefixes "under", "anti", "counter". The underground's language of love and peace was the antithesis of the rhetoric of aggression and war, yet the internalised violence of the counter-culture's more extreme activities, such as the Destruction in Art Symposium of 1966, shows that the polarities were not as fixed as was supposed. In a period of prosperity it was possible for a substantial number of people to live off the general surplus, their voluntary unemployment a symbol of the new leisure available to a society that was moving from a production to a consumption economy, and where middle-class values in particular were shifting. The hippies celebrated autonomy and individualism, living parasitically off the dominant economy while arguing against its values.

The celebration of the irrational – be it in the Theatre of the Absurd and its successor the Theatre of Cruelty, the honouring of schizophrenia by the anti-psychiatrists led by David Cooper and R. D. Laing, or the rediscovery of Eastern mysticism through the writings of Alan Watts – was a dialectical response to the increasingly materialistic and technocratic society that created the margins in which the counter-culture could develop a parallel economy, and a parallel press. *IT* (International Times), launched in October 1966, and *Oz* (January 1967) were the market leaders among the more than a thousand "alternative" magazines launched between 1965 and 1974, of which *Time Out*, much transformed from its original radical self, was to be the long-term survivor. The foundation of the Arts Lab in Drury Lane in 1967 by the American cultural shaman Jim Haynes inspired an anti-network of arts centres, and in 1968 there followed the self-described 'Anti-University'.

Precisely because of the underground's resistance to the verbal rationality of the "straight" world, it is difficult to abstract a coherent counter-cultural philosophy, though the movement had its sacred texts. These ranged from J. R. Tolkein's *The Lord of the Rings* (1954), Hermann Hesse's *The Glass Bead Game* (1943) and William Burroughs's *The Naked Lunch* (1959) to Wilhelm Reich's *The Function of Orgasm* (1942), Marcuse's *One-Dimensional Man* (1964), Alan Watts's writings on Zen, R. D. Laing's *The Divided Self* (1965) and *The Politics of Experience* (1967), Paul Goodman's *Growing Up Absurd* (1966), Jeff Nuttall's *Bomb Culture* (1968), Theodore Roszak's *The Making of a Counter-Culture* (1969), Joseph Berke's *Counter Culture* (1969) and Richard Neville's *Play Power* (1970). A limited number of people knew the work of the French situationist movement, through the artist Ralph Rumney, a founder member of the Situationist International in 1957, and later through the proselytising of the poet and novelist Alexander Trocchi.

The confusing and elusive values of what was an often deliberately ephemeral culture were well summed up by one of its opponents, the critic George Steiner: 'The violent illiteracies of the graffiti, the clenched silence of the adolescent, the nonsense-cries from the stage-happening, are resolutely strategic. The insurgent and the freak-out have broken off discourse with a cultural system which they despise as a cruel, antiquated fraud. They will not bandy words with it. Accept, even momentarily, the conventions of literate linguistic exchange, and you are caught in the net of the old values, of the grammars that can condescend or enslave.'[63] The point of most extreme contrast in values was on the question of drugs, which were the subject of increased legislation and increased consumption throughout the decade. In 1964 the Dangerous Drugs Act tightened control of cannabis and amphetamines. In 1966 LSD – an example of improved technology coming to the aid of the inner explorations of the underground – was made an illegal substance. In 1968 the Wootton Report recommending the decriminalisation of soft drugs was rejected, and legislation, which now gave the police greater powers to stop and search people on suspicion of possessing drugs, was further tightened by the Misuse of Drugs Act of 1970. Even the consumer society was prepared to set a limit to the indulgences its own attitudes encouraged.

The heady combination of sex, drugs and rock'n'roll that delighted the counter-culture was not the outcome of the revolution that the pioneers of the New Left had anticipated in the late fifties. In spite of a willingness to wear the icon of the Left's hero and martyr Che Guevara on their teeshirts, members of the underground eschewed conventional politics. Neither educated middle-class young nor newly financially empowered working-class youth showed much respect for symbols of authority of any kind, and those included those of traditional "good" culture. As Alan Sinfield has pointed out: 'The authority and consensual significance of "art" and "literature" collapsed together with other kinds of authority and consensus.'[64] The offerings of commercial culture were consumed with glee.

As was seen in Chapter IV, the New Left experienced a demoralising split in 1962, while some activists simply withdrew because of the need to answer the demands of developing careers. Instead of bringing the Left closer to the centre of power, the Labour election victories of 1964 and 1966 served to marginalise groups further to the Left, notably the International Socialists, which became the Socialist Workers' Party in 1969, and the International Marxist Group, formed in 1964. From the New Left's point of view, the Labour government did not bring socialism, but 'Wilsonism', and with it increasing impatience, especially with the Government's support for America's war in Vietnam. Raymond Williams, never consulted on matters of cultural policy by the government, left the Labour Party in 1966.

After the internal coup at the beginning of 1963 that left Perry Anderson in control of the *New Left Review* the expelled members of the board found a refuge in the quarterly *Views*, which ran from 1963 to 1966, and the annual *Socialist Register*, from whose pages E. P. Thompson attacked the review whose board he had once chaired. Perry Anderson justified his position by arguing that when the New Left had ceased to be a purely intellectual grouping, it had wasted its assets in trying to become a mass movement by taking over CND, and had thus been tied to CND's fate. Clearly Anderson did not intend that the *New Left Review* would ever again be 'at the mercy of a conjunctural fluctuation'.[65] In Anderson's view the cultural critique which had distinguished and, in many ways, inspired the formation of the New Left lacked the necessary rigour:

> Its almost complete failure to offer any structural analysis of British society is striking. Instead of a systematic sociology of British capitalism, it tended to rely on a simplistic rhetoric in which the "common people", "ordinary men and women" were opposed to the "interests", the "Establishment", etc. Described as "humanist", the idiom was, in fact, populist and pre-socialist.[66]

Anderson's target was E. P. Thompson, as was made clear in an attack on Thompson's contributions to the *Universities and New Left Review* and early numbers of the *Review*: 'Socialism, in them, gives way to a maundering populism. The categories of this thought are so vacuous and simplistic that it is difficult to credit that they are those of the same man who could write such overpowering concrete history.'[67] Although Anderson paid regular tribute to the work of Raymond Williams, he argued that the New Left's 'moral critique of capitalism' tended to become more and more concerned only with cultural issues, 'precisely those which most immediately and intimately affected its audience of teachers, writers, students'.[68] It had ended by becoming part of the problem it had set out to analyse.

Under Anderson's editorship, the *New Left Review* did not immediately become the arid, Stalinist 'paper emporium of a coterie of Marxist swots at the mercy of their own intellectual crazes' that its critics on the Left like David Widgery described.[69] The 'Motifs' section carried articles on the cinema and contemporary fiction, and a long series on modern jazz by Alan Beckett. Beckett specifically rejected Adorno's strictures on popular music.[70] There were approving references to Elvis Presley, Paul McCartney and Mick Jagger. In 1968 the *New Left Review*'s position was: 'Britain today is a society stifling for lack of any art that expresses the experience of living in it. Our theatre is a quaint anachronism, our novel is dead, and our cinema a mere obituary of it. Perhaps the only art form which has an authentic vitality in England is pop music.'[71] The 'anti-psychiatrists' R. D. Laing and David Cooper contributed to the *Review* in 1964 and 1965.

While gradually introducing a range of Continental thinkers to a British audience, Anderson, assisted by Tom Nairn, set out to develop an analysis of British history and identity that explained why Britain never had developed, and in the immediate prospect was unlikely to develop, the conditions for revolution. The answer lay in the historical accord reached between the middle class and a highly capitalistic aristocracy that headed off any prospect of a bourgeois revolution, the necessary antecedent to a proletarian one. Crucial to this analysis was Gramsci's concept of hegemony, which Nairn was responsible for first introducing into British thought. As was outlined in Chapter I, it could be shown that the dominant class maintained its power by diffusing its values beyond its own class, in the form of a ruling ideology that was absorbed into the value-system of society as a whole. The world view of the dominant class became internalised as everyday "common sense", so that the exercise of power was greeted with consent, and governments ruled by consensus. Anderson argued that the characteristic features of the English ideology were traditionalism and empiricism which 'fuse as a single legitimating system: traditionalism sanctions the present by deriving it from the past, empiricism shackles the future by riveting it to the present. A comprehensive coagulated conservatism is the result, covering the whole of society with a thick pall of simultaneous philistinism (towards ideas) and mystagogy (towards institutions).'[72]

The answer was to develop an authentic British Marxism, such as had not previously existed. This was not to be a crude, mechanical, "economist" Marxism, but would build on the tradition of Western European Marxism since the First World War, 'a tradition which has consistently been coeval with new forms of idealism, and a dialectical response to them with the evolution of Marxism itself'.[73] The sources of this tradition were Georg Lukács and Antonio Gramsci, and among living contemporaries, Jean-Paul Sartre, Marcuse, Lucien Goldmann, Theodor Adorno, Ernest Bloch and Louis Althusser. Articles by or about these theorists appeared with increasing density in the *Review.*

Disenchanted with the Labour Party, and sensing the growing political dissatisfaction with the government, in 1966 Raymond Williams, in concert with E. P. Thompson and Stuart Hall, began to organise a series of meetings among socialists, mainly academics, in order to discuss some form of broad opposition to Labour Party policy, without going so far as forming a new association or party. The result was a 'May Day Manifesto' edited by Williams, Thompson and Hall, and privately printed in 1967. Further and wider discussions led to the publication of a second version as a Penguin special in 1968, and in 1969 to the holding of a 'National Convention of the Left', chaired by Williams. This attempt to unite the Old, New and Anarchist Left foundered in 1970 on the Left's own characteristic factionalism, with a power struggle between the Communist Party and the International Socialists. This last gasp of the "old" New Left was, as Thompson put it, 'swept brusquely aside, in 1968, by the May events in Paris, by the revival of wages-based (but often a-political) industrial militancy, and the repression of the Prague "spring" '.[74] The failure of the National Convention made a bathetic end to the original ambitions of the founders of the *Universities and New Left Review.* For Williams this was the period when he shifted from confidence in an evolutionary socialism to hopes for a revolutionary one.

The extent to which revolutionary politics had taken over the original cultural concerns of the Left can be gauged from the title of a symposium organised by the Catholic Marxist review *Slant* in 1967, *From Culture to Revolution*. *Slant* appeared from 1964 to 1970, one of whose founder editors was Terry Eagleton, a graduate pupil of Raymond Williams's who published his first book, *The New Left Church*, in 1966. Taking its cue from the mood of liberalisation in the Catholic Church following the 1962–4 Conference of Cardinals known as Vatican II, *Slant* 'approached the idea of a socialist revolution ... as the central perspective within which the revolutionary message of the gospel can find articulation'.[75] At this time, for Eagleton, 'Christianity *is* that yet more radical movement that Marxism must move into', but he was later to develop a purely secular Marxism that joined the tradition that Anderson's *New Left Review* sought to foster.[76]

The *Slant* symposium of priests and academics (among them Raymond Williams and Stuart Hall) was a considerably more decorous affair than a two-week conference held at the Round House in July of that same year, under the title 'The Dialectics of Liberation – Towards a Demystification of Violence'. Through their organisation for the promotion of radical psychiatry, the Philadelphia Foundation, David Cooper, R. D. Laing, Leon Redler and Joseph Berke assembled a remarkable group of speakers, including the poet Allen Ginsberg, then at the height of his counter-cultural fame; the sinisterly charismatic leader of the exiled American Living Theatre, Julian Beck; Herbert Marcuse; Lucien Goldmann; the Americans John Gerassi, Paul Sweezy and Paul Goodman; the Marxist economic historian Ernest Mandel; and the Trinidad-born American advocate of black power Stokely Carmichael. In the parlance of the day the event was a cross between a "teach-in" and a spontaneous commune, for many of the audience camped out at the Round House for the fortnight.

The more coherent platform contributions were subsequently published by Penguin in 1968, but the event had the opposite effect to that intended. Violence – as in the attitude displayed by Stokely Carmichael – was romanticised rather than demystified. Marcuse was prepared to give his blessing to the attendant flower-bearing hippies as 'a serious phenomenon', but his argument that society should be liberated from the 'institutionalised violence' of the state served if anything to intensify the very sense of oppression from which the conference wished to be liberated.[77]

Nonetheless the strange, sometimes menacing atmosphere of the conference, captured by the archive recordings of the event, was consistent with the growing sense of disorder and unease at large.[78] The police had begun an aggressive campaign against drug-taking. The Vietnam War was gathering pace, and student troubles and demonstrations had begun. The first convention of the Radical Students' Alliance was held in January 1967. The London School of Economics experienced a riot in January and a sit-in in March. There was fighting between police and demonstrators outside the American Embassy in Grosvenor Square in October 1967 and March 1968 (illustration 11).

In May 1968 the *événements* in Paris were echoed by student protests across the world, and by June 1968 sixteen colleges and universities in Britain had had demonstrations and sit-ins attacking the authoritarianism of the educational establishment, the most serious at the art schools of Hornsey in London, and Guildford in Surrey. Student protests were to continue to erupt until 1970. In Birmingham, members of the Centre for Cultural Studies argued that they were a "Red Cell" with a responsibility to educate only the radicalised.[79] In 1969 there was a series of highly publicised "squats" in unoccupied buildings. Even Perry Anderson, a sceptical observer of British politics, was persuaded that something really was going on. In July 1968 he concluded his devastating survey of the intellectual nullity of contemporary British thought from anthropology to philosophy, 'Components of the National Culture', with some crumbs of comfort for the class of '68: 'A revolutionary culture is not for tomorrow. But a revolutionary practice within culture is possible and necessary today. The student struggle is its initial form.'[80]

1968 was not 1848. The student revolts were of the privileged rather than the oppressed and could be contained by the police and university authorities, once the limits of official tolerance were reached. Nonetheless, the political and cultural upheavals of 1968 were a manifestation of the subterranean changes that were taking place as consumption rather than production became the motor of the first-world economy, and social structures buckled under the stress. The mood of violence adumbrated in the arts through such events as Peter Brook's production of Peter Weiss's *Marat/Sade* in 1964, the Destruction in Art Symposium of 1966, Stuart Brisley's emetic performance art pieces or

Harrison Birtwistle's opera *Punch and Judy* in 1968, was not confined to young people. In April 1968 Enoch Powell, the Conservative Shadow Defence Spokesman, delivered a speech forecasting 'the River Tiber foaming with much blood' if Britain refused to curb immigration.[81] In August 1969 the British Army intervened in the growing sectarian strife in Northern Ireland. The violent response of the local authorities to a student-inspired civil rights movement was the catalyst for a revival of ancient hatreds and the beginning of an undeclared civil war that called into question concepts of "nationalism", "loyalism", "Britishness" and the unity of the British state, and which appeared to have found no proper resolution more than twenty-five years later.

At first the Arts Council tried to ride the tiger of the counter-culture. It was proud to draw attention to the presence of one of the Beatles at a lecture by Luciano Berio in its 1965–6 annual report. (In 1965 Harold Wilson had seen to it that the Beatles were awarded the MBE.) Lord Goodman and Jennie Lee encouraged the American cultural entrepreneur Jim Haynes, who had founded the Traverse Theatre in Edinburgh in 1962, to set up a London Traverse at the Jeanetta Cochrane Theatre in 1965. But Goodman withdrew his support for Haynes when he became involved with launching *IT* and the Arts Lab. As a gesture to "youth culture", in 1966 the Arts Council decided to appoint two junior members to each of its advisory panels, but when another of *IT*'s editorial board, Barry Miles, was invited to join the Literature Panel, Goodman insisted on his removal because of the paper's advocacy of the pleasures of drugs.

Goodman believed that the Arts Council, as the state's patron of the arts, had a moral responsibility towards the young. He told the House of Lords in April 1967: 'Young people lack values, lack certainties, lack guidance; . . . they need something to turn to; and need it more desperately than they have needed it at any time in our history – certainly, at any time which I can recollect. I do not say the arts will furnish a total solution, but I believe the arts will furnish some solution. I believe that once young people are captured for the arts they are redeemed from many of the dangers which confront them at the moment.'[82]

The Arts Council demonstrated its liberal credentials by joining in the campaign for the abolition of the Lord Chamberlain's censorship of the theatre. By the end of the decade the prevailing view in the arts establishment was: 'To shock has always been one of the beneficial social functions of art, an inevitable by-product of the fresh vision which characterises a good artist and which helps to protect society from inertia and paralysis.'[83] This was the opinion of a working party set up by the Arts Council as a result of a conference on the laws governing obscenity which it had organised in 1968. Lord Goodman believed the legal situation was 'total nonsense' because juries were being asked to decide on questions of ethical values rather than fact, but the Council carefully distanced itself from the ensuing report which called not for reform but repeal.[84] In 1968 the publisher John Calder finally won his appeal against the prosecution of Hubert Selby's novel *Last Exit to Brooklyn* (Lord Goodman's firm had conducted the defence), but it was in that year that he launched the Society for the Protection of Arts and Literature because he feared a reaction to the permissive atmosphere of the sixties was building up. In 1969 the government formally rejected the recommendation that existing legislation on obscenity should be repealed.

The Arts Council also tried to adjust its practices by acknowledging that new forms of art had been thrown up which did not respect the traditional academic categories and which found fresh creativity in mixing its media in the form of "installations", "environments" and "happenings". In October 1968 a New Activities Committee was set up under the chairmanship of a former Conservative Education Minister, Lord Boyle, to investigate what should be done. In the face of their chairman's disagreement, the committee recommended that a New Activities and Multi-Media panel be set up with a budget of one hundred thousand pounds. Lord Goodman balked at a new panel, and instead gave the committee fifteen thousand pounds to spend in 1969.

There followed an embarrassing series of disputes which demonstrated the mutual distrust of the underground and official culture. Goodman tried to laugh off the whole business of these 'Eldritch proceedings': 'Why, I was asked, have you subsidised a collection of weirdly attired, hirsute bohemians, whose principal joy in life is to revile you and the Council? . . . Meetings were invaded by demonstrators, long and protracted arguments about protocol, propounded by citizens of terrifying solemnity, and clamourings for justice, meaning thereby a large share of our depleted funds.'[85] But the supplicants to the committee, who formed themselves into the Friends of the Arts Council Co-operative, had a serious point, in that they wished to challenge the whole system by which the Arts Council awarded grants. As Goodman had the grace to admit: 'It would be hypocrisy to pretend that the young have our total trust.'[86] In the view of the young the process should be democratised by handing over decisions about the patronage of contemporary art to an Artists Council. Their case for democratisation had the implicit backing of a report in 1968 by a House of Common Estimates Committee which had recommended that the Arts Council should find ways for artists to be more directly represented. In 1969 the new chairman of the New Activities Committee, Michael Astor, tried to accommodate FACCOP by inviting six of its members to join the committee, but when these tried to act, not as individual advisers, but as delegated representatives, the experiment came to an end, and an exasperated Lord Goodman saw to it that the New Activities Committee was wound up, although an Experimental Projects Committee survived until 1973 and "community arts" continued to be funded until devolved to the Regional Arts Associations in 1981. FACCOP were not the best advocate of their case, but they were an early warning of repeated attempts during the seventies to make the Arts Council's procedures more open and democratic.

By the end of the decade the energies of both the political radicals and the counter-culture were by no means exhausted, but there were signs of growing distaste for their activities amongst "ordinary" people, and a distinct reaction from the Right. *IT, Oz* and a number of underground publications became the target for prosecutions from 1970 onwards. Mrs Mary Whitehouse, who had set up the National Viewers' and Listeners' Association as a censorious pressure group in 1965, widened her activities into a moral crusade, known as the Festival of Light, which held its first rally in 1971. Like the "demystifiers" of violence at the Round House, who only further romanticised it, Mrs Whitehouse's moral campaigns served rather to heighten interest in the eroticism of everyday life than to pour cold water on it.

The mood of the country was changing. Economic confidence had been dented when the government was forced to devalue sterling in 1967 and there was an international monetary crisis in 1968. In 1969 there were the first exchanges in the long battle over industrial relations and trades union power which was to preoccupy both Labour and Conservative governments in the seventies, when Wilson was forced to withdraw the reforms proposed in the White Paper *In Place of Strife.*

In June 1970, contrary to expectations, Labour lost the general election, and Britain had a new Conservative Prime Minister, Edward Heath.

In spite of the international headlines that it attracted, and the longer-term shift in cultural assumptions that it initiated, the counter-culture was a largely metropolitan phenomenon; the people who made it happen were little more than a hundred in number, and its audience was limited to the under-thirties, although that generation would retain at least some of its influences as it moved into middle age. The institutions of high culture – the Royal Opera House, Sadler's Wells Opera (which moved to the Coliseum in 1968, becoming English National Opera in 1974), the National Theatre, the Royal Shakespeare Company, the major orchestras, and the national museums and galleries – benefited even more than the underground from the expansion in public arts spending from 1964 onwards.

Owners of country houses, especially those who had adapted to the demands of motorised leisure, flourished until the economic crises of the early seventies. The National Trust continued to acquire properties under the Country House Scheme, and had launched a campaign to conserve the coastline, Enterprise Neptune, in 1963. The Trust was storing up trouble in the shape of a backlog of repairs, but its popularity as an institution continued to grow. There can be few better examples of the hegemony of aristocratic values that Perry Anderson decried in the *New Left Review* than the importance of the country house to the British sense of identity. One of the most popular television programmes between 1970 and 1975 was the drama series *Upstairs, Downstairs*, set in the Edwardian period, and showing masters and servants living in mutual dependency.

While the counter-culture was reaching its apogee in 1967 and 1968, Kenneth Clark was making the television series *Civilisation*, thirteen hour-long programmes transmitted by the BBC in 1969 and 1970. The timing was not entirely coincidental. Clark, for whom 'popular taste is bad taste, as any honest man with experience will agree', was at first reluctant to undertake the project.[87] Clark recalled that when he was approached by the then controller of BBC2, David Attenborough, 'he used the word *Civilisation*, and it was this word alone that persuaded me to undertake the work. I had no clear idea what it meant, but I thought it was preferable to barbarism, and fancied that this was the moment to say so.'[88]

Clark's view of civilisation was confined principally to the surviving

high-art artefacts of Western Europe, plus music and philosophy, but
excluding the ancient worlds of Egypt, Greece and Rome. In spite of
the patrician confidence that he displayed as he addressed the camera
from a succession of ravishing locations almost entirely devoid of living
people, Clark's theme, from the title of the opening programme, 'By
the Skin of Our Teeth', onwards, was the fragility of civilisation. His
script was peppered with disparaging remarks about the present day,
and showed a deepening pessimism as the programmes approached the
twentieth century. He confessed his bafflement at developments in
contemporary art, his horror at modern destructiveness and its intellectual justifications in ' "theatres of cruelty" and so forth'.[89] His closing
remarks managed a little cheerfulness about 'these bright-minded
young people' who 'think poorly of existing institutions and want to
abolish them' (Clark was filming in Paris in May 1968) but his conclusion was profoundly gloomy.[90] Quoting Yeats's 'Things fall apart;
the centre cannot hold', he added: 'The trouble is that there is still no
centre. The moral and intellectual failure of Marxism has left us with
no alternative to heroic materialism, and that isn't enough. One may
be optimistic, but one can't exactly be joyful at the prospect before
us.'[91]

The Marxist reply to Clark, indirectly, was to be John Berger's television series *Ways of Seeing* in 1972, but Clark was not the only writer
of mandarin persuasion who felt a void opening at the centre. In 1971
George Steiner synthesised many of the themes of his essays collected
in *Language and Silence* (1967) into a short polemic, *In Bluebeard's
Castle*. The subtitle, 'Some Notes Towards the Re-definition of Culture', was acknowledgement of his intention to reassess T. S. Eliot's
plea for order. Clark's civilisation had given way to what Steiner called
'post-culture': 'Our present feeling of disarray, of a regress into violence, into moral obtuseness; our ready impression of a central failure
of values in the arts, in the comeliness of personal and social modes;
our fears of a new "dark age" in which civilisation itself, as we have
known it, may disappear'.[92]

Steiner found the roots of this disorder in the nineteenth century
and its grimmest confirmation in the Holocaust (which, he pointed out,
Eliot had failed to mention): 'No less than our technical competence to
build Hell on earth [the death camps], so our knowledge of the failure
of education, of literate tradition, to bring "sweetness and light" to
men is a clear symptom of what is lost. We are forced now to return

to an earlier, Pascalian pessimism, to a model of history whose logic derives from a postulate of original sin.'[93] This profoundly conservative position aligned Steiner with Eliot, though without Eliot's Christian inflections: 'The democratisation of high culture – brought on by a crisis of nerve within culture itself and by social revolution – has engendered an absurd hybrid.'[94] The retreat from the word (in spite of the increasing specialisation of literary criticism) and the arrival of the counter-culture, signified the end of any kind of agreed hierarchy of values: 'It is the collapse, more or less complete, more or less conscious, of these hierarchised, definitional value-gradients (and can there be value without hierarchy?) which is now the major fact of our intellectual and social circumstance.'[95] This 'deep reordering or disordering of long-established frontiers' was, implicitly, the consequence of Alloway's arguments for a long front of culture.[96]

Steiner had no solution to offer to the recognition that previous models and definitions of culture were no longer useful, except to press on with the process of investigation, discrimination and evaluation with a kind of tragic gaiety, continuing to open the doors in Bluebeard's castle. But to raise the issue of the collapse of value in 1971 was timely; his coinage 'post-culture' and his analysis of its conditions anticipated the debate about post-modernism that was to absorb critics in the later seventies and the eighties as the structural shift in social and economic relations became more evident.

The contribution of Pop Art theory to the derogation of the traditional hierarchy of values was explicitly acknowledged by the critical contributions to *Pop Art Redefined* in 1969. Although still treated with suspicion in conservative quarters, Pop was given the accolade of a major exhibition at the Arts Council's Hayward Gallery, while David Hockney enjoyed a retrospective at the Whitechapel. There were no signs of anti-Americanism at the Hayward; the show celebrated its ability to mount a major retrospective of American Pop artists alongside the British. The American co-curator, Suzi Gablik, drew attention to the impact of Pop on 'the erosion of a previously established hierarchy of subject matter (Mondrian and Mickey Mouse are now equally relevant)' and to 'the expansion of art's frame of reference to include elements considered until now as outside its range, such as technology, kitsch and humour'.[97] But it was John McHale, a member of the ICA's original Independent Group, who drew out one of the consequences of establishing a long front of culture: 'The fine arts as institution may no longer be accorded the prime role in conveying the myths or defining edge of innovation in society. The visionary "poetry" of technology or its "symphonic" equivalent is as likely to be seen on TV, or in the annual report of an aerospace company, as in the book, art gallery or concert hall. The arts, as traditionally regarded, are no longer a "*canonical*" form of communication.'[98]

Suzi Gablik – and the agenda of the whole exhibition – did not wish Pop to lose its high-art status. The display stressed the connections between Pop and other avant-garde art forms, especially hard-edged and minimal art. She pointed out that Pop's 'main methodological assumptions are being expanded into a new dimension by the Minimalists, who have reduced its iconographic content to the essential structures which constitute the language of technology, and by the Situationalists [*sic*], who explore industrial materials for their inherent properties and act directly on the environment – by digging a "sculpture", for instance, directly in the desert'.[99]

The reference to minimalism was timely. 1969 saw the first issue of the journal *Art-Language* and the first major Anglo-American show of minimalist work at the ICA, 'When Attitudes Become Form'. It was also significant, for the simplicity and directness of Pop Art, which dispensed with any need for narrative interpretation, was a step towards dispensing with the need for an art object at all. The very materialism of Pop served to dissolve the material of art into purely conceptual form, so that even the category of aesthetic evaluation disappeared. Art began to be emptied of values from within. As John McHale put it: 'Generally, as the new cultural continuum underlines the expendability of the material artefact, life is defined as art – as the only contrastingly permanent and continuously unique experience.'[100]

Yet if art as a material object was about to disappear, the institutions which were empowered to define what constituted art were not. In 1976 the Tate Gallery found itself pilloried for buying Carl Andre's arrangement of one hundred and twenty fire-bricks, *Equivalent VIII*. Since the official acceptance and promotion of abstract expressionism in the fifties, artists had become accustomed to their principal patrons being not private collectors, but that paradoxical construction, the "museum" of modern art. While a few of the individual members and organisations of the underground were imprisoned, prosecuted or otherwise harassed into silence, a far more effective tactic against it was the gradual institutionalisation of the avant-garde.

The success of Pop in confusing aesthetic categories, satirising high-art procedures and celebrating kitsch was a key factor in establishing a long front of culture and widening the definition of what was admissible as culturally significant at all. But making room for every category of artistic value – and non-value – undermined the idea of value itself, as George Steiner had noticed. The danger of the long front of culture was that it could fragment into a rootless pluralism.

According to the critic Tim Hilton, the year 1969 'quite clearly marked the end of the English Pop scene'.[101] Far more noticeably than the end of the forties or the fifties, the end of the sixties was marked by critical obituaries, as though there was a desire to draw a line beneath the activities of an overstimulated decade. *Time* magazine's 'swinging meritocracy' bade farewell from the glossy portraits of David Bailey's *Goodbye Baby and Amen: A Saraband for the Sixties* (1969). The Beatles began to go their separate ways in 1970. Christopher Booker in *The Neophiliacs* (1969) and Bernard Levin in *The Pendulum Years* (1970) produced their conservative and largely negative assessments of the decade, agreeing that the illusions of the sixties would have to give way to a new realism.

The truth was that while the progressive consensus of the sixties had replaced its conservative predecessor with a more expansive and liberal cultural regime, it was undermined by, on the one hand, the forces calling for more radical change than it was willing to grant and, on the other, by reaction against the changes that had been achieved. More profoundly, the British economy was proving less and less able to meet the demands for consumption that had been unleashed, while the structure of British society began to be forced into adaptations not envisaged in the cultural critiques of the late fifties and early sixties.

The consensus began to fragment. Culturally, the crisis of 1968 was within the meritocracy, swinging or not, for culture was the property of the culture-making class. Economically, the trades unions, which had been brought into the management of the economy in 1940, began to be excluded (by a Labour government) because their demands and their power were perceived to be a threat. After 1970 there was serious industrial unrest, with the miners' strikes of 1973 and 1974, which brought down the Heath government, and the "winter of discontent" that brought down the Callaghan government in 1979. Socially, feminism, gay rights and racial equality were all themes announced during the sixties, but only fully developed in the seventies. The eroticism of the underground had sensitised people to their bodies, as vehicles for expression, or as objects of exploitation and suppression. Individual, rather than collective identity, began to be a political issue.

Yet for those for whom the political changes of the sixties had not gone far enough, there was a sense by 1970 that whatever had been thought was going to happen in 1968 was not going to happen after all. The political drama, heightened by anger at the Vietnam War, obscured the fact that what was often called a "cultural revolution" had been just that. Political failure thrust the issue of "culture and society" back into the cultural arena, thus making it even more of a political battleground. The struggle became once more about the nature of culture itself, the ideological significance of aesthetic value, the uses of culture in the maintenance of hegemony, and the function of the arts and popular culture in what the Situationists called "a society of spectacle". These questions called for a fresh approach.

Assessing the events in Paris in May 1968, an editorial in the *New Left Review*, bearing all the hallmarks of Perry Anderson's prose style, concluded that France had shown that the proletariat could be mobilised on the side of revolution, if correctly led. The success of the French students in provoking mass action was due to their access to a "reservoir" of Marxist ideas that the English Left lacked. The editorial was a self-justification for the line the *New Left Review* had taken. It also pointed to the direction that the cultural debate was to take: 'The production and circulation of theory is thus itself an indispensable preliminary practice.'[102] "Theory" became the watchword of the seventies. Practice was to turn out quite otherwise.

VI

The Uses of Subculture
Britain in the 1970s

'The devaluation of 1967 more than anything else confirmed Britain's "decline" in the public mind.'[1] This assessment, made in 1987 by the political and economic historian Alan Sked, places the moment at which post-war optimism gave way to pessimism alarmingly early. By this calculation the period of "affluence" which produced both social change and cultural expansion lasted less than ten years. Sked's use of quotation marks correctly stresses that Britain's economic decline has been relative to that of a prospering Europe and North America, not absolute, but when it comes to questions of national morale, the *perception* of decline is as important as its reality. In Sked's view: 'Since 1967 the British seem to have lived in an era of perpetual economic crisis, fearing that growth will never permanently return and that absolute decline may be just around the corner. That period is still continuing.'[2] The years since 1987 have given no cause to alter that judgement.

The economic crises of the seventies – the collapse of fixed exchange rates in 1971; the take-off of inflation; the oil price rises of 1973 and the world recession that followed; the rise in unemployment and slow-down in growth which created insecurity and industrial unrest – served only to reinforce the sense of decline that set in after 1967. The Labour government's recourse to the International Monetary Fund in December 1976 and the profound industrial unrest in the "winter of discontent" of 1978–9 produced international humiliation and domestic dissension. Strikes brought down both the Conservative government of 1970–74 and the Labour government of 1974–79. Neither government had held a sufficiently large majority to give a clear lead or make a firm change of direction.

The shocks to the world economic system in the seventies were severe. They resulted in a reorganisation of production, so that on the one hand multi-national companies increasingly transcended national economies by globalising their operations, while on the other mass production became a much more fragmented process. At the same time the established features of the social order in the West, from the dominant position of the United States to the traditional family structure, no longer seemed secure. Thus there was a crisis of social democracy as well as of capitalism. In 1973 the American social critic Daniel Bell published *The Coming of Post-Industrial Society*:

> In Western society we are in the midst of a vast historical change in which old social relations (which were property-bound), existing power structures (centred on narrow élites), and bourgeois culture (based on notions of restraint and delayed gratification) are being rapidly eroded. The sources of the upheaval are scientific and technological. But they are also cultural, since culture, I believe, has achieved autonomy in Western society. What these new social forms will be like is not completely clear. Nor is it likely that they will achieve the unity of the economic system and social structure which was characteristic of capitalist civilisation from the mid-eighteenth century to the mid-twentieth. The use of the hyphenated prefix *post-* indicates, thus, that sense of living in interstitial time.[3]

After Steiner's 'post-culture' of 1971, and Daniel Bell's 'post-industrial society' of 1973, the prefix became securely attached to the unifying drive that until then had characterised the twentieth century: modernism. That drive had first faltered, and then come to a stop. Bell's 'interstitial time' turned out to be the post-modern age.

In Britain the increase in unemployment beyond one million in 1975, shortly after inflation had touched 24.1 per cent, meant that the unwritten contract underpinning the consensus by which both parties had governed since the war was breaking down. The consequences were more far-reaching than the trades union militancy which broke both the Conservative and Labour governments of the seventies. The collapse of consensus also undermined the British sense of identity that rested upon it. It is significant that when Labour was returned to power as a minority government in February 1974 (achieving an overall majority of only four in a second election in October) it turned the unwritten understanding between government, capital and labour into an overt commitment, the "Social Contract", which tried unsuccessfully to rebuild a corporatist version of the post-war consensus, by bringing the trades unions into formal bargaining between the state and industrial capital, in exchange for nationally negotiated wage restraint. The Social

Contract broke down, and Callaghan's desperate "Concordat" with the Trades Union Congress in February 1979 was swept away by the Conservative election victory in May.

The breakdown of consensus provoked a crisis of identity that was national, regional and social. In 1973 Britain formally committed itself to Europe by joining the Common Market, although it was not until 1975 that a referendum confirmed that same commitment nationally, by a sixty-eight per cent yes, against thirty-two per cent no, in a high turn-out. In 1973 J. B. Priestley raked the embers of his wartime role as social commentator in a coffee-table book, *The English*. Its general tone was genial. 'The English Secret', he announced, echoing Orwell, was that they depended 'much more upon instinct and intuition than other Western Europeans do'.[4] Yet Priestley acknowledged: 'Englishness is not as strong as it was even thirty years ago.'[5] He sensed a crisis, for he wrote: 'England should discover her own living identity, something rather better than a tourist attraction.'[6] What he called 'Admass', an indirect description of Americanisation and commercial greed, was a threat to 'what remains of a characteristically English sense of community, decent fellow-feeling, fairness'.[7] The talismanic values of Deep England were under siege again, and the nation was failing itself: 'There has been little, or no appeal from deep feeling to deep feeling, from imagination to imagination. Recent years have "robbed us of immortal things".'[8] The final image in the book is of a stripper in a crowded working-men's club.

The weakening of English identity that Priestley noticed coincided with a strengthening of nationalism in Northern Ireland, Scotland and Wales. Though semi-quarantined by the Irish Sea, the undeclared civil war in Northern Ireland exacerbated the atmosphere of uncertainty and tension, especially during periodic IRA bombing campaigns in mainland Britain. While Labour tried to appease Welsh and Scottish nationalism by offering devolution, both Conservative and Labour governments were forced to maintain direct rule in Northern Ireland from 1972 onwards. The revival of the Scottish National Party and Plaid Cymru had begun in the early sixties, but the success of the Scottish Nationalists in the October 1974 election, which gave them eleven seats, was alarming to Labour, whose majority depended on holding Scottish seats. The offer of devolution measures to both Wales and Scotland fell well short of the dissolution of the United Kingdom but, like the issue of Europe, it divided both the country and the

Labour Party itself. In *The Break-Up of Britain*, published in 1977 at the height of the nationalist debate, the *New Left Review* contributor Tom Nairn argued: 'Politically speaking, the key to these neo-nationalist renaissances lies in the slow foundering of the British state, not in the Celtic bloodstream.'[9] Within England itself, local government reorganisation, introduced by the Conservative government in 1973, had its own disturbing effect on regional identity, extinguishing local entities such as Rutland, and creating the large metropolitan county councils that, ironically, would be abolished by another Conservative government in the eighties.

The breakdown of the political consensus meant that there was a far more extreme division between the Left and the Right, with both the main parties moving away from their previously centrist positions, and the extreme fringe parties gaining members in the early seventies. In terms of rival ideas of national identity, the Right was far more success-ful; Stuart Hall noted in December 1978: 'As we moved through the seventies, the popular mood shifted decisively against the Left.'[10] Hall attributed this to the backlash against the provocations of 1968, and specifically to the rhetoric of Enoch Powell, 'speaking over the heads of the party factions to "the people", helping to construct "the people" in their most patriotic, racist constitutional disguise'.[11] Margaret That-cher, who became leader of the Conservative Party in 1975, personified the move to the Right, but her success was the result of a deeper movement with a much longer trajectory.

Writing of the growing sensitivity of racial issues during the seventies, Arthur Marwick remarked in *British Society Since 1945* (1982): 'One great irony, and perhaps a revealing one about British society, may be that while class was now being openly spoken about when it was no longer the supreme factor in social inequality that it had been in the thirties, the well-bred reticence that once enveloped discussion of class now switches itself to discussion of race, just when race was becoming an especially potent cause of inequality.'[12] Yet race could not be politely ignored, for it was a fundamental reference point in measuring social identity. Paul Gilroy argued in *There Ain't No Black in the Union Jack* (1987) that 'the new racism' which developed in Britain had the capacity 'to link discourses of patriotism, nationalism, xenophobia, Englishness, Britishness, militarism and gender difference into a com-plex system which gives "race" its contemporary meaning'.[13]

Measured by the progress of the National Front, formed in 1966 out of the residue of a number of earlier extreme right-wing parties, race became an issue after the ostensible source of racist alarm, primary black immigration, had been virtually brought to a halt by government legislation. The 1971 Immigration Act removed the privileged access which had made it easier for Afro-Caribbeans and Asians from Commonwealth countries to settle in Britain. The expulsion of Asians from Uganda in 1973 provoked a further immigration scare, but the real focus of anxiety was the communities that had already settled in Britain, and who were moving into their second generation. By 1976 1.85 million people in Britain were classed as non-white, just over three per cent of the population, of whom forty per cent had been born in the United Kingdom. (The 1991 census showed that the ethnic groups classed as Black African, Caribbean and coming from the Indian sub-continent made up five and a half per cent of the population.) British government policy had been on the one hand gradually to restrict immigration, while on the other to legislate against overt racial discrimination. The *Empire Windrush*, the ship that had brought the first West Indian migrant workers in 1948, had not been made welcome, and as early as 1951 the Labour government was considering measures to limit immigration. The Institute of Race Relations was established in 1958, the year of the first serious racial disturbances in Nottingham and Notting Hill Gate. The Immigration Act of 1962 imposed immigration quotas, and controls were gradually tightened until the 1971 Act permanently ended primary black settlement. Labour left those provisions in place, although the 1976 Race Relations Act declared all discrimination illegal and set up the Commission for Racial Equality.

In the seventies the National Front grew sufficiently in strength to field fifty-four candidates in the February 1974 general election, thus qualifying for a television electoral broadcast. In May the Front polled significantly in some London boroughs and in October had ninety candidates in the second general election. The deliberately aggressive tactics of the Front in areas with a high non-white population and the counter-demonstrations they provoked added to the sense of social unease. But the activities of the Front were only an overt expression of the covert resentment of blacks and Asians that made the "assimilation" that was supposed to justify controls on immigration difficult, if not impossible. Non-white communities clustered rather than dispersed;

conditions of housing and employment remained worse for them and they were the first to suffer from the effects of growing recession. In compensation West Indians, who did not have the recognisable culture and languages of the Indian sub-continent, created their own cult of separateness, Rastafarianism, although this only increased their visibility to the police, who used the Vagrancy Act – commonly known as "sus" – as a regular means of harassment.

In 1970 the arrest and trial of so-called "black militants" associated with the Mangrove Restaurant in Notting Hill Gate marked the beginning of a series of bitter confrontations between the black community and the authorities, in particular the riots at the Notting Hill Gate Carnival in 1976, 1977 and 1978 (illustration 12). Against these set-piece confrontations was the constant anxiety about "mugging", which was seen as a particularly "black" crime. Paul Gilroy has argued that the years between Enoch Powell's 'rivers of blood' speech of 1968 and the "long hot summer" of 1976 'saw the definition of blacks as a low crime group turned round one hundred and eighty degrees. They also witnessed the formation of a politicised roots culture among the black populations of the inner city.'[14]

While the black and Asian population were the target of very real discrimination, and suffered the most from the economic and social difficulties of the seventies, they also served a significant psychological purpose for the majority white population: they became a scapegoat for the anxieties of the whites. The sociologist Michael Brake has argued: 'The mugger, according to the media, was part of "un-British" youth, a product of black immigration, part of the menacing "dangerous classes" gathering in the gloom of the collapse of the British Empire.'[15] In *The Break-Up of Britain* Nairn suggested that racism was a substitute for a true sense of national identity, in that the English, unlike most Western nations, lacked a myth of "the People" that could be mobilised for political ends. (As both Orwell in wartime and Humphrey Jennings at the beginning of the fifties had pointed out, the English version of the myth centred not on "the People" but "the family".)

Nairn demonstrated that Enoch Powell, the "legitimate" spokesman for racism who, unusually for a politician, was both a poet and a former Professor of Greek, had long contemplated the nature of English identity, for instance in the introduction to his *Biography of a Nation*, written with Angus Maude in 1955. Powell's cultural origins, as his own verse showed, lay in the 'conservative dream-world founded on an insular vein of English romanticism', developed by the Georgian poets in the Imperial Indian summer between the Boer War and 1914.[16] Such national imagery could be summoned up in wartime, as Chapter II shows, but in the absence of national dramas such as wars, 'the only *new* experience, going sharply counter to tradition, has been that of the coloured immigration of the fifties and sixties. Hence, Powell realised, it has become possible to define Englishness *vis-à-vis* this internal "enemy", this "foreign body" in our own streets.'[17] English self-confidence could be restored by defining its superiority to the new menace.

The connection between racism and extreme right-wing views and the growing popularity of romanticised versions of pastoralism and "heritage" as an embodiment of Englishness in the seventies is not fanciful. The "country" magazine *This England*, launched in 1968 ostensibly to celebrate "the poetry of the English countryside", took an increasingly sour attitude to contemporary developments during the seventies, criticising black immigration and recommending that its readers join the right-wing National Association for Freedom, and in the eighties printing articles by Stuart Millson, well known for his ultra-right views.[18] "Culture", meaning an unspecified but easily recognised idea of Englishness and an unspoken horror of blackness, was the essential link in Margaret Thatcher's cautious, but crucial, comment on racial politics in a television interview in January 1978. Raising the possibility that Britain's coloured population could reach four million by the year 2000, she said: 'Now that is an awful lot and I think it means that people are really rather afraid that this country might be swamped by people with a different culture.' People didn't agree with the National Front, she said, but 'at least it is talking about some of the problems'.[19]

Ironically, Thatcher's political rise contributed to the National Front's decline. Their vote in local elections began to fall in 1978, and all their candidates in the 1979 general election lost their deposits. While the racialist vote returned to the Conservative Party, splits developed in the National Front, with the British National Party emerging as the focus of the racist ultra-right.

Enoch Powell's intellectual honesty about his views led him into the political wilderness, but he played an important role in breaking the Conservative Party's attachment to consensus. As the Conservative historian Maurice Cowling has commented: 'It is doubtful whether "Thatcherism" could have been successful without him.'[20] Powell demonstrated his rejection of the Keynesian economic management pursued by both parties when he resigned as Financial Secretary to the Treasury in 1958. Ten years later what came to be known as his 'rivers of blood' speech led to his dismissal from the Shadow Cabinet and his exclusion from Heath's government in 1970. His opposition to the Common Market as a threat to Britain's constitution and cultural identity was so intense that he recommended voting Labour in February 1974 (and did so himself), thus breaking his links with the Conservative Party, although he returned to Parliament as an Ulster Unionist that October. Powell's monetarism, opposition to Europe and passionate right-wing patriotism attracted the sympathy of what Cowling has called 'an embryonic intelligentsia' of political journalists associated with the *Daily Telegraph* and the *Spectator*, among them Andrew Alexander, George Gale, Anthony Lejeune, Ronald Butt, Patrick Cosgrave, Colin Welch, T. E. Utley and Frank Johnson.[21] Just as the New Left had helped to prepare for a Labour government before 1964, intellectual revival on the Right helped to prepare for 1979. In 1975 the young Conservative MP Jonathan Aitken founded the Conservative Philosophy Group as a private forum for dons and journalists, among whose members were John Casey, editor of the *Cambridge Review* from 1975 to 1979, and Roger Scruton, who was to become editor of the *Salisbury Review*, launched in 1982. Margaret Thatcher's mentor as leader of the opposition was another "intellectual" politician, Sir Keith Joseph, with whom she established the Centre for Policy Studies. This and the monetarist Institute for Economic Affairs, joined later by the Adam Smith Institute, laid the ground for the social and economic policy changes that were to be enforced in the eighties.

On the outer edge of Conservative politics there appeared organisations like the Middle Class Association, the volunteer "militia" Civil Assistance, and the National Association for Freedom. The NAFF was officially launched by Norris McWhirter in November 1975, a week after his brother Ross had been assassinated by the IRA. Mrs Thatcher spoke at a fund-raising dinner for the Association in January 1976, against the background of the Association's support for the owner of the factory in Grunwick where a bitter ten-month dispute, culminating in June and July of that year in battles between mass pickets and the police, proved a psychological defeat for the Left. Although not overtly "political", the activities of Mrs Mary Whitehouse – especially her successful instigation of a prosecution for blasphemy of the homosexual newspaper *Gay News* in 1977 – were an important symbolic focus for cultural conservatives and had an inhibiting effect on broadcasting.

Several of those associated with the intellectual shift to the Right had been Labour supporters: the historian Hugh Thomas, the journalist Paul Johnson, editor of the socialist *New Statesman* between 1965 and 1970, and the novelist Kingsley Amis. Amis's trajectory from Fabian pamphleteer in 1957 to Conservative Political Centre lecturer in 1967 can be traced through his increasing disenchantment with the state of higher education. To Amis and many others the university – as opposed to the polytechnic – was the one place where a certain view of culture held true, yet the expansion of higher education during the sixties had led to a dilution of standards. 'More will mean worse,' he had warned in 1960, and by 1967 he felt his prediction was justified.[22] As Ian Carter has pointed out in his study of post-war British "campus novels", 'civilised culture' was identified as 'the central value justifying universities' existence. In return those places are seen as culture's ultimate refuge.'[23] As Carter also pointed out, however, Oxbridge culture was hostile to 'proletarians, scientists, women and foreigners', an aristocratic culture masquerading as a general culture.[24]

It is a characteristic right-wing response at a time of apparent dilution of standards and declining respect for tradition to reassert the value of literature as a moral discipline. Such a view was as much Leavisite as aristocratic in its inspiration, and it was one of the key themes of an early manifestation of the counter-attack of the Right, the pamphlets that reversed the imagery of government policy documents to call themselves *Black Papers*: 'Our central concern was with the breakdown of traditional authority in both schools and higher education.'[25] The writer is C. B. Cox, whose career shows how the same roots in Leavisism that led to the development of a radical critique of contemporary culture could lead in an entirely different direction.

The autobiography of C. B. (Brian) Cox, *The Great Betrayal* (1992), reveals a cultural formation and career that echoes, though with different inflections, that of Richard Hoggart. Of his working-class childhood and Methodist upbringing in pre-war and wartime Grimsby Cox wrote: 'The puritanism of the Methodist church penetrated deep into my blood; I have never completely rid myself of this inheritance.'[26] Military service brought him, like Hoggart, into army education, where he used the materials supplied by the Bureau of Current Affairs. A college scholarship and a grant made possible by the 1944 Education Act took him to Cambridge to read English, where he took part in Leavis's seminars, though Leavis was no longer at the height of his powers. 'Strongly influenced by Leavis, I wanted to write literary criticism.'[27] A first in English was followed by post-graduate research, teaching for the WEA and in 1954 an assistant lectureship at Hull, where his colleagues were Richard Hoggart, Philip Larkin and Malcolm Bradbury. Cox continued to teach for the WEA; he canvassed for the Labour Party, joined CND and marched from Aldermaston, but resigned in disagreement with the direct-action policies of the Committee of 100.

At Cambridge Cox had become a friend of a fellow English student and future teacher, Tony Dyson, whose attitudes closely paralleled his own: 'Like Wordsworth, Coleridge and T. S. Eliot, we have held fast to Plato's belief in absolutes of truth, goodness and beauty, towards which all human action should aspire.'[28] The remark places Cox and Dyson exactly in the conservative cultural tradition that Williams had anatomised in *Culture and Society*, but this was not incompatible with support for Labour and concern for liberal issues. Dyson had become a founder member of the Homosexual Reform Society in the fifties. Nor did Cox and Dyson accept Leavis's élitist conception of a saving remnant who would retain exclusive hold on the keys to literature: 'For all of us in the tradition of Matthew Arnold, T. S. Eliot, I. A. Richards and F. R. Leavis, great books possessed an absolute and inalienable value, and we believed that any culture or class of society to which they were irrelevant must be miserably impoverished. Our intent was to make even the rarest of literary artefacts accessible to as wide a readership as possible; we saw this as a truly democratic ideal.'[29]

In 1958, provoked by an anecdotal and belle-lettriste lecture at a British Council summer school by the former Apocalyptic poet and critic G. S. Fraser, Cox and Dyson decided that a successor to *Scrutiny*, which had folded in 1953, should be founded to reassert the moral importance of literature. *Critical Quarterly* was launched in 1959, using office space lent by Larkin at Hull University Library, and with Hoggart among their advisers. Where *Critical Quarterly* differed from *Scrutiny* was in the editors' commitment to publishing contemporary poetry as well as criticism; the journal featured not only Movement poets such as Larkin, but was an early champion of Ted Hughes and Sylvia Plath.

Like *Scrutiny*, the journal found that its five thousand or so readers included many English teachers in schools, who took part in the regular conferences that the editors organised. In 1963 they launched *Critical Survey* as a companion publication aimed at teachers. They were therefore closely in touch with developments in schools, and they did not like what they saw: 'We had observed in the schools the growing influence of progressive education in breaking down faith in high culture, in reason and disciplined learning. Emphasis on activity and self-expression easily became associated with the immediacy and sensationalism of neo-modern art.'[30] The student revolts of 1968 (Cox had seen the unrest at Berkeley, California as a visiting lecturer in the early sixties; he became a Professor at Manchester in 1966) were the last straw.

A more mundane reason for launching the *Black Papers* was the need to raise the subscription price for *Critical Survey*; a special issue of some kind was called for. The decision was taken to produce an anti-government White Paper, attacking the destruction of grammar schools by comprehensivisation, the student sit-ins and 'the new fashionable anarchy'.[31] Contributors included Kingsley Amis, Robert Conquest and the Conservative MP Angus Maude. The editors were making a political, as well as critical intervention: a copy of the first *Black Paper*, published in March 1969, was sent to every MP and the project was launched with a controversial press conference. Hoggart felt obliged to resign as an adviser to *Critical Quarterly* shortly afterwards. The decision by Labour's Education Minister Edward Short to attack the *Black Paper* at a National Union of Teachers conference gave it even more publicity and showed that it had hit its mark. A second *Black Paper* followed in October and a third in November 1970, titled 'Goodbye Mr Short' in celebration of Short's departure from office and the appointment of Margaret Thatcher as the Conservatives' replacement. Further *Black Papers* were published in 1975 and 1977.

The sociologist Bernice Martin, herself a contributor to *Black Paper* Number 4, has commented: 'The first Black Papers were certainly seen as the educational equivalent of the Festival of Light and Mrs Whitehouse's National Viewers' and Listeners' Association – the vicious backlash of the articulate culture of control against the progressives who were busy carrying off their neighbour's landmarks. Indeed, in part they were just that, and it is very significant that most of the prominent contributors to the Black Papers were first-generation grammar school and university products.'[32] The puritanism of this new meritocracy had its parallel in the prosecution in 1971 of the 'School-kids issue' of *Oz* which led to the magazine's demise, and the simul-taneous prosecution of the English edition of Soren Hansen and Jesper Jensen's *The Little Red Schoolbook*.

Although Cox declared in his autobiography, 'as a liberal, I held that study of literature helps readers to free themselves from repressive ideologies,' Cox and Dyson's appeal for a reassertion of authority – the official-sounding body set up to promote their ideas was called the National Council for Educational *Standards* (italics added) – drew them to the Right.[33] "Authority" was part of the rhetoric of the Conservative conference at the Selsdon Park Hotel in 1970 that led to the journalists' invention, "Selsdon Man". Cox joined the Conservative Party that year and was soon brought into contact with Margaret Thatcher at the Department of Education. A new recruit for *Black Paper* Number 2 was the former comprehensive-school headmaster (and Labour Councillor) Robert Rhodes Boyson, who became a Conservative MP in 1974. Boyson became a very active supporter of the campaign, and introduced Cox and Dyson to Ralph Harris at the Institute of Economic Affairs, and to Norris and Ross McWhirter. They discussed proposals to pub-lish *Black Papers* on a wide range of topics, including the National Health Service, but Cox and Dyson withdrew when they discovered that Angus Maude (a close ally of Thatcher's) was considered insuf-ficiently right-wing by their proposed partners.

Cox's specific claim for the *Black Papers* campaign was that it broke the left-liberal consensus on state education. It set the agenda for the "Great Debate" on education launched by Callaghan in 1978, and eventually to the Education Reform Act of 1988. The specific plans for a National Curriculum, however, led to Cox's disenchantment with the 'extreme right-wing views, out of touch with real classrooms' that were allowed to prevail over his own advice as chairman of the National Curriculum English Working Group and in his report on the teaching of Standard English.[34] The 'Betrayal' in the title of his autobiography refers as much to the right-wing politicians of the eighties as to the left-wing ones of the sixties. Yet Cox bears some responsibility for the ideological shift that produced the changes of the eighties. As Maurice Cowling has commented, the *Black Papers* 'showed that there was a reactionary public waiting to be tapped'.[35] Cox has admitted as much: 'The *Black Papers* liberated a repressed ideology which eventually was to play a part in making Mrs Thatcher Prime Minister in 1979.'[36]

—

As Secretary of State for Education during the whole term of Edward Heath's government, Margaret Thatcher had ultimate responsibility for funding of the arts and heritage through the Minister of State – first Lord Eccles (who was also Paymaster General) and then briefly Norman St John-Stevas – who had inherited the small department established by Jennie Lee. She does not seem to have taken a close interest in cultural policy, but it is possible to see hints of future developments. Unexpectedly, Thatcher resisted pressure from the Treasury to carry out the final wish of Iain MacLeod, who died shortly after becoming Chancellor in 1970, not to proceed with the Open University. It had been set up by Labour, but still needed the funds to launch itself. The Open University may have appealed to her as an aid to self-improvement after the manner of the Victorian advocate of self-help, Samuel Smiles. Thatcher did, however, carry out MacLeod's decision to impose entry charges on all the national museums, in order to reduce their dependence on the state, and the government's own expenditure. All the museums, with the exception of the Imperial War Museum, were opposed to charging. Mrs Thatcher fiercely defended the government's proposals in June 1971, but the time taken to introduce the necessary legislation meant that the turnstiles were only in operation between January and March 1974. This was long enough to discover that the charges were not meeting the cost of their collection. Attendances fell from sixteen million in 1973 to 14.8 million in 1974, and rose to 17.6 million in 1976.

The art historian John Pope-Hennessy, then director of the Victoria and Albert Museum, which was directly answerable to the Department of Education, noticed the change when Jennie Lee was replaced by Lord Eccles: 'The small office responsible for the arts was expanded into a mini-ministry (staffed, like Arts Ministries in other countries, by dead-end civil servants with no promotion prospects), and the obstinate, egocentric personality of a minister with cultural pretensions impinged more heavily on the Victoria and Albert than it did on trustee-controlled museums.'[37] Lord Eccles's personal contribution to the development of government cultural policy was the establishment of the Crafts Council with a budget of £45,000 in 1971, in order to fill the perceived gap between the activities of the Arts Council and the Design Council.

The cosy relationship between the Arts Council and the government was also ended by the change of party. The civil servants at the

Department of Education immediately took their revenge for Lord Goodman's direct access to Jennie Lee by hauling the Arts Council before the Parliamentary Public Accounts Committee on the grounds that it had violated civil service procedures by promising money it did not have, and allowing Sadler's Wells Opera (while moving to the Coliseum and preparing to change its name to English National Opera) to go into deficit. Goodman has described the proceedings as resembling 'an Asian bazaar far more than a judicial tribunal'.[38] The Council was exonerated on all counts. More serious was the attitude displayed by the new Arts Minister, Lord Eccles, who not only lacked 'any particular affection for artists, but . . . regarded them as members of the community who could be dealt with on a summary basis'.[39] Goodman discovered that the easy exercise of the arm's-length principle which had been made possible by the close relationship between himself and Jennis Lee was not so easy to maintain. He and Lee 'deceived ourselves that an arrangement empirically excellent was theoretically so'.[40] Under Eccles the principle that the Minister did not interfere with the policies of the Arts Council's clients came under strain: 'Knowing little about the theatre, Eccles was firmly convinced that it was a cesspool.'[41] Eccles expressed this view more judiciously in the House of Lords in February 1971 when he made public his disquiet about the use of public money to fund 'works which affront the religious beliefs or outrage the sense of decency of a large body of taxpayers. . . . If the Arts Council could reach some understanding with their clients that takes into account the moral views of those who are putting up the money, I should be very glad.'[42] Eccles wanted the Arts Council to exercise censorship by withholding funds from offending companies, an idea that Goodman firmly resisted, though he passed on a general reminder to clients.

In 1972 Goodman, who had had his original five-year appointment as Chairman extended by two years, retired and was replaced, predictably enough, by a more conservative chairman, Lord Gibson, whose other cultural interests included the National Trust, the Victoria and Albert Museum, the Redundant Churches Fund, the Gulbenkian Foundation, the National Art Collections Fund and Glyndebourne. In the view of the Arts Council's Literature Director, Charles Osborne: 'His was not an expansive personality, but he gave an impression of quiet confidence. He was cold, polite and occasionally lost his temper.'[43]

In a valedictory introduction to the Arts Council's report for 1970–71 Goodman wrote of the Council's 'enemies – few, but potent' whose 'pent-up rage was released on us and we found ourselves in positively mortal battle to defend the integrity and wisdom of our administration'.[44] He also admitted that the Council was a long way from completing the pattern of provision it wanted to see: 'We have, perhaps, been most remiss in our failure to improve the living conditions of the creative and performing artist.'[45] Conditions for the arts themselves, however, had improved enormously during his time as chairman. Goodman's main achievement was with the national companies, where a healthy rivalry was possible in opera between Covent Garden and the Coliseum, and in the theatre, where the Royal Shakespeare Company had become firmly established in London, and work on the new building for the National Theatre on the South Bank had begun in November 1964. Both the Hayward Gallery and the Serpentine Gallery were new creations added to the Council's portfolio.

Without a committed minister to battle on its behalf, the Arts Council began to feel the effects of the growing economic crisis. A commitment to three-year funding was abandoned before the end of the first three years, and the Council's report for 1973–4 warned: 'The effect of inflation on wages and other overheads now threatens the survival of many of our supported companies. Several have made it clear that they cannot continue to exist without larger grants than we have been able to allocate them.'[46] Economic difficulties proved as effective a form of censorship as the disapproval of Lord Eccles, for new activities such as "community arts" had to be curbed. The report for 1974–5 warned that, in spite of an agreed grant-in-aid for 1975–6 of twenty-five million pounds, it was already clear that 'this year many of our supported companies are going to face serious deficits'.[47] The chaos at the National Theatre's building site, where endless technical delays, soaring costs and appalling industrial relations were an emblem of the economic and industrial chaos of the country at large, provoked a financial crisis in the Council's theatre allocations, and in October 1975 sudden cuts were decided that hit the "fringe" theatre especially hard. The RSC secured an emergency two hundred thousand pounds, while costs at the still unopened National Theatre reached sixteen million pounds. The 'period of restraint' forecast in the Council's report for 1975–6 was to go on until the late eighties. The report was titled *The Arts in Hard Times*; the following year's report was presciently called *Value for Money*.

—

While the Goodman years have become retrospectively known as a golden age for the Arts Council, an independent investigation of the whole field of funding for the arts for the Gulbenkian Foundation by the Master of University College, Oxford, Lord Redcliffe-Maud, concluded in 1976 that there were 'no grounds for complacency. . . . Large areas of Britain constitute a Third World of underdevelopment and deprivation in all the arts and crafts. Architecture, almost everywhere, is the worst example.'[48] It was hardly surprising to read: 'What artists and the arts in Britain most of all need is money.'[49] Redcliffe-Maud however saw local authorities rather than central government as the most important potential source of funding, and the report caught the devolutionary spirit of the times by calling for entirely separate Arts Councils for Scotland and Wales, and a far greater devolution of responsibility to the regions. He hoped to see the arts becoming the responsibility of a minister of Cabinet rank who would also take charge of education, sport and leisure, but emphasised that the arm's-length principle which, as was shown in Chapter II, his report formally codified, was essential for the whole system.

Lord Goodman, who succeeded Redcliffe-Maud as Master of University College, Oxford in 1976, has shown in his own account that the successful promotion of the arts by the government through a surrogate body was only a variation on the very old tradition of state patronage: "enlightened" rulers exercising their preferences and pleasures, and gaining public approbation as a result. But with the widening division between Right and Left during the seventies the arts could not escape the politicisation that the conventional bipartisan approach of consensus government had sought to deny. In 1977 the official Labour Party document *The Arts and the People* declared: 'Politics are inextricably sewn into the fabric of the arts.'[50] Having benefited substantially from the first Wilson administration, the Arts Council found the second far less comfortable. With Jennie Lee now in the House of Lords, Wilson chose as his Arts Minister the combative Member for Putney, Hugh Jenkins.

Jenkins was the first – and to date, last – Minister for the Arts who had a sound knowledge of the internal workings of the Arts Council. A former official of the actors' trades union, Equity, Jenkins had helped to set up the Theatres Advisory Council in 1962 as a forum for British theatres, an increasing number of whom depended on Arts Council support. He served on the Council's drama advisory panel between 1962 and 1966 and sat on the Council itself from 1968 to 1971, returning to the drama panel from 1972 to 1974. When Lord Eccles was replaced as Conservative Minister for the Arts by Norman St John-Stevas in December 1973, Jenkins replaced the actor-MP Andrew Faulds as Labour's opposition spokesman, and became Arts Minister in March 1974. Because of a technicality he was not made a Minister of State, but was given a lesser post as an Under-Secretary, with an office in Belgrave Square which he tried to run 'as an autonomous republic within the Education and Science kingdom'.[51]

Jenkins had no less trouble with the civil servants responsible for the arts as a minister than Lord Goodman had had as chairman of the Arts Council. Jenkins did not want to abolish the Arts Council, as did some people in the Labour Party, but he did wish to democratise it. He had secured a commitment in the October 1974 Labour manifesto 'to make the Arts Council more democratic and representative of people in the arts and entertainment'.[52] This proposal had a long pedigree. The 1949 Select Committee on Estimates examining the Council had reported sympathetically on a proposal from Equity that a proportion of members of the drama panel should be elected, and that the panels should elect the members of the Council. Twenty years on in 1968 another Estimates Committee report recommended that the Council should be more representative and should investigate ways of becoming so – though the Council did nothing. Jenkins was of the opinion that the Arts Council should no longer be appointed by the Minister for the Arts. Instead the advisory panels would be made up of people chosen one third from trades unions and managerial bodies in the arts and entertainment, one third elected by a conference of local authority arts and entertainment committees, and one third of ministerial appointees. These would then elect the Council. Such a change would involve ending the Royal Charter, and replacing it with legislation establishing a new government department of Arts, Communications, Entertainment and Sport, with a Cabinet Minister and one or more junior ministers. The Conservative Department of National Heritage, created in 1992, thus has its origins in Labour thinking, for these ideas are to be found in Labour's *The Arts: A Discussion Document for the Labour Movement* in 1974, the Trades Union Congress's working party report on the arts in 1976 and *The Arts and the People* in 1977, although this went further than Jenkins in proposing the abolition of the Arts Council altogether.

While serving on the Council Jenkins had been unable to persuade Lord Goodman of the virtue of his ideas: 'The Council as a whole still believed in the curious proposition that to retain its independence *from* government it was necessary for it to be appointed *by* the government. There was also a more rational objection. Appointment ensured that the Arts Council consisted of persons dedicated to the arts. When the Arts Council emerged from CEMA there was no demand for democratic control. . . . It was not until the Council had grown into a great influence in the land and government patronage was taken for granted that complaints began to be heard that this enormous power, this decisive influence, was exercised by a small group of appointees answerable to no one but themselves.'[53] Jenkins further objected that these appointees were not necessarily very good: 'The Council is a group assembled by a series of chances, a collection of random choices made by a very tiny and ingrown electorate advised by the Council's own bureaucracy and finally approved by a Secretary of State or Prime Minister who knows little about the people concerned and naturally opts for what he is told is safe, which means the arts establishment.'[54]

Jenkins's own officials were no more interested in democratising the Council than the Council itself, and he found he had to instruct his Deputy Secretary, Willy Wright, who attended Council meetings on his behalf, to put forward Labour government policy, not his own views. Jenkins however was not above putting the ministerial powers of appointment, of which he disapproved, to his own use. He wanted the former WEA lecturer and Professor of Adult Education Roy Shaw, who was already a Council member, to succeed Lord Gibson as chairman, but Shaw pre-empted him by taking the post of Secretary-General of the Arts Council in 1975, and Gibson 'won Shaw for the anti-democratic cause'.[55] Shaw defended the Council's position in his annual report for 1976–7 by stressing the virtues of the arm's-length principle as defined by Lord Redcliffe-Maud in his Gulbenkian report, and it is from this period that the arm's-length principle became a familiar term in the Council's rhetoric. In this context the arm's-length principle was being deployed as a defence against democratic rather than government interference.

Jenkins unsuccessfully proposed Stuart Hall as a Council member, and secured Council places for Richard Hoggart and Raymond Williams, who joined the Council in December 1975. Williams later revealed that he had been appointed to the Council to act as a ministerial mole: 'On the specific understanding I had reached with the Minister, I was present to observe and to attempt reform.'[56] He was horrified by 'the usual mellow dusk' in which appointments to the Council and the advisory panels were made.[57] Though in principle in favour of 'intermediate' bodies such as the Arts Council claimed to be, he concluded that in no way was the Council's distance from government genuine: 'The true social process of such bodies as the Arts Council is one of administered consensus by co-option.'[58] The Arts Council was perfectly suited to this task, and true to Antonio Gramsci's description of hegemony as a compromise equilibrium, the Council gently adjusted to events. Williams observed that in spite of the 'mood of bewildered consensus' when it came to taking actual Council decisions, where in practice the officers knew far more than the Council to which they were responsible, the politics of the Arts Council did shift with the political wind.[59] When the Conservative-appointed chairman, Lord Gibson, gave way in 1977 to the Labour-appointed Kenneth Robinson, a former Labour Minister of Health, 'the observable character of the Council was subtly but significantly changed'.[60]

The Arts Council's equilibrium nonetheless would not shift so far as to admit democracy, and Jenkins became increasingly frustrated in his efforts to 'loosen the grip of the snobocracy on the arts scene'.[61] Lord Gibson refused to allow advisory panels to elect their own chairmen, who would then become members of the Council, and circumvented Jenkins by going directly to the Chancellor of the Exchequer Denis Healey, or to Harold Wilson. Jenkins therefore tried to engineer Gibson's removal, but as he had to admit in a letter to his superior, the Secretary of State for Education Fred Mulley: 'At the moment when I am beginning to undermine them [the snobocracy], I find myself being undermined.'[62] Jenkins had made himself generally unpopular by vociferously supporting a Wealth Tax and agitating for the introduction of Authors' Public Lending Right. Without consulting him, Wilson had asked Harold Lever, Chancellor of the Duchy of Lancaster, to investigate new ways of funding the arts, and Gibson was in contact with Lever. Gibson, backed up by Lord Goodman and others, proved more powerful than Jenkins, and the Minister's departure from office was being widely predicted when in April 1976 Wilson himself decided to resign. Creating a new administration, his successor James Callaghan appointed Lord Donaldson Minister for the Arts. Jenkins's comment was: 'Jack Donaldson . . . was a figure acceptable to the Establishment, while I was acceptable only to artists, to their organisations and to the artistic left, which includes most of the critics.'[63] It was not a strong enough alliance to shift the hegemony of the arts establishment.

Jenkins's frustration within the corridors of power was as nothing to that of those with little hope of ever entering them. Although left-wing groups like the Socialist Workers' Party grew significantly in numbers in 1972 and 1973, and drew encouragement from the miners' strikes of 1972 and 1974, a second dose of "Wilsonism", still less the Callaghanism that followed, was not what the Left was looking for. According to the political historian David Marquand: 'The Labour movement – indeed the whole progressive tradition in British politics – was collapsing from intellectual anaemia.'[64] While the Right profited from the growing sense of crisis, the Left felt increasingly thwarted. This was very evident in the work of the new wave of playwrights brought to prominence by the burst of theatrical activity encouraged by the removal of censorship and expansion of subsidy in 1968. In 1974 Howard Brenton declared that the "fringe" had failed: 'Its failure was that of the whole dream of an "alternative culture" – the notion that within society as it exists you can grow another way of life, which, like a beneficent and desirable cancer, will in the end grow throughout the western world, and change it. What happens is that the "alternative society" gets hermetically sealed, and surrounded. A ghetto-like mentality develops. It is surrounded and, in the end, strangled to death.'[65]

Brenton wanted to see writers more politically engaged, not less, but he and his fellow playwrights seemed fascinated by political failure: in 1972 David Hare's *The Great Exhibition* explored the disillusion of a Labour MP; Brenton's *Magnificence* of 1973 charted the failure of the Angry Brigade, and in the same year Trevor Griffiths's *The Party* conducted a post-mortem on the dreams of 1968. Jim Allen's television series *Days of Hope* (1975), directed by Ken Loach, the left-wing conscience of the BBC, sought to revive the tradition of working-class radicalism, but it could do so only by turning to the past and the period between the First World War and the General Strike.

The elegiac note is unmistakable in the title David Widgery gave to his introduction to the anthology *The Left in Britain 1956–1976*, 'Farewell Grosvenor Square'. Widgery was unusual not only in that he was a GP working in the East End, but also in that he straddled the gap between the "alternative society" and the radical and puritanical Left by combining membership of the Socialist Workers' Party with writing for, and on occasion editing, *Oz* magazine. It was therefore with some authority that he asked: 'Where have all the marchers gone? . . . Nowadays it is the memory of political waste which summons a reckoning of time misspent.'[66] A stern critic of the 'Marxist swots' of the *New Left Review*, Widgery concluded: 'The middle-class New Left has finished. Labour's New Left will not begin.'[67]

The uncompleted revolution of the New Left provided the theme for Malcolm Bradbury's satirical novel *The History Man*, published in 1975, where the object of the satire was the sexual and political amorality of a new breed of intellectuals – what might be called the "polytocracy" – who flourished in the new polytechnics and universities established in the sixties, and who in Bradbury's eyes were quite prepared to sacrifice their responsibilities as teachers to their personal and political ambitions. Set in a new university that is a judicious fictional mix of Sussex and Essex (though the plot has parallels with an actual scandal at Lancaster), the 'history man' (a reference to Hegel) is Howard Kirk, a radical sociologist. Kirk's social origins, and those of his wife, are northern, almost parodically Hoggartian, and their working-class puritanism is reinforced by grammar-school education and university at Leeds. But during the sexual revolution of the sixties the Kirks discover their erotic selves, and come to see that people like themselves 'had been chosen for élite privilege'.[68] They had access to wider social freedoms and could claim them for others.

Then came 1968, 'the year when what the Kirks had been doing in their years of personal struggle suddenly seemed to matter for everybody. Everything seemed wide open; individual expectation coincided with historical drive; as the students massed in Paris in May, it seemed that all the forces for change were massing everywhere with them.'[69] But Bradbury actually set the action of his novel in 1972, when the dream of 1968 has faded. The 'intimacy, warmth and consensus of that year, seems hard to recover. They look for it; they have a strong sense of something that was undelivered then, and a hazy dream still shimmers ahead of them: a world of expanded minds, equal dealings, erotic satisfactions, beyond the frame of reality, beyond the limits of the senses.'[70]

In fictional form, the novel played out the tension between literature and sociology that Bradbury had explored in his book *The Social Context of Modern English Literature* (1971) which took a liberal and empirical rather than theoretical approach to the sociology of literature. In the novel, Kirk sets his sexual sights on a new member of the English faculty, the self-described liberal, Miss Callendar. Metaphorically, sociology sets out to seduce literature. Bradbury's moral position was Callendar's rather than Kirk's: Kirk's campaigns triumph, but Bradbury implies that the personal cost – not least to Kirk's wife – is too great.

In *The History Man* sexual and academic politics went hand in hand. The politicisation of sexuality, especially for women and homosexuals of both sexes, was both a cause and effect of the social tensions of the seventies. But if the personal was also the political – as the Kirks would agree – the politics of sexuality brought into question issues of individual identity and suggested new directions for activism. The Gay Liberation Front was formed in 1970, the same year that a conference at Ruskin College, Oxford demonstrated that the Women's Movement which had been taking shape during the sixties was ready to make a new analysis of the conditions that structured the activities of both Left and Right.

To speak of a Women's Movement in Britain, however, gives the developing feminist argument an appearance of greater coherence than it had. It grew out of a cluster of disparate campaigns and events: the example of the Women's Movement in America; industrial disputes such as that over trawler safety in Hull and the claim of female machinists at Ford's in Dagenham to be graded and paid the same as men; the arguments for sexual freedom based on the theories of Wilhelm Reich, as in Germaine Greer's bestselling *The Female Eunuch* (1970); the popularity of Simone de Beauvoir's *The Second Sex* (first translated into English in 1953); the radicalising effect which the student campaigns had on women members of the International Socialists and the International Marxist Group; the growth of women's groups; the impact of demonstrations such as that against the Miss World Contest in London in 1970. Attempts to co-ordinate the movement as a whole through committees and annual conferences broke down, indeed the preferred structure of small groups and a co-operative network expressly avoided a hierarchical or disciplined organisation, as might have been the "masculine" model.

Although most British feminists emerged from a background in left-wing politics (and were mainly middle-class), a feminist analysis showed that male oppression existed in *all* classes, cutting across the customary class-based method of Left-cultural analysis. The issue of separatism not only divided feminists from the male world of class-based politics, but split the movement itself between "socialist feminists" who saw capitalism as the source of oppression regardless of sex, and the "radical feminists" who wished to establish a purely feminine sphere opposed to men.

These limiting differences were not yet serious at the conference at Ruskin College in February 1970. The reasons for the conference show what forces the new cultural critiques of the fifties had helped to unleash. E. P. Thompson's arguments for "history from below" had encouraged the formation of the 'History Workshop' movement at Ruskin where, as an independent college funded by the trades unions with a strong working-class intake, Labour history and oral history were part of a socialist agenda. Raphael Samuel, one of the founders of the *Universities and Left Review* in 1957, became a tutor in social history at Ruskin in 1963 and, critical of the examination system 'and the humiliations which it imposed on adult students', he encouraged working men and women to write their own history.[71] Under his aegis a series of annual History Workshops began to be held from 1967. (The term was a homage to Joan Littlewood's Theatre Workshop, and became generally adopted by the Left as an emblem of democratic good practice.) Women participants however became unhappy at the male-dominated nature of these events, and their discontent led them to organise the first National Women's Conference at Ruskin in 1970. The conference, attended by both men and women, created a focus that had been lacking and effectively launched the movement, although the Women's National Co-ordinating Committee which it established collapsed the following year. The annual National Women's Liberation Conferences that followed as a result of the Ruskin conference ended in 1978 when the divisions between the radical, separatist wing and the socialist feminists could no longer be bridged.

The feminist viewpoint began to be expressed both in terms of creativity and criticism. The director Buzz Goodbody, trying to make her way in the masculine world of the Royal Shakespeare Company, helped to start the first Women's Street Theatre Group in order to take part in the first Women's Liberation March on International Women's Day in March 1971. In 1973 a Women's Theatre Festival led to the formation of the Women's Theatre Group and women dramatists such as Caryl Churchill, Micheline Wandor and Pam Gems found they had a new and supportive context for their work as the status of women within the theatre began to be reconsidered. Women artists similarly began to work together to claim the attention that they had been denied: in March 1971, also coinciding with the women's liberation demonstration, the Woodstock Gallery in London mounted a show by the Women's Liberation Art Group. When the Artists' Union was formed in 1972 a Women's Workshop was established as a separate chapter of the union, and a Women's Art History Collective was also associated with the union. In 1973 a joint show at Swiss Cottage Library, 'Womanpower', drew the hostile attention of the Festival of Light because it included paintings of women (including one described as God) giving birth. 'Womanpower' asserted not only that women (including mothers) had the right to be professional painters, but that their experience gave them access to subjects closed to men, which could be presented in a specifically feminist way.

The growing recognition that women were disadvantaged by the male domination of art and its institutions led to five women artists being invited to be the selectors of the Arts Council's second 'Hayward Annual' show of contemporary art in 1978. The art historians Rozsika Parker and Griselda Pollock describe this as 'the major breach into official culture on behalf of women in Britain'.[72] The publication of Lisa Tickner's article 'The Body Politic: Female Sexuality and Women Artists since 1970' in the second issue of the journal *Art History* in 1978 made a similar break in the defences of academic art history.

One of the differences between feminist criticism and traditional approaches was that feminists were ready to celebrate as well as criticise. Part of the project was to rediscover and recover from the past women artists and writers who had, in the title of Sheila Rowbotham's 1971 study, been *Hidden from History*. This became a significant element in the work of the growing women's press (both *Spare Rib* and *Cosmopolitan*, the magazines of what might be called the radical and the consumerist wing of the Women's Movement, were launched in 1972). The Virago imprint first appeared in 1975 and became an independent publishing house in 1977, the Women's Press followed in 1978.

Many of the hopes with which the Women's Movement began in 1970 were not realised. The "four demands" agreed at the Ruskin conference – equal pay, equal education and opportunity, twenty-four-hour nurseries, and free contraception and abortion on demand – remained largely unmet. An Equal Pay Act was passed in 1970, imposing conditions of equal pay for equal work that were to come into force in 1975, but women's average pay has remained less than that of men, and the employment of women in part-time jobs meant that many of them were low paid. The Sex Discrimination Act and the creation of an Equal Opportunities Commission in 1975 were further official recognition of women's disadvantaged position, but material progress was slow.

The effect of the Women's Movement was to raise, from a particularly acute angle, the question of the relationship between social and individual identity, and the effect of cultural practices as mediators of that relationship. Reading groups gathered to study the ideas of Karl Marx, Antonio Gramsci and Louis Althusser. Juliet Mitchell's *Psychoanalysis and Feminism* (1975) drew on Jacques Lacan's theory of "subject formation" to show how the signifying practices of culture and language helped to construct feminine identity and define sexuality. Sheila Rowbotham's *Woman's Consciousness, Man's World* (1973) demonstrated that women suffered under a masculine, as well as capitalist, hegemony:

> Values linger on after the social structures which conceived them. Our ideas of what is "feminine" are a strange bundle of assumptions, some of which belong to the Victorian middle class and others which simply rationalise the form patriarchy takes in capitalism now. Either way the notion of "femininity" is a convenient means of making us believe submission is somehow natural.[73]

The feminist insistence that the personal was also the political served to reinforce the general argument on the Left that political oppression operated at, and could be challenged at, the level of the cultural. The effect of the failure of the "cultural revolution" of 1968 was therefore to make culture more important, not less. The aim of "culturalism", as it became known, was to graft the theories of continental Marxism onto the essentially empiricist British tradition of textual criticism and moral judgement. In order to pursue the political agenda of the cultural criticism developed by the New Left, however (namely, the democratisation of culture as part of a broader socialist programme), it was essential that culture should be seen to have a genuine autonomy, so that it could be shown to be acting on, and not just reacting to, social and economic conditions as a whole. The original Marxist model of an economic base that determined the nature of a cultural superstructure was therefore too limiting, for it left no room for culture as an autonomous, material practice.

On the Continent, twentieth-century Marxist thinkers – Antonio Gramsci, Georg Lukács, Walter Benjamin, the Frankfurt School, Jean-Paul Sartre, Lucien Goldmann and Louis Althusser – had long been refining the cultural theory that Marx himself had left only in outline, but it wasn't until the seventies that this became fully available for adaptation into the British tradition. This process can be traced in the work of Raymond Williams himself, from his essay on Lucien Goldmann in the *New Left Review* in 1971; to his rethinking of the theory of base and superstructure in 1973, again in an essay in the *New Left Review*; to his critique of the "Cambridge" approach to English literature in *The Country and the City* (1973); and finally to *Marxism and Literature*, published in 1977. An autobiographical introduction described the assimilation of Marx's historical materialism to what Williams called 'cultural materialism'.[74] Though a variation on Marxist theory, it was nonetheless explicitly Marxist: culture itself is seen as a form of production, producing ideas and institutions which have their own material effects, notably the maintenance (and on occasion disruption) of hegemony. Literature and literary criticism have their place within cultural materialism, but the theory logically emerges not in literary, but in cultural studies.

The seventies was the decade in which the advocates of cultural studies fought to establish a proper place for themselves within higher education. The older university bastions of the academy were largely resistant, except where cultural studies could be smuggled in as art history, or social history. The long-felt concern about the effect of the mass media had provided opportunities for media studies: the University of Leicester established a Centre for Mass Communication Research in 1966, the same year that Leeds set up a Centre for Television Research. The first chair in film studies was established by London University in 1967. The University of Glasgow's Media Group was to follow in 1974; in 1977 Cardiff became another centre for communications research and the Open University launched a course in mass communications and society. The most significant moves towards establishing cultural studies as a separate academic entity, however, were at Birmingham, where Hoggart's Centre for Contemporary Cultural Studies, in the words of Stuart Hall, ceased to be 'a dependent intellectual colony' of its suspicious patrons, the departments of English and Sociology.[75]

That this was so was due to Hall himself, and it was under his direction that, as the only university post-graduate institute specifically addressing cultural issues, the Centre became the most important and influential location for the cultural studies debate. In 1968 he had taken over as acting director of the Centre when Hoggart took up a temporary post as assistant director-general of UNESCO. Hall was confirmed as director in 1972 after Hoggart's appointment at UNESCO was extended and he decided not to return to Birmingham. The university conducted an inquiry into the Centre before confirming Hall's appointment, but at the same time the Centre was released from its ties to the English Department and was given a base within the Faculty of Arts. Richard Johnson, a senior lecturer in social history, joined the staff from the Department of Economic History; Michael Green, who had divided his time between the Centre and the English Faculty, became a full-time lecturer in 1976. Under Hoggart such Leavisite practices as exercises in close reading had been continued, but under Hall literary studies were redefined within what, in the Centre's report for 1968–9, Hall called ' "a centre for the study of culture". Culture, then, not as a body of work, or particular media, or even as a set of ideal standards and rules, but rather as lived experience, the consciousness of a whole society: that peculiar order, pattern, configuration of valued experience, expressed now in imaginative art of the highest order, now in the most popular and proverbial of forms, in gesture and language, in myth and ideology, in modes of communication and in forms of social relationship and organisation.'[70]

By the time Hall left Birmingham in 1979 for the Open University, the Centre for Contemporary Cultural Studies had more than doubled in size, with three staff members, three research fellows and over forty post-graduate students, several of whom were to become authorities in their own right in the eighties. In addition to academic work, the Centre also undertook commissions – for instance, research on education policy for the Labour Party and on television for UNESCO – and contributed to Workers' Educational Association day schools. In 1971 Hall instituted the regular publication of *Working Papers in Cultural Studies*, producing ten issues by 1977, when Hutchinson began to publish an annual series focusing on different aspects of the Centre's work. The main fields of study were popular culture, the media, language and women's studies, but what distinguished the Centre was the collective nature of its undertakings and its intensive programme of seminars. Most post-graduate academic research is conducted in lonely isolation, but at the Centre both research and publication were shared responsibilities. (This could be carried to extreme lengths: when a group presented its work at a conference, each paragraph of a paper might be read by a different member of the group.) The origins of this approach lay in a 'General Theory Seminar' where the debate over methodology raged furiously as the importation of continental theory gathered pace. Hall has admitted: 'There is no doubt that the Centre was, for a time, over-preoccupied with these difficult theoretical issues.'[77]

The general seminar became too large, and spawned a series of working sub-groups – 'Work Group', 'Literature Group', 'History Group', 'Mugging Group', etc. – which met to co-ordinate individual research and attempt to produce a collective view. This was not always possible. The Women's Studies Group, formed in 1974, found itself battling for a feminist identity within the Centre as well as trying to establish the validity of women's studies outside it, and much energy was devoted to the question of the inclusion or exclusion of men from the group. The group eventually settled on a project to develop a Marxist approach to the subordination of women, which was to emerge as the collective publication *Women Take Issue* in 1978. Political differences continued, however, and the editors warned: 'These political differences make it impossible for us to agree on a conclusion.'[78]

Although the intellectual and emotional intensity of the Centre's collective work during the seventies undoubtedly achieved Hall's aim of putting cultural studies on the academic map, Hall was always careful to emphasise that the Centre's intention was never to impose an orthodoxy, or even to establish cultural studies as an academic "discipline". Rather, it was the point of intersection between a number of disciplines, from anthropology and sociology to literary criticism, and the intersection was often explosive. Hall recalled in 1990: 'There is no such thing as the Birmingham school. . . . My memories of Birmingham are mainly of rows, debates, arguments, of people walking out of rooms.'[79]

Many of these debates were about the role of structuralism. The first collective practical research group, established in 1968, applied the theories of Claude Lévi-Strauss and Roland Barthes to a study of *Woman* and *Woman's Own*. Essays by Barthes and Umberto Eco appeared in translation in early numbers of *Working Papers*. But where French structuralists tended to reduce all signs to a system of language, Hall and his colleagues modified and developed the structuralist approach by locating language within social practice. Culture, as a system of signs located in "texts" that could be verbal, visual or institutional, was treated as a "signifying practice", with its own ideological significance that related to other material practices in society. To this extent, structuralism and theories of ideology derived from Althusser were absorbed into and modified the "culturalist" tradition. Hall has recorded this guarded acceptance: 'Whatever else it could or could not do, structuralism displaced "man in general" from the full intentional centre of the cultural project. It thus ended a certain theoretical innocence, whatever the critiques of structuralist theories which then had to be made. It made culture, in its expressive sense, conditional – because conditioned. It obliged us to rethink the "cultural" as a set of practices: to think of the material conditions of signification and its necessary determinedness.'[80]

The penetration of structuralism was such that by 1974 the Centre appeared to have broken almost completely with the literary tradition that had shaped its founder, Richard Hoggart. The contents of *Working Papers* Number 6, titled 'Cultural Studies and Ideology', explained its collective six editors: 'signify our experience in this Centre, of a theoretical shift in our approach to cultural studies. . . . We are signalling retrospectively, from an emerging Marxist perspective, the theoretical and political limitations of the liberal radicalism from which "cultural studies" and the Centre emerged.'[81] This philosophical development, influenced by Althusser, was an attempt to come to terms with a theory of ideology that, among other things, exposed the "humanist" thrust of literature-based cultural studies as one more form of ideological domination. Semiology helped to explain the relationship between ideological meanings and social practices. But the abstract nature of this approach limited its concrete application, and at a moment of acute political sensitivity, at least in the radical circles from which most of the Centre's cadre was drawn, the editorial collective of *Working Papers* Number 6 could not escape their sense of historical responsibility: 'Cultural studies proceeded in the context of: firstly, the recognition of cultural domination as a special area of politics; secondly, the emergence of "cultural politics" as a distinctive movement; and thirdly, the failure of the revolutionary left to take even a minimal cognisance of the political implications of this context.'[82]

This is a restatement, in the characteristic language of the Centre, of the sense of frustration and blockage, noted earlier, that was felt throughout the radical Left in the early seventies. 'The academic environment tends to absorb our politics; the local political group tends to define too narrowly the focus of our theory,' the editors complained.[83] 'We have as yet no adequate analysis of the nature and extent of cultural hegemony in this society.'[84] It is in this context that Stuart Hall's comment should be recalled, made in 1990 and quoted in Chapter IV (p. 113), that although the formation of the Centre for Contemporary Cultural Studies was a retreat from the direct engagement of the New Left in the early sixties, 'it was politics by other means'.[85]

The task of the Centre was to understand the failure of the hopes of 1968, to account for the ability of ruling interests to absorb pressures for change and frustrate challenges to their authority, to reveal the systems of domination which held social progress in check. All this could be done by conducting an analysis of 'the nature and extent of cultural hegemony' of whose inadequacy the editors of *Working Papers* Number 6 complained. Thus Gramsci's theory of hegemony became one of the Centre's principal organising ideas. In the collective publications *Resistance Through Rituals* (1975) and *Policing the Crisis* (1978) the Centre anatomised the breakdown of the consensus that had sustained British governments since the war:

> This is no longer a period of ruling-class hegemony: it is the opening of a serious 'crisis in hegemony'. And here, of course, not only do the social contradictions begin to multiply in areas far beyond that of the economic and productive relations, but here, also, the varying forms of social resistance, class struggle and dissent begin to reappear. There is certainly no overall coherence to these forms of resistance – indeed, in their early manifestations, they resolutely refuse to assume an explicitly political form at all. The British crisis is, perhaps, peculiar precisely in terms of the massive *displacement* of political class struggle into new forms of social, moral and ideological protest and dissent, as well as in terms of the revival, after 1970, of a peculiarly intense kind of economism – a defensive working-class syndicalism.[86]

Faced with what was identified as 'the birth of a law-and-order society' students and teachers at the Centre were drawn to the study of those groups which manifested resistance to the dominant sources of power, the "subcultures" whose challenge to authority was expressed not politically, but culturally.[87] The main roots of subcultural theory lay in sociology and the study of juvenile delinquency. The methodology also was sociological, in that it relied heavily on "participant observation" and the "ethnographic" practices of anthropology. During the sixties "delinquency" had come to be seen as taking too criminological an approach to the subject, especially when drug-taking became a recreation amongst the middle classes (including sociologists). The term "deviancy" was preferred, which lost none of the concept's oppositional inflections. In 1968 the National Deviancy Conference was established to encourage a more sophisticated approach that took in the effects of "labelling" on subcultures by the mass media and public opinion. Stan Cohen's study of mods and rockers, *Moral Panics and Folk Devils* (1972), examined the way in which the reporting of events shaped the perception of certain subcultures as "folk devils" and provoked "moral panics" which articulated and contained the anxieties of society.

From the 'emerging Marxist perspective' of the Centre for Contemporary Cultural Studies, the study of subcultures was a way of reintroducing the idea of class – meaning the working class – which had been fashionably discounted during the affluent sixties, when class was argued to be no longer an issue, because "embourgeoisement" had blunted the workers' revolutionary potential. Not only did the group question this thesis, the argument from subcultures also gave them a more subtle case to make: 'The idea of the "disappearance of the class as a whole" is replaced by the far more complex and differentiated picture of how the different sectors and strata of a class are driven into different courses and options by their determining socio-economic circumstances.'[88] The interest lay in the way these circumstances were imaginatively transformed through cultural expressions of identity and creative adaptability. It was both culture as "a whole way of life" and culture as "a whole way of struggle":

> The latent function of the subculture is this – to express and resolve, albeit "magically", the contradictions which remain hidden or unresolved in the parent culture. The succession of subcultures which this parent culture generated can thus all be considered as so many variations on a central theme – the contradiction at an ideological level, between traditional working-class puritanism, and the new ideology of consumption: at an economic level between a part of the socially mobile élite, or a part of the new lumpen.[89]

The work of the Subcultures Group was therefore to dismantle the broad term "youth culture" which had been applied in the sixties and examine more carefully the way a whole range of subcultures – Teds, Mods, Skinheads, Drug-users, Commune Dwellers, Rastafarians and Rude Boys – created their own subculture within the "parent" culture of their class and in relation to the hegemonic subordination of that class as a whole.

The issue that remained unresolved, however, was to what extent the 'magical' resolutions that these different ritualistic assertions of identity represented were truly capable of resisting domination. In spite of their belief in the 'objective oppositional content of working-class subcultures',[90] none of the contributors to Hall and Jefferson's volume of essays on youth subcultures, *Resistance Through Rituals*, either in that volume or in work developed from it – notably Paul Willis's *Learning to Labour* (1977) and *Profane Culture* (1978), and Dick Hebdige's *Subculture: The Meaning of Style* (1979) – were able to demonstrate that there was a 'subcultural solution' to the economic and educational disadvantages of the working class: 'Subcultural strategies cannot match, meet or answer the structuring dimensions emerging in this period for the class as a whole.'[91] Those 'structuring dimensions' were economic anxieties about inflation and unemployment, fear of social breakdown provoked by industrial unrest and the rise in reported crime, and the crisis of national identity, all of which found expression in the "moral panic" about race and the supposedly black crime of mugging. In *Policing the Crisis*, the Centre for Contemporary Cultural Studies produced a masterly account of the constituent elements in the crisis, and correctly forecast an authoritarian response to it. In the circumstances, to be right was small consolation.

Faced by the evident decay of the present, it is no surprise that many people should have sympathised with the views of Kenneth Clark in *Civilisation* and shown a preference for the past. With the encouragement of a powerful and effective lobby the word "heritage" began to acquire a special resonance as a source of value and reassurance. While this development had political overtones – in her first speech as leader of the Conservative Party at its annual conference in 1975 Margaret Thatcher criticised 'the deliberate attack on our heritage and our great past'[92] – the turn to the past that became manifest in the seventies was a widespread response. The attempted modernisation of the British economy in the sixties and the destructive effect it had on the environment in terms of new developments, new roads, and the loss of familiar patterns of life was unsettling. The change to decimal coinage in 1970 was just one more rupture with ancient traditions. Modernisation in the sixties was followed by recession in the seventies, and the growing perception of national decline. As Roy Strong, Director of the Victoria and Albert Museum and a leading member of the rapidly forming heritage lobby, wrote in 1978: 'We are all aware of problems and troubles, of changes within the structure of society, of the dissolution of old values and standards. For the lucky few this may be exhilarating, even exciting, but for the majority it is confusing, threatening and dispiriting. The heritage represents some form of security, a point of reference, a refuge perhaps, something visible and tangible which, within a topsy and turvy world, seems stable and unchanged. Our environmental heritage . . . is therefore a deeply stabilising and unifying element within our society.'[93]

Indications of this search for reassurance and a sense of authenticity based on tradition ranged from the cult of the country house as a fetish of Englishness, to the foundation of the Campaign for Real Ale in 1971. Industrial archaeology became a recognised discipline in the seventies, preservation societies of all kinds flourished and new museums opened at the rate of one a fortnight. In 1975 the Council of Europe organised European Architectural Heritage Year, which encouraged the creation of a new kind of institution, the "heritage centre". Unlike museums, heritage centres were not intended to hold large collections of artefacts and were usually established in a redundant building such as a church – as was the very first one, in Chester – in order to serve as a focus for the celebration of local history and identity. The original social purpose of the heritage centre became distorted by the pressures of the tourist industry, which treated them simply as cosmetic "attractions", profitably reviving the past to compensate for the poverty of the present.

The political element in the growing heritage industry became evident when the second Wilson government attempted to introduce a wealth tax on personal fortunes of over one hundred thousand pounds, based on valuations of investments, land, houses, copyrights, goods and chattels. Had the tax been imposed, it would have led to a far greater redistribution of wealth than anything achieved by the Labour government of 1945. Special exemptions were to be made for artworks and houses on display or accessible to the public – as was already the case with death duties – but it was likely that many "heritage" items in private hands would have been sold to meet the tax. First suggested in a Labour Party policy document in 1969, the proposal for a wealth tax was presented in Denis Healey's March 1974 budget, followed by a Green Paper published in August.

Even before the Green Paper was released a protest organisation, Heritage in Danger, established by the art dealer Hugh Leggatt, was in action. The parliamentary committee set up to examine the proposal was confronted by a barrage of hostile evidence from the great and the good. The case for Heritage in Danger was presented by Lord Goodman, and evidence was submitted by the Country Landowners' Association, the Historic Houses Association, the Museums Association, the Tate Gallery, the British Museum, the Historic Buildings Council, the Standing Commission on Museums and Galleries, the British Tourist Authority, the Reviewing Committee on the Export of Works of Art, the National Art Collections Fund and the Antique Dealers' Association. The Arts Council expressed its concern about the tax's effect on living artists. The National Trust submitted a memorandum that summed up the argument: 'The National Trust's anxieties arise from the fear that private owners, in whose ownership the bulk of the national heritage at present lies, may be forced by the new taxes and inflation to dispose of their property and that as a result the national heritage will be greatly reduced or dispersed.'[94] The argument that this property might pass into public ownership, or be made more accessible to the "nation" as a result of securing exemption from the tax did not carry much weight.

The lobby successfully forged the emotive issue of "the national heritage" into a shield against new taxation on any kind of private property. The select committee was unable to agree, producing five conflicting draft reports, which were debated in December 1975. Hugh Jenkins, who, unlike his civil servants, was against exemption for works of art from the tax, noted: 'Throughout the whole debate the Tories plugged the idea that anyone who possesses a valuable work himself becomes precious.'[95] Wilson had, however, ceased to favour the idea of a wealth tax by the time the select committee reported, and although still officially Labour policy – it was one of the concessions offered to the unions in the Social Contract – the proposal was quietly abandoned.

The idea that Britain's heritage – and therefore a significant element in national identity – was in danger proved a resonant theme. At the height of the wealth tax debate in the autumn of 1974 the Victoria and Albert Museum mounted a special exhibition entitled *The Destruction of the Country House 1875–1975*, a covert piece of propaganda against the wealth tax and a lament for the disappearance of a genteel way of life. Roy Strong argued in his introduction to the exhibition: 'The great houses of England and their occupants represent a continuity within our society. . . . Country-house owners are the hereditary custodians of what was one of the most vital forces of cultural creation in our history.'[96] The country house certainly had a powerful hold on the English imagination, as novels, plays, films and television programmes testified. It represented the pastoral virtues of Deep England over against the corruptions of the City; it embodied "history" as the steady accretion of layers of memory associated with family life and an extended community surrounding it. It gave visible form to both change and decay. It also embodied hierarchy, within itself, in terms of the social organisation of the architecture, and in the gradations of scale from hunting lodge to the splendours of Blenheim or Castle Howard (illustration 17). Tom Nairn has argued that the country house contains all the attributes of the nation – and vice versa. 'Great Britain herself is the stately home: the State which is also Home, a power-structure which could not so convincingly be either of these things without the Crown, and a family still in residence. Where appearance is itself a dimension of power, only through them can an apparatus of authority be made to seem so profoundly homely to its subjects.'[97]

Yet such powerful symbols (and the reality they express) appear most significant when they are most "in danger". Anniversaries have their own imperatives, but there is significance in the way in which events are selected and presented for celebration. In 1976 a quarter of a century had passed since the Festival of Britain, and the Victoria and Albert Museum mounted a commemorative exhibition. In the catalogue the design historian Reyner Banham reflected on the changes that twenty-five years had brought: 'Partly, there is now a kind of mixture of sentimentality and astonishment about the whole enterprise. The idea of leadership in public taste with an almost formally constituted establishment is now almost as incredible as it is, to some minds, attractive – especially in the picture it presents of an apparently orderly structure of social castes who "knew their place" in a way that teenagers, trades-unionists and trend-setters, among everybody else, no longer do.'[98] A similar mixture of sentimentality and regret – though less astonishment – accompanied the twenty-fifth anniversary of the accession of Queen Elizabeth II in the following year.

In 1969 the Queen and her advisers had repeated the double strategy of attempted modernisation on the one hand and the assertion of traditional authority on the other that had been deployed in the Coronation celebrations of 1953. As nationalist fervour grew in both Scotland and Wales, the Queen decided to fulfil a commitment made in 1958 to invest her eldest son at the age of twenty-one as Prince of Wales – historically, an ancient symbol of English domination of the Welsh. Prince Charles was temporarily withdrawn from Trinity College, Cambridge in order to study Welsh at University College, Aberystwyth, so that he could make a speech in Welsh at the 1969 Eisteddfod. Preparations meanwhile went ahead for his investiture at Caernarfon Castle on 1 July where, as Constable, his uncle by marriage, the photographer Lord Snowdon, was in charge of devising a ceremony which would also be the first major television outside broadcast in colour. The only previous time this ceremony had been staged was in 1911, for the future Edward VIII, when the Prime Minister Lloyd George was strongly suspected of seeking to exploit royal authority during the disestablishment of the Welsh Church. The atmosphere in 1969 was similarly politically charged, for the investiture was greeted in Wales with resentment and threats of violence. There were fifteen bomb incidents in the run-up to the investiture, culminating with the deaths of two bombers on the eve of the ceremony, which was very nearly cancelled as a result, although on the day it passed off without incident.

On the night before this anachronistic event, however, the Crown played its modernising card, with the transmission of the television documentary *Royal Family*, which presented the Queen and her offspring as just that, in an informal atmosphere of barbecues and country pursuits. The programme was highly successful, but as Charles's biographer Anthony Holden has remarked, it turned out to be 'a Frankenstein's Monster, creating a public demand for private royal titbits far in excess of supply'.[99] *Royal Family* proved to be the opening episode in the royal soap opera that Malcolm Muggeridge had warned about in 1955. Its first victim was Princess Margaret, divorced in 1978, and it reached its nadir with Prince Charles's divorce in 1996.

By the time of the Queen's Silver Jubilee in 1977, the sense of national decline and dissension was endemic. By 1976 inflation had become so bad, and Britain's international economic position so low, that total collapse of the economy could only be prevented by negotiating a loan from the International Monetary Fund, the price of which was large cuts in government spending and a first taste of monetarism from a Labour government. Having lost his majority through by-elections, and with his first devolution proposals in ruins, in March 1977 James Callaghan avoided defeat by making a pact with the Liberals. As Phillip Whitehead has written: 'The celebration of Elizabeth II's Silver Jubilee as Queen of the United Kingdom of Great Britain and Northern Ireland seemed a chancy affair at such a time. In the event the British, and two-thirds of the Northern Irish, decided that one way to confront a future that might not work was with the trappings of a past which had worked.'[100] The journalist Norman Shrapnel was of a similar opinion: 'The event seemed to fill a number of unconscious needs, chiming fortunately for one thing, with the current taste for nostalgia. . . . The celebrations in the summer of 1977 were in most respects quite unlike modern life, with a brassy Edwardian air reminiscent of Elgar and a cheerfulness which British cities had not seen for years.'[101]

British "cheerfulness" in adversity had been one of the constant themes of wartime propaganda, and along with bell-ringing and bonfires, the most characteristic popular way of celebrating the Jubilee was the street party, of which there were four thousand in London alone. Street parties were a happy memory of the end of the war, and their revival was a half-conscious echo of the social solidarity of that time, an attempt to restore a sense of community even, as at Queen Street, Rugely, when the community no longer existed. Queen Street had been demolished and redeveloped, but the former residents came together for a party on the site. What both the monarch and her subjects seemed to be celebrating above all was the sheer fact of survival. The historian David Cannadine has concluded: 'The jubilee was an expression of national and imperial decline, an attempt to persuade, by pomp and circumstance, that no such decline had really taken place, or to argue that, even if it had, it really did not matter.'[102]

Yet what the celebrations were intended to mask or to deny did matter, and it found its expression in a collision between the most enduring icon of national identity and a subculture which did not even exist in 1972, but which by 1977 had become the encapsulating image of the British crisis. The contrast between a ritualised, even magical, past and an uncertain and violent present was captured in Derek Jarman's film *Jubilee*, shot in 1977 as 'a fantasy documentary fabricated so that documentary and fictional forms are confused and coalesce'.[103] The framing concept of the film parodied New Elizabethanism, in that Queen Elizabeth I is transported forward into the age of Queen Elizabeth II, to find herself in a desolate and derelict cityscape where guerrilla warfare has broken out between a fascist police force and armed punks. A rock version of 'Rule Britannia' parodies the political paranoia of the times as Britannia's bumps and grinds turn into a goose-step and Hitler's voice is heard against the howl of Stukas (illustration 13). A media mogul has taken over the world and bought Buckingham Palace from the liquidators; the only safe place is a cordoned-off Dorset, cleansed of blacks, homosexuals and Jews.

The history of punk is characterised by its intensity, and its brevity. Largely identified with the career of one particular group, the Sex Pistols, it began in the autumn of 1975 with their first live performance, and reached its apogee with the break-up of the group in the autumn of 1977. In February 1978 their bass guitarist, Sid Vicious, died from a drug overdose in New York while out on bail after being charged with the murder of his girlfriend Nancy Spungen. Other punk bands and singer-song-writers, notably the Buzzcocks, the Jam, the Clash, Mark E. Smith of the Fall and Elvis Costello, proved more durable, but it was the sudden explosion of groups inspired by the Sex Pistols, and their almost equally sudden disappearance or transmutation that marked the "moment" of punk.

Punk might have been created for the benefit of cultural theorists: it was the ultimate expression of "youth" culture in that it repelled most adults, provoked moral outrage in the popular press, and seemed intent on the destruction not only of middle-class values, but of itself. It was deviancy of a high degree, it confirmed the predictions of liberal sociologists concerned by the alienation of contemporary youth, and more than met the expectations of the media eager to generate a moral panic about law and order. Punk communicated itself entirely in cultural terms: in dress, where rips, zips and bondage-wear combined with the self-mutilation of tattoos and safety-pin punctures provided material ripe for the interpretations of the anthropologist; and in music, where the harsh sounds and brutal lyrics supplied a text supplemented by the crude artwork on record sleeves and teeshirts and in the self-generated "fanzines", all material ripe for the social historian.

"Participant observation" could be dangerous fun. But the curiosity of punk was the self-consciousness of these features. As Dick Hebdige, in *Subculture: The Meaning of Style*, has commented: 'Punks were not only directly *responding* to increasing joblessness, changing moral standards, the rediscovery of poverty, the Depression, etc., they were *dramatising* what had come to be called "Britain's decline". . . . The punks appropriated the rhetoric of crisis which had filled the airwaves and editorials throughout the period and translated it into tangible (and visible) terms.'[104]

Punk might have been invented for the cultural theorists – and the partial truth is that it was. The Sex Pistols were "authored" by their manager, Malcolm McLaren, who, with his partner the fashion designer Vivienne Westwood, was interested in having a group that would promote their clothes shop in the King's Road, which they had run under various names since 1971. McLaren's authorship of the Sex Pistols was inscribed in their contract, stating that 'the name "Sex Pistols" was created by the Manager and that such name belongs to and is owned by the Manager'.[105] McLaren had studied at a number of art schools, without graduating from any of them, but learning enough of the language to present himself convincingly as an artistic entrepreneur. In 1968 he and a fellow student, the graphic designer Jamie Reid, had led a sit-in at Croydon Art School that coincided with the more celebrated one at Hornsey. From Reid, McLaren picked up the principles of situationism, the anarchist movement that had been instrumental in setting off the *événements* in Paris in 1968. The particular appeal of situationism was the use of outrageous and symbolic acts to expose the sham of the "society of spectacle" which concealed the realities of capitalism. McLaren had participated in one such event in December 1968 when a group organised by the British situationist offshoot King Mob Echo went into the toy department of Selfridges' store and started handing out the toys as presents to passing children.

McLaren's *post-hoc* justification for his actions as manager of the Sex Pistols was the film *The Great Rock'n'Roll Swindle* which presented his activities as a situationist *détournement*, a deliberate act of provocation intended to turn things inside out, in this case exploiting the gullibility and rapacity of the recording business. He claimed to be exacting rock'n'roll's revenge on the capitalist industry for exploiting the anarchic values of rock'n'roll and turning it into a commodity like any other. In true situationist manner, this was not entirely true, for McLaren was himself an adept manipulator who wanted to make money and promote his products.

Punk's historians have acknowledged the managerial manipulation that went into the creation of punk: it was, in Greil Marcus's phrase, an 'art project', and was launched with performances in London art schools.[106] Jon Savage has described McLaren and Westwood using teenagers as experiments in social engineering, yet also writes of 'the cultural resistance that was Punk'.[107] The impact of punk cannot be accounted for by the activities of McLaren and Westwood alone. In a few months the example of the Sex Pistols had spawned a score of bands, revived the British recording industry and given fashion designers a whole new repertoire. However mediated, punk ritualised a resistance that was genuine. Hebdige has argued that punk needed to happen: 'The various stylistic ensembles adopted by the punks were undoubtedly expressive of genuine aggression, frustration and anxiety. But these statements, no matter how strangely constructed, were cast in a language which was generally available – a language which was current. This accounts, first, for the appropriateness of the punk metaphor for both the members of the subculture and its opponents and, second, for the success of the punk subculture as spectacle: its ability to symptomatise a whole cluster of contemporary problems.'[108]

The burden of Hebdige's argument was that punk was in itself a language in which it was possible to articulate a crisis in the British sense of identity, a language which "spoke" the actions of the actors and which, in true semiotic manner, was conveyed not merely in words, but in clothing and customs, in *style*. Style was the magical resolution to the question of subcultural resistance, for through constant innovation in codes of dress and behaviour, subcultures would continually challenge the hegemony of the norm and the recuperative powers of the dominant culture.

There are difficulties with this argument, but there were material (as opposed to purely linguistic) events which seemed to confirm punk's metaphorical power. The Clash's first single, 'White Riot', was a response to witnessing the riot that ended the 1976 Notting Hill Gate Carnival, a riot that was in part a response to the decision to have sixteen hundred policemen on duty to prevent disorder. The purest example of punk's subcultural resistance was the decision to release the Sex Pistols' 'God Save the Queen' to coincide with the climax of the Jubilee celebrations on 4 and 5 June 1977: 'God save the Queen/ She's not a human being/ There is no future/ In England's dream' (illustration 14).[109] For impure, commercial reasons, McLaren managed to engineer a situationist confrontation designed to infuriate authority. Consciously or unconsciously (and McLaren would never have used these words) a subculture set out to expose the official and unofficial operations that preserved the hegemony.

If that was indeed McLaren's aim, he succeeded. The resistance he met was not only cultural, but brought in hegemony's other instrument, coercion. The project encountered censorship, firstly when two record-processing plants refused to manufacture the disc, then when the BBC refused to play it, the Independent Broadcasting Authority banned its transmission on commercial television or radio, and major retailers refused to stock it. This did not prevent two hundred thousand copies being sold by the end of Jubilee week, but what appears to have been a quiet conspiracy within the record business meant that the Sex Pistols were deprived of the accolade of being number one in the sales chart.[110] The collision was more than symbolic. The Sex Pistols were arrested after a Thames riverboat party on Jubilee night; John Lydon and Jamie Reid, who designed the record cover, were later separately attacked and beaten up. Fights between the respective subcultures of punks and Teds became a regular feature on the King's Road.

The civil war in the background to Jarman's 'fantasy documentary' *Jubilee* was not explained in any way, but explanations were unnecessary, for something like a war was brewing between the supporters of the narrow Britishness of the National Front, and those most active on the Left, led by the Socialist Workers' Party. There was street fighting between the two groups in April and August of that year. The anarchic violence of punk, which had begun by deploying the visual rhetoric of swastikas and black leather as part of its shock tactics (Sid Vicious wrote the lyric 'Belsen Was a Gas' in 1976), and its aggressively proletarian style could easily have been recruited to the cause of the National Front, as were a number of skinhead bands. Yet punk's musical affinities to reggae – most markedly in the case of the Clash – also drew it towards an identification with the oppression of the blacks.

The Socialist Workers' Party successfully mobilised punk, not as a subcultural theory, but as a useful weapon against the National Front. The radical and libertarian associations of rock'n'roll had always sat uneasily with its function as the motor of a multi-million-pound entertainment industry. The career of Elvis Presley from "poor white" singing black songs, to hero of conservative middle-America topping the bill at Las Vegas is just one example of the ambiguities of popular music as a medium for protest – a problem the Sex Pistols were never to have to deal with. In 1976 two British stars brought rock'n'roll's supposed radicalism into question when the guitarist Eric Clapton made remarks in favour of Enoch Powell during a rock concert, and the singer David Bowie, then flirting with the stylistic repertoire of fascism during his "Berlin" period, made some questionable comments during an interview in *Playboy* magazine. In August 1976 a group of photographers and designers working at the printshop that produced *Socialist Worker* wrote letters to the popular music press in protest: 'Rock was and still can be a real progressive culture, not a packaged mail-order stick-on nightmare of mediocre garbage. Keep the faith, black and white unite and fight.'[111] The letters heralded a new vehicle for political activism, Rock Against Racism.

Most attempts by political parties to harness the energies of popular music founder on the structural differences between political and musical populism. Throughout the sixties the puritanism of the radical Left and the hedonism of the counter-culture had been the cause of mutual suspicion, but Rock Against Racism had none of the Left's traditional contempt for the products of the capitalist entertainment industry. This was partly due to the contribution of David Widgery, Socialist Workers' Party member *and* former occasional editor of *Oz*. Widgery did not wish merely to reclaim young rock fans who were straying into the paths of racism, but to reclaim what had originally driven rock'n'roll in the sixties. 'We aimed to rescue the energy of Russian revolutionary art, surrealism and rock and roll from the galleries, the advertising agencies and the record companies and use them again to change reality, as had always been intended. And have a party in the process.'[112]

Like punk, Rock Against Racism used the art school network to launch itself, making propaganda by organising "two-tone" events where black and white bands appeared on the same stage while stalls sold political literature. At the celebrations which Rock Against Racism organised in 1977 to mark the first time May Day became an official public holiday in Britain – at that quintessentially sixties venue the Round House – the team of graphic designers and photographers at the heart of the movement launched their newsletter *Temporary*

Hoarding, using many of the devices of the collaged, photo-litho-and-staples fanzines that had grown up around punk (illustration 15). The SWP, while undoubtedly directing events, were careful to respect the "do-it-yourself" element of punk, which had put so many fanzines, and bands, on the street. Punk, as the most anarchic, the most subversive, and potentially the most popular music of the moment, 'provided the circuitry', in Paul Gilroy's phrase, for connections to be made between love of music, hatred of racism and the various youth styles that represented more than mere consumption.[113] Punk's cry, 'No Future', was adapted to 'National Front: No Fun'.

Between 1977 and 1978 Rock Against Racism organised some two hundred events, among them a major rock concert for one hundred thousand people at Victoria Park in the East End of London after a march from Trafalgar Square in April 1978, and a series of smaller concerts in provincial cities. Just as "race" had become a figure for the crisis of identity felt in mainstream Britain since 1968, Rock Against Racism used racism as a symbol of the capitalist crisis and all the unacceptable social relations it was against, be it the neo-fascism of the National Front, or the idea of the nation projected by the popular nationalism stimulated by the Jubilee. In November 1977 RAR activists were instrumental in establishing a broader-based coalition, the Anti-Nazi League, which drew Labour MPs, actors, writers and academics into a single-issue electoral campaign aimed at defeating the National Front. RAR continued to organise events alongside and in support of the Anti-Nazi League which, like CND before it, felt obliged to present an older and more sober image than the anarchic appeal of punk's anti-politics. The rhetoric of national identity deployed by the Anti-Nazi League, as the name suggests, drew on the imagery of wartime solidarity, to which the National Front replied with its own xenophobic patriotism, neither side fully acknowledging the changes that had taken place since 1945.

Although the Anti-Nazi League's device of organising through interest groups – Teachers Against the Nazis, Dockers Against the Nazis and so on – lent itself to parody (and the National Front answered RAR with its own Rock Against Communism), the campaign did confront and harass the National Front at a moment when it seemed that it might establish a real political foothold. It is difficult to know whether the Anti-Nazi League or Margaret Thatcher should have more of the credit for the decline of the National Front after their losses in the 1979 general election, but with that election the political moment had passed for both sides, and while RAR and the Anti-Nazi League never formally stood down (resurfacing in 1993 in response to the rise of the British National Party), the Conservative victory forcefully changed the agenda for the Left as a whole.

Writing in 1981, David Widgery saw RAR as a victim of its own success: 'What is required of the political Left is the imagination, the patience and the political clarity to relate to all that passion. And perhaps save it from getting wasted. Otherwise we are waltzing with ourselves in a political hulk which may look imposing but which is sinking under the dead weight of its own outmoded cultural and political forms. At least the *Titanic*, they say, had a good band.'[114] Rock Against Racism's success in securing a temporary alliance between pop and politics was not forgotten: it provided a precedent for the charitable campaigns of the eighties, Band Aid and Live Aid. Though no less urgent a problem or worthy a cause, starvation in Africa was a simpler issue to address than the complex politics of race in Britain.

While the "moment of punk" shows that a subculture could indeed become the prism through which feelings of anxiety, alienation and opposition were concentrated in a single resonant image, the moment, though glorious, was brief. The "resistance" of punk, situated as it was within a set of meanings that were not of its creation, still could not escape the overarching power of the hegemony, as its symbols – in this case a musical style and code of dress – were turned into exploitable commodities. As Dick Hebdige pointed out: 'It is through this continual process of recuperation that the fractured order is repaired and the subculture incorporated as a diverting spectacle within the dominant mythology from which it in part emanates.'[115] Once that had happened, some new form of "resistance" might be devised, as in the sexual ambiguities of the "new romantics" who succeeded punk, or the heightened sense of "black British" identity in reggae, dub and rap. But the 'cycle leading from opposition to defusion, from resistance to incorporation encloses each successive subculture'.[116]

In his conclusion to *Subculture: The Meaning of Style*, Hebdige was forced to admit that 'we should be foolish to think that by tackling a subject so manifestly popular as youth style, we have resolved any of the contradictions which underlie contemporary cultural studies'.[117] The most fundamental of those contradictions was between the two methodologies which his own book had employed: the "culturalist" approach, which began with a specific social experience, examined the ways in which this was translated into the "signifying practices" of culture, and how this interacted with social experience as a whole; and the "structuralist" approach in which the signifying practices of language and ideology determined the specific experience. Crudely, the difference lay between an approach that treated culture as the determinant of ideology, and one that treated ideology as the determinant of culture. The original justification for what Williams had called 'cultural materialism' had been that culture was an autonomous practice with its own power to influence society as a whole. Structuralism ultimately denied that autonomy, and its humanistic impulse, since it held that culture was no more than an "effect" of language.

During the seventies the differences between these two approaches became more extreme, to the point where in 1979 Richard Johnson, a research fellow at the Birmingham Centre for Contemporary Cultural Studies, could write: 'The two traditions do not merely coexist but actively interrupt each other.'[118] There had indeed been fierce controversy between the Centre and writers associated with *Screen* magazine, who had most eagerly adopted the structuralist approach in the hope of developing a unified theory that demonstrated the links between signifying practices, ideology and individual subjectivity. But as structuralism moved into its "post-structuralist" phase, in response to the contemporary work of Julia Kristeva, Jacques Derrida and Michel Foucault, the gap that their work claimed to reveal between reality and representation grew so wide that it became possible to doubt whether meaning existed at all. Not only was our perception of what we take to be reality said to be so structured by language that reality existed only *in* language, but the very idea of a discrete, individual subject as the unified centre of perception dissolved into a slippery sea of floating signifiers. Structuralism, which had seemed to offer new ways of understanding the experience of culture, appeared ultimately to deny the possibility of experience altogether.

In the later seventies the *Screen* group began to lose faith in its methodology, as the possibility of producing a unified theory that would account for the relationship between subjectivity, signification and ideology appeared to recede, and the very search for a totalising explanation became suspect. "Theory" became an end in itself, so that, as Richard Johnson put it in 1979, it was difficult to know 'how to situate oneself within increasingly fractured sets of theoretical problematics. While theory has been overdeveloped and has tended to acquire a dynamic of its own, studies at a lower level of abstraction have tended to be neglected.'[119] Critical theory, as developed during the seventies, appeared to have no relation to any body of contemporary artistic or literary practice.

The struggle for supremacy between "culturalists" and "structuralists" found dramatic expression at Oxford in December 1979, when an evening debate at the thirteenth annual History Workshop was devoted to the issues raised by E. P. Thompson's *The Poverty of Theory*, published in 1978. Thompson, pained by a 'real sense of isolation and even of alienation' from the post-1968 new New Left,[120] had produced an excoriating attack on the extreme structuralist position of Althusserianism:

> This particular freak . . . has now lodged itself in a particular social *couche*, the bourgeois *lumpen-intelligentsia*: aspirant intellectuals, whose amateurish intellectual preparation disarms them before manifest absurdities and elementary philosophical blunders, and whose innocence in intellectual *practice* leaves them paralysed in the web of scholastic argument they encounter; and bourgeois, because while many of them would *like* to be "revolutionaries", they are themselves the products of a particular "conjuncture" which has broken the circuits between intellectuality and practical experience (both in real political movements, and in the actual segregation imposed by contemporary institutional structures) and hence they are able to perform *imaginary* revolutionary pyscho-dramas (in which each outbids the other in adopting ferocious verbal postures) while in fact falling back upon a very old tradition of bourgeois élitism for which Althusserian theory is exactly tailored.[121]

Thompson was invited to defend his thesis in a three-sided debate with Stuart Hall and Richard Johnson before a partisan audience which would not take kindly to being termed "lumpen-intelligentsia", assembled in a chilly disused church. While Hall spoke for Thompson against the 'theoretical terrorism' of Althusserians, but against his quasi-mystical elevation of "history", Johnson spoke for the uses of theory and against Thompson's 'absolutism'. Thompson, rising magisterially to the occasion, 'proceeded on a demolition job on his critics which caused evident personal pain and discomfort to many of those present', as Raphael Samuel has recorded. 'The aftermath of the Saturday night's fusillade hung like a pall of smoke over the rest of the conference.'[122]

Stuart Hall's view in 1980 was: 'Neither "culturalism" nor

"structuralism" is, in its present manifestation, adequate to the task of constructing the study of culture as a conceptually clarified and theoretically informed domain of study.'[123] Dick Hebdige had put it more bluntly: 'We are in society but not inside it, producing analyses of popular culture which are themselves anything but popular.'[124] Encouraged by Hall, the general response at Birmingham to the culturalist/structuralist impasse was a return to a more concrete form of research into political and civil institutions, as signalled by the publication of *Policing the Crisis* in 1978, where the analysis of "Thatcherism" as an organised and articulate fraction of the radical Right *within the leadership of the Conservative Party itself* (italics his) begins to be made.[125] When Hall left the Centre in 1979 to take up the chair of sociology at the Open University he was succeeded by Richard Johnson, who was committed to a more historical approach, to the point of calling for 'histories of cultural studies to trace the recurrent dilemmas'.[126] That Hall, who began by studying English literature, should become responsible for a department of sociology was evidence of the changes that had taken place in both fields, and of the rising influence of cultural studies. In the eighties, through his association with *Marxism Today*, Hall, like E. P. Thompson with his campaign for European Nuclear Disarmament, would make his political position an explicit, as opposed to implicit, feature in his writing.

In 1968 Perry Anderson in the *New Left Review* had called for 'the production and circulation of theory'.[127] It is clear that during the seventies the radical intelligentsia produced little else. Yet in spite of the sophistication of their theories, the tide of events was flowing against them, and it is possible to see the influence of those events in the self-doubt that the assessments of 1979 and 1980 convey. David Widgery, no theoretician, recorded in 1979 that 'there has been a certain faltering of impetus' both in the revolutionary Left and the Women's Movement in the face of the Rightwards shift in the popular mood.[128] 'The student visions of 1968, the working-class insurgency of 1972 and 1974, the socialist parties which tried to fuse them – all three hit an impasse in the late 1970s.'[129] In the very different circumstances of 1988, Dick Hebdige's view of "the moment" of theories of subcultural resistance had changed: 'The idea of subculture-as-negation grew up alongside punk, remained inextricably linked to it and died when it died.'[130]

In spite of the achievements of the Birmingham Centre for

Contemporary Cultural Studies in what, thanks to the educational policies and politics of the eighties, was to turn out to have been its heyday, the spread of cultural studies as an academic subject was limited to a dozen polytechnics, while the universities largely ignored it. Cultural studies were on the map, but still in an uncertain border territory between better-established disciplines. The prevailing attitude at the older universities was summed up by the dispute at Cambridge in 1980, when a temporary lecturer, Colin MacCabe, author of a book on structuralism and a former editor of *Screen*, was refused a permanent post by the English Faculty, thus bringing to a halt moves to shift the English Tripos towards becoming a cultural studies degree. In addition to the only marginal acceptance of cultural studies within academe, it was not encouraging for a new subject that from 1979 onwards there was a growing sense that all universities and polytechnics were under threat from the abrasive attitude to higher education shown by the new Conservative government.

Yet there was a more profound reason for the uncertainty and self-questioning of the cultural theorists. One of the effects of the Marxist-structuralist debate in the seventies – particularly in its Althusserian inflection – was to demolish the authority of English literature as the central source of cultural value within the British tradition – the source it had been before Matthew Arnold and after Richard Hoggart, and whose authority the promoters of the *Black Papers* had campaigned to restore. In *Criticism and Ideology*, published in 1976, Terence Eagleton argued:

> There is no "immanent" value – no value which is not *transitive*. Literary value is a phenomenon which is *produced* in that ideological appropriation of the text, that "consumptional production" of the work, which is the act of reading. It is always *relational* value: "exchange-value". The histories of "value" are a sub-sector of the histories of literary-ideological receptive practices – practices which are in no sense a mere "consumption" of a finished product, but which can be studied as a determinate (re)production of the text. We read ("consume") what an ideology reads ("produces") for us.[131]

The question of value troubled not only literary critics. In 1978 the art critic Peter Fuller, at that stage in his career still nominally a Marxist, observed: 'Paintings and sculpture acquire an ever more drained out, vacuous character, as if artists were voluntarily relinquishing the skills and techniques which they had previously possessed.'[132] The emptying out of material and spiritual values left the "art-shaped hole" that Fuller, moving culturally to the Right, later tried to fill with neo-natural theology and worship of the English landscape feeling, but Fuller had a point (borrowed from John Berger) when he argued that leftist artists and critics of the sixties and seventies achieved the opposite of their intentions: 'These commentators *think* they are radicals, hard-headed socialists, producing a devastating critique of "bourgeois" Fine Art. But I think what they are in fact doing merely theorises that ideologically-blinded way of looking characteristic of late monopoly capitalism. They talk about paintings as *if these were advertisements*.'[133]

The effect of the attempted demolition of the notion that art and literature had an intrinsic, ideal value was not only to put into question the teaching of English literature as an ideological practice, it also put into question the practice of teaching as a whole. As Richard Johnson has pointed out: 'Cultural studies is necessarily and deeply implicated in relations of power. It forms a part of the very circuits which it seeks to describe.'[134] Through a process of on the one hand revealing the ideological determinations that constructed judgements of value, and on the other calling into question the very existence of an independent, judging self, the idea of value as the foundation of both moral and aesthetic discriminations was emptied of meaning, and with that the function of the teacher and critic. The dissolution of any belief in absolute standards of value into a free-floating relativism marks the shift from the modern to the post-modern condition.

In November 1977 the Labour government, able to continue in office only because of a formal political pact with the Liberals, made one more attempt to resolve the nagging question of national constitutional identity by offering devolution to Scotland and Wales. A first attempt to create separate elected Scottish and Welsh assemblies (though giving a real measure of power only to that in Scotland), while retaining Scots and Welsh representation at Westminster, had failed in February. Thanks to the Lib-Lab pact, fresh legislation was passed in 1978, but it depended for implementation on the outcome of a referendum to be held in March 1979.

In September 1978, to the surprise of many, James Callaghan announced that he would not be holding a general election that year. He was gambling that a fall in inflation, an improvement in the balance of payments thanks to North Sea Oil revenues and a successful outcome to the referendum on devolution would improve Labour's chances of winning an election the following year. A general election would in any case have to be held by November 1979. He miscalculated. The trades unions rebelled against his government's attempt to impose a five per cent pay norm, and there followed a series of strikes by public-sector trades unions whose low-paid workers would receive the smallest benefit from such a deal. Severe winter conditions combined with strikes by transport drivers, hospital workers and rubbish collectors marked the aptly named "winter of discontent", but it was the outcome of the referendum on devolution that finally led to Labour's demise. Wales voted against, the vote in Scotland was only lukewarm in favour, and the overall yes vote did not reach the forty per cent of the total voting population required by the legislation to bring the new assemblies into being. The Scottish National Party withdrew its support for Labour, and at the end of March the government fell on a motion of no confidence.

The general election of 1979 opened a new era of British politics, the "crisis of hegemony" was resolved in favour of the Right. The winter of 1978–9 had demonstrated the collapse of consensus and raised real fears about the ungovernability of the country. On the steps of Number 10 Downing Street the new Prime Minister, Margaret Thatcher, looked a vulnerable figure as she recited the words of St Francis of Assisi: 'Where there is discord may we bring harmony. Where there is error, may we bring truth. Where there is doubt, may we bring faith. And where there is despair, may we bring hope.'[135] There was an unusually dramatic irony to these words, for they had been written out for her by her speech-writer, the playwright Ronald Millar. St Francis spoke of reconciliation, but this was quite opposite to what was in Margaret Thatcher's mind. One kind of discord was about to be replaced by another. In February she had told the *Observer*: 'I am not a consensus politician, or a pragmatic politician, I'm a conviction politician.'[136] Standing amid the ruins of the post-war consensus, she was determined that it should never be reconstructed.

VII

The Enterprise Culture

Britain in the 1980s

In 1979 the Conservative Party election manifesto had declared: 'The years of make-believe and false optimism are over. It is time for a new beginning.' That final phrase reappears, unacknowledged, in the introduction to *The Downing Street Years*, Margaret Thatcher's testament of more than a decade in office. As her introduction also makes clear, however, that new beginning was conditioned by the sense of disorder and decay that had marked the seventies: 'Everything we wished to do had to fit into the overall strategy of reversing Britain's economic decline, for without an end to that decline there was no hope of success for our other objectives.'[1] As Nigel Lawson recorded in *The View From No. 11*, his testament to a somewhat shorter period in office as Chancellor of the Exchequer: 'By 1979 Britain was pitied abroad and mired in an all-pervasive defeatism at home. This was the culmination of trends that had begun long before the Labour government of 1974–9, but which by the end of that period had become pathological. That was what we set out to reverse.'[2]

A primary cause of the pathological condition into which Britain appeared to have fallen was the collapse of the post-war consensus that Conservative as much as Labour governments had helped to create, but which neither had been able to sustain during the seventies. Rather than attempting to restore the consensus, Thatcher and her closest colleagues came into office convinced that this consensus had itself been one of the causes of Britain's decline. When in 1981 the former Conservative Prime Minister Edward Heath attacked his successor's abrasive approach, Thatcher's answer was: 'To me, consensus seems to be: the process of abandoning all beliefs, principles, values and policies in search of something in which no one believes, but to which no one objects; the process of avoiding the very issues that have to be solved, merely because you cannot get agreement on the way ahead. What great cause would have been fought and won under the banner: "I stand for consensus"?"[3]

Yet because the old order of values had collapsed, it was necessary to construct a new one, a 'new beginning' which would secure sufficient consent to keep the country governable and the Conservatives in power. A new form of consensus had to be built around the values of what was already known as "Thatcherism". The term had been coined by Stuart Hall even before Thatcher came to power, and explored in articles for *Marxism Today*, the British Communist Party journal reinvigorated under the editorship of Martin Jacques. But as Lawson pointed out in his memoirs, the expression was quickly adopted by Thatcher's supporters. It was a mistake to treat Thatcherism as simply what Thatcher did or said: 'The right definition involves a mixture of free markets, financial discipline, firm control over public expenditure, tax cuts, nationalism, "Victorian values" (of the Samuel Smiles self-help variety), privatisation and a dash of populism.'[4] Lawson's retrospective catalogue makes it clear that although the new consensus was to be built around the arguments for monetarism that Thatcher had absorbed since 1974, Thatcherism was a moral and ideological project that set out to release new energies and produce cultural change. Lawson continued: 'A subsequent formulation of the government's supply-side policy objective . . . much used by Margaret was the recreation of the "enterprise culture" in the UK. The model in this case was the United States – although that country had in turn derived it from the vigorous enterprise culture of Victorian England and Scotland, and developed it further. As far as I know the "enterprise culture" was my coinage and the "dependency culture" was Margaret Thatcher's.'[5]

In the enterprise culture, full employment based on a manufacturing economy was to be abandoned in favour of control of money supply and the achievement of zero inflation, with the expansion of the service industries as compensation for the decline in manufacturing, and the full integration of the British economy into the world economy by the abandonment of controls on the flow of capital. Unemployment became what John Major's Chancellor, Norman Lamont, was to call "a price worth paying", even though the cost in benefit payments meant that public expenditure was not to shrink as a proportion of Gross Domestic Product, as was intended by the proponents of "supply-side" economics, who believed state expenditure squeezed out private initiative. While manufacturing was to suffer, the international financial institutions of the City of London were to prosper, particularly after the "Big Bang" of deregulation in 1986. Reliance on the City was a reassertion not so much of nineteenth- as of eighteenth-century mercantile-capitalist values and it dealt with the problem of industrial decline by not treating it as a problem. When the playwright Caryl Churchill wrote her satire on the corruption of the financial markets, *Serious Money*, in 1987 she modelled the play, complete with the deliberate archaism of rhyming couplets, on an eighteenth-century "City comedy".

The alleged authority of history is a useful tool in the construction of a new set of values: the past – however distorted – supplies a framework of justification for the present. As the political historian David Marquand has written: 'Thatcherism was born of the sense of despair, almost of panic, which a generation of apparent national decline had provoked in a certain section of the political class. Its central purpose was to make Britain great again; since the heyday of market liberalism had coincided with the heyday of the British Empire, it assumed that market liberalism was the key to greatness.'[6] The new beginning therefore involved a return to certain old principles: a free economy and a strong state.

The authority of the state was to be used to free the economy, and that meant using the authority of the state against any centres of opposition to the free market, such as the trades unions, and to all centres of opposition to the new idea of the state: local democracy, a liberal intelligentsia and any institution that derived authority from the collectivist years. The new consensus was to be constructed on themes of law and order, on the traditional family and patriotism, in contrast to collectivism and the "permissive society". The new beginning would not only rediscover economic greatness, it would rediscover a secure identity. Thatcherism, wrote Marquand, was about 'British (or rather English) nationhood as well as the profit motive; about history, identity, and above all, authority as well as economics. For most Thatcherites, the strong state, English nationhood and authority come first.'[7] In one field, the reassertion of Britain's greatness involved replaying one of the themes that had served to seal the post-war consensus, anti-communism, leading the Soviet press in 1976 to dub Margaret Thatcher the "Iron Lady", a title she was happy to accept.

Thatcher came to power determined to reverse Britain's decline, a decline measured in both economic and moral terms. The health of the economy was not merely treated as a measure of progress or decline, but was a focus of national anxiety. Increasingly, all aspects of social life – including the arts – were seen through the lens of economic anxiety. Yet although Thatcherism was presented as an economic doctrine, the underlying moral philosophy was more important. As Thatcher told the *Sunday Times* in 1988: 'Economics are the method. The object is to change the soul.'[8] The British soul was to be remade, by creating a new myth of economic individualism to replace the old ideas of community and collectivism. 'The basis of the enterprise culture lies with the restoration of the age of the individual,' declared Lord Young of Graffham, a former director of Thatcher's Policy Studies Institute who became Secretary of State at the Department of Trade and Industry (which he attempted to retitle "the Department of Enterprise").[9] The individual, empowered through the sovereignty of the consumer, was to be liberated by the freedom of the market not only from the dependency culture of collectivism, but the old hierarchies of deference, status and taste.

There is a strong element of utilitarianism in the morality of the free market. When the aristocratic justifications of privilege are destroyed the sheer utility of making money gives access to power to anyone who can make a profit. But the freedom of the individual is purely economic: there is freedom to make money, but also freedom to starve. The market becomes the only sphere of social action, and the economic becomes the only motive of morality. Ultimately, economic activity becomes the principal form of human expression. As the obsession with "style" during the eighties shows – exemplified by the magazine *The Face* launched in 1980 – you are what you buy. The citizen is redefined as the consumer, as a paying customer for public services which previously were available by right, and which the individual may now opt out of helping to provide for others. One of the first acts of the 1979 Conservative government was to switch the emphasis from direct to indirect taxation by raising the rate of Value Added Tax from eight per cent to fifteen per cent, and cutting the basic rate of income tax from thirty-three per cent to thirty per cent, the top rate from eighty-three per cent to sixty per cent. Further cuts were to follow.

Ironically, the "permissive society" had made a contribution to the new culture of consumption. The counter-culture, as Bernice Martin has pointed out, 'contains elements which are increasingly appropriate to a complex, mobile and privatised social system in which ego rather than any natural "tribal" group forms the basic unit'.[10] The trajectory of the magazine *Time Out* from hippy noticeboard and radical news-sheet in the sixties to consumer style-file in the eighties is a case in point. Yet as David Marquand has argued: 'The range of identities legitimised by the enterprise culture is very limited. It gives increased scope for one's identity as a consumer, but not to other identities. Indeed, it is positively hostile to identity-choices that threaten the authority of the entrepreneur and the supremacy of entrepreneurial values.'[11]

The attraction of Thatcherism was that it drew on the authority of an imagined past while weaving in strands of contemporary ambition and desire so as to create a distinctive brand of contemporary populism. As *Marxism Today* was forced to admit in October 1988: 'Increasingly, at the heart of Thatcherism, has been its sense of New Times, of living in a new era. While the Left remains profoundly wedded to the past, to 1945, to the old social democratic order, to the priorities of Keynes and Beveridge, the Right has glimpsed the future and run with it. As a result, it is the Right which now appears modern, radical, innovative and brimming with confidence and ideas about the future.'[12]

There was, however, always a danger that the various strands of Thatcherism could unravel, for although Thatcher was the first British Prime Minister to have a political philosophy named after her, she was not a conceptual thinker. She called herself an 'instinctive Conservative' and there is no doubt that the force of her personality – magnified by the influence of the media – played a key role in stamping her name on the events of the decade.[13] An inherent contradiction in her personal philosophy was between its two founding concepts, the free economy and the strong state. As the *Economist* asked in 1993: 'Why was a politician who celebrated the individual over the state such a relentless centraliser of government power, and so careless of civil liberties? . . . The reason is that Thatcherism was never a coherent set of economic and political ideas (though it often had pretensions to be). Rather, it was a list of instinctively selected friends and enemies. At a rough approximation, the friends were the property-owning (and would-be property-owning) middle, lower-middle and aspiring working classes. The enemies were trade unions, public-sector workers, the intelligentsia and (as she saw them) spongers of every kind who were content to live off the state.'[14]

Such prejudices were the key to Thatcher's populism, for there was clearly a constituency in the country instinctively to the right of the liberal consensus which even the Conservative Party subscribed to, and which gave her three election victories in a row. Phillip Whitehead has pointed out that during her time as Leader of the Opposition, when under the tutelage of Sir Keith Joseph and others she was acquiring the rudiments of monetarist economic theory, Margaret Thatcher 'actively sought out this constituency and addressed it. Her speeches, when published, carry the credits of those who influenced her: F. A. Hayek, Keith Joseph, Arthur Seldon, Paul Johnson, Robert Conquest. Her achievement was to use words which brought these thinkers the mass audience they would not otherwise have enjoyed.'[15]

Thatcherism as a political philosophy was a product of the galvanising relationship between the "instinctive" Margaret Thatcher and the intellectuals of the New Right. Paul Johnson has recorded admiringly: 'There's no doubt that Mrs Thatcher is more interested in intellectuals and hearing what they have to say and listening to them than any other Prime Minister I have come across. . . . Under Mrs Thatcher, ideas were paramount and that gave a completely new zesty tang to intellectual life in this country and explains, of course, the way in which she was loved and hated because the left intelligentsia hated her and the right loved her. So we had quite a battle of ideas in Britain.'[16] The battle had begun in the seventies, with the emergence of the New Right and the growing influence of right-wing think-tanks: the Institute of Economic Affairs, founded in 1957, the Centre for Policy Studies (1974) and the Adam Smith Institute, which moved to London from America in 1979. The historian of the New Right, Maurice Cowling, has been anxious to stress its disparate origins: 'The New Right has been conducted by about fifty people (mainly graduates, and mostly men) who have come from no one type of social, sexual or intellectual background and who include among them a smattering of atheists and agnostics; a few converted, a few practising and a few lapsed Catholics; a handful of Jews, observing or otherwise; some Dissenters and Evangelicals; a fair number of observing and a number of converted Anglicans; and a contingent for whom religion is of little significance. In opinion there has been a lack of stereotype.'[17]

What did unite them was that on the whole they did not have patrician origins, but more often had the provincial puritan background that shaped the attitudes of Brian Cox or Roger Scruton. Several, such as the former editor of the *New Statesman*, Paul Johnson, had the fervour of converts from the Left. Importantly, many earned their living as journalists, and so were in a position to communicate their ideas to a significant public. Even when they were academics, like Scruton, they wrote regularly in the press. In addition to writing for *The Times*, Scruton became editor of the quarterly *Salisbury Review* in 1982, which provided intellectual justifications for the economic appetites of Thatcherism. In answer to Raymond Williams's criticism of the "market" as the solvent of community, Scruton countered: 'It is a mechanism of distribution operated entirely by the voluntary transactions of individuals, each of whom secures his advantage by soliciting the agreement of those with whom he deals. "Consumer sovereignty" is another name for that day-to-day "equality of being" which allows each person's choice to influence the outcome of the social process. The result is not very edifying – but the results of democracy seldom are.'[18]

The *Salisbury Review* was not widely read, but the house-magazine of the New Right, the *Spectator*, was, and the overall heavy weighting of the British press to the Right was undoubtedly helpful in shifting opinion towards the new consensus. The support of Rupert Murdoch, who added *The Times* and the *Sunday Times* to his portfolio of the *Sun* and the *News of the World* in 1981 (thus gaining access to the entire British social spectrum represented in the press), was important – as was the government's help to Murdoch – but there was an ideological as well as an economic confluence of interests. As an Australian, Murdoch did not subscribe either to the collectivist or the patrician tradition. In his words: 'I am suspicious of élites, including the British broadcasting élite, which argues for special privileges and favours because they are supposed to be in the public interest as a whole. Such special pleading tends to produce a service which is run for the benefit of the people who provide it, rather than the viewers who want it.'[19] Margaret Thatcher expressed almost identical sentiments, as will be seen.

Progress towards establishing a new consensus around the values of Thatcherism was made easier by the fragmentation and demoralisation of the Left, a condition captured in David Edgar's 1983 play, *Maydays*. There was a fierce battle for power within the Labour Party between radical and conservative wings, while the trades unions continued to believe that "direct action" in the form of strikes would achieve their ends. These struggles culminated in the splitting-away of David Owen, Shirley Williams, Roy Jenkins and Bill Rodgers and others to form the

Social Democratic Party in 1981. Marquand – who was then a Labour MP and joined the SDP – has pointed out that the desire for a new beginning extended beyond the immediate circle of Thatcherism: 'Like her, [David Owen] spoke to and for the raw, down-to-earth, thrusting New Men who saw themselves as the harbingers of a new age of realism and enterprise: for the self-proclaimed "achievers", whose ambitious climb up the status hierarchy seemed blocked by a patronising old Establishment which they half-despised and half-envied.'[20] If it is one of the characteristics of a successful hegemony that its values are held by others than those immediately in power, then the penetration of the rhetoric of the enterprise culture suggests that – even as she condemned the term – Thatcher was well placed to make progress in establishing a new consensus.

The early years of Thatcher's government seemed designed to demonstrate the end of the old order. A historian of her first administration wrote that it 'formally abandoned the pretence that full employment and economic growth were in the gift of the government'.[21] In the face of a world recession prompted by a further rise in oil prices, in 1980 inflation rose to a peak of 21.9 per cent, the minimum lending rate went up to seventeen per cent and unemployment passed two million for the first time since the thirties. As recession deepened, manufacturing output shrivelled, and there was a swathe of cuts, closures and bankruptcies across industry. While unable to reduce public spending – and increasing it on defence and the police – the government prepared to confront the power of the unions with the Employment Acts of 1980 and 1981.

The social stress in the country found its expression in serious riots in St Paul's, Bristol, in April 1980, and Toxteth, Liverpool, in July 1981. The only distraction from an increasingly grim situation for both Government and people was the marriage of the Prince of Wales to Lady Diana Spencer in the same month as the Toxteth riots. Public opinion surveys showed the deep unpopularity of both the government and the Prime Minister by the end of 1981. Only a minority of Thatcher's first Cabinet wholeheartedly agreed with her, but she took steps to secure her position with a reshuffle that removed "one nation" Tories (redefined by her as "wets") like Sir Ian Gilmour and brought in hardliners such as Norman Tebbit. In 1982, thanks to budget and trade deficits in the United States, the economy began to show signs of recovery, and then, on Friday 2 April, the completely unexpected happened. Argentina invaded the Falkland Islands.

The following day the House of Commons sat on a Saturday for the first time since the Suez Crisis in 1956, and the almost unanimous decision was taken to secure an Argentinian withdrawal, by force if necessary. On 5 April HMS *Hermes* and *Invincible* weighed anchor. In an atmosphere of war, Parliament and the country raised the ghost of an earlier consensus. Tom Nairn had written presciently in 1977: 'England needs another war. This alone would recreate the peculiar spirit of her nationalism, rally her renegade intelligentsia (as in the thirties), and reconcile the workers to their lot.'[22] The Falklands Crisis briefly revived a much-desired wartime feeling of solidarity. As the historian Kenneth Morgan has pointed out: 'By the eighties, the late war was almost as much a part of a thriving "heritage" industry as were Tudor manor houses or medieval cathedrals.'[23]

The expedition was also an opportunity to reverse the international humiliation of Suez. The rurality and ethnicity of the eighteen hundred Falklanders, this second 'island race' (a phrase of Churchill's adopted by Mrs Thatcher), appealed to the deep-seated pastoralism of the British, even though the Conservative government's new Nationality Act had deprived the Falklanders of their British citizenship two years before.[24] That the crisis was the result of the government's own oversight was quickly forgotten as the task force set out. Mrs Thatcher's personal determination and the successful short military campaign, in which British losses were relatively light, turned popular opinion around, and the return of the task force and the Victory Parade through the City of London struck deep chords. The political commentator Anthony Howard wrote later that the reversal of the humiliation of Suez 'translated Thatcher into Boadicea, an international figure in her martial chariot virtually invulnerable (at least until her cabinet chieftains turned against her) to her domestic political opponents' (illustration 16).[25]

The significance of the Falklands Campaign and its revival of deep English myths was not lost on Thatcher. On 3 July 1982 she addressed a Conservative rally at Cheltenham race course. Harold Wilson had once appealed to 'the Dunkirk spirit', but Thatcher was altogether more triumphant. While acknowledging the international support Britain had received, 'we also fought alone – for we fought for our own people and for our own sovereign territory'.[26] This evocation of 1940 and 1941 led to a comparison with the situation in 1980 and 1981. Even when attacking the 'fainthearts' who believed 'that our decline was irreversible – that we could never again be what we were', Thatcher was acknowledging the distance that had been travelled. To deny that 'Britain was no longer the nation that had built an Empire and ruled a quarter of the globe' is to admit the possibility that it was. The whole thrust of the speech turned on an evocation of the purposefulness and solidarity of wartime, when 'the sterling qualities which shine through our history' appeared. But: 'Why does it need a war to bring out our qualities and reassert our pride?'

Making a transition via a quotation from Winston Churchill expressing a similar sentiment about working together in peace and war, Thatcher fell into bathos with an attack on the leaders of the train drivers' union ASLEF for calling a strike, and then appealing to nurses and ancillary hospital workers to accept their recent pay award. There was 'a new mood of realism in Britain' and the train drivers (and by implication all trades unionists) should take note. Her final peroration returned to the high rhetoric of national recovery and national identity: 'What has happened is that now once again Britain is not prepared to be pushed around. We have ceased to be a nation in retreat. We have instead a new-found confidence – born in the economic battles at home and tested and found true eight thousand miles away. That confidence comes from the rediscovery of ourselves, and grows with the recovery of our self-respect. . . . Britain has found herself in the South Atlantic and will not look back from the victory she has won.'

It was from this point, through this moment of briefly recaptured imperial glory, that Margaret Thatcher was able to consolidate her position and enforce the imperatives of the enterprise culture, as she prepared for her second general election in 1983. Her modernising drive was now appropriately presented in borrowed terms of "Victorian values" – her original expression was 'Victorian virtues' – of patriotism, hard work, thrift and private charity.[27] It has been frequently pointed out that Thatcher's interpretation of what constituted Victorian values was highly selective, but the appeal to the authority of history is important. Jonathan Raban wrote in a commentary on her address to the General Assembly of the Church of Scotland in 1988:

> Her own break with the past has been radical to the point of being revolutionary, yet . . . she continually employs "history" as the great licensing authority, to validate every departure from historical practice. Her notions of what actually happened in history are often eccentric, sometimes downright

ignorant – perhaps necessarily so, since no one who knew much about the Victorian period could possibly ascribe Margaret Thatcher's meaning to the term "Victorian values". At fonder moments ... she substitutes the phrase "our heritage" for "history" – and "heritage" expresses her meaning more accurately. For a heritage is something we have possession of after the death of the original owners, and we are free to use it as we choose.[28]

What is significant is that Thatcher, for all her appeals to the past, saw herself as a revolutionary. The general election of June 1983 increased the overall Conversative majority to one hundred and forty-four, the second largest in post-war history, while with two hundred and nine seats Labour had the smallest representation since 1935. After her deep unpopularity of 1980 and 1981, Margaret Thatcher could now properly begin the task she had set herself: 'There was a revolution still to be made, but too few revolutionaries.'[29]

Before examining how that revolution was experienced in the world of the arts, it is important to appreciate the extent to which Thatcherism was itself the product of a revolutionary situation: the break-up of the old capitalist and industrial system. It was possible to think in terms of a new order precisely because the old consensus had already broken down, in the disorder and fragmentation of the seventies. The opening sequence of Derek Jarman's film *Jubilee* (1977) depicts a ravaged, semi-derelict city. On a wall above a group of leather-jacketed rioters appears the graffiti 'post-modern'. The scrawl is never explained, but it was clearly intended to convey the contemporary sense of disintegration and social breakdown. Post-modernism, a term which came into use at just this period, was a response to the loss of confidence in the underlying economic and social structures which had previously supported the idea of progress and improvement throughout the post-war period.

Though deeply unsettling, the changes that began to manifest themselves during the seventies as the consequences of economic and technological development took effect represented a mutation within capitalism, rather than an external crisis or revolution. One of the effects of the new technology of communication, whether by information satellite or jet plane, was what the geographer David Harvey has called 'time–space compression', which he relates specifically to the new global organisation of capitalism.[30] The rapid movement of capital around the world, the universal exchange of the dominant currencies, the distribution of identical products, the appearance of the same television programmes in different countries, heralded the emergence of a universal network of exchange no longer rooted in any one source of production. It is significant that both Fredric Jameson, a critic of the 'cultural logic of late capitalism', and Jean Baudrillard, a celebrant of the new cultural conditions created by the 'ecstasy of communication' made possible by the development of information technology, should use the metaphor of the screen and its electronic imagery to express the new mythology of capitalism, where the visual display unit had become the basic tool of commodity brokers and market makers (illustration 18).[31]

Capitalism appeared to have transcended all national boundaries and identities. As Terry Eagleton has written, capitalism 'no longer, so to speak, has to pass through consciousness; instead, it simply secures its own reproduction by a manipulative, incorporative logic of which human subjects are the mere obedient effects. It is not surprising that the theoretical ideology known as structuralism should have grown up in just this historical epoch.'[32] Structuralism argued that ideas were the products of the language systems that conveyed them; culture was a product of the capitalism that made it possible. Culture was not a bulwark against capital, but merely one of its "effects".

The shift that began in the seventies from an emphasis on the production of things to the production of images and ideas, where information in itself became a precious commodity, made culture as important an item of consumption as any other. The information industry, driven by the needs of advertising to stimulate consumption, became the subject of intense globalisation during this period. Rupert Murdoch's worldwide network of interests through his company News Corporation is a prime example, embracing newspaper and magazine groups in key countries, terrestrial and satellite television stations, film studios and publishing houses. The emblematic success story of the eighties in Britain was that of the advertising agency founded by Charles and Maurice Saatchi in 1970, which in 1986 became the biggest advertising agency in the world, and the following year attempted to take over a bank. Success was temporary. In 1989 the company made a loss of £58.5 million, and by 1990 was no longer world leader. In January 1995 Maurice Saatchi was forced out as chairman, and the brothers sold their shares in the company.

It was no accident that at the time when his company was becoming the country's most influential distributor of commercial messages and, with its work for the Conservative Party, political images, Charles Saatchi became the most important British private collector of contemporary art. According to Fredric Jameson: 'Aesthetic production today has become integrated into commodity production generally: the frantic economic urgency of producing fresh waves of ever more novel-seeming goods (from clothing to airplanes), at ever greater rates of turnover, now assigns an increasingly essential structural function and position to aesthetic innovation and experimentation.'[33] The result has been a massive expansion of the "cultural" into the economic sphere, but where the "economic" is the principal expression of the cultural: 'Every position on post-modernism in culture – whether apologia or stigmatisation – is also at one and the same time, and *necessarily*, an implicitly or explicitly political stance on the nature of multinational capitalism today.'[34]

Given the all-pervasive influence of the changes within capitalism on the shaping of the new cultural order, post-modernism is easier to comprehend as a condition than as an agreed set of aesthetic principles or a coherent set of ideas. As originally deployed by American theorists in the early seventies the term was used positively, to indicate a break with the oppressive conventions of modernism – as in the subversive activities of Pop Art – and especially a liberation from the tyranny of the international modernist style in architecture.

To make the break with modernism was one thing: to define precisely what was replacing it another. The critic and advocate of post-modernism Charles Jencks defined it in architecture as a 'double coding: the combination of modern techniques with something else (usually traditional building) in order for architecture to communicate with the public and a concerned minority, usually other architects'.[35] In architecture, the end of modernism as the only acceptable style meant that all past styles became equally available for the architect's use. Paradoxically, an architect like Quinlan Terry, who abhorred the architecture of the modern movement and produced buildings that have all the appearance of having been designed in the eighteenth century according to the classical principles of Vitruvius, is thus a post-modern architect, for the buildings he designed could only have been commissioned in the late twentieth century. In this respect, the rediscovery and representation of the past as an entertainment mediated by the heritage industry is an aspect of the post-modern condition.

The interventions of the Prince of Wales in the field of architecture, seeking to revive classical ideals, have been similarly post-modern. In 1984 his attack on the proposed modernist design for an extension to the National Gallery as a "monstrous carbuncle" led to the scheme being dropped, and its replacement with a design that makes playful use of classical elements, by one of the early theorists of post-modernism, Robert Venturi. Charles Jencks has linked the Prince's rejection of modernism as the only permissible style in which to build a modern building to a broader rejection of seemingly monolithic solutions to cultural problems: 'Most people, and the Prince is one of them, are not satisfied with a status quo which limits choice, and they are asking their leaders and politicians difficult questions, interrogations which only increase the scope of choice, and therefore dissonance. Alternative medicine, alternative architecture, small businesses, inner-city renewal – these are the focused "issue-oriented" politics which typify our fragmented post-industrial society, and they happen to be the four areas on which the Prince is most outspoken.'[36]

In spite of the fragmentation to which Jencks alludes, there is a utopian aspect to the post-modern condition. The break-up of the old structures and hierarchies of culture means that the old conflict between high and popular culture is dissolved. Culture, given an added significance by its role within the information industry and consumption generally, becomes an information system without discriminating valuations within it. But when discussion of post-modernism moved to Europe in the later seventies, the view of the post-modern condition became more pessimistic. Playful post-modernists did not appear to have found anything substantial to put in modernism's place, for they lacked a radical social vision of their own. 'The American post-modernist avant garde,' wrote the critic Andreas Huyssen, 'therefore is not only the endgame of avant-gardism. It also represents the fragmentation and decline of the avant-garde as a genuinely critical and adversary culture.'[37] Once all styles become equal, and an avant-garde approach is just one approach among many, stylistic innovation becomes merely a new way of recycling old styles, and art – most noticeably in architecture – becomes a form of pastiche.

The price of the break with modernism was the loss of the vision of an improved future for mankind that modernism had helped to frame. After modernism, there was merely a void. This pessimistic view was reinforced by the political pessimism that spread among French intellectuals of the Left in the wake of the failed revolution of 1968. The cultural logic of structuralism and its appropriately named refinement, post-structuralism, led to the disappearance of faith in any single solution to the problems of oppression and exploitation that permeated society, its institutions and language. For Michel Foucault, power was not organised through a single state or social structure such as the class system, but was dispersed throughout a whole series of cultural constructions, ranging from the architecture of prisons and the organisation of universities to the definition of madness and of sexual identity itself, which was not unified, but polymorphous. Thus the operation of power, transmitted by the systems of knowledge – or "discourse" – that these institutions and ideas represented, was in a sense irresistible, except at a very local level, and certainly not in terms of the universal emancipation that modernism had projected. Modernism was in itself a totalising, and therefore totalitarian, system; resistance could only be piecemeal and led to further fragmentation.

It might be possible to retain some confidence in one's capacity to criticise and judge society and its institutions if one could be sure that what was written and said was what was actually meant. Jacques Derrida carried the structuralist argument that culture was determined by language a stage further, by arguing that the connection between the signifier (the word or symbol) and the signified (its meaning) was not simply arbitrary, but non-existent. In saying something we are only reconstituting previous texts into a new text whose meaning is immediately remade by those who hear or read it, a process entirely beyond our individual control. This way of thinking about texts and their meanings – "deconstruction" – argues that when we speak or write we communicate meanings that we do not intend, and we cannot convey what we do mean. Language (like Althusser's version of ideology) constructs us, we are merely texts in an infinite series of texts, and therefore we are not in control of our own perceptions, nor ultimately are we individual centred beings at all. All meanings are unstable, fragments that are open to reuse and reinterpretation as they pass from one person to another.

Such fragments of meaning as we are able to cling to, however, are divorced from any connection with the real world. According to the sociologist Jean Baudrillard, reality is unknowable, and we only deal with representations of reality, representations which hide reality from us: 'The very definition of the real becomes: *that of which it is possible to give an equivalent reproduction.*'[38] Our only knowledge of the world is gained through these reproductions – Baudrillard calls them "simulacra" – and we live in an "ecstasy of communication" within a network of electronic imagery where the image 'bears no relation to any reality whatever: it is its own pure simulacrum'.[39] Society, or rather the image of the social that we construct for ourselves, with the assistance of language, explodes into a mass of individual atoms held together by the depthless screen of hyper-reality, 'a nonreflecting surface, an immanent surface where operations unfold – the smooth operational surface of communication'.[40]

Thus, as Jean-François Lyotard has argued, any hopes of achieving a unified system of knowledge, a "grand narrative" that offers a universal explanation, have to be abandoned. There is no overarching meta-language in which all systems of knowledge can be contained. At best there are only partial knowledges, constructed by individual linguistic practices or intertextual exchanges. Given these attitudes and arguments, it is no wonder that the "discourse" of post-modernism becomes one of fragmentation and pessimism. Dick Hebdige summed it up as a discourse of negation: the denial of totalisation as a viable philosophical project, the denial of the possibility of discovering any teleology that would explain ultimate causes or ultimate ends, the denial of the possibility of a utopia towards which society might be moving. In this respect, 'post-modernity is modernity without the hopes and dreams which made modernity bearable'.[41] As Hebdige put it: 'The discourse of post-modernism is fatal and fatalistic: at every turn the word "death" opens up to engulf us: "death of the subject", "death of the author", "death of art", "death of reason", "end of history".'[42]

Within the yawning void of post-modernism, neither the artist nor the critic has any secure foothold. As the art historian Brandon Taylor has argued, what is artistic "expression" if there is nothing that can be expressed?

> "Expression" assumes, according to the argument, the very distinction between the "inner" and "outer" mind that characterised the old bourgeois humanist conception of the subject as an autonomous a-social being. Secondly, "expression" elevates the artistic style, trace or brushmark to a position of importance which it cannot in reality possess – since there can be no guarantee that the brushmarks of the artist give an *accurate* account of the state of his inner mind or character. This is an epistemological doubt. Thirdly, post-modernism proposes that the modernist's unique "style", his particular method of marking the canvas or the paper, derives principally from the market itself. The market fetishises the individual artistic

product . . . bestows rarity and singularity upon that which it wishes only to sell.[43]

Neither artist nor critic appears to be left with any purpose or function.

Demonstrably, the function of the critic did not disappear, for the subject of post-modernism in itself generated a critical outpouring. Nor did artists and writers stop work. By the eighties "theory" could be said to have achieved its own cultural autonomy, so that the connection between critical speculation and contemporary artistic practice, never a close fit, seemed looser than ever. In the hands of writers like Julian Barnes, Peter Ackroyd and Martin Amis the narrative assurance of the novel was broken up by authorial self-consciousness about the artificiality of the devices used to construct a "real" world through fiction. The conventional naturalism of English literature was further disrupted by more cosmopolitan voices: Salman Rushdie, Timothy Mo, Kazuo Ishiguro, and by fabulists like Angela Carter and extremists like Kathy Acker and Iain Sinclair. In *The Singing Detective* (1987) Dennis Potter even managed to break the iron conventions of naturalism on television. Derek Jarman and Peter Greenaway brought a respectively "hot" and "cold" painterly aesthetic to the cinema.

Artists began to investigate the new technology of video and photocopying; sculptors such as Tony Cragg, Bill Woodrow and David Mach responded to the breakdown of formal conventions by creating their work out of "found" objects and discarded industrial materials. Some of the most innovative work took place not within artistic disciplines, but between them. The "installation" became a characteristic form that moved between sculpture, environment and performance, creating a space where the artist is free to combine natural and constructed materials, might use film or video or slide projections, incorporate sound, or create a setting for actions performed by the artists or others. The installation blended into "live art", which depended on a time-based performance which is distinct from drama, in that the performers are not concerned to create theatrical illusions or simulate characters. The breakdown of traditional forms led to cross-fertilisation: dance companies like DV8 and Second Stride moved towards theatre, adding speech to action, while music, dance and mime became part of the repertoire of troupes like Théâtre de Complicité. One artist who did appear determined to declare the mortality of art was Damien Hirst, whose installations involving a rotting cow's head, fly larvae and an insect electrocutor, or dead animals suspended in formaldehyde, seemed designed to provoke morbid thoughts of death and inanition.

The debate about post-modernism had a stimulating effect on the area where there could be a fit between theory and practice: the teaching of cultural studies. While post-structuralist arguments undermined confidence in the claim that criticism could be scientific, and called into question academic discourse as a form of ideology in itself, the collapse of faith in the possibility of discovering a single explanatory system encouraged a lively pluralism. The "grand narrative" to suffer the most serious consequences of the questioning of such explanatory systems was Marxism, which had lost its authority as the ruling methodology in cultural criticism even before its collapse as a political system with the fall of the Berlin Wall and the reunification of Germany in 1989. In spite of the lively cultural debate that it had stimulated, *Marxism Today* ceased publication in January 1992.

The gradual disappearance of an explicitly Marxist politics from cultural studies appears to have encouraged institutional growth. Angela McRobbie has described how the academy began to absorb the previously marginal field of cultural studies during the eighties: 'Take a tradition of textual analysis long established in the English departments of a hundred US campuses, update it with the language of structuralism, post-structuralism and deconstruction, extend this mode to texts of popular culture (film, TV, video, popular fiction), add the blessings of cultural relativism which make it "legit" to take the popular seriously, canonise the new curriculum by appealing to feminism, black or popular politics (with the final of these acting as a kind of substitute for class) and we are all in business.'[44]

The principal growth in cultural studies was in the polytechnics, where joint and "modular" courses meant they could be combined with more traditional subjects. Between 1979 and 1989 the number of communications, media and cultural studies courses validated by the Council for National Academic Awards had increased from seven to sixteen, and the CNAA established a separate Communication and Cultural Studies Board. By 1993 there were more than seventy single or joint courses available in communication and media studies, and interdisciplinary or combined studies were a significant element in courses in English, social science, art and design. The Open University, whose courses were popular with secondary school teachers (and therefore an indirect influence on schools), launched their 'Mass

Communication and Society' course in 1977 and followed it up in 1982 with the highly influential 'Popular Culture' course, which ran until 1987. The popular culture course was taken by five thousand students, involved a team of fifty lecturers in setting it up and one hundred tutors across the country in teaching it. The course was a conscious attempt to reconcile the methodological and doctrinal differences between culturalism and structuralism by adopting a Gramscian approach: popular culture consisted 'not simply of an imposed mass culture that is consonant with the interests of the dominant class, nor simply of a spontaneously oppositional working-class culture; it is rather an *area of negotiation* between the two'.[45]

Ironically, in view of its pioneering work in the field, the Birmingham Centre for Contemporary Cultural Studies underwent disrupting change, partially as a result of the cuts in university funding imposed by the 1979 Conservative government. As a small independent unit it came under severe pressure to accept rationalisation and reabsorption into the English department, which it fiercely resisted. While Stuart Hall had always fought against the idea that Cultural Studies was a formal academic discipline, Richard Johnson was obliged to defend the Centre by arguing that it had now acquired that status. Ultimately it was the Department of Sociology, its other suspicious cousin, which collapsed, and the centre was reformed as the Department of Cultural Studies, and relocated within a Faculty of Commerce and Social Science. The decision to offer undergraduate as well as post-graduate degrees was a sign of the arrival of cultural studies as an accepted academic subject, but the consequent pressure on what had been the Centre's key activity, research, radically altered its nature.

By the end of the eighties the broad acceptance of a "cultural studies approach" to teaching in the humanities and the far greater popularity of the nineteenth and twentieth centuries as fields of study meant that, despite Stuart Hall's reluctance, the subject had achieved the status of a "discipline" like any other. In a study published in 1991, Anthony Easthope, Professor of English and Cultural Studies at Manchester Polytechnic, argued that the intense disputes about methodology that had characterised the seventies marked the moment of crisis in the transition from literary to cultural studies approaches. Easthope proposed that cultural studies were on the point of supplanting literature as the dominant critical paradigm: like the study of English literature before them, they had become a medium for social and moral criticism.[46]

It would be wrong, however, to assume there had been a resolution to the continuing debates within and around cultural studies. Like English literature, the new discipline had to negotiate a path between the extremes of, on the one hand, becoming a practice of technological expertise open to the professional few or, on the other, serving as a general humanistic approach lacking intellectual rigour. Disputes within the discipline were far from settled. In a historical survey published in 1990 Graeme Turner warned: 'While the culturalism/structuralism split may have now dissolved, the three-way split of economic versus cultural determination versus individual agency still dominates, in one form or another, arguments about the formation of culture and the role of ideology.'[47]

The important difference between cultural studies and English literature as a field of study was that culture had become the very site and medium for ever wider issues of politics, morality and national identity. Leavisite literary criticism addressed social issues from a distance, from within a tradition that opposed cultural values to those of society at large. But culture, as redefined by the theoretical work of the seventies, not only embraced a great deal more than literature; it could not be separated from the society that produced it, and whose values it served to express and define. When Terry Eagleton became Thomas Wharton Professor of English Literature at Oxford University in 1992, his appointment showed the penetration of a culturalist approach into the academic establishment, but the task before him was different to that of his predecessors, as he pointed out in his inaugural lecture:

> What has happened is that culture is less and less able to fulfil its classical role of reconciliation – a role, indeed, on which English studies in this society were actually founded. . . . For as long as the conflicts which such a notion of culture sought to mediate were of a material kind – wars, class struggle, social inequities – the concept of culture as a higher harmonisation of our sublunary squabbles could just retain some thin plausibility. But as soon as such contentions become themselves of a cultural kind, this project becomes much less persuasive. For culture is palpably part of the problem rather than the solution; it is the very medium in which battle is engaged, rather than some Olympian terrain on which our differences can be recomposed. It is bad news for this traditional concept of culture that the conflicts which have dominated the political agenda for the past couple of decades – ethnic,

sexual, revolutionary nationalist – have been precisely ones in which language, value, identity and experience have been to the fore.[48]

In the post-modern condition the interpenetration of the economic and the cultural was such that change in one could only be achieved through change in the other. This was what Margaret Thatcher meant when she said that economics were the method, but her object was the soul. As she prepared to launch a revolution after the election of 1983, the cultural and the economic were synthesised in a single phrase: the Enterprise Culture.

Assured in her leadership as a result of the Falklands War, and armed with a healthy majority following the 1983 election, Margaret Thatcher was in a position to drive home her attack on the domestic sources of resistance to her will. The most spectacular casualties were the miners, defeated in a bitter eleven-month battle after they went on strike in March 1984 in protest at the government's rationalisation of the coal industry. The technique for dealing with potential sources of opposition was direct legislation, as in the case of the trades unions, or a combination of legislation and economic destabilisation, as in the case of the National Health Service, local authorities, education and the nationalised industries. Where the object of change was less directly exposed, as in the case of the BBC, the universities, the Arts Council, the British Council and other cultural institutions, the process was to apply financial pressure, in the name of reducing government spending, and to use the power of appointment to ensure that institutions voluntarily bent to the government's will.

Yet although the rhetoric of Thatcherism spoke of "rolling back the frontiers of the state", the effect of this policy was to create a partial vacuum, which the government filled with its own centralising power. This was most clearly demonstrated in the government's attitude to quangos (Quasi-Autonomous Non-Government Organisations), which carried out a wide range of administrative and regulatory functions on behalf of the government, and were run by unelected boards. Thatcher began with the intention of cutting them back. In 1979 there were 2,410 "non-departmental public bodies", to use the government's narrow definition of a quango, and by 1983 five hundred had been wound up. But new ones were created almost as quickly, and from 1985 onwards they bred rapidly as the government moved power away from local authorities and began to break up the monolithic institutions of the welfare state. The creation of new regulatory bodies, the changes to the National Health Service and education led to a multiplication of public bodies towards the end of the decade. It was calculated in 1994 that nearly a third of all public expenditure was being channelled through 5,521 appointed bodies. While there were only twenty-five thousand elected local councillors, there were seventy thousand appointees, all owing their positions to a Conservative government.

Britain's cultural institutions had traditionally operated on the quango-model, at arm's length from government, their governors, trustees, board members or council members drawn from the voluntary army of the Great and the Good. But this instrument for administering the consensus was unsuited to the confrontational mode of government in the eighties. As Richard Hoggart has written: 'Quangos emerged from more than the consensus idea; they emerged from and could only work where there was an assumed pattern of values about the nature of the good society and the good life.'[49] For Margaret Thatcher the idea of the Great and the Good summoned up associations of 'favouritism, injustice and propping up the status quo'.[50] She echoed the opinion of Rupert Murdoch in her view that 'broadcasting was one of a number of areas – the professions such as teaching, medicine and the law were others – in which special pleading by powerful interest groups was disguised as high-minded commitment to some greater good'.[51]

The eighties proved a decidedly uncomfortable decade for the Great and the Good. In 1984 Bryan Appleyard observed of the cultural mandarins he met in the course of his work as an arts correspondent: 'There is a nagging doubt, an air of ennui and irritation. It arises partly from the battles they have fought and are reluctant to fight again and partly from a sense that the tide has turned against them in some indefinable way. They are no longer members of a confident priesthood officiating at the shrine of art with the support of an enthusiastic and aspiring congregation.'[52] The following year Peter Hennessy, an expert on the Whitehall scene, described the Great and the Good as 'the Lost Tribe of British Public Life'.[53] Though they were a creation of the Victorian era, Mrs Thatcher's values had no room for 'the auxiliary fire service of the ruling classes. . . . Loaded with honours, dripping with gravitas, oozing the accumulated experience of decades, [they] have become the most elevated and distinguished casualties of the Thatcher years.'[54]

Thatcher felt no inhibition about the policy that was adopted: 'One could only do so much by changing the framework of the system: it was the people who operated within it who were the key.'[55] Thus while cultural institutions retained their notional distance from government, a new breed of nabob – entrepreneurs, public-relations experts, newspaper executives – with a different concept of public responsibility took control. The art historian Martin Kemp, a trustee of the Victoria and Albert Museum who resigned in protest at changes there in 1989, wrote afterwards: 'The cosy clubs have been replaced by far more active, partisan and managerially-minded bodies, many of whose members do not hesitate to impose their views on the organisations for which they are caring. I do not think the present government has made any secret of the fact that it expects the boards to promulgate policies which reflect the economic values of the market.'[56]

Gestures of opposition such as Kemp's were rare, for as private individuals accustomed to the consensual tradition of public service, the Great and the Good had no collective, independent power once the government's favour was withdrawn. The "moving equilibrium" of hegemony had tilted away from them. The most public protest came from Thatcher's alma mater, Oxford University. In the autumn of 1984, after universities had experienced four years of reduced funding, redundancies, early retirements, frozen salaries and unfilled posts as a result of government policy, it was proposed that Oxford should follow tradition and offer the Prime Minister of the day an honorary degree. Normally this would have gone unquestioned, but two hundred and seventy-five dons signed a petition arguing that Thatcher had done deep and systematic damage to the whole public education system in Britain. Early in 1985, after an acrimonious debate, Thatcher's candidacy was rejected by 738 votes to 319.

The opponents of Thatcher's honorary degree had a point, for the universities were among the earliest institutions to feel a scouring wind of change. It was reported that one of the first questions asked by Sir Keith Joseph on becoming Secretary of State for Education was: 'How do you close a university?'[57] As was seen in Chapter II, the arm's-length principle had in a sense begun with the creation of the University Grants Committee (see p. 32), but in 1981 its chairman, Dr Edward Parkes, announced that in future the UGC would be taking a much closer interest in the internal affairs of universities. That year the UGC decided that student numbers would have to be cut by five per cent, and university budgets were reduced by an average of seventeen per cent. Some four thousand, four hundred senior lecturers took early retirement. By 1986 university funding had fallen by twenty per cent in real terms and twenty thousand student places had been lost. Polytechnics, then still funded by local authorities, were not cut in the same way, but suffered an erosion of resources through the pressure on local authority finance, and the demands made on them to make up the places lost at universities.

In 1985 the government embarked on major changes to the whole education system, which emerged as the Education Reform Act of 1988. Polytechnics were taken out of local authority control, and were later redesignated as universities. The University Grants Committee was replaced by the Higher Education Funding Council, whose membership was drawn from businessmen as well as academics. The concept of "contract funding" was introduced, which placed specific obligations and performance targets on teaching institutions, and their research "productivity" began to be regularly assessed. Academic tenure was abolished. The intention was now rapidly to expand higher education, but at as little cost as possible, and universities found themselves caught between rising demand and unpredictable funding. The same act abolished the Inner London Education Authority, allowed individual primary and secondary schools to opt out of local authority control, and introduced a National Curriculum. When the government announced its intentions in a Green Paper in 1985 the editor of the *Times Higher Education Supplement*, Peter Scott, wrote: 'Today large parts of higher education have moved into permanent opposition, even internal exile. Mrs Thatcher's rejection at Oxford was not some fluke engineered by Balliol bolshies. This alienation of organised intelligence from the government, and perhaps more generally from a state with apparently philistine values, will have serious consequences for the sensible conduct of public affairs well into the next century.'[58]

As the principal means of shaping information and opinion, broadcasting received particular attention from the government and its advisers. In November 1982 Channel Four began transmissions. It was a hybrid of the traditions of commercial television and public-service broadcasting, in that it carried advertising, but was insulated from market forces as it was financed by a levy on the independent television companies, and was expressly charged with carrying a proportion of programmes that would appeal to tastes not catered for on the main commercial channel. Channel Four enjoyed the support of William (later Lord) Whitelaw, a more traditional Conservative who became an important ally of Thatcher, and it appealed to Thatcher because it did not itself make programmes, but commissioned them, thus encouraging smaller production companies and breaking down the near-monopolistic character of the large commercial franchise-holders. The new channel succeeded both in terms of meeting minority tastes and encouraging independent production. Under the 1990 Broadcasting Act, Channel Four was pushed further towards private enterprise by being required to raise its own revenue through advertising, with the consequent pressure to increase its audience.

The proliferation of channels, with the government's encouragement of cable and satellite broadcasting, was one of the means of putting pressure on the BBC, long regarded as a disloyal, leftish organisation by many in the Conservative Party, and by Margaret Thatcher in particular. As the relatively liberal Home Secretary Douglas Hurd warned in 1988: 'As choice multiplies and the average viewer has more and more channels to chose from, it will become less and less defensible that he should have to pay a compulsory licence fee to the BBC.'[59] Thatcher was deeply hostile to the licence fee and would have liked to abolish it. In 1985 a committee was set up under the advocate of "consumer sovereignty", the economist Sir Alan Peacock, to examine alternative ways of financing the BBC. The 1986 Peacock Report rejected advertising on the BBC, but did suggest "privatising" Radios 1 and 2, and introducing subscription viewing. Balked of her objective, Thatcher decided in 1986 to 'make the BBC more cost-conscious and businesslike' by freezing the licence fee until 1988 and then index-linking it, so that the BBC was forced to economise.[60] In 1991 the licence fee was increased by less than inflation and then once more linked to the Retail Price Index. With Thatcher's departure from office the threat of a move from funding by licence fee to subscription receded, and the BBC's charter was renewed to its satisfaction in 1996.

The other means of bringing the BBC in line were the government's appointments to its board of governors, and the threat of using its powers of direct intervention. In 1985 the then Home Secretary Leon Brittan came close to this when he asked the governors to stop the transmission of a programme about terrorism in Northern Ireland, *Real Lives*. The governors complied, although a modified version was later transmitted. The first two chairmen of the BBC appointed by the

Conservative government, George Howard and Stuart Young (whose brother was a government minister), were both relatively inactive because of illness, so an important role was played by the board's vice-chairman, Sir William Rees-Mogg. Though by origin and inclination a member of the Great and the Good, he had no difficulty in adapting to the new conditions, for he was much in sympathy with the government's views. Appointed in 1981 on leaving the editorship of *The Times*, it was his opinion that the BBC was 'not an enterprise culture but a spending culture'.[61] Rees-Mogg's political conservatism was matched by a cultural conservatism and a moral disposition to censorship, which may explain why in 1982 he was also made chairman of the Arts Council. After retiring as a governor of the BBC in 1986 and from the Arts Council in 1988, he became the first chairman of the Broadcasting Standards Council, set up to monitor standards of taste (meaning sex and violence) on all channels in Britain.

On the death of the BBC chairman Stuart Young in 1986 the government appointed a former Times Newspapers executive with good Conservative connections, Marmaduke Hussey, as his successor, with the unofficial but widely acknowledged remit to "sort out" the BBC following the Peacock Report. This was done in no uncertain terms by firing the director-general, Alasdair Milne, in January 1987, replacing him with an accountant, Michael Checkland, and bringing in as his deputy a former commercial television executive, John Birt. It was Birt's role to reorganise and centralise the BBC's news services while Checkland restructured the finances and prepared for cuts in staff and facilities, a process carried on even more enthusiastically by Birt, who was nominated to succeed Checkland as director-general nearly two years before he actually did so in 1992. Marmaduke Hussey's chairmanship was extended for a further five years in 1991.

The changes forced on the BBC and the adaptation to the enterprise culture at the most senior level appeared to satisfy Thatcher for the time being – her comment was: 'The appointment of Duke Hussey as chairman of the BBC in 1986 and later of John Birt as deputy director-general represented an improvement in every respect.'[62] Following the 1987 election her attention switched to independent television. At a seminar for the most senior television executives at 10 Downing Street she accused ITV of being the last bastion of restrictive union practices, the first shot in a campaign to introduce more competition by encouraging satellite broadcasting and creating a market-led commercial system.

The 1990 Broadcasting Act introduced an auction system for the next round of commercial television licences (modified by a "quality" threshold), established a third commercial television channel (though the one bid for the franchise was unsuccessful) and replaced the Independent Broadcasting Authority with the Independent Television Commission and a new Radio Authority. These were supposed to have a regulatory "light touch", but at the same time the Broadcasting Standards Council and the Broadcasting Complaints Commission were both placed on a statutory footing, with oversight of both ITV and the BBC, while broadcasters were no longer exempted from the provisions of the Obscene Publications Act. The "free economy" of commercial deregulation was therefore accompanied by the "strong state", with closer government supervision.

As a satellite station, Rupert Murdoch's Sky Television, operating from 1982 but fully launched in 1989, was allowed to escape the limitations on cross-media ownership imposed on newspapers and "terrestrial" television companies, and in 1990 Sky was allowed to take over its only satellite competitor, BSB. The commercial consequences of the 1990 Broadcasting Act, which opened the way to mergers between companies, some of whom had overbid for their licence fees, were the subject of much dissatisfaction within the television industry. There appeared to be less commitment to quality and the "public service" tradition which had always been present in ITV, while the effect of mergers would be to encourage the tendency to turn a federal system into an oligopoly. At the end of the first year of the new franchises the Independent Television Commission felt it necessary to criticise two of the new companies, Carlton and GMTV, for their poor standards.

The cultural consequence of Thatcher's attitude to broadcasting was to replace quality with quantity, and end the confident duopoly that had been created when commercial television began in 1955. Arithmetically, it would become impossible for the BBC, except with its most popular programmes, to gain the fifty per cent of the total audience which had been accepted as justifying its funding by licence fee. Popularity was not supposed to be the only measure of a programme service's worth, but the moral defence of the principle of "public service" broadcasting was no longer so easy to make, for behind it lay paternalistic assumptions about what people should be allowed or encouraged to see, based on a consensus of opinion which Thatcher had made it her business to break up. The BBC's authority and self-confidence was thus directly attacked, but as the political commentator David Watt pointed out in 1985, Thatcherism 'also helped to create a polarised political and cultural climate in which Reithian aspirations find it hard to survive. The problem is really much deeper than political ideology. National consciousness is at present dissolved to the point where no single organisation can possibly "represent" it. Where there is no centre of cultural gravity, high-mindedness can indeed be labelled "pomposity". The protection of standards with which one disagrees becomes "pretentiousness", and the conscious attempt to spread them "flagrant bias". Any sign of self-confidence or independence is "dangerous self-assurance".'[63]

The difficulty of answering the challenge of Thatcherism was demonstrated by the problem of another institution which could lay some claim to represent national consciousness, the Church of England. That a majority even of churchgoers were not members of the established national church added to the perplexities of an organisation unsuccessfully coming to terms with a rapidly changing world. (David Hare's play *Racing Demon* (1990) uses the Church of England as an exemplar of the crisis of liberal institutions.) A few churchmen, notably the Bishop of Durham, Dr David Jenkins, were prepared to speak out against the Government. For Jenkins, to 'return to the ethos of nineteenth-century entrepreneurial individualism is either nostalgic nonsense or else a firm declaration that individual selfishness and organised greed are the only effective motivations for human behaviour'.[64] But as one of the keystones of the old Establishment, the Church of England was hampered by the values of the consensus that Thatcher was attacking, since its authority, like the BBC's, rested on its supposed political neutrality. Just as the BBC was criticised by Conservatives for quoting Argentinian claims during its reporting of the Falklands War, the Archbishop of Canterbury, Dr Runcie, gave offence at the Falklands victory thanksgiving service by recalling the Argentinian as well as British dead.

Dr Runcie caused further annoyance with the report of his Commission on Urban Priority Areas, *Faith in the City* (1985), which showed what the effect of economic restructuring was on the poor in the inner cities, and questioned the government's view of wealth creation which applied to private, but not public, investment. This call for a debate on the moral implications of economic decisions, and the Archbishop of York's further report, *Changing Britain: Social Diversity and Moral Unity* (1987), showed that the Church still held to the values of what the sociologist Kenneth Thompson has called 'organic communitarianism', a pre-industrial social tradition which set a limit to the appetites of capitalist individualism.[65] When Thatcher came into conflict with the Church of England she was also challenging one of the founding principles of her own party, for it too had traditionally claimed to be a defender of the organic unity of the nation against the depredations of industrialism and the disruptions of capitalism. But Thatcher was not a "one-nation" Tory, nor was she by origin a member of the Church of England. Her father had been a Methodist lay preacher, and her economic attitudes were flavoured not only by her childhood as a shopkeeper's daughter, but by the Calvinist justification by works that was a strong element in his faith.

In the adversarial climate of Thatcherism it was difficult for institutions like the BBC, the universities and the Church to defend their position, for subscription to the culture of consensus meant that they had no effective means of going onto the attack. No such political inhibitions affected the leaders of the large metropolitan local authorities which, because of the electoral cycle, had come under Labour control in the local elections at the time of the government's deep unpopularity in 1981. The loudest protests, and the most easily heard, since its headquarters lay directly across the river from the Palace of Westminster, were those of the Greater London Council.

The battle between the government and the GLC, together with the six metropolitan county councils which had been created by the Heath government in 1972, was a straightforward political struggle for control of local responsibility for the lives of the majority of the English population, clustered in the conurbations of London, Manchester, Merseyside, South Yorkshire, Tyneside, the West Midlands and West Yorkshire. These authorities represented alternative centres of political power to Whitehall, and had been the least amenable to attempts to curb public spending. Central government proved the stronger, and all were abolished in 1986, but not before an alternative cultural, as well as political, argument had been developed, most articulately by the GLC.

The cultural argument, which is the issue here, developed slowly. The arts hardly featured in the 160-page manifesto which the GLC Labour group published before winning power from the Conservatives in 1981, yet by 1986 the arts were seen as the leading edge of a radical social and economic agenda. Economic change and the restructuring of industry called for the development of a cultural policy to cope with the problems of an increasingly "post-industrial" city, where traditional constituencies were declining, and new ones emerging. The decline in traditional trades-union power had been one of the reasons why the left-wing group led by Ken Livingstone had been able to take control of the Labour block on the GLC. With the traditional working-class vote in decline, there was a need to establish links with new groups of voters: black British, Asians, middle-class people working in the public sector, and the small but articulate pressure groups of gays and lesbians. A cultural policy which addressed the interests of those groups became an alternative form of mobilisation and communication.

The GLC set up a new Arts and Recreation Committee under the chairmanship of a politically ambitious trades-union official, Tony Banks, who called a grand conference of London's arts organisations in November 1981. The GLC adopted a wider definition of the arts than the Arts Council's to include photography, video, electronic music and community radio, and sought to re-radicalise all the art forms by giving representation on its sub-committees to the most active practitioners. In addition to giving grants, the GLC organised its own festivals and events in order, in Banks's words, 'to project the GLC's image as a progressive, caring, socialist council'.[66] The arts were called into service for the GLC's Peace Year (1983), London Against Racism (1984) and Jobs Year (1985). According to Banks: 'We could, in other words, use the arts as a medium for a political message.'[67]

Support for organisations like Red Wedge, set up by leftist rock musicians Billy Bragg and Paul Weller in 1985 to try to regain the youth vote lost in the 1983 general election, placed an emphasis on communication, which in turn led to a concern for audiences. In 1982 Banks set up sub-committees for sport, community and ethnic arts, which were intended to push resources towards the constituencies identified: unemployed youth, women's groups, gay men's groups, the elderly and disabled, blacks, Asians, and other minorities, rather than respond to the demands of the particular art forms and their professional practitioners, including "community artists". The latter still proved more adept at negotiating their way through the complex maze of legal restraints on local authority funding. The budget for ethnic arts grew from four hundred thousand pounds in 1982–3 to two million

10. *Nouvelle vague*: The painter Peter Phillips in Ken Russell's 'Pop Goes the Easel' for the BBC's *Monitor* 1962.

11. Cultural struggle:
demonstration outside the American Embassy,
Grosvenor Square, 1968.

12. Racial struggle:
Notting Hill Gate Carnival,
1977.

13. Punk Britannia:
Derek Jarman's film *Jubilee*,
1977.

20. Cultural consensus:
street party 1945.

pounds in 1985–6, and proved a powerful stimulus to black theatre, benefiting companies such as Temba (1972–93), Tara Arts (1976–), Black Theatre Co-operative (1979–), and Talawa (1986–). Women's groups found their interests divided between the community and ethnic arts subs-committees, and the GLC's own internal pressure group, the Women's Committee.

The GLC also continued to play an important role in funding the more conventional arts and their institutions in London (the previous Conservative administration had threatened to withdraw its grant to the National Theatre because it had produced Howard Brenton's play *Romans in Britain*) and the arrival of the new regime caused some alarm. In a discussion paper for the Arts and Recreation Committee in July 1981, Banks reviewed the GLC's responsibility for the concert halls on the South Bank which it had inherited from the LCC: 'It is a sad fact that probably a majority of Londoners have never set foot inside those halls which their rates have helped to build and sustain. . . . Centres of excellence must not be allowed to remain the preserve of those who by good fortune or by privilege, recognise the true value of such facilities.'[68]

Because of the enormous expansion in the GLC's arts budget, which had more than doubled to over twenty million pounds by 1984, it was not necessary to cut traditional clients such as the National Theatre and English National Opera. The impact on the Royal Festival Hall and its environs, directly managed by the GLC, was memorable. An "open foyer" policy began in April 1983 and attracted a million visitors in its first year, substantially increasing the attendances in the concert halls themselves. David Widgery wrote: 'Whatever one's reservations about Ken Livingstone's GLC, it prised open the South Bank, the concert halls and the public parks and gave them over to popular performance. When Ranking Ann was toasting free on the stage of the Queen Elizabeth Hall, Misty was making the County Hall car park shudder, ragas tintinnabulated through the Purcell Room and ice-cream vans sounded outside, one began to hear what a socialist city might sound like.'[69]

Although the Arts and Recreation Committee found new ways to stimulate a wide range of activities, its approach was still conventional in that it depended on handing out grants or organising events. But the consequences of economic restructuring in the capital were such that the GLC also had to develop policies that would create wider opportunities. The GLC's Industry and Employment Committee worked with the Economic Policy Unit to develop an industrial strategy for London, to be implemented by a new agency, the Greater London Enterprise Board, in which the so-called "cultural industries" would play a part. A report outlining a cultural industries strategy criticised the Arts Council's practice of funding by meeting companies' deficits, and argued that arts funding could have little impact economically because it was not directed towards the economically viable. Instead, the GLC should work through, and not against the market. A Cultural Industries Unit was set up in 1984 to provide loans and equity investment. One beneficiary from a GLC loan was the co-operative that set up the listings magazine *City Limits* after most of the staff of *Time Out* revolted against the owner Tony Elliott's decision to end its collectivist tradition and the principle of equal pay. Although the co-operative went into receivership in 1990, and the magazine closed in 1993, it had managed to repay an eighty-thousand-pound loan from the GLC with interest.

The GLC's cultural industries budget was only six hundred thousand pounds in comparison with its arts budget of twenty million pounds, and the policy ran for little more than a year before the GLC's abolition, but in effect the GLC had begun to develop its own version of an enterprise culture. Tony Banks, who became an MP in 1983, argued: 'I say that money should be spent on the arts because it is one of the finest forms of public investment that any country can make. . . . We do not subsidise the arts, we invest in them.'[70] The progressive arts policy of the GLC and its attempt to empower minority groups was only one more reason for the Conservative government to wish to abolish it along with the metropolitan county councils. Their abolition became a 1983 manifesto commitment.

The loss of funding from both the GLC and the metropolitan county councils was potentially disastrous for many organisations, because this had made a major contribution to the increase in local-authority arts spending made possible by the 1972 Local Government Act. A brief consultative document from the Office of Arts and Libraries in October 1983 seemed unaware of the scale of the problem. Some extra money would be provided, but about a thousand arts organisations would have to look to the smaller successor authorities in the two tiers of local government that would remain. The Arts Council calculated that the total expenditure of the threatened authorities on the arts was forty-six million pounds a year, and it asked for thirty-seven million to help cover the loss, for it did not believe that the successor authorities with their more limited perspectives would be willing to make up the entire sum. The government eventually came up with an extra sixteen million pounds for the Arts Council, seventeen million for museums and galleries and one million for the British Film Institute.

Although arts spending represented less than one per cent of the condemned authorities' budgets, it became the focus of a defensive campaign that reversed the poles of the argument against Labour's wealth tax a decade before. In the autumn of 1984 the GLC tweaked the Arts Council's tail by giving it six months to quit the Hayward Gallery, forcing the Council to go to court under the Tenant and Landlord Act. When rate capping was introduced in 1985, by which central government set a limit to the amount local authorities could raise in local taxes, the GLC immediately threatened to withdraw funding from four hundred arts organisations, targeting the National Theatre, English National Opera and London Festival Ballet. When the National Theatre decided to close the Cottesloe Theatre later that year in order to draw attention to its insufficient funding, the GLC came to the rescue with a grant of three hundred and seventy-five thousand pounds.

The GLC was doomed, however, and in April 1986 it ceased to exist; its functions were dispersed to the thirty-three London boroughs and a host of other institutions. London became the only major capital in the world not to have some form of unified authority to harmonise its planning or represent its needs. The joint London Boroughs Grants Scheme for co-funding arts and voluntary activities was a totally unsatisfactory replacement for the GLC's cultural funding. It was riven by political disputes between Conservative, Labour and Liberal boroughs, and had great difficulty in setting even low budgets.

Ken Worpole and Geoff Mulgan, who were closely associated with the development of the GLC's cultural policy, concluded of the experiment: 'It was the first time that the doors of power had been so explicitly thrown open to new constituencies, many unfamiliar with the ways of power. This did not result in a mass outburst of sweetness and light. The relationship between organisations, the GLC bureaucracy and the politicians was often tense and contradictory.' Yet the hurly-burly of competing interests was preferable to the 'pacified democracy of secret criteria and even more secret decision-making' of the Arts Council or the BBC.[71] The white working class benefited less from the GLC's largesse than the newly discovered minorities, but it is clear that the GLC's experiment helped to widen the definition of the arts and what was appropriate for a cultural policy, and addressed a new audience in original ways.

Although there was a refreshing frankness in the GLC about the role in political communication that the arts could play, the arts were not so much "politicised", as given a social context where they could articulate the needs of disparate groups, often ones which had little or no voice in the traditional structure of patronage. This principle applied to political as well as cultural power, for the GLC was ready to work with activists to maintain a radical momentum, rather than settle into the old patterns of Labourist bureaucracy. The collective nature of this endeavour was in marked contrast to the privatising, individualistic approach of Thatcherism, where the freedom of the market masked the increasing authoritarianism of the state. One consequence of the GLC's provocative poster campaign in its own defence – an earlier campaign had asked: 'Where would Mrs Thatcher have got to if she had been black?' – was the provisions of the 1986 Local Government Act. This expressly curtailed the power of local authorities to spend money on publicity which could be deemed political – an inadvertent tribute to the impact of that campaign.

Although the cultural influence of the BBC was wider than the Arts Council's and its patronage of actors, writers, composers and musicians far greater, although the universities and polytechnics took the central educational role and although the combined cultural budgets of the local authorities were larger, the Arts Council was still the defining institution in national cultural policy, and so could not fail to be affected by the revolution that Margaret Thatcher intended to make. When the Arts Council declared in its strategy document *The Glory of the Garden* in 1985 that 'for some years the Council has been stuck in a groove', it did not realise that it was entering a period of disconcerting, destabilising change.[72] The 'strategy for a decade' turned out to be the beginning of ten years that would leave the Arts Council at its lowest point ever. Indeed, by 1995 the Arts Council of Great Britain would no longer be in existence.

As a busy, not to say hyperactive Prime Minister, Thatcher did not have much time to enjoy the arts, except as part of her official engagements. She was known to enjoy the novels of Frederick Forsyth and

John Le Carré and the company of the popular writer and active politician Jeffrey Archer. She approved of the profitable musicals of Andrew Lloyd Webber, who wrote the 1987 Conservative campaign theme, and who was later knighted. A parliamentary question from Tony Banks in October 1987 about her choice of works from the government art collection to decorate Number 10 Downing Street revealed the selection of a Van Dyke engraving of Oliver Cromwell, landscapes by Turner and the School of Norwich, views of Cornwall, a map of the approaches to the Falklands, two Gilmans, a Sickert, reproductions of Van Gogh's *Basket of Fruit with Blue Gloves* and Paul Klee's *Fish Magic*, and six Cibachrome landscapes by Paul Wakefield.[73] Mrs Thatcher was sufficiently a modernist to arrange for the loan of a Henry Moore sculpture from the Henry Moore Foundation, and a different Moore drawing or print would be hung beside it every three months. Thatcher's favourite was one of Moore's shelter drawings during the Blitz.

On a visit to the Tate Gallery, Thatcher was reported as saying that it was important to add to the heritage, as well as preserve it, but she had in mind private rather than public patronage. As she wrote in her memoirs: 'I was not convinced that the state should play Maecenas. Artistic talent – let alone artistic genius – is unplanned, unpredictable, eccentrically individual. Regimented, subsidised, owned and determined by the state, it withers. Moreover the "state" in these cases comes to mean the vested interests of the arts lobby. I wanted to see the private sector raising more money and bringing business acumen and efficiency to bear on the administration of cultural institutions.'[74]

Nevertheless, the state had some responsibility to the arts, as a matter of prestige: 'I was profoundly conscious of how a country's art collections, museums, libraries, operas and orchestras combine with its architecture and monuments to magnify its international standing.'[75] In 1988 the government, with Prince Charles acting at one point as an emissary, was involved in negotiations with the Swiss-based industrialist Baron Thyssen-Bornemisza to persuade him to move his large collection of Old Masters to Britain, possibly to be sited in Docklands. The government was prepared to release one hundred and fifty million pounds from the contingency reserve to achieve this, but in the event the Baron's Spanish wife caused the collection to be settled in Madrid.

The arts that brought prestige were unproblematic for a premier who became ever more regal in her bearing, but the contemporary had its dangers. Sir Peter Hall, director of the National Theatre from 1973 to 1988, has recorded that he had 'several argumentative meetings with Mrs Thatcher, public and private. It was like talking to a suspicious headmistress who feared that artiness among the boys and girls might lead to softness and possible left-wing tendencies; they should all aim to get a proper job instead.'[76] (Hall was admittedly not an unbiased witness, though he had voted Conservative in 1979.) To Thatcher's credit, she had supported the principle of a Public Lending Right, which would reward authors for the use of their books in public libraries, ever since she had been responsible for the arts as Secretary of State for Education under Edward Heath. An enabling bill was passed in 1979 and the decision taken to proceed in 1980, with the money coming from the government's arts budget. The first payments, mainly small sums, and none more than five thousand pounds, were made in 1984.

Her most significant spending decision for the arts was to give the go-ahead in 1980 for the construction of a new British Library on a site next to St Pancras Station. In December 1982 Prince Charles laid the foundation stone for a building he was later to anathematise. Colin St John Wilson's design was for the largest public building of the decade, but its construction was hampered by technical problems and the difficulties caused by being funded on an annual basis. The original plan, which would have meant that building continued until 2025, was curtailed, and a new deadline set for completion by 1996, but the official opening would not be until 1998. When completed, the building still would not be large enough to hold all its collections in one place, as was the original intention in moving out of the British Museum building in Great Russell Street. The total projected cost of the new building was more than five hundred million pounds, which placed a steadily rising pressure on the arts budget. It did, however, allow the government to claim that it was spending an increasing sum on the arts.

Though Thatcher may have been suspicious of state intervention in the arts, the foundations of the Department of National Heritage, established by her successor, John Major, were laid during her premiership. She told a House of Commons select committee investigating the funding of the arts in 1981: 'I have made it clear from the first that I am convinced of the need for the arts to have its own independent voice in government.'[77] Her first choice of Arts Minister was Norman St John-Stevas, who had briefly served in 1974, and then acted as Conservative Opposition Spokesman. In 1979 St John-Stevas became

Chancellor of the Duchy of Lancaster as well as Arts Minister, which meant that for the first time there would be an Arts Minister in the Cabinet. A separate Office of Arts and Libraries, with its own accounting officer, was created out of the former Arts and Libraries Branch of the Department of Education and Science. St John-Stevas, 'whose wit', in the words of Nigel Lawson, 'tended to get the better of his discretion', was a one-nation Tory, and the first of the "wets" to be dismissed, in January 1981.[78] He was invited by Thatcher to stay on simply as Arts Minister, but he declined. On his replacement by Paul Channon, the Office of Arts and Libraries disappeared into the DES again, but became independent once more in 1983, this time linked to the Privy Council Office and the Cabinet Office with Channon's successor, Lord Gowrie, also serving as Minister for the Civil Service.

The Arts Council began the Thatcher years at a low ebb. There were ideologues on the Right – Kingsley Amis among them – who argued that there should be no funding of the arts, and no Arts Council, while on the Left the Council was regarded with suspicion as a conservative, middle-class organisation. An internal investigation by a former Council vice-chairman, Jeremy Hutchinson QC, reported in 1979 that there was a widespread feeling of malaise, and uncertainty about the Arts Council's function. In 1977 the poet Roy Fuller had resigned from the Council, loudly protesting at its patronage of performance art, but there were equally others who thought it did too little for the innovatory and the avant-garde. The advisory system at the time, whereby there were large panels of advisers, but small inner groups with quasi-executive status who decided the grants, was confusing and cumbersome, and following the Hutchinson Report the number of advisers was halved.

The Council's secretary-general was Roy Shaw, first appointed in 1975. A former WEA lecturer under Sidney Raybould, he had become a professor of adult education before joining the Council. He had a staunch ally in his friend from WEA days, Richard Hoggart, who returned to England after serving as an assistant director-general of UNESCO from 1970 to 1975, became a member of the Arts Council in 1976 and its vice-chairman in 1980. Naturally Shaw pushed the cause of arts education, and in the face of considerable hostility established a small education unit within the Council. Though, like Raybould, a missionary for the arts – he explicity repudiated the W. E. Williams adage 'few but roses' – Roy Shaw was culturally conservative.[79] He was no friend of community arts: 'I know that Tony Banks, the redoubtable chairman of the Greater London Council's Arts and Recreation Committee, says that all arts are political and only an idiot denies it; but I am an idiot in this matter.'[80] Shaw's contract was extended in 1979 to pre-empt possible government changes, but this may not have been a wise move. Norman St John-Stevas records that 'between Mr Roy Shaw . . . and myself there appeared to be a temperamental incompatibility'.[81] Nor was Shaw popular with all the staff of the Council, his soubriquet among some officers being, according to the literature director Charles Osborne, 'Roy the Obscure'.[82]

While the Arts Council was in poor shape to defend itself, for Norman St John-Stevas 'the immediate problem facing me was that great expectations had been aroused by my activities in Opposition'.[83] This is hardly surprising, for he had called for the doubling of the arts budget. He had persuaded Margaret Thatcher to say a few words to a Conservative conference on the arts in 1978 and had reprinted a letter from her to the Chairman of the Arts Council, Lord Gibson, in a party policy document. On the subject of funding Thatcher had written: 'I don't believe in the present economic situation it will make sense for any government to look for candle-end economies that will yield a very small saving, whilst causing upset out of all proportion to the economies achieved.'[84] As soon as the government came into office, and without any consultation with St John-Stevas, the budget of the Office of Arts and Libraries was cut in mid-year by £2.6 million, of which the Arts Council had to bear a cut of one million. The apparent willingness of the government to make exactly the candle-end economies which Margaret Thatcher had previously rejected panicked the Arts Council into deciding in December 1980 to withdraw funding entirely, and without warning, from forty-one companies, even though the grant for 1981–2 was a slight increase in real terms, to eighty million pounds. The cuts – whose major casualties were the Prospect Theatre Company at the Old Vic, the National Youth Theatre, National Youth Orchestra and National Youth Brass Band, but also a number of left-wing theatre companies – were handled badly and brought great unpopularity, for the Council appeared to be behaving, not for the first time, with a blustering arrogance.

The Arts Council was not to escape the twin pressures of economic constraint and political redirection felt by larger institutions. Ministers would regularly claim that government spending on the arts significantly increased during the eighties, but this has to be set against the very real difficulties that most organisations faced during the decade, which culminated in major crises in 1989 and 1990. A report by the Policy Studies Institute (an independent body not to be confused with the Thatcherite Centre for Policy Studies) calculated that, at face value, there had been a substantial increase in spending on the arts and museums between 1978–9 and 1988–9: 'At constant prices (deflated by the GDP deflator), the growth in arts and museum revenue expenditure is impressive, increasing by forty per cent over the period. However, part of this increase up to 1987/8 does not represent an increased financial commitment to the arts and museums, but instead reflects changes in the structure of funding at central and local government levels.'[85]

The first cautionary note must be the use of the Gross Domestic Product deflator rather than the Retail Price Index as the measure of inflation. The former was the government's preferred measure, and was appropriate to bulk items, but the RPI, which most directly affected arts organisations, told a far less favourable story. Important factors in the government's claims were the construction of the British Library, and the additional funding necessitated by the abolition of the Greater London Council and Metropolitan County Councils, which represented a transfer rather than an increase in resources. Still using the GDP deflator, this reduces the increase for arts and museums to twenty-two per cent. Nor was the spending equal between the two sectors, and building work on museums meant that there was greater expenditure on the heritage than the arts. As far as the Arts Council was concerned, excluding replacement funding and using the Retail Price Index, the increase in its funding between 1979 and 1989 was just one per cent. Using a third measure of inflation, the Average Earnings Index, it suffered a cut of nineteen per cent.

These macroeconomic calculations were the subject of claim and counter-claim: the reality was that while the demand for the arts increased during the eighties, arts organisations had a harder and harder struggle to meet it. In spite of the difficulties placed in their way, local authorities increased their spending on arts and museums, although their policies were as patchy as the available statistics. If expenditure on public libraries is included, local authorities were spending more than central government by the end of the decade, some seven hundred and fifty million pounds a year. Following the departure of Nigel Lawson from the Treasury in 1989 and then the appointment of David

Mellor as Chief Secretary to the Treasury in John Major's first administration, there were real increases in the arts budgets, although the Arts Council was to receive a cash cut in real terms in 1994. In 1993–4 the total budget of the Department of National Heritage was just 0.4 per cent of central government expenditure.[86]

The Arts Council was not to be exempted from the politicisation of public appointments which characterised the decade. In 1981 the Conservative Party's Treasurer, Alistair (later Lord) McAlpine, joined the Council. McAlpine was a considerable collector and patron of the arts – he commissioned Quinlan Terry to erect a memorial to the defeat of Labour's wealth tax proposals in the garden of the house which he rented from the National Trust – but he did not believe in the public subsidy of the arts, and said so. When Roy Shaw pointed this out, it was indicated to him that McAlpine's nomination could not be questioned, since it came from Thatcher herself.[87]

McAlpine did not stay long on the Council, and made little impact, but his appointment was a harbinger of changes to come. When in 1981 the question of renewing Richard Hoggart's appointment to the Council arose, Shaw and the Chairman Kenneth Robinson explained to the Arts Minister, Paul Channon, that as Hoggart was the Council's vice-chairman, by custom his term would be extended. They were told that this was impossible: 'Number 10 doesn't like him.' For Hoggart, who tells this story, the point was obvious: 'It confirmed that governmental intervention in such bodies started very early in the eighties. Fiats from Number 10 and compliance from some of her ministers.'[88] In April 1982 the management of the Arts Council became much easier, from the government's point of view, when William Rees-Mogg took over as its chairman. One of his first acquisitions for the Council was a gavel, something that had not previously been thought necessary for Council meetings.

Roy Shaw's view of his new chairman was that his policy was 'undesirably close to the policy of the government', and he later accused him of conducting a 'secretive and despotic chairmanship' because of his plan to turn the Arts Council's Hayward Gallery over to the British Film Institute for its new Museum of the Moving Image.[89] (The plan was thwarted, and the museum squeezed under Waterloo Bridge instead.) Rees-Mogg accepted that funding was not going to expand, and that arts organisations had to develop other sources, including business sponsorship. 'I was also very concerned to lower arts companies' expectations about funding.'[90] The policy promulgated in *The Glory of the Garden* was accepted by his Council members; less welcome was his view that 'arts grants should primarily be a consumer and not a producer subsidy'.[91] Rees-Mogg admitted that he was occasionally 'depressed by the way in which many artists seem to be trapped in a dated and provincial set of attitudes, the post-Fabian Guardian consciousness of genteel academic English collectivism' and declared that he hoped they would reassert 'human and individual values against the twentieth-century collectivism'.[92] He began a decisive change in the distribution of power between the Council's chairman and its secretary-general, who until then had taken the lead. On Shaw's retirement in 1983, he chose the thirty-six-year-old director of the Association for Business Sponsorship of the Arts, Luke Rittner, to succeed him. Rittner, who described himself as 'in no sense an intellectual', encountered snobbish resistance to his appointment, from senior Council officers among others.[93]

Rees-Mogg's closeness to government policy led to the extension of his five-year appointment until 1989. It caused little surprise that his successor should be a millionaire, Peter Palumbo, whose substantial wealth (inherited from his father) was derived from business property. He was customarily described as a developer, but his one major project, to build an office block next to the Mansion House in the City of London, first to a design by Mies van der Rohe, and then by James Stirling, seemed permanently blocked by planning disputes, and work did not begin on clearing the site until 1994. Palumbo was a collector of twentieth-century art, and had been considered for the chairmanship of the Tate Gallery, until he made a public attack on the Tate's director, Alan Bowness. He told *The Times* that his personal commitment to private patronage was 'surely an eighteenth-century thing: perhaps I am a throwback'.[94] Palumbo was also a donor to the Conservative Party, and was awarded a peerage in Thatcher's resignation honours list, which was widely read as a reward for his political services, rather than for his service to the arts.

A much less public figure than Rees-Mogg, Palumbo had difficulty in adjusting to the bureaucratic and consultative culture of the Arts Council. In a typical gesture, he spent one hundred thousand pounds of his own money on decorating his offices in the Council's building. His personal interest in architecture led to the creation of an architecture unit at the Council. He caused consternation when he decided in 1989 that an unexpected legacy to the Council of £1.1 million should be used to set up a completely separate organisation, the Arts Foundation, of which he would be chairman. The purposes of the Foundation were to raise funds and stimulate innovation, but it remained embarrassingly inactive until 1993, as either raiser or dispenser of money. His relations with Luke Rittner were not good, and Rittner resigned in protest at government plans to hand over many of the Council's clients to the Regional Arts Associations in 1990. He was succeeded by the deputy secretary-general, Anthony Everitt.

The political nature of appointments to the Arts Council and elsewhere did not go unnoticed. Lord Goodman commented in 1989: 'There have been some rather startling appointments of people who have been appointed self-evidently more for their political judgement.' He pointed to the rejection of the former director-general of the British Council, Sir John Burgh, as a possible chairman of the Tate Gallery. Rees-Mogg, he added, 'would not have become chairman of the Arts Council if he had not been a proclaimed Conservative' (a view Rees-Mogg disputed, though the evidence seems incontrovertible).[95] Peter Hall observed a similar process at work in appointments to the board of the National Theatre: 'The government found acceptable as Board members only those they could call "one of us". The old idea of keeping a rough balance was gone. It was happening in all public institutions.'[96] After Margaret Thatcher's departure this principle continued to apply under John Major. When Lord Palumbo's five years in office ended in 1994, his successor was none other than a former arts minister, Lord Gowrie.

VIII

Value for Money
The arts under Thatcherism

Throughout the changes of Arts Minister during the eighties, the government's policy towards the Arts Council remained consistently that announced by St John-Stevas at a conference of Regional Arts Associations in November 1979. The government, he said, had decisively tilted away from the enlargement of the public sector to the enlargement of the private, and while the present level of support for the arts would be maintained: 'in the immediate future we will not be able to increase it'.[1] Lord Gowrie was to say much the same in 1985: 'As Culture Minister it is, I am afraid, also my duty to administer something of a culture shock. The party is not over, but the limits of hospitality have been reached. From now on, central government funding will remain broadly level in real terms.'[2]

Economic and political pressure, combined with public dissatisfaction, forced the Council more than once to review its procedures and ask itself what its purpose was. New guidelines were issued to advisory panels in October 1981 which showed that the contradictions in the Council's founding purpose had not been resolved: 'In their forward policy thinking, Panels and Committees should be concerned with both quality and access; the aim should be to identify quality (whatever the scale of the activity concerned) and to spread that quality as widely as possible.'[3] In what was in effect a *post-hoc* justification of the cuts of 1979, the Council solved the problem of "amateur versus professional" by concluding that their resources were so stretched that only the "professional" could be helped. It became policy gradually to withdraw from funding individuals. A choice between individual artists was always harder to make and justify than one between organisations.

A particular focus of complaint among the Council's critics was the Literature Department which, although – or because – it spent little

252 Culture and Consensus

more than one per cent of the Council's grant-in-aid, was regularly accused of indolence and favouritism. The general perception of the long-serving literature director, Charles Osborne, who had joined the Council in 1966, was that he was, in his own words, 'a charming, witty rat'.[4] There was great embarrassment in March 1980 when a new Council literary prize, worth seven and a half thousand pounds, was presented to the historian Hugh Thomas, who promptly refused it. Thomas had become chairman of Margaret Thatcher's Centre for Policy Studies, and he used the opportunity to criticise public funding of the arts. In 1981 the novelist Margaret Forster left the literature advisory panel, saying: 'I no longer believe that the Arts Council gives a damn about the literature panel. . . . The relationship between Council and panel is non-existent and between Council officials and the panel very – shall we say – difficult. . . . It is not that anyone is abusing the system, but that the system is an abuse in itself.'[5]

In October 1982 a parliamentary select committee on Education, Science and the Arts published the results of a year-long investigation into the entire field of arts funding. It found the division of responsibility between the Arts Council and the Office of Arts and Libraries uncertain, and brought the Department of National Heritage one step nearer by recommending that a Ministry for the Arts, Heritage and Tourism should be created, led by a minister of Cabinet rank, which would take responsibility for broadcasting as well as for the arts, libraries, heritage and tourism. As a consequence, 'the Arts Council will no longer be the sole channel of central government funding for the performing and creative arts'.[6] The report also heralded an important new theme: 'We are of the opinion that the considerable economic importance of the arts is not generally appreciated by local and national government.'[7]

The government gave a bland and dismissive reply to these proposals, but the report pointed to things to come. One suggestion was that the government should "earmark" grants to major companies, a proposal that worried the Arts Council, for it weakened the arm's-length principle. By 1982 the financial position of many companies was becoming desperate because of the recession. As Rees-Mogg warned the Arts Minister Paul Channon, many Arts Council clients 'are now operating at an uneconomic level, with long periods of closure; their buildings are becoming more dilapidated; and, most important of all, their creative scope is more seriously restricted than ever before'.[8] The growing deficits at the Royal Opera House and the Royal Shakespeare Company (which had just moved into new premises at the Barbican Arts Centre in London) were such that in December 1982 the Office of Arts and Libraries commissioned a financial scrutiny by an efficiency expert in the Prime Minister's office, Clive Priestley. His report confirmed that both organisations were seriously underfunded, by about twenty per cent, but decided that neither was inefficient or wasteful, as had been assumed. The government's response was to earmark an additional grant of £2.8 million for the two organisations. The Council was shocked: 'The report's suggestion that the activities of great national companies would be above political interference flies in the face of experience, even in this country. . . . The dividing line between earmarking and direct funding is so fine that the Council finds earmarking only less objectionable in principle.'[9]

The Arts Council had another setback when it commissioned a report on the effect of inflation on the arts. The conventional wisdom was that the arts suffered disproportionately, for they were unable to economise on labour. The report by the economist Alan Peacock concluded, however, that the differential effect of inflation between 1970 and 1982 had been comparatively slight. This was not what the Arts Council wanted to hear. Peacock has commented: 'Any case for increasing public subsidies to arts organisations solely because of differential inflation effects was destroyed. I am told that the ACGB was very taken aback and horror was expressed at the "enormous" cost of the study itself. The chairman is alleged to have remarked that the Survey would have been cheap at half the price, if it had come to the right conclusion.'[10] The report was not widely circulated.

The only way for the Arts Council to break out of the stasis and demoralisation that had gradually enveloped it since 1975, when expansion had effectively ceased, was to reorganise itself internally and devise a new policy that would fend off encroaching government interference. At the same time, the Council faced a challenge from another quarter: a further suggestion of the Education, Science and Arts Committee had been that more should be done by the Arts Council to devolve responsibility for clients to the twelve Regional Arts Associations in England.

The RAAs were voluntary associations which had begun to form following the decision by the Arts Council to close its regional offices in 1956. By 1973 Buckinghamshire was the only county not covered by one of the Associations, which brought together representatives of local authorities, local institutions such as universities, and individual members, who jointly elected their governing board. The RAAs did not make the same distinction between amateur and professional made by the Arts Council, and had a more democratic tradition, electing their chairmen and committees themselves. Local authorities contributed some funding and much of the ethos of the RAAs, but ninety per cent of funds came from the Arts Council. Since most of the Arts Council's clients were also funded by their local RAAs, there was inevitably a duplication of effort as the same government money reached a client in two different ways, while the slightly different criteria used could also lead to conflict.

For the Arts Council, devolution offered an opportunity to restructure itself, and make cuts. It would answer the justified complaint that too much of the Council's money was devoted to London, for twice as much was spent in London and the South-East as in the rest of the country. It would also demonstrate that it was the appropriate body to deal with the consequences for the arts of the impending abolition of the GLC and the metropolitan county councils. The horticultural metaphor of what was to be called *The Glory of the Garden* was already in place when the secretary-general Luke Rittner announced in November 1983 that a new strategy was to be developed which 'will help the Council to thin out the seed-bed to give more room . . . and for new seeds to be planted'.[11]

The title of the resulting strategy, published in March 1984, was taken from lines by Rudyard Kipling which combined a hierarchical version of the pastoral myth with a hint of the enterprise culture: 'Our England is a garden, and such gardens are not made/ By singing "Oh how beautiful!" and sitting in the shade.'[12] The Council proposed to transfer six million pounds in funding from London to the regions and to devolve forty-four of its clients to Regional Arts Associations. One of the four London symphony orchestras was to be "encouraged" to move to the east of England; ten music organisations, ten theatres and five touring companies would lose their grants; and the Royal Court Theatre was put on notice that it would lose its funding. Provision for training, arts centres and community arts would be reduced and the capital fund for housing the arts run down. No new clients would be taken on in London. The Literature Department would effectively be wound up.

The Glory of the Garden turned out to be rather less radical than it looked. All but one million of the six million pounds to be found by the cutting of organisations actually came from the cutting of regional companies. Several of the condemned organisations won a reprieve, and no London orchestra proved willing to move. In 1985 William Rees-Mogg admitted that the actual transfer of funds was only three per cent. The policy did solve the problem of what to do with Charles Osborne, for he was made redundant, thus freeing him to write his memoirs. The policy was also a bid for increased funds from the government, which were not forthcoming, yet the principal point of the exercise, to show that the Arts Council was capable of rethinking its position, was made.

For the first time the Arts Council introduced the idea of "challenge funding", by which it would make its grants conditional on matching sums being given by local authorities. This was crucial as the potential damage to the arts from the abolition of the GLC and the MCCs became apparent. (In 1986 the Arts Council claimed that it had secured replacement funding from successor authorities for the 'vast majority' of affected arts organisations.[13] Nonetheless abolition did do damage, especially on Merseyside.) Ironically, by convincing the Arts Minister Lord Gowrie that the Arts Council was the appropriate body to distribute the replacement funding that would be needed, and that it should take over ownership of the South Bank and other facilities from the GLC, the Council subverted the whole purpose of *The Glory of the Garden*, for its metropolitan responsibilities substantially increased. When the 'strategy for a decade' was first announced, the Council had one hundred and fifty-six annual revenue clients, and proposed to reduce these to ninety-four. But in 1989 the Arts Council had one hundred and forty clients, and was still spending forty-eight per cent of the money for England in London.

The Arts Council may have gained the trust of the government, but it lost that of many in the arts. The Regional Arts Associations complained that they were not getting the resources they needed, and ten London theatres protested that they were in crisis as a result of being given near standstill grants. In February 1985, having warned the Council not to go ahead with *The Glory of the Garden* because the lack of money made it unworkable, seven members of the Drama Panel resigned, saying: 'The Arts Council will never re-establish its position as an invaluable national asset until it is no longer perceived as an arm of government.'[14] As director of the National Theatre, which was menaced by a growing deficit, Peter Hall became a spokesman for the protestors. He declared that the Arts Council had become an instrument of the government: 'It is probably the first time in the history of the Arts Council that a powerful group of people have actually repudiated the Council as a body which can judge, influence, and finance them.'[15] Lord Gowrie, he wrote later, 'seemed to me far more concerned with pleasing Thatcher than with the creative potential of the arts'.[16] At a press conference at the National Theatre he stood on a coffee table to announce that the National's third auditorium, the Cottesloe, would be closed to save money and one hundred jobs would be lost. Earlier, the arts correspondent of *The Times*, David Hewson, had reported: 'The sense of anger, disillusionment and even betrayal now being expressed over the direction of the government's arts policy is virtually universal.'[17] In March, forty-two artistic directors passed a vote of no confidence in the Council. It was an indication of the Council's failure to act as an advocate for the arts constituency that a new lobby, with a professional staff, the National Campaign for the Arts, was launched in 1985.

The arts, however, were caught in an irresistible tidal change: the shift towards what Lord Gowrie's successor as Arts Minister, Richard Luce, called 'the culture of wealth creation'.[18] "Value for money" was now statutory policy, enforced by the 1983 National Audit Act which empowered the Auditor General to review the value for money given by central government departments and other public bodies in terms of economy, efficiency and effectiveness. Effectiveness was measured by the setting of "performance indicators" and setting specific activity targets in forward plans. While "value for money" entered the language of the arts, the arts themselves were entering the period when they became "cultural industries". Economists not only considered the genuinely industrial aspects of publishing, recorded music, television and radio, but looked at the arts in terms of their contribution to employment and as adjuncts to tourism. Guided by one of its special advisers, the cultural economist John Myerscough, the Education, Science and Arts Committee had taken the approach seriously, and the concept was further endorsed in the Priestley report on the RSC and Covent Garden. Roy Shaw, however, was dismissive of the "cultural industries" and their commercial appeal: 'These largely exploit the cultural inexperience of the majority, rather than help people to develop.'[19] It was an attitude that a new generation of arts administrators would feel forced to reconsider.

If the arts were to look elsewhere than to the government for patronage, then business sponsorship was an obvious starting point. While sponsorship of sports events was well established, less than one million pounds a year was going to the arts when the Association for Business Sponsorship of the Arts was formed under the chairmanship of Lord Goodman in 1976. Business sponsorship, which could be treated as part of a company's advertising costs, was hardly disinterested. Luke Rittner, a former director of ABSA, has said: 'Sponsors are not donors, the reason for sponsorship is a commercial one, not exclusively altruistic. They quite rightly expect a return.'[20] Business sponsorship was a means of acquiring a benevolent image; association with the more prestigious arts events and star names was an attractive means of entertaining clients. In some cases sponsorship offered a way of avoiding restrictions on the promotion of a product. ABSA was orginally housed in the offices of Imperial Tobacco, and its first secretary was an Imperial Tobacco employee.

Arts sponsorship had risen to approximately four million pounds a year by the time the Conservatives came into office in 1979. Norman St John-Stevas decided to stimulate it further by forming a "Committee of Honour" to promote the cause of sponsorship with a pamphlet, *The Arts are Your Business*, and gave ABSA twenty-five thousand pounds to expand its activities. Under Lord Gowrie, government subsidy of business sponsorship began on a regular basis with the introduction of the Business Sponsorship Incentive Scheme in 1984. Administered by ABSA, the scheme meant that once a sponsorship was agreed, further sums of government money could be added to the deal. By 1994 the government had contributed twenty-one million pounds, in response to forty-three million in sponsorship. In 1992 total business sponsorship for the arts rose to sixty-five million pounds, but fell back to fifty-eight million in 1993 in the face of recession.

The need to find business sponsorship became an established part of the economic thinking of arts companies: in 1989, on the advice of the consultants Strategic Sponsorship Ltd, the Arts Council set up its own sponsorship unit to seek sponsors, not for its clients, but for itself. Whereas at first sponsorship was treated as a useful source of additional funds, it became more and more part of the core funding of organisations.

In 1994 the Royal Shakespeare Company announced that at the end of six years of sponsorship from Royal Insurance worth a total of £3.3 million, it had found fresh sponsorship from Allied Lyons (now Allied Domecq), a further £3.3 million for three years, making it the largest arts sponsorship deal in Britain. The RSC's artistic director Adrian Noble confirmed that sponsorship was no longer just an add-on: 'There has been a shift towards sponsorship supporting the core activities of the company. It is a historical movement that is unstoppable.'[21]

In a lecture early in 1985 appropriately titled *The Political Economy of Art*, the Arts Council's chairman showed that he had adopted the rhetoric of the cultural industries: 'The Arts Council gives the best value for money in job creation of any part of the state system. . . . The arts are to British tourism what the sun is to Spain.'[22] Later that year the Council published fifteen thousand copies of a glossy brochure, *A Great British Success Story*, designed to look like a company report and launched at the Fortune Theatre in an atmosphere of a shareholders' meeting. The Council's finance director, Anthony Blackstock, told the *Sunday Times*: 'You have to talk to this government in the language it understands.'[23] Describing itself as 'an invitation to the nation to invest in the arts', the 'prospectus' used the language of the enterprise culture freely, talking of 'product' rather than productions, 'customers' rather than audiences, and 'investment' rather than subsidy.[24]

The Council was hoping that speaking in this language would persuade the government to raise its grant-in-aid to £161 million for 1986–7. The government produced only £135.6 million, but the Council decided to repeat the exercise in 1986 with *Partnership: Making Arts Money Work Harder*. This time the emphasis was on urban renewal and the development of links with local authorities in the wake of the abolition of the metropolitan councils. The arts would, in order of priority, 'bring new life to inner cities/expand and develop the cultural industries and, consequently, the number of jobs/improve the quality and quantity of arts provision outside central London/ help develop the skills and talents of ethnic minorities and other specific communities/ enhance the cultural and economic potential of rural areas.'[25] The list revealed not only the extent to which arts were now being presented in terms of economic policy, but showed where most anxiety was being felt about the consequences of economic restructuring: unemployment and urban decay.

The Council believed that one of the solutions to the problems of the arts was 'better marketing', and in its bid to the government, this time for £164 million, included five million for 'marketing and entrepreneurial schemes'.[26] In its administrative reorganisation after *The Glory of the Garden*, the Council had created a new Marketing and Resources Department, headed by a former account executive at Saatchi and Saatchi, while the directorates of the arts departments had been grouped together in a single division. The government's response to the 1986 bid was £138.4 million for 1987–8. In the light of the Council's earnest efforts to extract more money from the government it was ironic that in September 1985 Lord Gowrie should resign from his post as Minister for the Arts, saying that he could not live on his ministerial salary of thirty-three thousand pounds.[27] His successor, Richard Luce, who had resigned as a junior minister at the Foreign Office at the beginning of the Falklands War, immediately reminded his new constituency that 'there is no bottomless pit for funds', and repeated the views of his predecessors that the arts would have to look elsewhere for growth.[28] But it wasn't until his reappointment after the 1987 election that he went on the offensive.

Shortly after Margaret Thatcher was returned as Prime Minister for a third time, with a majority of over a hundred, Luce told the annual conference of the Regional Arts Associations: 'I must say that the recent general election provided precious little evidence for the proposition that increased public expenditure on the arts has become a higher priority than hitherto in the minds of the electorate as a whole.'[29] The speech marked a new stage in the implanting of the enterprise culture, with the announcement that there would be a new system of "incentive funding". But Luce was not yet entirely satisfied that the new values had been accepted:

> The most important thing is for the arts world to accept the economic and political climate in which we now operate. . . . There is no argument that enables us to claim that the arts are sacrosanct and should be insulated from the real world. . . . There are too many in the arts world who have yet to be weaned from the welfare state mentality – the attitude that taxpayers owe them a living. Many have not yet accepted the challenge of developing plural sources of funding. They give the impression of thinking that all other sources of funds are either tainted or too difficult to get. They appear not to have grasped that the collectivist mentality of the sixties and seventies is out of date.[30]

The Arts Council evidently could be excluded from these strictures, for it had already agreed with Richard Luce that £3.5 million pounds would be earmarked in the Council's £150 million grant for 1988–9, for an incentive scheme that would be used to encourage organisations to increase their own earnings through better marketing, management, box office and other commercial receipts. Higher standards of work appeared to be secondary. The Council set aside five thousand pounds per applicant to the scheme for the cost of employing management consultants to prepare their submissions, and appointed their own consultant to introduce the scheme. In 1991, when the Council received a substantial increase in funds to £194 million, "incentive" funding was replaced by "enhancement funding", which turned out in practice to be a discreet way of helping to pay off the seventeen million in accumulated deficits of some of the Council's major clients. The Royal Opera House and the RSC were in serious trouble: in November 1990 the RSC shut down its operations at the Barbican for four months to save money.

As the Arts Council bent to the government's bidding it found itself rewarded with less, rather than more, independence from the centralising tendencies of Thatcherism. When the prospect of Labour being returned to power loomed before the 1987 election, the Council organised a grand international conference on the theme of *The Arts: Politics, Power and the Purse*. The covert purpose of the conference was to stave off the creation of a Ministry of Culture, which Labour proposed. William Rees-Mogg concluded his introduction to the conference record: 'While Great Britain has something to learn from the successes born of political commitment to the arts in high places on the one hand [meaning France], and of the decentralisation of funding on the other [meaning the United States], the cardinal feature of the British system – the arm's-length principle – should be honoured and pre-served.'[31] Rees-Mogg's true distance from government policy seems questionable, but the ideology of power is such that hegemony is best maintained by the appearance of independence, and is even more effective when those who exercise it believe that they genuinely are independent. At the conference Tony Banks dismissed the arm's-length principle as a myth: 'This is very much a conference that marks the end of the arm's-length principle. . . . The mere fact that this conference is being held is at least a tacit acknowledgement that the arm's-length principle is dead.'[32]

While the threat of a Labour Ministry of Culture receded, the pressure from the Conservative government did not. At the end of the decade the Arts Council found itself facing a challenge to its position from a far more thorough-going devolution of its clients than the botched *Glory of the Garden*, and at the government's behest. In December 1988 Richard Luce commissioned the civil servant at the head of the Office of Arts and Libraries, Richard Wilding, who was about to retire, to review the relationship between the Arts Council and the Regional Arts Associations. His report, delivered in September 1989, was correctly judged by Lord Goodman to be 'a plan that for practical purposes spelt the end of the Arts Council'.[33]

The main thrust of Wilding's report was that the existence of two tiers of funding was indeed administratively costly, and caused duplication and friction. Wilding believed that two million pounds a year could be squeezed out of the system in administrative costs alone, by reducing the number of Regional Arts Associations (to be renamed Regional Arts Boards and brought under much closer ministerial control), merging the Arts Council with the Crafts Council, and cutting back on staff throughout the system. Wilding proposed that all but thirty of the Arts Council's clients should be devolved to the new Regional Arts Boards, and that the Arts Council should not consider any project with a budget of less than five thousand pounds. In a new "federal" system, the Arts Council would be responsible for the "national" companies and major touring companies, and the encouragement of innovation. It would vet the plans of the Regional Arts Boards, but its own task would be to develop links with broadcasting and the wider world of Europe. In Wilding's opinion, the Council had no long-term view of how the arts should develop: 'What the hungry sheep look up for, but do not get enough of, is vision.'[34]

It took until 1994 for Wilding's vision, and Goodman's nightmare, to come at least partially true. In July 1990 Luce retired from government, and was replaced as Minister for the Arts by David Mellor. Mellor was a very different personality, an enthusiast for the arts, and much less of a devolutionist than Luce. Hardly had he begun to review Luce's post-Wilding negotiations with the Arts Council, however, than Margaret Thatcher resigned, and Mellor was rewarded for his part in John Major's successful campaign to succeed her, with promotion to Chief Secretary to the Treasury. Mellor was replaced as Minister for the Arts by Timothy Renton, demoted from Chief Whip, who took a more acerbic view of the Arts Council and a more favourable view of

Wilding's devolution proposals. At the Treasury Mellor, in co-operation with the Chancellor, Norman Lamont, was able to secure substantial increases in arts funding for 1991 and 1992, increases that were badly needed by most of the Arts Council's clients, as the second recession began to bite. Renton's view of the Arts Council became even more sour when he found that Lord Palumbo, who had cultivated his connections with Mellor, was bypassing his office in order to secure more money from the Treasury. In the run-up to the 1992 general election Renton was publicly contemplating the abolition of the Arts Council, and it was a small group of his advisers who worked on the plans for a Department of National Heritage which became a manifesto commitment in the 1992 election.

In March 1990 Luke Rittner resigned as Arts Council secretary-general, warning that the Wilding proposals would be deeply damaging to the Council's position. Not having any choice in the matter, his successor Anthony Everitt opened negotiations with the Office of Arts and Libraries and the Council's clients as to the precise number to be devolved – the new term was "delegated" – to the Regional Arts Boards which, ten in number, came into existence in October 1991. These negotiations were protracted as Ministers came and went, and clients objected to what they saw as a loss of status as they passed out of metropolitan control. The process was not completed until April 1994, by which time the Arts Council retained responsibility for the four "national" companies (Covent Garden, English National Opera, the National Theatre and the RSC), the South Bank, the London and main regional orchestras, and the major touring companies, with a total of one hundred and twenty-five annual revenue clients in all. All the Council's other drama clients, excepting the Royal Court, were devolved to their respective RABs. The structure of art-form departments (including a literature department, revived in 1987) remained, and these continued to fund one-off projects by companies not funded on an annual basis, but many of the specialist units that the Council had developed in the eighties to promote general policies such as cultural diversity, the role of women in the arts and attention to disability, were wound up.

At the beginning of 1994 the Arts Council calculated that it had spent up to six million pounds since the delivery of the Wilding Report on restructuring, relocation, redundancies and the cost of internal and external management enquiries. At least five hundred thousand of this

can be accounted for by the elaborate consultation exercise to devise
'A National Strategy for the Arts and the Media', which sought to
prove that the Council was indeed capable of the 'vision' which Wilding
believed it lacked. Beginning in the spring of 1991 (with similar exercises carried out by the Scottish and Welsh Arts Councils) the Arts
Council, in collaboration with the Regional Arts Boards, the Crafts
Council (which had survived Wilding's merger proposal), the British
Film Institute and the Museums and Galleries Commission, issued
forty-five discussion documents and then held seminars and conferences up and down the country, to produce a draft document a year
later. Following a further round of consultation a final document, titled
A Creative Future: the way forward for the arts, crafts and media in England,
was published in January 1993.

The final document was wise to drop any claim to be a strategy in
the technical sense, for it was long on good intentions, but lacked
any proposals as to how they might be achieved structurally, and any
estimate of what they might cost. The long-recognised division between
professional and amateur artists and arts organisations was to be dissolved, and the traditional hierarchy of forms within the arts (in practice
already abolished) was to be discarded. There was to be a renewed
emphasis on artistic innovation, on individual artists and artistic entrepreneurs, as opposed to the now almost exclusive reliance on organisations and bureaucracies. There was to be better recognition of the
linguistic and cultural diversity of the United Kingdom, the arts were
to be made more widely available, and there was to be a new emphasis
on the arts in education. There was to be greater openness about
decision-taking, and more consultation. Yet the only practical proposal
as to how any of this might be achieved was limited to the suggestion
that the funding of the arts by local authorities should be a statutory,
as opposed to discretionary, responsibility. Since this proposal had
already been pooh-poohed by the Secretary of State for National Heritage, Peter Brooke, it is not surprising that it, along with the rest of
the report, was ignored by the Department of National Heritage.

The truth of the matter was that after David Mellor was forced to
resign, for personal reasons, as Secretary of State for National Heritage
in September 1992, the Arts Council lost a key ally in government with
a direct line to the Prime Minister, John Major. The new Department
of National Heritage was eager to prove itself by bearing down on the
forty-five different organisations of which it was sponsor, and of which

the Arts Council was the biggest, in order to produce "efficiency savings" and ensure "accountability" – a term which, in spite of regular ministerial acknowledgements of the arm's-length principle, implied much closer supervision and direction on the part of the Ministry. Peter Brooke was not the advocate of the performing arts that Mellor was. At the Treasury, the new Chief Secretary was the right-wing Michael Portillo, who appears to have taken revenge on the liberal Mellor by deciding in the autumn of 1992 that the Arts Council's projected grant for 1993–4 should be reduced to £225 million, an increase below the rate of inflation that meant a cut in real terms, and that it should be cut by a further five million in 1994–5. This cut was later reduced to £3.2 million, but far from endorsing the Council's vision, the government appeared to have decided to make it even harder for it to carry it out. As a final blow, in March 1993 the Department of National Heritage announced that in the following year the Arts Councils of Wales and Scotland, technically sub-committees of the Arts Council of Great Britain, would be funded directly by the Scottish and Welsh Offices, and the Arts Council in London would become the Arts Council of England only. Lord Goodman's prophecy had been fulfilled.

The last year of the Arts Council of Great Britain's existence was the most humiliating in its history. Although the passage of the National Lottery Act in 1993 created a new source of funding, and the Arts Council was to be responsible for overseeing the distribution of lottery funds to capital projects in the arts, the Council was having to prepare to make real cuts in its revenue funding, and was required by the government to make £560,000 savings in its administration costs. A further requirement was to reduce the number of Council members from twenty to sixteen. Having invested so much money and prestige in *A Creative Future*, the Council was determined to prove that it had one, by "funding fewer better". But attempts to achieve this by switching spending priorities between art forms, so that dance, visual art and education were to gain, while music and drama were to lose, ended in fiasco. First a proposal to cease funding up to ten regional theatres was leaked, provoking another theatres revolt that forced the idea to be withdrawn. The Council then tried, not for the first time, to reduce its funding of the four London symphony orchestras, and invited an outside committee, chaired by an appeal court judge, to decide which two should lose their grants altogether. The verdict was inconclusive, and all four continued to receive funds, though at substantially different levels. The Council's music director, Kenneth Baird, and the chairman of the music panel, Bryan Magee, resigned.

In February 1994 the secretary-general, Anthony Everitt, announced his resignation also. His stated reason was that his departure, coinciding with that of Lord Palumbo at the end of March, would leave the new chairman of the new Arts Council of England, Lord Gowrie, with a clean slate, but at the end of a period in which the Arts Council had lost the confidence of both the government and the arts constituency, Everitt's resignation had been widely called for. Just short of its fiftieth anniversary, and the publication of an official history commissioned at a cost to the Council of sixty thousand pounds, the era of what Everitt described as 'Maynard Keynes's idiosyncratic creation, a neo-Bloomsbury, free-standing, mini-ministry of culture, led not by politicians but by practitioners and lovers of the arts' had come to an end.[35] It seemed unlikely that the government would dispense entirely with the useful fig-leaf provided by the existence of an Arts Council and the device of the arm's-length principle, but having done so much to undermine the old system of patronage, the Department of National Heritage could be expected to move further into the void it had created.

Just as the institutions responsible for the future of Britain's cultural identity underwent a thorough reconstruction during the eighties, so did those responsible for the presentation and perception of the nation's past. It might at first appear that the appeal to the past manifested by the multiplication of museums, heritage centres and commercial attractions – calculated to give an ever more pleasing "experience" of a past that was in fact irrecoverable – contradicted the call to mobilise national enterprise and secure the future. In practice, the emphasis on the past served both as a mask for the revolution of the present, and as a compensation for it.

The past was reinvented, so that the social conflicts of the industrial revolution were consolingly reintegrated into the picturesque and pastoral narrative that became the consumer's version of the national story. Cotton mills and coal mines were painted into a picture-book history as decorative artefacts, redundant relics of lost communities. The machinery still stood, but its brutal *raison d'être* was at best dimly recalled in the act of fantasising "the way we were". The parallel cult of the castle and the country house appealed directly to the authoritarian side of Thatcherism. The inheritance of the past was projected as "common", yet it excluded many people, notably immigrants and their British-born children. Uncritical reference to the past served unconsciously to reproduce older patterns of deference and class. Few, if any, people owned the landscape, properties and artefacts that were presented as "their" heritage, and they were increasingly expected to pay for access to them.

The official status of the word "heritage" within the prevailing ideology received powerful reinforcement with the National Heritage Acts of 1980 and 1983, though in neither case was a formal definition of its meaning part of the legislation. The different intentions of the two acts were symptomatic of the cultural shift that Thatcher's government was trying to engineer. The 1980 National Heritage Act was a belated recognition of the visionary nature of Hugh Dalton's 1946 National Land Fund. During the major public expenditure crisis of 1976 the Labour government had concluded that it could not afford to accept the offer of Mentmore House, together with its contents, in lieu of death duties on the estate of the 7th Lord Rosebery's father. This magnificent nineteenth-century Rothschild mansion could have been acquired "for the nation" for three million pounds but after protracted negotiations the government was only prepared to release one million from the National Land Fund. In May 1977 the house was put up for sale and its contents dispersed in an auction that raised £6.25 million for the contents alone. The nation acquired some pictures and furniture, but it was plain that a bargain had been missed, and the essential unity of house and contents broken.

The Mentmore scandal – and Mentmore was only one of a number of great houses in need of "saving" – became a *cause célèbre* for the heritage lobby as another part of the nation's past was first threatened and then destroyed. It also drew attention to the failure to use the National Land Fund for the purposes for which it had been intended. In spite of the Treasury's raid in 1957 (see Chapter II, p. 47) there was still eighteen million pounds in the Fund, and with heritage issues now playing a much larger part in public awareness, it was time to rethink the administration of the Fund. Following an investigation by a Parliamentary Select Committee, which reported in June 1978, and a government White Paper in February 1979, fresh legislation was in preparation when the Labour government fell.

The National Heritage Act was therefore introduced in December

1979 by Norman St John-Stevas, who was pleased to announce that in this area at least, extra investment had been found. The National Land Fund was to be reconstituted as the National Heritage Fund (the word Memorial was added as an afterthought at the committee stage) and handed over to the control of independent trustees. The chairman and ten trustees were to be, in St John-Stevas's words, 'cultured generalists' – possibly the last time the Great and the Good received official acknowledgement.[36] The trustees would have at their disposal, not the original fifty million pounds of 1946, still less the six hundred million-plus it could have become had it not been tampered with, but a basic endowment of £12.4 million, to be topped up by annual grants from the Department of the Environment and the Office of Arts and Libraries, initially £5.5 million from each. The Fund would no longer compensate the Treasury when properties or artefacts were accepted in lieu of death duties. Instead, it would acquire property, and in practice anything else it chose, from Books of Hours to submarines, on behalf of other organisations that would become responsible for their care. The National Trust, the Wildfowl Trust, the Nature Conservancy Council, national and provincial museums and galleries were typical beneficiaries. Where necessary, as in the case of country houses, the National Heritage Memorial Fund was empowered to add an endowment for upkeep. Under the 1993 National Lottery Act, the Fund has become the principal body responsible for the distribution of funds raised by the lottery in the field of heritage and conservation.

The 1980 National Heritage Act was an enlightened piece of legislation that added the use of endowment funding to the range of funding methods, the advantage of an endowment being that the Fund's income was not entirely dependent on the vicissitudes of annual government spending battles to decide the level of grant-in-aid. The 1983 National Heritage Act was a more calculated manoeuvre. It was one of the government's declared aims to reduce the size of the Civil Service; a thousand civil servants were employed at the Department of the Environment, carrying out the department's duties in the field of planning, the protection of listed buildings and ancient monuments, the distribution of government grants for archaeology and repairs to privately owned listed buildings, and looking after the historic castles and ancient monuments which, as Crown property, were the department's responsibility. By hiving these duties off to a new quango, the Secretary of State, Michael Heseltine, would be able to claim an increase in the efficiency of his department.

At the same time, the new Historic Buildings and Monuments Commission for England, created by the 1983 Act, would take a more dynamic approach to the presentation of monuments and buildings such as Stonehenge or Tynemouth Castle, in order to exploit their money-making potential. The heritage would be packaged and marketed, as well as protected. The HBMC was launched in April 1984 under the chairmanship of Lord Montagu of Beaulieu, one of the pioneers of the heritage industry who had shown the potential profitability of the past at Beaulieu Abbey and its associated Motor Museum. Beaulieu and his fellow commissioners – fewer "cultured generalists" and more business men among them – decided that for marketing purposes, the Commission should use the more evocative title, English Heritage. Between them, the trustees of the National Heritage Memorial Fund and the commissioners of English Heritage would follow their own taste in empirically deciding what Britain's heritage was and would be.

As a further step towards reducing the apparent number of civil servants, the 1983 National Heritage Act also changed the constitutional arrangements of the Royal Armouries, and the Science and Victoria and Albert Museums, whose staff were government employees. In future these institutions, like the fifteen other national museums, would continue to be directly funded by the government, but their administration became the responsibility of independent (though government-appointed) trustees. All three institutions were to find themselves actively embracing the values of the enterprise culture, as the national museums collectively experienced the now familiar tactics of financial pressure and politically calculated appointments of trustees and senior staff. In 1984 all purchase grants for new acquisitions were frozen, and then cut by an average of thirteen per cent; as with arts organisations, consistent underfunding forced museums to put more effort into marketing, sales and finding business sponsorship.

By the mid-eighties it looked as though the Conservative government would achieve by stealth what its predecessor in 1970 had attempted to do by compulsion: the universal introduction of entry charges. It was a long-standing tradition that, with the exception of special exhibitions, entry to national museums and galleries should be free, as an act of popular education. The British Museum, the National Gallery and the Tate Gallery held to this belief, and their visitor numbers soared as a result. Those museums that introduced charges saw on average an immediate fall of forty per cent. The first to introduce a compulsory charge was the National Maritime Museum at Greenwich, in April 1984. The Imperial War Museum and the Victoria and Albert followed with "voluntary" charges. The Natural History Museum started charging in 1986, and the Science Museum, whose new director, Neil Cossons, had first introduced charging at Greenwich, followed suit.

Most museums funded by local authorities resisted this trend, but the many new privately managed independent museums had no choice but to charge as a matter of course, for while it was relatively easy to find the capital to launch a museum, it was much harder to achieve the revenue to keep one going, as the effects of recession and market saturation at the end of the decade were to show. It was a sign of the shift in attitudes during the eighties that in June 1990 a compulsory charge was introduced for visitors to St Paul's Cathedral.

The effect of the changes that were being enforced in the museum world was seen most dramatically at the Victoria and Albert Museum. In October 1985 the V & A's director Sir Roy Strong, in company with the chairman of its new board of trustees, the former Conservative Foreign Secretary, Lord Carrington, held a press conference to announce the emergence of 'a more consumer-orientated V & A': 'We have to face the reality of a fundamental shift and like any well-run organisation in the private sector, learn how to capitalise on what is a market-oriented society.'[37] By going into business and merchandising products based on designs in the gallery, Strong believed that 'the V & A could be the Laura Ashley of the 1990s'.[38] The comparison was apt, for while in the sixties the designer Terence Conran had introduced a "contemporary" look into the British domestic interior through the Habitat shops, in the eighties Laura Ashley had caught the public eye and made a fortune by reviving fabrics and furnishings from the Victorian and Edwardian period. At the same time as signalling the V & A's embrace of the enterprise culture, Sir Roy also announced that from November the museum would be introducing a voluntary entrance fee. Visitors would not be obliged to pay, but in practice they were firmly encouraged to do so.

In spite of his adoption of consumerist values, Sir Roy Strong's direction of the V & A had placed him at odds both with his senior curators and the trustees, and in 1987 he took early retirement. Significantly his successor, Elizabeth Esteve-Coll, had never held a curatorial post in a museum, having previously been in charge of the V & A's library. The move into the market gathered pace. Promotional displays by Sotheby's, Burberry's and the Sock Shop were featured in the museum, and its new marketing director capped Sir Roy by saying that the V & A 'should always be seen as the Harrods of the museum world'.[39] With Maurice Saatchi serving as a trustee, it was not long before the museum was being promoted in television and billboard advertising as 'an ace caff with quite a nice museum attached'.

The changes at the museum were, however, more than matters of marketing and presentation. "Consumer orientation" was to penetrate the entire structure. Professor Martin Kemp, who became a trustee in 1985, has recorded: 'The nadir of this approach was reached when one of the smart young men from Saatchi and Saatchi was introduced . . . to present a series of propositions on virtually every aspect of the Museum's operations. Each proposition was written on a single sheet of paper in large letters, and the Trustees were taken through these like a primary-school reading class. Needless to say the selling of assets and compulsory admission charges featured prominently in the presentation.'[40]

In January 1989, now under the chairmanship of Sir Robert Armstrong – the former Chief Secretary to the Cabinet who had coined the phrase 'economical with the truth' during the government's unsuccessful attempts to prevent the publication of Peter Wright's allegations of security service wrongdoings in *Spycatcher*[41] – the trustees were given half an hour to consider plans for a radical reconstruction of the V & A's administration. The museum's federal structure of individual subject collections, each headed by a senior curator, was to be changed to a division into two departments, with curatorial duties separated between scholarship and "housekeeping", meaning the physical management of the collections. All serious research was to be hived off into the ill-defined "Research Department". These proposals had the full support of Richard Wilding at the Office of Arts and Libraries, and it was clear that there was strong pressure from the OAL to carry them through. The immediate effect of this restructuring, which left the museum's purely administrative, non-curatorial personnel untouched, was that nine senior curatorial staff, including five heads of department, were offered "voluntary" redundancy. Eight, under pressure, accepted. The initial three hundred thousand pounds which these redundancies cost was found – ironically in view of the V & A's fifty-million-pound backlog in repairs – from the building and maintenance budget.

The plan, which ultimately proved unworkable, provoked an international protest which severely damaged the museum and its director's standing. Even those, like the connoisseur Denys Sutton, who supported Margaret Thatcher, thought things had gone too far: 'It is an error to believe that a museum is comparable to a business: it is not required to make a profit. If state museums are to exist, then they should be properly funded; and to accept the notion that they should rely too heavily on finance from the private sector is a fatal error.'[42] Professor Kemp, however, was the only trustee to resign, declaring: 'I had not been able to perform my duties as a trustee on behalf of the public.'[43] It is unlikely that Kemp would have sanctioned the decision in 1991 to allow eighteen hundred square metres of the museum to be hired out for private venture exhibitions over which the V & A had no curatorial control. *Visions of Japan*, part of the Japan Festival, was judged to be a success, but an exhibition of sporting trophies and *Sovereign*, celebrating the fortieth anniversary of the Queen's succession, were critical and commercial embarrassments.

Just as the furore over the V & A was reaching its height, a new museum opened whose context and creation epitomised the new museum economy. Like a mutant strain, it had been nurtured since 1982 within the viscera of the V & A. This was the Boilerhouse Project, a separately funded exhibition space in the museum's old boiler rooms which emerged, once matured and fully fledged, as the Design Museum, settling on the south bank of the Thames below Tower Bridge at Butlers Wharf. As a sign of the official approval of this creation of the enterprise culture it was formally opened by Margaret Thatcher in July 1989. The principal funding for the project came from a foundation established by one of the V & A's trustees, Sir Terence Conran, which he had set up following the highly profitable flotation of the Habitat chain in 1981. The Conran Foundation met most of the Design Museum's seven million pounds' capital costs, but although sponsorship and entry charges were expected to cover a substantial amount of the running costs, there was still a call on public funding from the English Tourist Board, the London Docklands Development Corporation and the Department of Trade and Industry.

The Design Museum was a natural extension of the sphere of cultural consumption that Sir Terence had made distinctly his own. It also served to stimulate the kinds of consumption that were the business of its commercial sponsors: Perrier, Olivetti, Sony, Coca-Cola, Courtaulds, Kodak, Addis, Apple, Fiat, Black & Decker. In her speech at the opening ceremony Margaret Thatcher praised Sir Terence for bringing 'new quality of standards, value for money and culture to people who could not otherwise have had it', but she recognised the building for what it was, describing it as a 'Design Exhibition Centre. . . . I call it an Exhibition Centre and not a museum – a museum is something that is really rather dead, and this is a *living exhibition*.'[44]

What it exhibited, in its first 'agenda-setting' temporary exhibition, was the thorough interpenetration of 'Commerce and Culture'. Sir Roy Strong's vision of the commercial future of museums was no longer a rhetorical flourish, but an established fact, for the exhibition's argument was that the elision of commerce and culture was virtually complete: 'One day, maybe, stores and museums will become the same . . . with everything for display, inspection and sale.'[45] Less obviously, the Design Museum was itself a marketing device, for it was at the centre of a two-hundred-million-pound redevelopment project undertaken by Conran. A redundant warehouse had been remodelled as a Bauhaus pastiche, a form of cultural gentrification preparing the way for the offices, shops, apartments and hotel that were intended to occupy the rest of the Butlers Wharf site. While the rhetoric of the Design Museum celebrated shopping as 'one of the legitimate cultural pursuits of the eighties', advertising for the development declared: 'The Design Museum sets the tone for retailing at Butlers Wharf.'[46] At the Design Museum, culture and commodities became one.

The exploitation of the Design Museum as part of the commercial redevelopment of Butlers Wharf – itself part of the regeneration of London's docklands – was an example of the new use of culture as a form of economic inducement. Arts and museum facilities were attractions intended to encourage private investment in run-down areas. The consequences of economic restructuring were most severe for the great manufacturing cities that had flourished in the nineteenth century, and from which traditional industry had retreated, leaving behind the populations that had once served them. From time to time the decay of inner cities was dramatically highlighted by riots whose racial overtones nagged at the question of national identity, but the deprivation was more often felt as a kind of ugliness and apathy, marked by rising figures for long-term unemployment, crime and homelessness, and engendering a general despair.

The institutions most appropriate for dealing with these problems should have been the local authorities. Since 1945 they had become the main providers of the services of the welfare state: housing, education, public health, social services, planning, libraries, arts facilities and recreation, and they had substantially increased their share of public expenditure as a result. But the difficulties that local authorities faced as a result of the decline in their revenues caused by the very decay they wished to arrest, were compounded by a government that wanted to cut public spending, and which saw the local authorities as bureaucratic expressions of the "welfare state mentality" and the "dependency culture" they intended to eradicate.

By 1989, Margaret Thatcher's government had passed forty-six separate bills directed at controlling the activities of local authorities. Government control of local authority budgets was much tighter, and central government's financial contribution fell. "Rate-capping" was introduced in 1985, local authority control of education was severely weakened by the Education Reform Act of 1988. The 1988 Local Government Finance Act abandoned local taxation through the rating system: instead there was the community charge or "poll tax". At the same time, the government took into its own hands the setting of local taxation for businesses. The poll tax, introduced into Scotland in 1989 and England and Wales in 1990, proved so unpopular that it, more than anything, led to the decision within the Conservative Party to force Thatcher's resignation in 1990. In 1992 the poll tax was replaced by a new system of banded property tax, the council tax, but the severe financial constraints on local authorities remained. The 1988 Local Government Act also introduced a new element of censorship: an amendment by right-wing MPs, Clause 28, expressly forbade local authorities to use their money or facilities to 'promote' homosexuality, a proviso which affected public libraries, the discussion of gender in schools, and the presentation of plays, films or visual art that dealt with homosexual topics in local-authority-owned arts facilities.

The response of central government to the problems of the inner cities was a whole range of piecemeal measures that did not constitute a coherent geographical or administrative strategy, and which for the most part tried to exclude local authorities by limiting their powers or removing them altogether, as in the case of the creation of Urban Development Corporations. Some schemes were literally cosmetic: "garden festivals" on reclaimed derelict industrial land were held in Liverpool, Stoke, Glasgow, Gateshead and Ebbw Vale. While the definition of unemployment was regularly redrawn in such a way as to reduce the overall figure, the Manpower Services Commission increased its expenditure by five hundred per cent, reaching £3.1 billion by 1987, in order to create work-related training schemes such as the Community Programme to reduce the number of registered unemployed. Museums, which made wide use of this semi-voluntary labour, were thrown into confusion when the Community Programme was abruptly wound up in 1988, and the Manpower Services Commission became the Training Agency. Tourism, until 1985 the responsibility of the Department of Trade, was transferred to the Department of Employment, until a fall in unemployment at the end of the decade caused it to be handed back to the DTI, and thence to the Department of National Heritage in 1992.

There was also a European dimension to inner-city regeneration. Although access was tightly controlled by the Department of the Environment and the Department of Trade and Industry, the European Community's Regional Development Fund and the European Social Fund provided money for training and job-creation schemes, and grants and loans to encourage businesses, services and tourism. Newcastle Theatre Royal, the Bradford Alhambra, Cardiff New Theatre and the Lyceum Sheffield were all refurbished with the help of European Community money.

The drive for urban regeneration was given a fresh impetus in June 1987 by a chance remark of Thatcher's at the triumphant close of her third election night, when she indicated that there was a job to be done in the inner cities. In Thatcher's mind the "job" was political rather than social, but it was a cue for a fresh flurry of activity that led to the launch of *Action for Cities* the following year. The government declared its intention to spend three billion pounds on a range of projects in 1988–9, but on closer examination, most of the money came from existing programmes. Overall, government spending on urban programmes had increased by fifty-eight per cent since 1979, but most of this increase was aimed at securing private investment rather than spending on social or community projects. The major innovation of

Action for Cities was the creation of a private consortium of eleven major construction companies, British Urban Development, headed by Thatcher's special adviser on the environment, Hartley Booth. The plan was to create "partner enterprise zones" run by the private sector. BUD was involved in half a dozen projects which were either never started, or from which it later withdrew, and it ceased operation in 1990. The ten billion pounds spent by the government on urban renewal between 1988 and 1992 failed to create an economic renaissance.

While the arts received a pat on the head in *Action for Cities,* there was no new money or policy for the arts, and the initiative had to come from elsewhere. In February 1988 the Arts Council launched its pamphlet *An Urban Renaissance* which caught the tone of the times with its claim: 'The arts create a climate of optimism – the "can do" attitude essential to developing the "enterprise culture" this government hopes to bring to deprived areas.'[47] The following month it published *Per Cent for Art*, urging the adoption of the American principle by which a percentage of any building development was spent on decorative features and artworks for new buildings. Neither pamphlet committed the Arts Council to spending any money itself – after all, it had none to spare. The "Per Cent for Art" scheme was taken up voluntarily in a number of places, notably Birmingham where the results were the "public art" in Centenary Square, but whereas in America "Per Cent for Art" was enforced in many states and cities by legislation, in Britain compulsion would have been regarded as an infringement of commercial freedom.

The American model for inner-city regeneration – strongly advocated in a three-year programme of seminars and publications by the British–American Arts Association, begun in 1986 – was nonetheless influential in Britain. The aim was to promote partnerships between local authorities, business, arts and conservation groups, and developers. Projects tended to concentrate on the more picturesque run-down commercial areas – docklands, quaysides, warehousing and the central city itself – with the idea of creating "cultural districts" that would combine entertainment with retail and office development. Spurred on by Thatcher's apparent interest in the subject, in October 1988 there were no less than four separate international conferences in Britain on the urban role of the arts.

While the arts undoubtedly claimed a place on the economic agenda of the inner cities, the advocates of this approach were hampered by the lack of hard evidence as to the actual effect investment in arts facilities might have. In 1983 the Policy Studies Institute published the first edition of *Facts About the Arts*, edited by John Myerscough, the cultural economist who had acted as an adviser to the 1982 House of Commons select committee enquiry into arts funding. This was the first time that any serious attempt had been made to collate statistical material on the subject: the sources were so widespread and the reasons for their collection so different that not a single table was directly comparable with another throughout the study. The Policy Studies Institute went on to produce increasingly sophisticated data, published since 1989 as the quarterly, *Cultural Trends*.

In 1985 the Policy Studies Institute was commissioned to conduct the first-ever audit of the arts in the United Kingdom, using a team led by John Myerscough. The funds came jointly from the Gulbenkian Foundation and the Office of Arts and Libraries, with additional money from the Arts Council, the Museums and Galleries Commission and the Crafts Council. A pilot study was carried out on Merseyside, where the abolition of Merseyside Metropolitan Council made the need for information especially urgent. This was followed by a detailed study of Glasgow and, for a "rural" comparison, Ipswich and Suffolk. These findings were fed into a statistical survey of the whole country.

Published in 1988, *The Economic Importance of the Arts in Britain* made a persuasive case for the implicit argument of its title. Its basic conclusions were that overall the sector had 'a turnover of ten billion pounds, amounting to 2.5 per cent of all spending on goods and services by UK residents and foreign buyers, and giving direct employment to almost half a million people. . . . The arts are placed fourth among the top invisible export earners. Public funding . . . represents eighteen per cent of income for the sectors; the balance is shifting from central government to local authorities and from public funding to private finance. The large element of small businesses in the sector makes it a seedbed for future growth and a place for research and development.'[48] Twenty-seven per cent of overseas earnings were specifically attributable to the arts. In total, the "cultural industries" contributed 1.28 per cent of gross domestic product, roughly the equivalent of the motor industry.

The report stressed the common European aspect of this approach to the arts. Arts spending by central governments had been levelling off all over Europe, and arguments for their support based on their educational value or intrinsic worth had lost their force. The purely economic value of the arts had seemed to provide fresh justification, but Myerscough wished to take this further:

> In retrospect, the early 1980s' stress on the economic value of the arts reads like special pleading by those defending the arts against threatened reductions in public spending. It was set in no particular policy frame and might have applied equally to any area of public spending, to defence as much as to drama companies. In the space of a few years, the argument has moved on to higher ground, by relating the role of the arts to the fact that we live in an era of industrial restructuring characterised by the growing importance of the service industries (especially in the areas of finance, knowledge, travel and entertainment), and of industries based on new technologies exploiting information and the media. The success of cities in the post-industrial area will depend on their ability to build on the provision of services for regional, national and international markets.[49]

To make the point, Myerscough developed arguments about the "multiplier effect" of arts spending, to show how indirect spending and employment were generated by direct spending on the arts, and to demonstrate the importance of the arts in persuading businesses to settle in a city. He ended on a note of 'national prestige and value to the public': 'It is an important conclusion of this report that the arts sector is capable of great expansion which will benefit the economy. It is an even more significant fact that this will increase the artistic experience of the British people for present and future generations.'[50]

This was exactly what his sponsors wanted to hear, and while Myerscough's sincerity should not be questioned, his use of the statistics was. The economist Gordon Hughes argued that the definition of the cultural industry was so broad that only ten per cent of the estimated overall ten billion pounds was generated by conventional arts activities. Twenty-five per cent came from 'mechanical performance' (video, cinema, broadcasting), thirty-six per cent came from cultural products such as books and records, and twenty-five per cent was attributed to arts-related expenditure such as food, drink and hotels that might well have happened anyway. Myerscough's "multiplier effect" was questionable, and 'the claim in the report that arts spending is a cost-effective means of job-creation is highly suspect'.[51] The problem was that additional consumer spending on the arts was only an internal shift of resources from another area of the economy, so there would be loss elsewhere. Sir Alan Peacock made similar criticisms, arguing that if one city were to attract a business through its art policies, another city would logically be losing it. Sir Alan, who had recently disappointed the Arts Council with his report on inflation in the arts, warned: 'The economist, so it is argued, might become a hired gun for the cultural establishment.'[52]

The Economic Importance of the Arts nonetheless supplied local politicians with arguments that justified cultural spending as a means of renewing the vitality of their cities. In the sixties the emphasis had been on comprehensive redevelopment and road schemes which more often than not destroyed the character of a city rather than enhanced it. In the eighties there was a concerted effort to revive the pleasures of city living, with pedestrian schemes, shopping malls and improved arts facilities. But the change was more one of image than economic substance. As Franco Bianchini and Michael Parkinson argued in their 1993 study: 'The direct impact of eighties cultural policies on the generation of employment and wealth was relatively modest, in comparison with the role of culture in constructing positive urban images, developing the tourism industry, attracting inward investment, and strengthening the competitive position of cities.'[53]

The Greater London Council had begun one experiment in cultural regeneration, only to be abolished. Other cities in Britain adopted a more conventional approach that emphasised prestige buildings and the presence of "flagship" companies. Bradford, Leeds, Newcastle, Swansea and Cardiff all built new facilities or refurbished old ones. Sheffield created a "cultural industries quarter" around the Leadmill Arts Centre, opened in 1982, hoping that training and employment in the field of film, video and music recording would compensate for the decline of steel making. One hundred and fifty million pounds was invested in new, world-class sports facilities in order to house the 1991 World Student Games, but the Games made an operating loss of ten million and the new facilities left the city saddled with debt.

The most determined efforts to use the arts for economic leverage were in Birmingham, the largest local authority in England, and Glasgow, which with the Strathclyde region held most of the population of lowland Scotland. Both cities had suffered from the decline of industry – motor cars and engineering in Birmingham, steel and ships in Glasgow – but they retained strong local identities, even if these were often negatively perceived in the rest of Britain. Birmingham tried to turn its notorious sixties road system to advantage by holding grand prix races, made a bid to host the Olympic Games and created indoor arenas and exhibition centres. As part of a £100-million conference centre a new concert hall was built for the City of Birmingham Symphony Orchestra, whose chief conductor, Simon Rattle, was widely regarded as one of the city's greatest assets. The Sadler's Wells company of the Royal Ballet was persuaded to relocate and become the Birmingham Royal Ballet, and the D'Oyly Carte Opera Company was given a home at the Alexandra Theatre. Birmingham Repertory Theatre built a £4.5 million extension as part of the general refurbishment of Centenary Square, which became one of the largest public art projects in the country. Festivals were created celebrating jazz, film and television, and literature, and in 1990 the Birmingham Symphony Orchestra launched its 'Towards the Millennium' project, a cross-arts celebration of the separate decades of the twentieth century.

Birmingham was the first city council to establish a 'Joint Arts Culture and Economy Committee' which expressly linked the cultural with the economic aspects of policy at a senior level. In addition to its construction programme (which drew European Community assistance) the arts budget rose to ten million pounds a year. But the emphasis on culture – and "high" culture at that – had its downside. Birmingham claimed to be putting its own people first, rather than trying to present a new face to the world in the manner of Glasgow, but small-scale, locally motivated activity such as fringe theatre declined. In 1991 the seven-year-old Handsworth Carnival, a midlands version of the Notting Hill Gate Carnival (Handsworth was the home of the Kokuma Afro-Caribbean Dance Company, launched in 1980), found itself renamed the Birmingham International Carnival and its local organising committee was wound up. In 1992 a study at Birmingham Polytechnic concluded that the policy of regeneration through prestige projects had failed. The government accused the city of underspending its education budget, and following a change in Council leadership in 1993, policy was switched towards dealing with the £200-million back-log of repairs and maintenance needed by the city's schools. For all of Birmingham's commitment to culture, the Alexandra Theatre went into receivership in 1994, and the City of Birmingham Symphony Orchestra had a deficit of two hundred and fifty thousand pounds.

While the success of Birmingham's cultural policy remained in question, Glasgow could claim to have substantially remade its image during the eighties. Between 1975 and 1989 Glasgow, a city with a grim reputation for violence and deprivation, lost twenty-three per cent of its population as its old industries declined. Reconstruction began with slum clearance, the refurbishment of central Glasgow and one of the largest urban renewal schemes in the world in the east of the city. In 1983 the city government and a local business organisation, Glasgow Action, launched a public relations campaign, 'Glasgow's Miles Better', which was initially aimed at changing the attitudes of Glasgow residents themselves. In the same year a new building was opened to display the paintings and furniture gathered by a former industrial magnate, the Burrell Collection, and an annual arts festival, Mayfest, was launched in 1984 as a local reply to Edinburgh's international festival. A section of nineteenth-century warehousing and office buildings near the City Hall was reinvented as "The Merchant City" as a location for artists' studios, cafés, restaurants and shops. The gentrification of this "cultural quarter" by Glasgow's bohemia was so successful that by the time John Myerscough conducted his survey of the Policy Studies Institute he had to report: 'Rising rents may now jeopardise further developments along these lines.'[54]

In 1986, following a campaign by Glasgow District Council and Glasgow Action, the city was chosen by the European Commission to serve for a year as 'Cultural Capital of Europe' in 1990. Unlike the cities that preceded it – Athens, Florence, Amsterdam, Berlin and Paris – Glasgow's reputation was not strongly associated with the arts. The appointment of Saatchi and Saatchi to promote the year was an indication that it was to be used, not just to celebrate the arts, but to market Glasgow and improve its image. In addition to prestige building projects – including a £24-million concert hall and a £3-million refurbishment of the McLellan Art Gallery – the programme for the year cost £53.5 million, with the bulk of the funds coming from the District Council and Strathclyde Regional Council.

Yet when the director of the city's Festivals Unit, Robert Palmer, started work in 1987, 'no cultural plans or blueprints existed. There were no formal criteria concerning arts expenditure in any city council policy documents.'[55] The decision was taken to conduct a double strategy for 1990 of attracting high-profile international performing companies – Peter Brook's production of *The Mahabharata* was presented in Glasgow before the year had even started – and encouraging activity among more than one hundred and fifty local arts organisations, notably the Citizens Theatre and Scottish Opera, together with a determined programme of community arts and activities. Visitors driving in from the city's airport were greeted with a sign: 'All around Strathclyde there's culture.'

This was culture in its broadest sense, but it did not stop a group of local intellectuals, led by the novelists Alasdair Gray and James Kelman, protesting at the way the city's radical tradition – the "Red Clyde" of the twenties and thirties – had been neutralised by performances such as Bill Bryden's *The Ship*, and the special exhibition *Glasgow's Glasgow*, at £4.6 million the most expensive special project in the programme, which rapidly became the year's costliest failure. The sociologist Sean Damer, a supporter of the 'Workers City' (as opposed to Merchant City) group, protested: 'The culture of the city's working class is now being repackaged as some kind of anodyne and quaint survival instead of the result of two centuries' struggle.'[56]

It could be argued that Glasgow's year as European capital of culture was only the culmination of a process that had been under way for some time. Although perceived as a manufacturing centre – in 1951 the Festival of Britain's 'Exhibition of Industrial Power' had been sited in Glasgow – Glasgow's economy was already mainly one based on business and service, with more people working in the arts than in ship-building, as John Myerscough's survey discovered. Supported by the Scottish Development Agency, far enough away from London (and contemptuous of Edinburgh), Glasgow had both the arts facilities and the underlying security of identity to make a cultural policy work. How far that reached from the city centre into the outlying housing estates was open to question, as Sean Damer argued: 'Glaswegians are entitled to garden festivals, riverside walkways, more and better galleries, good restaurants, decent, comfortable pubs, civilised drinking hours, good entertainment, a wide range of shops, foods and goods and, in general, a clean, attractive and safe city. Nobody denies them that; it is their right as citizens. But the question has to be asked: Glasgow's Miles Better for Whom? The short answer is: not for the bulk of Glaswegians.'[57]

Although a follow-up survey by John Myerscough appeared to justify the cost of Glasgow 1990 in terms of visitor numbers and expenditure, estimating a "profit" of between ten and fourteen million pounds, in 1993 local unemployment was fifteen per cent, there was a glut of empty office space, and the city still had some of the most deprived urban areas in Europe. Immediately after the year of culture the Third Eye arts centre went bankrupt and Scottish Opera got into financial difficulties. The year undoubtedly served further to improve the city's image, but the direct economic benefit was short-term. In their post-1990 study Peter Booth and Robin Boyle concluded that the city still lacked an integrated cultural policy that would turn city-marketing into a secure arts-based local economy linking mainstream and local development: 'As a result, there is confusion about the nature of the next step in the regeneration process – whether it is further city promotion, cultural specialisation or some form of physical initiative.'[58]

While Glasgow was able to build on its distinct identity, Liverpool, the English city whose recent history suggested that it had the greatest cultural potential, spectacularly failed to use the arts either to remake its tarnished image or rebuild its collapsing economy. Liverpool demonstrated the limits to cultural regeneration; its social, political and economic problems were too great for the cosmetic effects of an artificially stimulated culture. Economic decline had created extreme political instability, and the "workerist" administration of the early eighties was hostile to what were perceived as middle-class arts. Between 1983 and 1987 the City Council was dominated by the far left Militant Group, which threatened to bankrupt the city in its confrontation with the government. It was not until November 1987 that a more moderate leadership proposed a cultural industries strategy for Liverpool, intended to exploit the city's sixties links with pop music, and use money from the government's Urban Programme to encourage film, video and broadcasting. The abolition of Merseyside Metropolitan Council had damaged the system of arts funding to the extent that the area's seven museums and galleries had to be "nationalised", and directly funded by the government as the National Museums and Galleries on Merseyside. The successor authorities were too poor, or too preoccupied with other matters, to fund Liverpool's theatres properly. The Liverpool Playhouse was only saved from bankruptcy in 1990 by a deal with a commercial producer; and the Liverpool Everyman went bankrupt in 1993.

While Liverpool City Council faced intractable problems of inner-city deprivation and decay, underscored by the riots in Toxteth in 1981, it also had the government working directly on its doorstep through the Merseyside Development Corporation, which had been given responsibility for reclaiming and if possible making profitable

Liverpool's semi-derelict docks. Thus the main cultural investment in Liverpool, the 1984 Garden Festival on reclaimed industrial land, and the refurbishment of the Albert Docks as a home for the Merseyside Maritime Museum and an out-station for the Tate Gallery, 'the Tate of the North', together with shops, restaurants and a local television studio, was nothing to do with Liverpool's local government, for the Development Corporation, run by government appointees, had complete control over the territory staked out for them.

The cultural significance of the Merseyside Development Corporation, or indeed of similar corporations later set up in Tyne and Wear, Teeside, Trafford Park, Central Manchester, the Black Country, Cardiff, Leeds, Sheffield and Bristol was, however, slight in comparison with that of the London Docklands Development Corporation, set up in 1981. The LDDC took over control of eight and a half square miles of land on either side of the Thames below Tower Bridge, including fifty-five miles of waterside frontage. ("Docklands" only properly acquired that name once there were no more working docks.) Parcels of land making up twenty-five per cent of the area of the boroughs of Southwark, Tower Hamlets and Newham passed into the control of the corporation, together with seven per cent of their population. The LDDC had none of a local authority's responsibilities for housing, education or the social needs of those who lived within or on its borders, though it was prepared to make philanthropic gestures such as that of supporting the Docklands Sinfonietta and local arts and community groups. Its cultural purpose was far greater, to prove that private enterprise was capable of creating a new business district that would serve as capitalism's version of the New Jerusalem. At the heart of Docklands was an 'Enterprise Zone' where all planning restraints were removed to allow the free play of market forces.

In view of the emphasis on private enterprise, it was remarkable how much public money was required. In its first decade the LDDC received nearly a billion pounds from government grants and the sale of land. The Department of Transport spent £638 million improving access to the area, and the extension to the Jubilee underground line was costed at a further billion. John Redwood, then a junior minister in Margaret Thatcher's government, conceded the point in his book *Popular Capitalism* (1988): 'The paradox is that because state action is responsible for so much of the activity and ownership in the area it takes state action to get the thing right. The government has been prepared to live with the paradox in the interests of getting things done.'[59] While commercial developers required all sorts of financial inducements such as ten-year rates holidays and one-hundred-per-cent tax-deductible capital allowances, the government, in its eagerness to see Docklands succeed, was prepared to forgo any share in the potential profits. By agreeing to contribute to road and rail projects, the developers of the key site at Canary Wharf were able to buy the land at half the market price.

In its first phase, Docklands threw up a rash of speculative housing and clumps of bulky sheds, but as the financial deregulation of the stock market in 1986 approached, and the need grew for offices capable of handling the new electronic hardware of the information industry, steel- and glass-walled buildings sprang up in a variety of developer's *moderne*, an architecture which could hardly appeal to the classical and conservative aesthetic principles of the advocate of the free market, Roger Scruton. The president of the Royal Town Planning Institute, Chris Sheppey, condemned the architecture and layout of Docklands as 'an irredeemable failure'.[60]

For a time Docklands did not appear to be a great financial success either, but the prospects were transformed when the largest and richest property development group in the world, the Canadian-based Olympia and York, took over the Canary Wharf site in 1987. Construction began on what was intentionally the tallest office block in Europe, to a design by Cesar Pelli at the centre of a masterplan by the American firm Skidmore, Owings and Merrill. The eight-hundred-foot tower and the twenty-four surrounding buildings were planned to create twelve million square feet of floor space, capable of accommodating fifty thousand office workers. With only one British architect involved, the conception and appearance of Canary Wharf was an American transplant, a reproduction of Chicago or Battery Park City which Olympia and York had built in New York. Sir Roy Strong – who dismissed the rest of Docklands architecture as 'Dolly-mixture land'[61] – was responsible for the streetscape, commissioning iron railings and street furniture and supervising the planting of mature trees to create an instant – but eerily empty – environment for the expected hordes of office workers (illustration 19).

Margaret Thatcher closely associated herself with Canary Wharf. She laid the foundation stone in 1987, and drove the first pile in 1988. Cesar Pelli's tower was topped out in November 1990, just before Thatcher's fall from government. In 1988 John Redwood had written:

'Perhaps one day Heron Quay, Mudchute and Canary Wharf will be names as well known worldwide as Trafalgar Square, Marble Arch and Charing Cross.'[62] By 1993 Canary Wharf was to become well known worldwide as one of the most spectacular business failures of the decade.

When, in August 1989, the Arts Council announced that it was giving two bursaries of eleven thousand pounds to chartered accountants, the enterprise culture, emblematically at least, appeared to have triumphed. Everywhere, the accountants were taking over, and the values of the market had penetrated so deeply that it seemed impossible, or futile, to discuss the merits of the arts in anything but economic terms. In 1993 the American Economic Association officially admitted a new category to its classification of economic disciplines, that of "cultural economics", but this was only formal recognition of the transformation that had taken place in the eighties. The language of the arts had changed; productions had indeed become "product", audiences "consumers", public patronage "investment". A member of the staff of the British Council – which had had a similar experience to the Arts Council's of Margaret Thatcher's social revolution – wrote in the Council's magazine: 'From the Corporate Plan downwards, Council documents seem to be couched more and more in management-speak. "Corporate", "business", "products" and other unlovely terms have become as much part of our vocabulary as "cultural manifes-tation", "functional" and "specialist tourist". So all-pervasive is this new terminology that an impression has been created that the Council is little more than a commercial firm with the same purposes and ethos as, say, Marks & Spencer's.'[63]

The rhetoric of the enterprise culture was heard in surprising places. In 1988, faced with the need to raise seven million pounds to solve their financial problems, the Dean and Chapter of Hereford Cathedral decided to realise their most valuable asset, a thirteenth-century map of the world, the *Mappa Mundi*. Their adviser was Lord Gowrie who, two years after resigning as Minister for the Arts, had become chairman of Sotheby's. According to Lord Gowrie, attempts to arrange a "private treaty" sale to the British Museum had failed, and the map was placed for auction at Sotheby's. Following a public outcry, the map was with-drawn, and instead there was an attempt to sell one-thousand-pound shares in '*Mappa Mundi* PLC'. The share issue failed, and Hereford

Cathedral's problems were more conventionally solved by money from the National Heritage Memorial Fund and the private patronage of John Paul Getty.

During the "boom" years between the beginning of economic recovery in 1982 and the stock market crash of October 1987 it did appear that there might be some substance behind the passion for consumption. Although the boom excluded many people, manufacturing output did not regain its 1979 level until 1987, and unemployment did not fall below three million between January 1982 and July 1987. The imagery of new money, new technologies, new office blocks and shopping malls did encourage the belief that an economic transformation based on the service industries – of which the arts, as an extension of tourism, was one – was taking place. These were the years of "style", whether manifested in magazines like *Arena, I-D* or *The Face*, in the fashion revolution in the high street, or the remaking of corporate identities by suddenly sought-after experts in graphic design. Displayed on the 'smooth operational surface' of the depthless screen of Baudrillard's post-modernism, this conspicuous consumption created a simulacrum of prosperity. While "post-" was the popular prefix, "designer" was the most desirable adjectival noun. New labels were found for new social categories: the "Sloane Ranger", the "Yuppy", the "Young Fogey". In January 1985 a new club opened in Soho, the Groucho, intended to appeal to the new breed of literati. It was rapidly swamped by directors of independent television production companies, style consultants and media executives. After financial services, the smart professions were marketing, advertising and public relations, whose services had rapidly become essential to politicians of all persuasions.

As an adjunct to this superficial culture of consumption, the arts, redefined as the cultural industries, benefited from a climate where everything – ideas, images or goods – was available for display, inspection or sale. The commercial theatre, epitomised by blockbuster high-tech musicals, such as *Cats, Starlight Express* and *Miss Saigon*, prospered. London auction houses enjoyed dominance over the rest of Europe, and though most of the trade was in Old Masters, Impressionists or the early classics of modernism, contemporary art prices shared in the upswing. Myerscough's survey, *The Economic Importance of the Arts*, reported in 1988: 'After a lull in the early eighties, audiences for the arts have expanded so that most areas of the arts are trading at higher levels in the mid-eighties than prevailed ten years previously.'[64]

In the terms of the enterprise culture, they were also trading more efficiently, for the increase was driven mainly by the box office, not by public subsidy. In 1980–81 an Arts Council-funded organisation was receiving on average forty-five per cent of its income from the Council, by 1988–9 that proportion had fallen to thirty-five per cent, the balance being made up by increased earnings and sponsorship. No national museum was receiving one hundred per cent of its running costs in grant-in-aid. All were making up the difference through trading, sponsorship and, increasingly, entrance charges. The Royal Shakespeare Company made a Faustian bargain with the most successful theatrical producer of the decade, Cameron Mackintosh, by providing the theatre and company resources to mount the musical *Les Misérables* at the Barbican in 1985, before its transfer to the West End. The RSC enjoyed a share in the subsequent profits, but the attempt to repeat the process with the musical *Carrie* in 1988 was a humiliating failure.

Both the Royal Opera House and the South Bank Centre tried to cash in on the property boom of the mid-eighties with schemes to redevelop parts of their sites into offices and shops. First planning difficulties and then the government's refusal to contribute to the cost held up the proposals for Covent Garden; the collapse of the property market put an end to a scheme to encase the South Bank in a shell of commercial development. It was not until the arrival of the National Lottery that such major capital projects could be contemplated, using this new source of public funds.

Business sponsorship of the arts made the closest connection between commerce and culture, and served subtly to shape artistic programmes and policy, more by what was not sponsored – and therefore not seen – than by what was. Even though such sponsorship increasingly became part of the core of arts funding, as Adrian Noble acknowledged, sponsors were not willing to take on the entire responsibility. In 1989 the Arts Council turned the tables on the government by printing in its annual report an article by Ian Rushton, chief executive of Royal Insurance, whose sponsorship of the RSC had been keeping the company going in the face of a mounting deficit. Sponsors still looked to the government to maintain the assets that private enterprise was able to exploit. Rushton warned: 'The arts have rightly been encouraged to follow an entrepreneurial course. But encouraging business attitudes requires in return business discipline and formal planning. No business could operate successfully when a major source of revenue – in this case the government – expects high standards of excellence and of quality of output but is not willing to offer forward guarantees on income. This is made even worse when the government allows that revenue to be reduced in real terms. A business faced with such a position would surely go bankrupt or have to debase its standards.'[65]

From the government's point of view, one justification for not increasing state patronage was that lower tax rates, especially for the highest earners, allowed individuals to resume the responsibility once accepted by the aristocracy. Businessmen, notably foreign businessmen, did indeed make some impressive gestures of philanthrophic patronage, as opposed to commercial sponsorship, and their names were duly honoured: the Clore Gallery at the Tate, the Sainsbury Wing at the National Gallery, the Sackler Gallery at the Royal Academy, the T. T. Sui Chinese gallery at the V & A, the Joseph Hotung gift to the British Museum. John Paul Getty, Lord Wolfson, Lord Rayne, Lord McAlpine, Sir Terence Conran, Paul Hamlyn and the Heinz family were all true patrons in this sense. Yet the government did very little to assist individual patronage by creating a tax regime that encouraged it, as in the United States, offering only modest measures of tax relief in the 1986 and 1990 budgets.

The shift of emphasis from production to consumption within society at large was felt within cultural theory as well as cultural practice. In the seventies the stress had been on the study of texts – albeit "texts" much more widely defined than the literary texts of F. R. Leavis's Great Tradition. These products of popular culture were the subject of analysis by the privileged academic reader; their significance for the popular consumer for whom they were created tended to be forgotten. In the eighties the development of audience studies challenged the implicit élitism of cultural studies and attempted to bring the abstractions of high theory closer to the real lives of those whom sociologists and cultural critics had always wished to understand.

Audience studies recalled Raymond Williams's warning: 'There are in fact no masses, but only ways of seeing people as masses.'[66] The approach tried to recapture the initiative from consumer culture by treating consumption as a form of subcultural resistance. As Dick Hebdige pointed out, cultural conservatives since the mid-thirties had feared Americanisation – the most deleterious form of "mass culture" – on the grounds that it would lead to cultural homogenisation. But

Hebdige argued: 'American popular culture – Hollywood films, advertising images, packaging, clothes and music – offers a rich iconography, a set of symbols, objects and artefacts which can be assembled and reassembled by different groups in a literally limitless number of combinations. And the meaning of each selection is transformed as individual objects – jeans, rock records, Tony Curtis hairstyles, bobby socks, etc. – are taken out of their original historical and cultural contexts and juxtaposed against other signs from other sources.'[67] Thus the humble commodities of mass consumption became, through their use, part of the "signifying practices" that constituted individual cultural identities.

The primary site for the study of audiences was television, where popular soap operas like *Coronation Street* or *EastEnders* appeared to supply contemporary society with an equivalent to the folk mythology of the past. The doings of fictional characters whose lives echoed – albeit in a dramatically exaggerated form – those of the viewers were a common topic of conversation and interest. Groups of viewers were surveyed and interviewed in an effort to understand what meanings were being created. In 1982 Dorothy Hobson published the results of her study of followers of the soap opera *Crossroads* as she watched with them in their own homes: '*Crossroads* viewers contribute to their own understanding of the programme and make their own readings of what the production sets out to communicate. They work with the text and add their own experiences and opinions to the stories in the programme. It seems that the myth of the passive viewer is about to be shattered. They do not sit there watching and taking it all in without any mental activity or creativity.'[68]

Hobson wished to free television from forms of criticism carried over from the "high" arts, arguing that ultimately it could only be understood in terms of what the audience made of it in the light of their own experience. But by looking at a single programme, she ignored the way in which television worked as a continuous flow, containing many messages that served to create a framing interpretation of the world, including the discrete viewer's own experiences. Nor did she give much consideration to the material offered up for interpretation, a conventional set of dilemmas that found conventional solutions.

The question of what was offered up, even for subversive consumption, was even more important to the viability of Paul Willis's case in his study, *Common Culture* (1990). Willis appeared to have discovered a new, and more authentic, culture among the young, based on consumption and resistant to the official culture promoted through the traditional arts: 'There is now a whole social and cultural medium of interwebbing common meaning and identity-making which blunts, deflects, minces up or transforms outside or top-down communication. In particular, élite or "official" culture has lost its dominance. It has certainly always been honeycombed with subterranean resistances and alternatives but now the very sense, or pretence, of a national "whole culture" and of hierarchies of values, activities and places within it is breaking down.'[69] Whereas the arts were inert, having nothing to offer but the repetition of their internal aesthetic codes, the objects of commercial culture – fashion, music, dance, television – were intended to be used, and this use involved creativity in the production of symbolic meanings: 'Cultural commodities are catalyst, not product; a stage in, not the destination of, cultural affairs. Consumerism now has to be understood as an active, not a passive, process.'[70]

The nub of Willis's argument was: 'Consumption is itself a kind of self-creation – of identities, of space, of cultural forms – with its own kinds of cultural empowerment.'[71] While it may be possible to agree that there is 'a kind of cultural production all within consumption', it very much matters what is being consumed, and what 'symbolic identities' are constructed out of them.[72] The source of the material to be creatively consumed is the market, and that market is shaped by powerful ideological forces that condition the production and reception of ideas. As the American cultural critic Herbert Schiller has argued in *Culture Inc.* (1989): 'Whatever the unique experiential history of each of the many subgroups in the nation, they are all subject to the rule of market forces and the domination of capital over those market forces. This is the grand common denominator that insures basic inequality in the social order, an inequality that the pluralists and the active-audience culturalists most often overlook.'[73] Just as structuralism had surfaced at a moment when the transcendence of capitalism provoked a particular feeling of helplessness on the part of the individual, what might be called "consumption theory" appeared as a response to the consumerism of the eighties. The identity most successfully constructed was precisely that of the consumer. But the creativity of his or her consumption was limited by access to the market, and what the market made available for consumption. A growing proportion of the population were actively disempowered by this process. Sheer poverty gave them no identity choices at all, so that they became, not a creative, resistant subculture, but a sullen underclass.

However much the enterprise culture succeeded in changing the language of the arts and, it would appear, in reshaping at least some aspects of cultural theory, to be truly successful, it had to deliver the benefits of material achievement. This, Margaret Thatcher's government conspicuously failed to do. The stock-market crash of October 1987 heralded a second, and even longer recession. Unemployment and inflation rose once more, while the boom in house prices, which had done so much to encourage the feeling of prosperity in the middle class, began to collapse eighteen months later. The slump in property prices was felt acutely in Docklands. The largest housing developer, Kentish Property Group, went into receivership in August 1989. The shopping development carved out of the listed warehouses at Tobacco Dock went into receivership in November 1990, Sir Terence Conran's development at Butlers Wharf followed in December. The London Arena, which had brought rock concerts and sporting events to Docklands, closed in December 1991, and in May 1992 the previously inconceivable happened, when the entire Canary Wharf project, less than half-built – and that only half-occupied – went into receivership with the rest of the Olympia and York empire.

It was left to Margaret Thatcher's successor, John Major, to attempt to pick up the pieces, for in November 1990 she had been forced to resign, when a majority of Conservative MPs concluded that they would not win the next election under her abrasive leadership. When Thatcher left office the real tax burden was higher than it was in 1979 (and was to rise further under Major), unemployment was higher, public expenditure had not been reduced, and as much as a quarter of the country's manufacturing capacity had been lost, leaving fewer resources for growth in the future. The trade deficit was widening and the government's need to borrow increasing. The restructuring of the British economy in favour of international capital had produced low growth, long-term unemployment, low wages, and a new underclass. In 1994 none other than the director of the Confederation of British Industry, Howard Davies, pointed out that the changes since 1979 had produced a more unequal and poverty-stricken society. The average income of the top tenth of earners had risen by sixty-two per cent, that of the bottom tenth had fallen by fourteen per cent. The number of people needing income support had risen from three to four million, the 1.3 million increase in jobs was accounted for entirely by part-timers, mainly women. The *Economist* had already concluded: 'Whatever the cause, after the longest recession for decades, few people in Britain any longer believe in the Thatcher miracle.'[74] Having committed herself to ending decline, Thatcher had only deepened the disillusionment of the post-war years.

That Thatcher should be driven from office by her own party and, notwithstanding the subsequent Conservative victory in 1992, that John Major's government should quickly descend into disarray, suggests that the Conservatives of the eighties failed to establish a new hegemony. As Andrew Gamble has argued: 'True hegemony requires the economic dominance of a successful regime of accumulation to be combined with the winning of political, moral and intellectual leadership in civil society.'[75] Thatcherism produced neither economic success nor moral leadership. In spite of their dominance of the House of Commons, the Conservatives never had more than forty-four per cent of the popular vote. In terms of public opinion, support for collective provision to answer social needs, paid for by public expenditure, actually increased. Margaret Thatcher's was a personal regime that could only temporarily contain the contradictions between belief in a free market and maintenance of a strong state within the force field of her own dominating personality.

This is not to say that her regime did not produce change. As Paul Heelas and Paul Morris argue in *The Values of the Enterprise Culture*, Thatcher's 'counter-revolution has led to the rejection of Keynesianism by all the major political parties in Britain and their acceptance of significant elements of the enterprise culture, including a greatly enhanced place for the market'.[76] Labour was faced with irreversible changes such as the sale of council houses, the denationalisation of public-sector industries including gas, water, electricity and the telephone services, and the reorganisation of industrial relations, and it consciously remodelled itself into a centrist, social-democratic party that advocated partnership between the state and private capital. Even *Marxism Today* was prepared to argue in its 1988 'New Times' edition that there was much to be learnt from Thatcherism. The welfare state's emphasis on planning and economies of scale had foreclosed flexibility and choice, and was no longer suitable to the new post-industrial conditions. There was room for autonomy and decentralisation, as people took responsibility for their lives over against the progressive expansion of the state sector. Under Thatcher the old social divisions of class had been replaced by an emergent meritocracy – even if that meant one form of stratification was replaced by another, and the economic divisions between top and bottom had become even wider.

The root cause of Thatcher's overall failure to achieve hegemony, however, lay in the divisive nature of what she had set out to do. While happy to wrap herself in the Union Jack, as in her post-Falklands speech at Cheltenham, Thatcher had a vision of Britain that excluded many people. In attacking the "permissive society" and asserting "family values" she was denying the pluralism that had developed in the seventies, a diversity of gender and race that could not be included in the revived, unified nation. This divisiveness made her initially popular, and it fuelled her attack on the previous consensus. But what began as the break-up or weakening of all the previous power blocks and vested interests – the trades unions, the local authorities, the institutions of the welfare state, the liberal intelligentsia, the BBC, the Church, the Great and the Good – led to the gradual unravelling of all institutions, including those she depended on for power and legitimacy.

The nationalism of Thatcherism was at odds with the internationalism of her economic policy, which surrendered all national economic interests to those of the free movement of international capital. The British Empire was no longer available as a source of unifying symbolism, and even the union of the United Kingdom was in question. The Anglo-Irish agreement of 1986 left Ulster Unionists on their own, Scotland and Wales had few Conservative representatives and even the major English cities were no longer under Conservative rule. The question of British identity in relation to Europe divided the Conservative Party against itself.

Ultimately, Thatcherism was a challenge to the traditions of Conservatism. "One Nation" Tories, recharacterised as "wets", were seen off. The Establishment, traditionally perceived as a largely conservative institution embracing the civil service, the media and other cultural organisations, was treated with suspicion. The idea of a governing class contained in the expression the Great and the Good was treated with contempt. Yet it was these institutions which had provided the country with leadership and a sense of identity, legitimising customary ways and values and organising collective consent.

Although extreme libertarians among the new Conservatives were disappointed that, far from rolling back the frontiers of the state, Thatcher's government filled the vacuum of its own making with ever-greater central control, Thatcher's belief in economic individualism proved corrosively subversive of the traditions and social restraints that the Conservatives had relied on in the past to protect their claim to be the natural party of government. Once Margaret Thatcher had outlived her political usefulness, and could no longer impose unity through the force of her will, the Party descended into faction, with each minister for himself, quick to reach for the pen to record the treacheries of the time.

The destructive forces that Thatcher unleashed ran out of control. The popular press which had revelled in Thatcher's iconoclasm went on to bring down the icon of their own making, the modern monarchy. As the old symbols of national identity collapsed one by one, so that – alarmingly – the only one to retain some respect was the Army, no new binding myth or image emerged to replace them. Tolerance, mutual respect and co-operation, the value of community and belief in the possibility of common purpose, all dissolved. Instead there was a pervasive sense of national bewilderment and decline. In 1987 Thatcher had said: 'There is no such thing as society. There are individual men and women, and there are families.'[77] It was her achievement to encourage this fragmentation. Her great cause had been fought under the banner: "I do not believe in consensus", but by completing the breakdown of the post-war consensus, she also broke the binding framework that had secured a collective sense of national identity since 1940.

IX

The Public Culture

Britain in the future

On 31 October 1996 the people of Britain were given a glimpse of the future. At Greenwich Borough Hall the firm Imagination Ltd., chosen to design a Millennium Exhibition as the focal point for the national celebrations in the year 2000, unveiled its plans to convert 181 acres of derelict and polluted land at the end of the Greenwich peninsula into the symbolic gateway to the next millennium. The principal feature of the scheme was a vast temporary structure supported by masts and wires, 320 metres in diameter and 50 metres high at its centre, a 'Millennium Dome' that would be the largest structure of its kind in the world. Within this tented space the twelve segments of its circle would house pavilions celebrating the exhibition's theme of Time: Action Time, World Time, Dream Time, Fun Time, Past Time. Up to fifty thousand people would be able to enter the Dome and enjoy its restaurants, theatres, galleries, plazas, multi-media studios and 'entertainment environments'. Twelve and a half million visitors were expected during the year 2000; The Dome would cost £42 million to build, but the final cost of the whole project was put at anything between the official figure of £700 million and more cynical estimates of over £1 billion.

The architectural echoes sounded by the design of the Millennium Dome and its setting were loud and clear: here, vastly bigger, was the inflated son of the Dome of Discovery built for the Festival of Britain. The riverside site, the masts and wires, the pavilions and public transport, even the conversion of derelict land on the south bank of the Thames, recalled the transformation that had taken place at the end of Waterloo Bridge in 1951. It was also true that Britain was as in need of investment and renewal at the close of the twentieth century as it had been at the end of the Second World War. But the mechanism for bringing the Millennium Exhibition into being and the way it was to be financed showed the distance that had been travelled between the hopes of 1951 and the commercial calculations of the year 2000.

The Festival of Britain had been an imaginative act of government. The Millennium Exhibition too was government-inspired, but whereas in 1951 the costs had been met from national resources, the Millennium Exhibition was supposed to be financed by corporate sponsorship and a game of chance. The National Lottery, which had been launched at the end of 1994, was to provide £200 million, and a further £150 million was expected to come from business organisations who would sponsor the pavilions and displays within the Dome's embracing canopy. Entrance and media fees were to cover the rest. But when the plans for the Dome were first revealed, the private finance was not in place. Emblematically, the interior of the Dome was empty.

A similar emptiness lay at the heart of the organisation created to devise the celebrations of the Millennium. The Millennium Commission was a new cultural quango, responsible for distributing one fifth of the proceeds of the National Lottery. When it was appointed in February 1994 it was given a number of tasks in addition to coordinating the year 2000 celebrations. It was to help finance about a dozen appropriate large building projects suitably dispersed about the United Kingdom and Northern Ireland, it was to assist many smaller millennial schemes, and establish bursaries to encourage the development of individual talent. But it was inhibited by its terms of reference from actively seeking particular proposals for the use of its money, or to propose projects on its own behalf. Constrained to act only "in response" to the ideas of others, the Commission was remarkably reluctant to indicate what it thought the Millennium might mean, or indeed what this arbitrary date, significant only in the Christian calendar, was for. Expected to rely on the vision of others, the Commission appeared to have no vision of its own. At the display of plans for the Millennium Dome in Greenwich the accompanying video material showed a nation of consumers dedicated to having a good time, a parodic echo of Humphrey Jennings's 1951 *Family Portrait* that endlessly repeated the surging chords and chorus of a borrowed pop song: 'Altogether now, altogether now, altogether now, across the land': a Millennium anthem combining the cosy reassurance of a building society advertisement with the ersatz communitarianism of a Coca-Cola commercial.

Although the commission which had accepted Imagination Ltd's bid to mastermind the creation of the Millennium Exhibition was an arm's-length organisation, its closeness to government was ensured by the presence of two ministers, one of them the chairman, on the nine person board. The opposition was allowed to nominate one member: Labour chose a former chairman of the English Tourist Board. The other six commissioners were chosen to represent what was believed to be a carefully balanced regional and social mix: a Scottish Earl, two businessmen, a former editor of *The Times*, a lady astronomer and a black, female QC. The government places were filled by the deputy Prime Minister, Michael Heseltine and, *ex officio*, whoever filled the post of Secretary of State for National Heritage. A change of government would mean a change in the political balance of the Commission as the new Secretary of State took over. In December 1996 there were frantic negotiations between the government and Labour when the financial instability of the Millennium Exhibition became clear. Labour won the right to review the scheme in office; the government agreed to guarantee it with public money. The market solution to the millennium had failed.

The Millennium Commission combined the two innovations of cultural policy in the 1990s: the National Lottery and the Department of National Heritage. In April 1992 John Major won a general election that gave the Conservative Party 14.1 million votes, the highest number ever recorded for one party. This was, however, still only forty-two per cent of the popular vote. Labour and the Liberal Democrats together won fifty-two per cent. In the harsh accountancy of the House of Commons, the Conservative majority was reduced to twenty-one. Since this was the fourth consecutive Conservative election victory, the Party's hegemony could be said to have held, but the government was soon in trouble as the *annus horribilis* of 1992 unfolded.

Major had been seen as a relief after Margaret Thatcher, his ordinariness a stabilising influence following an extraordinary decade of revolution that had harried artists into adopting the values of the enterprise culture. His public persona encouraged this view. His first official prime ministerial portrait, painted by Peter Deighan, showed him in jacket and slacks, leaning informally against a bookcase. That the book in his hand was more probably *Wisden's Cricketer's Almanac* than his favourite novelist, Trollope, gave reassurance, though he was no stranger to culture: his wife Norma wrote popular biography and was a lover of the opera. The painting, with its clear light and bland naturalism seemed intended to illustrate Major's personal message in the 1992 Conservative manifesto: 'That, I believe, is the way we all want to live – a decent life in a civilised community.'[1]

Where Thatcher had viewed support for the arts largely in terms of national prestige, Major's conception of cultural identity was altogether more intimate and comfortably nostalgic. In a speech in 1993, given on – of all days – St George's Day and to – of all people – the Conservative Party European Group, he was happy to evoke his England with the help of his speech-writer's borrowings from George Orwell: 'The long shadows falling across the county grounds, the warm beer, the invincible green suburbs, dog-lovers and pools-fillers . . . old maids bicycling to Holy Communion through the morning mist.' But the absurdity of that final image lifted from *The Lion and the Unicorn* revealed the distance between the ideal and reality. By 1993 few old maids felt they could bicycle safely, at any time of the day, and Holy Communion had become a source of division. Major's emphasis on a classless society and a nation at ease with itself was an admission of the menace of their grimmer, and much more evident opposites: a society divided between ever-richer haves and more destitute have-nots, a nation that had lost not only its direction but its sense of identity.

One way for Major to convey his concern that people should be able to lead a civilised life in a decent community was through the state's provision for the material expressions of culture: the arts and heritage. To that end, he introduced a new and transforming source of funding, and a new department of state for the management of cultural policy. Announced in the 1992 manifesto, but not given its title until after the election, the Department of National Heritage would reassemble responsibilities previously carried by half a dozen ministries, and bring them together into a powerful new instrument of government whose minister would have a permanent place at the Cabinet table. That this new department should go under the comforting, retrospective label of "heritage" was a reflection of the civilising reassurance that Major hoped to bring.

The Department of National Heritage was intended to be, in its first Secretary of State David Mellor's phrase, more than 'the Office of Arts and Libraries on wheels'. To the responsibility of the Office of Arts and Libraries for the performing arts, museums and galleries, and the National Heritage Memorial Fund, were added English Heritage from the Department of the Environment, sport from Education, film from Trade and Industry, and tourism from Employment. By focusing the former peripheral activities of other ministries, Major was shaping the 'big beast' that Mellor, in his informal, 'unstructured conversations' with the Prime Minister before the election, had argued would have both financial and political clout.[2]

Not only did this create a cultural budget approaching one billion pounds, one of the department's first tasks was to devise a National Lottery for good causes which would provide an entirely new source of funds for charities, sport, the arts, heritage and a Millennium Fund which, in the words of the 1992 manifesto, would 'restore the fabric of the nation'.[3] Until the National Lottery Act was passed in October 1993, Margaret Thatcher's residual Methodism had ensured that Britain was the only country in Europe without a state lottery. Any fears that Thatcher had about the impact of this new attraction on a nation of inveterate gamblers were entirely justified: between 1994 and 1995 the amount spent on gambling increased by forty-one per cent, largely because of the National Lottery. In the first two years since it first came into operation in November 1994, a total of seven billion, three hundred and nine million pounds was spent on £1 stakes for the weekly draw televised on BBC1, together with the instant gratification of scratch-cards. Thirty million people over the age of sixteen became regular lottery players, and the average household was soon spending more on lottery tickets than bread or books. The distribution of players by social class showed that not only were the poor playing more frequently than the rich, they were spending a higher proportion of their income. In spite of protests from the Churches, from charities who claimed they were losing out in the switch from charitable giving, from football pools companies suffering direct competition, and critics of the substantial profits made by the private operating company Camelot, the government pronounced the National Lottery a great success, and happily gathered in one billion, one hundred and seventeen million pounds in additional revenue in the first two years from the twelve per cent tax on every pound wagered.

The financial success of the Lottery, which far exceeded expectations, however proved an embarrassment for those charged with distributing the proceeds that were left after prizes, expenses and tax: £2.7 billion in the first two years. In addition to the Millennium Commission, a National Charities Board was created as compensation for the voluntary bodies whose previous patterns of fund raising were affected by the

Lottery. The arts, sport and heritage became the responsibility of the four arts councils (with a fixed proportion for each country), the Sports Council and its respective subsidiaries, and the National Heritage Memorial Fund. The NHMF had a nationwide remit, and divided its organisation between its traditional responsibilities, where the "memorial" aspect was to be emphasised, and a new Heritage Lottery Fund. The five sectors covered by the Lottery each received a fifth of the income paid by Camelot into the National Lottery Distribution Fund, which by the end of 1996 was averaging five to six million pounds each a week.

The five principal distributing bodies therefore each had an annual income greater than that of the American Ford Foundation or the Getty Trust. But the sheer volume of money, and the weight of demand for it, completely altered the nature of the organisations themselves, shifting the balance of their activities towards this new form of capital funding. The Arts Councils, Sports Council and the NHMF had to increase their staff substantially and take on more advisers. The Arts Council of England calculated that by the year 2000 it would have received up to 6,000 applications amounting to four billion pounds. Outside accountants and consultants found renewed prosperity either assessing lottery bids on behalf of distributors, or advising clients on how to make their applications to the distributors they advised.

What had been conceived as important safeguards in the distribution of lottery funds proved in practice to be major hazards. The first of these was the level of outside financial participation needed to unlock a successful lottery application. It was argued that it was necessary for there to be a degree of partnership in any scheme to prove that it was really wanted (just as it was necessary for the successful applicant to demonstrate it had a secure financial future). The Millennium Commission demanded that fifty per cent of the cost of its major building projects be met from the resources of the applicant or from other donors. The Arts Council set a level of twenty-five per cent for any project costing more than a hundred thousand pounds, ten per cent for sums below that. Only when these matching sums were found could the lottery money be drawn down. Such was the competition for these matching funds – foundations, business sponsors, or local authority capital budgets – that there were severe doubts that there would be sufficient matching money to go round. None of the first major projects to which the Millennium Commission committed funds in principle –

the Tate Gallery of Modern Art at Bankside, the Great Court for the British Museum, the Earth Centre at Doncaster, the refurbishment of Portsmouth Harbour – had sufficient funds in place to guarantee at the outset that they would indeed go ahead.

The second, and defining, safeguard was that, with the exception of the National Charities Board and the Millennium Commission's bursaries, awards could be made by the distributing bodies for capital projects only. The logic of this decision was firstly, that Britain's cultural plant and equipment, in terms of museums, galleries, theatres and concert halls, was in desperate need of refurbishment. (The Arts Council's Housing the Arts fund had dried up in 1984, the government's Property Services Agency had systematically neglected museums and galleries, and local authority arts budgets were steadily reduced.) Secondly, by making lottery funding flow in a distinct stream towards capital projects, it would be possible to ensure that government-funded organisations did not suffer a loss of grant-in-aid for their running and performing costs. It was expected that annual revenue funding would be maintained by the Treasury, regardless of any capital windfalls from the lottery. This principle of "additionality" – that lottery funding did not count as public expenditure and was additional to, and separate from, revenue funding – was reiterated several times by the Prime Minister himself. 'The money raised by the Lottery will not replace existing government spending', Major told an English Heritage conference on 16 September 1994, while calling for a 'national outbreak of lateral thinking' on how the money should be spent.

This commitment was made before the amount of money that would be available became apparent, and the disparity between the revenue and lottery streams of cultural funding turned out to be so extreme. The disparity was exacerbated by the government's failure to respect its own commitment to maintain revenue funding of the arts and heritage. While at the end of the 1980s there had been a significant increase in government cultural spending, so that between 1989 and 1992 the Arts Council's grant-in-aid increased by twenty per cent, and it had a further increase after two years of restraint in 1995, the 1995/6 grant in aid of £191.1 million marked a peak in the Arts Council's revenue funding. In the 1996/7 budget allocation, the first year during which lottery funding was also on stream, the Arts Council's grant was cut by £5 million to £186.1 million, and held at that figure for 1997/8, with reductions planned for future years. Because of inflation, in real terms the Arts Council's grant was twenty-five million pounds less than it had been in 1992. Government spending on museums and galleries was also reduced, with the effect that the Victoria and Albert Museum introduced a compulsory entrance fee in October 1996, and in the light of the 1996 budget the British Museum and other free galleries were forced to consider both charging and reducing their staff. Reductions in the Department of the Environment's contribution to local authority finance put additional pressure on local museums and arts facilities.

The Department of National Heritage's overall spending allocation for 1997–8 fell by sixty-three million pounds to exactly one billion, which gave the lie to the government's promise to maintain revenue funding of the arts and heritage, and underlined the absurdity of restricting Lottery funding so tightly. Even though he was a former Conservative Minister for the Arts, Lord Gowrie as Chairman of the Arts Council had to protest: 'we are not allowed to use the Lottery to look after the arts themselves. We can build shining new palaces of culture. . . . But we cannot fund what goes on inside them. On top of this, the funding consensus, which has always governed the Council, has in effect broken down.'[4] David Mellor concluded that the 1996 budget signified the Treasury's desire: 'no longer to be bound by the undertaking I gave . . . that money from the Lottery would not be taken into account when determining support for the arts, sports and the heritage.'[5]

While continuing to insist that the principle of additionality had not been breached (and in the same breath trumpeting the amount of money going towards the arts from the lottery) the government appeared to be aware of the problems that were emerging. Under new directions that came into force in 1997 the Arts Council was permitted to use lottery money for an experimental 'stabilisation fund' that would enable arts organisations to get onto a more secure financial footing – the most likely way being to clear long-term deficits. Dance and drama students who, unlike music and art students, did not qualify for mandatory local education authority grants were to be given help through the Lottery. Commissions to artists linked to new building projects were to be treated as capital investments; lottery money was to be made available to encourage more touring by theatre companies and to subsidise access to the arts for young people. £20 million was committed to a fresh scheme 'Arts For Everyone', to fund new projects by established organisations, and give small grants to groups which had never been funded before, thus allowing a small amount of lottery money to go to people rather than buildings. The Arts Council also decided substantially to increase its commitment in the one area where lottery money had already been going to artists, feature film production, where the Council had previously had no remit. In the heritage field a new act was brought in to widen the application of lottery funds and allow private owners of heritage properties as well as charitable trusts to apply for grants.

All this however was merely tinkering, and did not address the paradox of cultural institutions dying of revenue thirst while drowning in lakes of capital funding. The complications and restrictions surrounding the bureaucratically elaborate procedures for obtaining a lottery grant were not easily understood by the general public, who were constantly being told how much the Lottery had raised for the arts. The alternative story was told by the popular press, who were quick to seize on a number of early high profile awards – £13.25 million for the purchase and preservation of the pre-1945 papers of Winston Churchill from the Heritage Lottery Fund; £55 million from the Arts Council to the Royal Opera House, with a conditional extra £30 million to follow – to claim that the poor were funding the pleasures of the rich. This was not true: as with the rest of the subsidised arts, the public at large was funding the pleasures of the literate middle classes. The Arts Council was almost overscrupulous in ensuring that 75 per cent of its awards were for sums of less than £100,000, and nearly every brass band in the country appeared to be acquiring new instruments. Nor was there an excessive bias of funding towards London which, being the capital, inevitably housed a number of major beneficiaries, but whose local arts organisations did not do conspicuously well in the early years.

Whatever good the Lottery did to those who successfully negotiated the complex path between application and completion, in general it seemed to make the arts less, rather than more popular, as it became an excuse for the venting of envy and crude philistinism. Nor did it have a restorative effect on the government's popularity. This was recognised in an article by the journalist Hugh Colver at the time of his resignation from a brief period of service in the press department of Conservative Central Office. He asked: 'How can you lose on a policy which created over 100 millionaires in its first year and gave £1 billion to good causes and another £1 billion to the Treasury? It is a prize example of how to turn a public-relations triumph into a disaster.'[6]

Responsibility for the National Lottery lay with its creator, the Department of National Heritage. The new ministry had been shaped to the tastes of Major's friend and ally, David Mellor, an enthusiast for the arts, especially music, and a keen follower of football. Although he did not choose its title – he has said he was not a 'heritage man' – Mellor was plainly delighted with his new department of state, the first such creation (apart from the Northern Ireland Office) since Harold Wilson's Department of Economic Affairs in 1964 – a somewhat unfortunate precedent. The Department quickly became known as the "Ministry of Fun", but the joke turned sour when in July 1992 Mellor was revealed to have been having an affair with an actress, Antonia de Sancha. Mellor's immediate offer of resignation was rejected, but the Prime Minister's loyalty could not save his friend, and the scandal early laid the government open to deeply damaging accusations of sleaze and corruption.

Mellor's replacement was Peter Brooke, recalled from the back benches. The fifty-nine-year-old Brooke *was* a heritage man, but he was not ambitious for himself or his department in the way that Mellor had been. He warned in a lecture to the Royal Fine Art Commission in December 1992: 'We are not about to enter the era of Ludwig of Bavaria, or Louis XIV.'[7] This proved to be the case, and with the departure of Mellor the Department of National Heritage became a mere staging post for politicians on the way up, or the way down. In a reshuffle in July 1994 Brooke was replaced by the younger, and – in Conservative terms – more left-wing high flyer, Stephen Dorrell, who remained true to Conservative belief that the arts should earn their keep through contributions to the tourist industry and broadcasting. Dorrell's service was brief, for in July 1995 he was promoted to the Department of Health, whose incumbent, Virginia Bottomley was demoted to National Heritage. Mrs Bottomley lost no opportunity to promote the benefits of the National Lottery, but was incapable of defending her ministry against the demands of a tax cutting Chancellor of the Exchequer, as the reduction of her Department's budget at the end of 1996 showed. Mellor's 'big beast' turned out to be a neutered tom.

The raising to cabinet rank of the former post of Arts Minister meant that the Labour Party had to follow suit with the status of its opposition spokesmen, but it also followed a similar pattern with its appointments. While the pre-1992 arts spokesman Mark Fisher continued to serve in a junior capacity, the lack-lustre Anne Clwyd was soon replaced by Mo Mowlam, who was in turn followed in 1994 by Chris Smith. Smith showed considerable zeal for the job, but was promoted the following year to cover the Department of Social Security. He was replaced by Jack Cunningham, who had failed to be elected to the Shadow cabinet, and had little affinity with the post. The Labour Party was very slow to produce any clear commitments to a future arts policy that went beyond the familiar pieties of access and economic regeneration. Its vision for the Department of National Heritage appeared to be that of a cultural equivalent of the Department of Trade and Industry. Plans to use former Millennium Commission funds for educational and social spending were open to the same charges of breaching "additionality" as those levelled against the government.

As the party in power the Conservatives were able to be judged by their actions rather than by their words, which showed that the arts and heritage were of little importance when it came to reducing public expenditure in preparation for a general election. It took some time for the Department of National Heritage to assemble its constituent parts and forge their different parts into a coherent whole. It too was reluctant to commit itself to a particular vision of its responsibilities. One senior official remarked: 'It is not part of our culture to think in terms of a cultural policy.'[8] In May 1993 the department did at least acquire an identifiable geographical personality, when it moved into offices in Cockspur Street, just off Trafalgar Square. The building had begun life as the Royal Bank of Canada, but behind the listed, 1929 neo-classical facade lay a typical eighties interior tricked out in developer's post-classical, with a salmon-pink marbled and columned entrance hall leading to an atrium with waterfall, weeping fig-tree and glass-sided lift. The location was curiously appropriate for a department that had chosen the resolutely English term "heritage" for its title: here was a restored facade and an ersatz interior. Ironically, one of the first responsibilities thrust upon it in November 1992 had been to deal with the consequences of the Windsor fire.

In almost any other country, this new department would have been called a Ministry of Culture, but the British have shown themselves uncomfortable with the idea of Culture, whereas they have become entirely comfortable with the word "heritage". "Culture" still suggests at best the preoccupation of a snobbish intellectual élite, at worst a Stalinist state imposition promoting official artists backed by an overweaning bureaucracy. "Heritage" sounds patriotic, even nationalistic, and summons up the splendours of the past – Shakespeare and Windsor Castle, Elgar and Chatsworth – a world of secure values and an unthreatening social order where the arts supply colourful illustrations to the national narrative. But the secret of the profound attraction of the rich imagery of heritage is that it helps to disguise the poverty of the present. By entrusting what its third Secretary of State Stephen Dorrell called: 'those activities which shape our sense of national identity' to a Department of National Heritage, what should be a living culture was thus officially defined as traditionalist, retrospective, nostalgic and entropic.[9]

But a Ministry of Culture the Department of National Heritage nonetheless is, and it is the culmination of a process that began more than fifty years ago, when the Council for the Encouragement of Music and the Arts was launched in January 1940. In a disguised act of modernisation, Britain has been following a practice common throughout the developed world. Over the last hundred years government patronage has successively supplanted the patronage of the Church, the Crown, the aristocracy, and lastly that of the late nineteenth- and early twentieth-century bourgeoisie. The important difference between the modern form of patronage and those that preceded it, however, is that the state does it with other people's money, through taxation.

The degree to which the state has in return allowed the taxpayer a say in the way in which cultural patronage is exercised has varied from country to country, and there has been a rich variety of "intermediate organisations" to supervise its distribution. The degree of the state's direct intervention in cultural matters has also varied. There has been the aggressive *Kultur* of Nazi Germany and the oppressive "command culture" that dominated the former Soviet Union and Eastern Europe until 1989. Following historically entrenched cultural patterns, France developed centralised bureaucratic control, while post-war Germany preferred a system that encouraged benign competition between individual cities and federal states. True to its own traditions, Britain has evolved a distinctive "mixed economy", where funding by central and local government, the National Lottery, the activities of the Arts Councils and Regional Arts Boards, business sponsorship and the box office, all play their part.

The system operating in the United States is different, but in one respect essentially it is not. The dominance of private patronage through corporations, foundations and the donations of individuals is only possible because public policy encourages it. It is still government patronage, in that it is exercised in the form of federal and state taxes forgone. During the Cold War American cultural policy played an important part in promoting the "values of the free world" – hence the triumph of Abstract Expressionism and the School of New York in the fifties and sixties. The United States has had its own version of the Arts Council, the National Endowment for the Arts, since 1965. Across the world, culture has become a matter of public policy.

At the same time that governments have gradually supplanted earlier forms of cultural patronage, the definition of what is meant by culture has changed. Culture has always been more than the activities of painters, poets, playwrights, novelists and performing artists. Anthropologically it applies to the customs and beliefs of a whole people, which exist in a moral, even religious, dimension. Both artists and their patrons have felt themselves involved in a social activity that has moral as well as aesthetic value. Culture was Matthew Arnold's 'the best that has been said or thought in the world'. It was a positive ideal to be opposed to the development of a barbarian industrialised society.

Such a definition, with its emphasis on "the best" was inevitably élitist. As mass production, mass organisation and, significantly, mass education multiplied alongside the spread of democracy, attitudes to this ideal culture became increasingly pessimistic, so that for T. S. Eliot or F. R. Leavis, culture became merely a saving remnant in a brutish world. Kenneth Clark's television series *Civilisation* of 1969 showed élite culture apparently in retreat in the face of a debased mass culture – George Steiner's 'post-culture' – promoted by the forces of commercialism.

Yet in the sixties, a new and more positive definition of culture had also emerged: what Raymond Williams termed culture as 'a whole way of life'. Not merely the artefacts and ideals of high culture beloved by Kenneth Clark, but a wide range of activities, institutions and creative practices began to be seen as having cultural – and moral – significance. The traditional élitist pyramid of highbrow, middlebrow and lowbrow mass popular culture was replaced by a different model, Lawrence

Alloway's 'long front of culture', which exchanged a hierarchy of taste for a democracy of access to the arts. In Pop Art, the iconography of vulgar popular culture was translated into high art.

The increased elasticity of the definition of what constitutes culture coincided with a momentous change in the developed world from mass production to mass consumption as the primary focus of economic activity – consumption being necessary to maintain and extend production. In this fundamental shift from the ruling condition of modernism to that of post-modernism, culture ceased to be a fixed ideal, and as such was susceptible to ever greater distortion under the pressures of commercialisation and the ambitions of national policy.

At the same time that culture began to be an object of economic and social concern, its assumed transcendental value was being hollowed out from within. From roughly 1968 onwards, culture as an ideal was the subject of ever more destructive definitions from the Left. Marxists developed Gramsci's conception of culture as one of the means by which a ruling class maintained its control over the rest, in such a way that culture was no longer seen as a virtue, but as an ideology, a set of ideas, images and values that served to keep certain interests in power, not just by force, but by consent. Culture increasingly became a site of contention, where issues of identity, class and social power were disputed through the images and language of the arts as much as through those of politics, which turned out to be culture by another name. Structuralists and post-structuralists attacked not only the ideological basis of cultural value, but announced the death of the author and made the job of the critic impossible, by arguing that there was no longer such a thing as the unified centred and judging individual, only decentred prisoners of language. In a final ecstasy of communication, the elasticity of the "grand narrative" of modern culture snapped, and the fragments plunged into the black hole of the free-floating relativism of post-modernity.

The void was partially filled by the commodification of culture, so that it became a matter of public policy. In effect, this squared the circle of culture-versus-society and culture-as-expression-of-society. Whether funded by the government or not, high art has been absorbed into the general circulation of commodities; mass or popular culture is what it became after the Industrial Revolution, an entertainment produced for, and not by the masses. Both élitist and popular culture, be it the Royal Opera House or Wembley Arena, the South Bank or Shaftesbury

Avenue, have become part of the same, unified ruling culture. This form of culture has been termed by Donald Horne 'the public culture'. In his book *The Public Culture: The Triumph of Industrialism* (1986) Horne argued:

> In a modern society there is no longer the dichotomy of ruling-class culture and folk culture. In modern industrial societies (if in varying degrees) traditional folk culture has been attenuated into a few last souvenirs. The culture that dominates the public scene is not a ruling-class culture of triumphal display, but a fabricated "public culture" that purports to be the culture not just of the rulers but of all the people.[10]

In Horne's view, such a public culture 'might be seen as the "language" used to enact the dominant "myths" of a society'.[11] In other words, the public culture is an effective instrument of hegemony.

Horne has stressed the distance between the reality of contemporary life and the image currently projected on to it: 'The public culture of a modern industrial society is not a representation of that society.'[12] Significantly, the emergence of a public culture has been criticised from the Right as well as from Horne's position on the Left. In *L'État Culturel: Essai sur une Religion Moderne* (1992) the French cultural historian Marc Fumaroli has described the evolution of such a culture as: 'a subtle perversion of the public realm, mixed with a will to power of a politico-administrative oligarchy, then the organisation from above of a mass culture, pretentious in content, egalitarian in its design'.[13]

Although Fumaroli traced this development to the creation by President de Gaulle of a Ministry of Culture under André Malraux, his targets were President Mitterand and his Minister of Culture, Jack Lang. In France, Fumaroli argued, state patronage has become so pervasive that there was no space for other forms: 'Culture is another name for propaganda.'[14] While this may well be true of official culture in France, there seems little structural difference between this and the corporate culture of the United States or the United Kingdom where, with the spread of business sponsorship – ironically, promoted at the taxpayers' expense – "culture" has become another name for advertising.

One of the features of the public culture, whatever the political system in place, has been that no one appears directly to own the resources at its disposal. Instead they are controlled by professional bureaucracies such as the Arts Council, who appear unaccountable to anyone, protected as they are by the pretence that they are at arm's length both from government and from the constituency of artists they are supposed to serve. This is one of the reasons why the public culture has become strangely rootless and bloodless. Grand cultural events, be they the Edinburgh Festival, a gala at Glyndebourne, Shakespeare at the Barbican, or a concert at the Albert Hall, become a matter of routine. They are part of official culture, a celebration of the country's power to sustain cultural activity and tradition, yet empty of meaning beyond that.

The same process can be seen in the institutionalisation of the avant-garde, which has led to that contradiction in terms, the museum of modern art. Even when an artist sets up in opposition to the status quo the work is seized upon for earnest discussion on television and featured in glossy magazines, and the rebel artist is quickly turned into a celebrity. For Marc Fumaroli, this reached its apotheosis in France, where under Jack Lang the avant-gardists of 1968 completed the institutionalisation of modernity into the official state religion, with its national cathedral the Centre Pompidou and its bishops seated in every Maison de la Culture and *espace culturel*. Horne goes so far as to argue that most people are positively excluded from real cultural activity: ' "Art", if it happens at all, is something that for many citizens is done *for* them and *to* them. The idea of actually going so far as to *make* art could seem impertinent. Indeed a great deal of art is presented in such a way that it is done *against* the citizens.'[15] Fifty years before, the "missionary" faction in CEMA had been producing similar arguments which were gradually silenced by Keynes and the fledgling Arts Council.

One very evident consequence of the emergence of a public culture is that when the arts are captured by public policy, they become subject to its ruling concerns, which are primarily economic. This has been especially true in Britain, where there is a general perception of economic decline. In the late twentieth century economic activity has become the principal form of public expression. Cultural engagement is conceived of as cultural consumption, and indeed culture is seen more and more as a commodity like any other. The market place has become the model of culture, and through the operation of the enterprise culture, the long front of culture has become a supermarket of styles.

The problem created by the argument that the arts are a source of urban regeneration, or that the taxes they yield show that subsidy is really "investment", is that the arts become entirely instrumental, a matter of "value for money". In the public culture the traditional opposition between culture and industrial society has disappeared. Instead of preserving the classical and conservative values of western civilisation, which resisted the socially destructive drive of industrialisation, cultural activity now has the authority of the state to encourage the citizen's indulgent consumption, no longer tempering the naked greed of the market by appeals to the spiritual and moral values of art, but extracting as much profit as possible, looking to the arts as a means of economic recovery. Where Matthew Arnold held up the values of high culture against the anarchy of the market, high culture is now a niche market all of its own.

A tragic hedonism has become the characteristic feature of the contemporary arts in the nineties. Within the market place certain kinds of art – notably visual art that has broken free of the conventions of easel painting and academic sculpture – have flourished, and the culture of consumption has increased the number of buyers and sellers. On a broad definition of what constitutes cultural activity, 80 per cent of Britain's adult population takes part in one way or another, with cinema going (45 per cent) and stately-home visiting (33 per cent) the most popular cultural recreation, folk-dancing (3 per cent) and poetry reading (2 per cent) the least. On a narrower definition, taking in just seven "serious" arts forms – theatre, art, classical, ballet, opera, jazz and contemporary dance – some seventeen million adults enjoy the arts in one way or another. According to the 1991 census, while the number of economically active people in the country had hardly changed as a whole since the previous census in 1981, the number of individuals describing themselves as having cultural occupations went up by 34 per cent. Six hundred thousand people, about as many as are employed in banking and finance, are working in the cultural sector as a whole. This figure includes those employed in the media and fashion industries, but there has been a significant increase in the number of artists, designers, performing artists, producers and directors.

The cutting edge of creative – as opposed to interpretative – arts activity is necessarily small, although it attracts a disproportionate amount of publicity. For the rising generation of artists like Damien

Hirst or writers like Irvine Welsh social surrealism rather than social realism is the appropriate medium through which to convey the random raptures of post-industrial society, where the breakdown of previous social and aesthetic order has created the opportunity to make new patterns out of the chaos. Yet their themes are often the impossibility of, even the death, of art, or the ecstatic insanity of a world of fraught personal relationships, menaced by violence and poisoned by sexual and physical abuse.

The fragmentation and insecurity of the late twentieth century is more than subject matter for contemporary artists, it is the condition that has helped to create them. At a time when no job is safe and no career certain, the risk involved in choosing to strike out on a creative path seems lessened, although the chances of a safe arrival are no greater. This new pattern was set in the eighties. In the previous decades creative energy had gone into the formation and expansion of cultural institutions – the founding of the National Theatre, the construction of facilities like the Hayward Gallery, the establishment of a regional network of repertory theatres, arts centres, galleries and concert halls. This network was never completed, and after 1979 institutional expansion effectively ceased. Young artists found that they had to strike out on their own, exploiting the gaps in the official culture and ignoring the formal demarcations between one artistic discipline and another. Those that succeeded have been left with very little commitment to structures – either in terms of organisations or buildings such as theatres or galleries – a personally liberating form of economic individualism, but one which implies that there may be no solidity or permanence for the arts as a whole. There is a feverish excitement about much of this work, but it needs more secure roots if it is genuinely to flourish and grow.

The official policies of the nineties, while attempting to claim the credit for the hectic and youthful culture that has become known as "cool Britannia", have done nothing to ensure that this apparent talent and appetite for the arts is given any security within which to develop. Just as in industry, where the British have proved good at research and development, but poor at investing in the results, artistic innovation is rarely given the opportunity to mature. The network of buildings and organisations which create the context for new work – if only as a context to react against – is in danger of collapse. The National Lottery may in certain cases arrest physical decay of the buildings, or even provide new ones, but so far it has proved a massive distraction from the real crisis of a lack of investment in training, experiment and performance. It must be radically revised to allow for the creation of endowment funds that would give arts organisations a genuine independence, and free them from the procrustean bed of the government's annual spending decisions.[16]

The crisis of the arts – and the crisis of national identity they embody – cannot be resolved without the development of a cultural policy that is free of the instrumental imperatives of market forces. The arts embody values – imagination, independence of mind, creativity of expression, shared experience, cooperation, above all a sense of mutual worth and common identity – that are not the values of the marketplace and which are not susceptible to market-led solutions. The failure of the public culture has been to generate values to which insufficient numbers of people can subscribe. Instead, we have been offered values that are transitory, individualistic, atomised and destructive of community. It is the failure of these values that has produced the crisis of national identity, and this in turn has fed back into individual discontent.

The public realm – the space between the individual and the state – has, like the space beneath the Millennium Dome where we might have shared in an altogether more uplifting rite of passage into the next century, been privatised, so that we are indeed becoming only individual men and women and – if we are lucky – families. The crisis of national identity is a reflection of the destruction of a common space in which to express it; the need for its reaffirmation is all the more urgent in order to counter the utter alienation of post-modern globalisation and homogenisation. In *Culture and Society* Raymond Williams argued: 'We lack a genuinely common experience, except in certain rare and dangerous moments of crisis. What we are paying for this lack, in every kind of currency, is sufficiently evident. We need a common culture, not for the sake of an abstraction, but because we cannot survive without it.'[17]

A common culture need not be a conformist one. A plural society would be a better guarantee of collective liberties, and a closer reflection of contemporary realities. What is needed, however, is the acceptance of a value-system which would allow for the creation of a public realm within which pluralism could flourish. This calls for the sustenance, not of a "welfare state", but a commonwealth, in which individual and communal responsibility would work to reconcile self-interest with public interest in order to produce social justice. A social order of this kind can only be generated by genuine citizens, not subjects, clients or customers. Its value-system demands a fresh calculus: a public account-ability, not a private accountancy, of social goods: common services, environmental health, education and culture as a common activity, a means of securing old identities and creating new ones.

A common culture is also a critical culture, for it becomes the arena for argument, a space for the competing and collaborating forces that shape the 'compromise equilibrium' of the national consensus. Specific ideas of national identity are a reflection of this consensus, and like consensus, like hegemony, are mobile and therefore open to be renewed. To create this new realm and the new consensus in which pluralism could thrive, it is necessary to discover a new national narra-tive, one that uses continuity as a bridge to the future, not as a dead weight from the past.

The search for a secure sense of national identity will always be an open and incomplete process, just as our culture is not a closed canon or a reliquary for past values, but a way of thinking about the possibilit-ies of a better life. Whatever are the larger political processes that will be required to establish a new consensus and a regenerative national narrative, those relating to our national culture will play an even greater part in the debate, for it must be understood that culture *is* the national narrative, the ground of identity and the support of society. What we should be arguing for is not value for money, but money for values.

Notes

I: Dis-United Kingdom

1. *Windsor: The Great Fire* (no author credit), Pitkin Pictorials Ltd, 1992, p. 2.
2. *Ibid.*
3. *Sunday Express*, 15 November 1992.
4. M. Jones, 'Royals need new role in nation racked by doubt', *Sunday Times*, 7 February 1993.
5. I. Jack, 'Comment: Flames that illuminate an autumn of unease', *Independent on Sunday*, 22 November 1992.
6. *Windsor: The Great Fire, op. cit.*, p. 2, p. 10.
7. Lord Goodman interviewed by Terry Coleman, *Guardian*, 21 August 1993.
8. M. Jacques, 'The Erosion of the Establishment', *Sunday Times*, 16 January 1994.
9. W. Rees-Mogg, 'More Grey is Forecast', *The Times*, 10 February 1994.
10. R. Hughes, *The Culture of Complaint: The Fraying of America*, Oxford University Press, 1993, p. 109.
11. M. Warner, *Managing Monsters: Six Myths of Our Time* (The 1994 Reith Lectures), Vintage Books, 1994, p. 92, p. 91.
12. *Windsor: The Great Fire, op. cit.*, p. 2.
13. *Hansard, Parliamentary Debates* (25 November 1992), 6th Series, Vol. 214, columns 619, 620.
14. Quoted in H. Hopkins, *The New Look: A Social History of the Forties and Fifties in Britain*, Secker & Warburg, 1963, p. 285.
15. T. Nairn, 'Britain's Royal Romance', in *National Fictions, Patriotism: The Making and Unmaking of British National Identity*, Vol. 3, ed. R. Samuel, Routledge, 1989, p. 76.
16. *The British System of Government*, HMSO, 1992, p. 8.
17. *Ibid*, p. 9.
18. L. Marks and M. Bailey, 'Her Majesty invites . . .', *Observer*, 2 May 1993.
19. A. Barnett, *Iron Britannia*, Alison & Busby, 1992, pp. 87–8.

20. D. Gervais, *Literary Englands*, Cambridge University Press, 1993, p. 30.
21. *Ibid*, p. 39.
22. P. Larkin, 'Going, Going', in *High Windows*, Faber & Faber, 1974.
23. M. Warner, 'The puzzle of the monarchy', *The Times*, 15 May 1993.
24. D. Horne, *The Public Culture: The Triumph of Industrialism*, Pluto Press, 1986, pp. 57–8.
25. A. Gramsci, *A Gramsci Reader: Selected Writings 1916–1935*, ed. D. Forgacs, Lawrence & Wishart, 1988, pp. 205–6.
26. *Ibid*, p. 211.
27. *Ibid*, p. 194.
28. *Ibid*, pp. 306–7.
29. A. Gramsci, *Selections from Prison Notebooks*, trans. and ed. Q. Hoare and G. Nowell-Smith, Lawrence & Wishart, 1971. For an account of Gramsci's reception in Britain, see D. Forgacs, 'Gramsci and Marxism in Britain', *New Left Review*, no. 176 (July/August 1989), pp. 70–88.
30. A. Gamble, *The Free Economy and the Strong State: The Politics of Thatcherism*, Macmillan, 1988, p. 207.
31. G. Orwell, *The Lion and the Unicorn: Socialism and the English Genius*, reprinted in *The Collected Essays, Journalism and Letters of George Orwell*, ed. S. Orwell and I. Angus, Penguin, 1970, Vol. 2, p. 77.
32. P. Addison, *The Road to 1945: British Politics and the Second World War*, Jonathan Cape, 1975, p. 14.
33. See Anthony Seldon's introduction to D. Kavanagh and P. Morris, *Consensus Politics from Attlee to Major*, Blackwell, second edition, 1994, p. viii.
34. A. Gamble, *op. cit.*, p. 24.
35. D. Kavanagh and P. Morris, *op. cit.*, p. 14.
36. See B. Pimlott, 'The Myth of Consensus', in L. Smith (ed.), *The Making of Britain: Echoes of Greatness*, Macmillan, 1988.
37. A. Gamble, *op. cit.*, pp. 170–1.
38. See A. Gramsci, *A Gramsci Reader, op. cit.*, pp. 346–7.
39. Quoted in P. Heelas and P. Morris (eds.), *The Values of the Enterprise Culture*, Routledge, 1992, p. 17.
40. A. Smith, *National Identity*, Penguin, 1991, p. 16.
41. S. Hall, 'Subcultures, Cultures and Class', in S. Hall and T. Jefferson, (eds.), *Resistance Through Rituals*, Hutchinson, 1976, p. 12.
42. *Ibid*.
43. D. Hebdige, *Subculture: The Meaning of Style*, Methuen, 1979, p. 17.
44. A. Smith, *op. cit.*, pp. 69–70.
45. R. Williams, *Culture and Society 1780–1950* (first published Chatto & Windus, 1958), Penguin edition, 1961, p. 320.
46. M. Girouard, *Windsor: The Most Romantic Castle*, Hodder & Stoughton, 1993, p. 39.
47. S. Greenberg, letter to *The Times*, 27 November 1993.
48. 'House of Windsor: Little focuses public attention so well as a fire', *The Times*, 23 November 1992.

II: Deep England

1. H. Dalton, *High Tide and After: Memoirs 1945–1960*, Frederick Muller, 1962, p. 118.
2. A. Calder, *The Myth of the Blitz*, Jonathan Cape, 1991, p. 182. The phrase was coined by Patrick Wright. See P. Wright, *On Living in an Old Country: The National Past in Contemporary Britain*, Verso, 1985, pp. 81–7.
3. N. Aldred, 'A Canterbury Tale', in D. Mellor (ed.), *A Paradise Lost: The Neo-Romantic Imagination in Britain 1935–1955*, Lund Humphries/ Barbican Gallery, 1987, p. 118.
4. T. S. Eliot, *The Complete Poems and Plays of T. S. Eliot*, Faber & Faber, 1969, p. 197, lines 235–7.
5. H. Dalton, *op. cit.*, p. 119.
6. K. Morgan, *The People's Peace: British History 1945–89*, Oxford University Press, 1990, p. 28.
7. P. Hennessy, *Never Again: Britain 1945–51*, Jonathan Cape, 1992, p. 52.
8. G. Orwell, *The Lion and the Unicorn: Socialism and the English Genius*, reprinted in *The Collected Essays, Journalism and Letters of George Orwell*, ed. S. Orwell and I. Angus, Penguin, 1970, Vol. 2, p. 105.
9. *Ibid*, p. 118.
10. *Ibid*, p. 77.
11. *Ibid*, p. 88.
12. *Ibid*, pp. 98–9.
13. T. Harrisson, *Living Through the Blitz*, Collins, 1976, pp. 314–15.
14. Army Bureau of Current Affairs, *Current Affairs*, No. 28, 10 October 1942.
15. C. Barnett, *The Audit of War: The Illusion and Reality of Britain as a Great Nation*, Macmillan, 1986, p. 12, and see p. 25.
16. Quoted in P. Addison, *The Road to 1945: British Politics and the Second World War*, Jonathan Cape, 1975, pp. 215–16.
17. *Social Insurance and Allied Services* ('The Beveridge Report'), Cmd. 6404, HMSO, 1942, p. 6.
18. Home Intelligence Report No. 114 for 1–8 December 1942, quoted in C. Barnett, *op. cit*, p. 29.
19. C. Barnett, *op. cit.*, p. 33.
20. G. Orwell, *op. cit.*, p. 83.
21. P. Addison, *op. cit.*, p. 166.
22. A. Calder, *op. cit.*, p. 15.
23. Quoted in H. Dalton, *op. cit.*, p. 119.
24. Quoted in F. M. Leventhal, ' "The Best for the Most": CEMA and State Sponsorship of the Arts in Wartime, 1939–1945', *Twentieth Century British History*, Vol. 1, No. 3 (1990), p. 293.
25. *Ibid*, p. 303.

26. Lord Redcliffe-Maud, *Support for the Arts in England and Wales*, Calouste Gulbenkian Foundation, 1976, p. 24.
27. *Ibid*, pp. 24–5.
28. R. Williams, 'The Arts Council', reprinted in R. Gable (ed.), *Resources of Hope: Culture, Democracy, Socialism*, Verso, 1989, p. 44.
29. *Ibid*, p. 49.
30. Quoted in E. White, *The Arts Council of Great Britain*, Davis Poynter, 1975, pp. 25–6.
31. M. Arnold, *Culture and Anarchy*, ed. J. Dover Wilson, Cambridge University Press, 1961, p. 6.
32. M. Glasgow, 'The Concept of the Arts Council', in W. M. Keynes (ed.), *Essays on John Maynard Keynes*, Cambridge University Press, 1975, p. 261.
33. J. B. Priestley, *Postscripts*, Heinemann, 1940, p. 53.
34. M. Glasgow and B. I. Evans, *The Arts in England*, Falcon Press, 1949, p. 47.
35. H. Dalton, *The Fateful Years, 1931–1945*, Frederick Muller, 1957, p. 479.
36. K. Clark, *The Other Half: A Self-Portrait*, John Murray, 1977, p. 26.
37. *Ibid*, p. 27.
38. C. P. Landstone, *Off-Stage: A Personal Record of the First Twelve Years of State-Sponsored Drama in Great Britain*, Elek, 1953, p. 67.
39. M. Glasgow, *op. cit.*, p. 267.
40. Quoted in F. M. Leventhal, *op. cit.*, p. 29.
41. C. P. Landstone, *op. cit.*, p. 58.
42. *Ibid*, p. 59.
43. J. E. Morpurgo, *Allen Lane: King Penguin*, Hutchinson, 1979, pp. 120–1.
44. Quoted in E. White, *op. cit.*, p. 41.
45. Quoted in F. M. Leventhal, *op. cit.*, p. 308.
46. *The Charter of Incorporation Granted by His Majesty the King, Ninth Day of August 1946*, p. 3.
47. J. M. Keynes, 'The Arts Council: Its Policy and Hopes', *Listener*, Vol. 34, No. 861 (12 July 1945), p. 31.
48. *Let Us Face the Future*, Labour Party, 1945, p. 9.
49. J. M. Keynes, *op. cit.*, p. 32.
50. A. Peacock, *Paying the Piper: Culture, Music and Money*, Edinburgh University Press, 1993, p. 118.
51. *Ibid*, pp. 118–19.
52. K. Clark, *op. cit.*, p. 129.
53. C. Connolly, editorial for *Horizon*, July 1947.
54. C. P. Landstone, *op. cit.*, p. 60.
55. R. Williams, *Politics and Letters*, Verso, 1979, p. 73.

III: New Britain

1. C. Connolly, editorial for *Horizon*, July 1947.
2. Quoted in the *Independent*, 16 December 1991.
3. For 'the strategic retreat of the Left' see R. Hewison, *Under Siege: Literary Life in London 1939–45*, 2nd (revised) edition, Methuen, 1988, p. 79.
4. H. Dalton, *High Tide and After, Memoirs 1945–1960*, Frederick Muller, 1962, p. 187.
5. T. S. Eliot, *Notes Towards the Definition of Culture*, Faber & Faber, 1948, p. 19.
6. P. Ackroyd, *T. S. Eliot*, Hamish Hamilton, 1984, p. 269.
7. T. S. Eliot, *For Lancelot Andrewes: Essays on Style and Order*, Faber & Gwyer, 1928, p. ix.
8. T. S. Eliot, *Notes, op. cit.*, p. 83.
9. *Ibid*, p. 37.
10. *Ibid*, p. 31.
11. *Ibid*, p. 103.
12. *Ibid*, p. 108.
13. *Ibid*, p. 100.
14. W. Moberley, *The Crisis in the University*, Student Christian Movement Press, 1949, p. 25.
15. *Ibid*, p. 294.
16. D. F. Pocock in a 'symposium' on Eliot's *Notes, Scrutiny*, 1950, Vol. 17, No. 37, p. 275.
17. *Scrutiny*, 1953, Vol. 19, No. 4, p. 327.
18. G. R. Barnes, 'The Aims of the Programme', *Listener*, Vol. 36, No. 924, 26 September 1946, Third Programme Supplement, pp. i–ii.
19. Quoted in W. Harrington and P. Young, *The 1945 Revolution*, Davis Poynter, 1978, p. 115.
20. J. B. Priestley, *The Arts Under Socialism*, Turnstile Press, 1947, p. 9.
21. R. Williams, '1956 and all that', *Guardian*, 2 April 1981.
22. R. Williams, *Culture and Society 1780–1950* (first published Chatto & Windus, 1958), Penguin edition, 1961, p. 238.
23. K. O. Morgan, *The People's Peace, British History 1945–1989*, Oxford University Press, 1990, p. 71.
24. Quoted in R. Weight, 'The Festival of Britain 1947–51', paper presented to the Institute of Historical Research, 10 February 1993, p. 2.
25. B. Donoghue and G. W. Jones, *Herbert Morrison: Portrait of a Politician*, Weidenfeld & Nicolson, 1973, p. 492.
26. *Ibid*.
27. Quoted in E. R. Chamberlain, *Life in Wartime Britain*, Batsford, 1972, p. 111.
28. Quoted in a wall placard at a festival anniversary exhibition, Royal Festival Hall, September 1991.

29. Ian Cox, *The South Bank Exhibition: A guide to the story it tells*, HMSO, 1951, p. 8.
30. *Ibid.*
31. *Ibid*, p. 67.
32. *Ibid*, p. 68.
33. *Ibid.*
34. For a discussion of the Royal College of Art and the Lion and Unicorn Pavilion, see A. Seago, *Burning the Box of Beautiful Things*, Oxford University Press, forthcoming.
35. *The Man in the White Suit*, directed by Alexander Mackendrick, Ealing Films, 1951. Charles Barr describes the film as 'a story of frustration, blockage and stagnation', C. Barr, *Ealing Studios*, Cameron & Tayleur, 1977, p. 135.
36. Quoted in M. Banham and B. Hillier (eds.), *A Tonic to the Nation: The Festival of Britain 1951*, Thames & Hudson, 1976, p. 35.
37. Introduction to Arts Council of Great Britain, *Sixth Annual Report, 1950/51*, p. 3.
38. B. Donoghue and G. W. Jones, *op. cit.*, p. 493.
39. M. Frayn, 'Festival', in M. Sissons and P. French (eds.), *The Age of Austerity*, Hodder & Stoughton, 1963, p. 320.
40. *Ibid*, p. 323.
41. *Ibid*, p. 320.
42. M. Banham and B. Hillier, *op. cit.*, p. 197.
43. *Family Portrait*, written and directed by H. Jennings, produced by Ian Dalrymple for Wessex Films, 1950.
44. H. Jennings. All quotations are taken from the soundtrack of *Family Portrait*.
45. G. Orwell, *The Collected Essays, Journalism and Letters of George Orwell*, ed. S. Orwell and I. Angus, Penguin, 1970, Vol. 2, p. 88.
46. L. Anderson, in M. L. Jennings (ed.), *Humphrey Jennings: Film Maker, Painter, Poet*, British Film Institute, 1982, p. 59.
47. *Ibid.*
48. Quoted in M. Banham and B. Hillier, *op. cit.*, p. 38.
49. T. Nairn, *The Enchanted Glass: Britain and its Monarchy* (first published, Radius, 1978), Picador, 1980, p. 269.
50. *Ibid*, p. 115.
51. *The Twentieth Century*, Vol. CLIII, No. 916 (June 1953), p. 403.
52. *Ibid*, p. 404.
53. P. Gibbs, *The New Elizabethans*, Hutchinson, 1953, p. 18.
54. *The Times*, 2 June 1953. I am grateful to Boris Ford for drawing my attention to Masefield's poem.
55. Quoted in C. Frost, *Coronation June 2 1953*, Arthur Barker, 1978, p. 26.
56. E. Shils and M. Young, 'The Meaning of the Coronation', *The Sociological Review* (new series), Vol. I (December 1953), p. 70.
57. *Ibid*, p. 67.

58. *Ibid*, p. 72.
59. *Ibid*, p. 74.
60. *Ibid*, p. 76.
61. N. Birnbaum, 'Monarchs and Sociologists', *Sociological Review*, Vol. 3 (New Series), No. 1 (1955), p. 19.
62. I. Hayden, *Symbol and Privilege: The Ritual Context of British Royalty*, Tucson, University of Arizona Press, 1987, pp. 157–8.
63. E. Shils and M. Young, *op. cit.*, p. 78.
64. Lord Harewood, *The Tongs and the Bones*, Weidenfeld & Nicolson, 1981, p. 138.
65. *The Times*, 18 June 1953.
66. Lord Harewood, *op. cit.*, p. 134.
67. *Ibid*, p. 135.
68. B. Britten, *Gloriana: Opera Guide No. 24*, John Calder, 1983, p. 103.
69. Quoted in P. Alexander, *William Plomer*, Oxford University Press, 1989, p. 272.
70. Interview with the author, 24 July 1991.
71. B. Britten, *op. cit.*, p. 99.
72. Interview with the author, 24 July 1991.
73. Lord Drogheda, *Double Harness*, Weidenfeld & Nicolson, 1978, pp. 239–40.
74. W. Plomer, 'Let's Crab an Opera', *London Magazine*, October 1965, p. 101.
75. D. Cairns, 'Gloriana', in *Responses: Musical Essays and Reviews*, Secker & Warburg, 1973, p. 79.
76. N. Dennis, *Cards of Identity*, Weidenfeld & Nicolson, 1955, p. 119.
77. N. Annan, 'The Intellectual Aristocracy', in J. H. Plumb (ed.), *Studies in Social History: A Tribute to G. M. Trevelyan*, Longmans Green, 1955, p. 244.
78. *Ibid*, p. 285.
79. *Ibid*.
80. *Ibid*, p. 286.
81. E. Shils, 'The British Intellectuals', *Encounter*, Vol. 4, No. 4 (April 1955), p. 6.
82. *Ibid*, p. 7.
83. *Ibid*, p. 10.
84. M. Kemp, 'A Loss of Balance: The Trustees and Boards of National Museums and Galleries', *Burlington Magazine*, Vol. 131, No. 1034 (May 1989), p. 356.
85. E. Shils, *op. cit.*, p. 11.
86. H. Fairlie, 'Political Commentary', *Spectator*, No. 6639 (23 September 1955), p. 380.
87. P. Hennessy, *The Great and the Good: An Inquiry into the British Establishment*, Research Report No. 654, Policy Studies Institute, 1986.
88. Lord Drogheda, *op. cit.*, p. 87.

89. J. E. Morpurgo, *op. cit.*, p. 190 and see p. 269.
90. Arts Council of Great Britain, *The Arts in Great Britain: Seventh Annual Report, 1951/52*, p. 3.
91. Arts Council of Great Britain, *Sixth Annual Report, 1950/51*, *op. cit.*, p. 31.
92. *Ibid*, p. 34.
93. Arts Council of Great Britain, *The Public and the Arts: Eighth Annual Report, 1952/53*, p. 12.
94. K. Clark, *op. cit.*, p. 135.
95. *Ibid*, p. 136.
96. E. Shils, *op. cit.*, p. 12.
97. T. Rattigan, in the introduction to *Collected Plays*, Vol. 2, Hamish Hamilton, 1953, p. xii.
98. E. Shils, *op. cit.*, p. 13.
99. *Ibid*, p. 9.
100. N. Pevsner, *The Englishness of English Art: an expanded and annotated version of the Reith lectures broadcast in October and November 1955*, Architectural Press, 1956.
101. *Ibid*, p. 11.
102. *Ibid*, p. 55.
103. *Ibid*, p. 61.
104. *Ibid*, p. 88.
105. *Ibid*, p. 114.
106. *Ibid*, p. 119.
107. *Ibid*, p. 186.
108. *Ibid*, p. 181.
109. *Ibid*, p. 192.
110. D. Mellor, *A Paradise Lost: The Neo-Romantic Imagination in Britain 1935–1955*, Lund Humphries/Barbican Gallery, 1987, p. 39.
111. E. Shils, *op. cit.*, p. 16.
112. N. Pevsner, *op. cit.*, p. 121.
113. Lord Harewood, interview with the author, 24 July 1991.
114. E. Shils, *op. cit.*, p. 9.
115. J. Osborne, *Look Back in Anger, Collected Plays*, Faber & Faber, 1993, Vol. 1, p. 83.
116. C. P. Snow, *Homecomings*, Macmillan, 1956, p. 283.

IV: The Uses of Culture

1. E. Shils, 'The British Intellectuals', *Encounter*, Vol. 4, No. 4 (April 1955), p. 15.
2. A. H. Halsey, 'British Universities and Intellectual Life', reprinted in *Education, Economy and Society*, ed. A. H. Halsey, J. Floud and C. A. Anderson, New York, Free Press of Glencoe, 1961, p. 505.

3. *Ibid*, p. 511.
4. *Ibid*, p. 505.
5. *Ibid*, p. 510.
6. S. Spender, 'On Literary Movements', *Encounter*, Vol. 1, No. 2 (December 1953), p. 66.
7. *Ibid*, p. 67.
8. K. Amis, Letter to the *Listener*, Vol. 52, No. 1326 (29 July 1954), p. 179.
9. M. Bradbury, 'The Rise of the Provincials', *Antioch Review*, Vol. XVI, No. 4 (December 1956), p. 470. Bradbury's novel *Eating People is Wrong* was published by Secker & Warburg in 1959.
10. M. Bradbury, *op. cit.*, p. 477.
11. Q. D. Leavis, *Fiction and the Reading Public*, Chatto & Windus, 1932, p. 271.
12. J. McIlroy, in R. Williams, *Border Country: Raymond Williams in Adult Education*, ed. J. McIlroy and S. Westwood, Leicester, National Institute of Continuing Adult Education, 1993, p. 276.
13. R. Hoggart, 'What Shall the WEA Do?', *The Highway*, Vol. 44 (November 1952), p. 48.
14. J. Harrison, 'The WEA in the Welfare State', in S. Raybould (ed.), *Trends in Adult Education*, Heinemann, 1959, p. 12.
15. R. Williams, *Culture and Society 1780–1950*, Penguin edition, 1961, p. 318.
16. R. Williams, 'The Common Good', reprinted in *Border Country*, *op. cit.*, p. 228.
17. R. Williams, *Politics and Letters*, Verso, 1979, p. 80. For a discussion of this issue, see R. T. Fieldhouse, *Adult Education and the Cold War: Liberal Values Under Siege 1946–51*, Leeds Studies in Adult Education, 1985.
18. R. Williams, 'Adult Education and Social Change', reprinted in *Border Country*, *op. cit.*, p. 257.
19. R. Williams, *Politics and Letters*, *op. cit.*, p. 78.
20. R. Hoggart, 'Where Have the Common Readers Gone?', *The Times*, 6 May 1992.
21. R. Hoggart, 'What Shall the WEA Do?', *op. cit.*, p. 49.
22. S. Hall, 'Cultural Studies and the Crisis of the Humanities', *October*, No. 53 (Summer 1990), p. 12.
23. R. Williams, *Politics and Letters*, *op. cit.*, p. 69.
24. R. Hoggart, *A Sort of Clowning: Life and Times Volume II*, Chatto & Windus, 1990, p. 96.
25. R. Williams, 'Adult Education and Social Change', reprinted in *Border Country*, *op. cit.*, p. 260.
26. E. P. Thompson, *The Making of the English Working Class*, Penguin, 1991, p. 14.
27. *Ibid*, p. 833.
28. Quoted in *Border Country*, *op. cit.*, p. 271.

324 Culture and Consensus

29. E. P. Thompson, *op. cit.*, p. 833.
30. R. Hoggart, 'Where Have All the Common Readers Gone?', *op. cit.*
31. R. Williams, *Politics and Letters, op. cit.*, p. 97.
32. R. Hoggart, *An Imagined Life: Life and Times*, Vol. III, Chatto & Windus, 1992, p. 73.
33. R. Williams, 'Culture is Ordinary', *op. cit.*, p. 9.
34. S. Hall, 'Cultural Studies and the Crisis of the Humanities', *op. cit.*, p. 15.
35. R. Hoggart, *A Sort of Clowning, op. cit.*, p. 110.
36. Q. D. Leavis, *op. cit.*, p. 117.
37. E. P. Thompson, *op. cit.*, p. 8.
38. The title of an article for the *Times Literary Supplement*, 7 April 1966.
39. E. P. Thompson, review of *The Long Revolution, New Left Review*, No. 9, 1961, p. 33. Thompson had been reluctant to review Williams's book because he feared it might endanger political relations in the New Left. See E. P. Thompson, 'The Politics of Theory', in *People's History and Socialist Theory*, ed. R. Samuel, Routledge, 1981, pp. 397.
40. R. Hoggart, *The Uses of Literacy*, Penguin edition, 1990, p. 194.
41. *Ibid*, p. 24.
42. *Ibid*, p. 213.
43. Q. D. Leavis, *Fiction and the Reading Public, op. cit.*, p. 211.
44. R. Hoggart, *The Uses of Literacy, op. cit.*, p. 180.
45. *Ibid*, p. 68.
46. *Ibid*, p. 63.
47. *Ibid*, p. 190.
48. R. Williams, 'The Uses of Literacy: Working-Class Culture', *Universities and Left Review*, Vol. 1, No. 2 (1957), p. 30.
49. R. Williams, *Culture and Society 1780–1950* (first published Chatto & Windus, 1958), Penguin edition, 1961, p. 244.
50. *Ibid*, p. 245.
51. *Ibid*, p. 253.
52. *Ibid*, p. 205.
53. *Ibid*, p. 323.
54. R. Hoggart, *The Uses of Literacy, op. cit.*, p. 193.
55. *Ibid*, p. 249.
56. A. Sillitoe, *Saturday Night and Sunday Morning* (first published Chatto & Windus, 1958), Pan, 1960, p. 109.
57. *Ibid*, p. 179.
58. *Ibid*, p. 158.
59. H. Ritchie, *Success Stories: Literature and the Media in England, 1950–1959*, Faber & Faber, 1988, p. 35.
60. R. Hoggart, *The Uses of Literacy, op. cit.*, p. 323.
61. R. Williams, *Culture and Society, op. cit.*, pp. 249–50.
62. *Ibid*, p. 12.
63. Quoted in D. Widgery, *The Left in Britain, 1956–1976*, Penguin, 1976, p. 90.

64. E. P. Thompson, 'The Politics of Theory', in *People's History and Socialist Theory*, ed. R. Samuel, Routledge, 1981, pp. 399–400.
65. S. Hall, editorial for *New Left Review*, No. 1 (Jan/Feb 1960), p. 1.
66. R. Williams and R. Hoggart, 'Working-Class Attitudes', *New Left Review*, No. 1 (Jan/Feb 1960), p. 29.
67. L. Anderson, 'Get Out and Push', in T. Maschler (ed.), *Declaration*, MacGibbon & Kee, 1957, p. 173.
68. R. Williams, *Politics and Letters*, *op. cit.*, p. 363.
69. Editorial, *Universities and Left Review*, No. 1 (Spring 1957), p. ii.
70. E. P. Thompson, 'Socialism and the Intellectuals', *Universities and Left Review*, No. 1 (Spring 1957), p. 35.
71. Advertisement in *Universities and Left Review*, No. 5 (Autumn 1958), p. 66.
72. Editorial, *Universities and Left Review*, No. 5 (Autumn, 1958), p. 3.
73. S. Hall, review of *Declaration*, *Universities and Left Review*, No. 6 (Winter 1958), p. 87.
74. B. Groombridge and P. Whannel, 'Something Rotten in Denmark Street', *New Left Review*, No. 1 (Jan/Feb 1960), p. 52.
75. *Ibid.*
76. K. Coppard, R. Williams, T. Higgins and P. Whannel, 'Which Frame of Mind', *New Left Review*, No. 7 (Jan–Feb 1962), p. 35.
77. T. Eagleton, *Criticism and Ideology: A Study in Marxist Literary Theory*, New Left Books, 1976, p. 7.
78. R. Williams, 'Culture is Ordinary', *op. cit.*, p. 7.
79. R. Williams, 'Culture and Revolution: a comment', in *From Culture to Revolution*, T. Eagleton and B. Wicker (eds.), Sheed & Ward, 1968, p. 296.
80. R. Williams, *The Long Revolution*, Chatto & Windus, 1961, p. xi.
81. *Ibid*, p. 48.
82. S. Hall, in S. Hall (ed.), *Culture, Media, Language: Working Papers in Cultural Studies, 1972–79*, Hutchinson, 1980, p. 19.
83. E. P. Thompson, 'Outside the Whale', reprinted in E. P. Thompson (ed.), *The Poverty of Theory*, Merlin Press, 1978, p. 13.
84. *Ibid*, p. 31.
85. E. P. Thompson, *Peace News*, 29 November 1963, reprinted in D. Widgery, *op. cit.*, p. 133.
86. R. Hoggart, *An Imagined Life: Life and Times*, Vol. III, Chatto & Windus, 1992, p. 90.
87. S. Hall, 'Cultural Studies and the Crisis of the Humanities', *op. cit.*, p. 12.
88. R. Hoggart, 'Schools of English and Contemporary Society', inaugural lecture at Birmingham University, 1963, reprinted in *Speaking to Others: Essays*, 2 Vols, Chatto & Windus, 1970, Vol. 2, p. 258.
89. *Ibid*, p. 255.
90. *Ibid.*

91. A. Sinfield, *Literature, Politics and Culture in Postwar Britain*, Oxford, Blackwell, 1989, p. 242.
92. *Ibid*, p. 243.
93. Launch brochure for Centre 42, 1961.
94. R. Williams, 'Culture is Ordinary', reprinted in *Resources of Hope*, Verso, 1989, p. 16.
95. S. Hall and P. Whannel, *The Popular Arts*, Hutchinson Educational, 1964, p. 15.
96. *Ibid*, p. 30.
97. *Ibid*, p. 48.
98. *Ibid*, p. 68.
99. S. Hall, editorial, *New Left Review*, No. 1 (Jan/Feb 1960), p. 1.
100. K. Tynan, review of *Look Back in Anger*, reprinted in *A View of the English Stage*: 1944–1963, Davis-Poynter, 1975, p. 178.
101. K. Whitehead, *The Third Programme: A Literary History*, Oxford, Clarendon Press, 1989, p. 2.
102. K. Amis, 'In Defence of Dons', in *Literary Opinion*, No. 3, BBC Third Programme, 9 June 1954, quoted in H. Ritchie, *op. cit.*, p. 213.
103. *Report of the Committee on Broadcasting 1960*, Cmmnd. 1753, HMSO, 1962, p. 60.
104. R. Williams, 'Culture is Ordinary', *op. cit.*, p. 11.
105. R. Shaw, *The Arts and the People*, Cape, 1987, p. 124.
106. Interview with Boris Ford, 18 January 1993.
107. A. Goodman, *Tell Them I'm On My Way*, Chapmans, 1993, p. 271.
108. W. E. Williams, *The First Ten Years*, Arts Council of Great Britain, 1956, p. 22.
109. Arts Council of Great Britain, *A Brighter Prospect, 17th Annual Report 1961–62*, p. 12.
110. Quoted in R. Hoggart, *An Imagined Life*, op. cit., p. 229.
111. P. Anderson, 'Critique of Wilsonism', *New Left Review*, No. 29 (Sept/Oct 1964), p. 26.
112. *Ibid*.
113. A. Goodman, *op. cit.*, p. 261.
114. *A Policy for the Arts: The First Steps*, Cmmnd. 2601, HMSO, 1965, p. 16.
115. *Ibid*, p. 15.
116. *Ibid*, p. 16.

V: A Swinging Meritocracy

1. R. Hoggart, 'Where Have the Common Readers Gone?', *The Times*, 6 May 1992.
2. C. P. Snow, *The Two Cultures and the Scientific Revolution: The Rede Lecture 1959*, Cambridge University Press, 1959, p. 4.

3. *Ibid*, p. 21.

4. *Ibid*, p. 25.

5. *Ibid*, p. 45.

6. F. R. Leavis, *Two Cultures? The Significance of C. P. Snow*, Chatto & Windus, 1962, p. 29.

7. *Ibid*, p. 10.

8. *Ibid*, p. 13.

9. *Ibid*, p. 15.

10. *Ibid*, p. 16.

11. *Ibid*, p. 24.

12. *Ibid*, p. 20.

13. *Ibid*, pp. 26–7.

14. A. Sampson, *Anatomy of Britain*, Hodder & Stoughton, 1962, p. xiii.

15. *Ibid*, p. 637.

16. T. R. Fyvel, *Intellectuals Today: Problems in a Changing Society*, Chatto & Windus, 1968, p. 26.

17. *Ibid*, p. 57.

18. *Ibid*, p. 212.

19. *Ibid*, p. 23.

20. H. Carleton-Greene, *The Third Floor Front: A View of Broadcasting in the Sixties*, Bodley Head, 1969, p. 13.

21. D. Thompson (ed.), *Discrimination and Popular Culture*, Penguin, 1964, p. 16.

22. R. Hoggart, 'Mass Communications', in B. Ford (ed.), *The Modern Age*, Penguin, 1961, pp. 452–3.

23. R. Williams, *Britain in the Sixties: Communications*, Penguin, 1962, p. 10.

24. Quoted in D. Thompson (ed.), *op. cit.*, p. 15.

25. T. W. Adorno, 'Culture Industry Reconsidered', in J. M. Bernstein (ed.), *The Culture Industry: Selected Essays on Mass Culture*, Routledge, 1991, p. 85.

26. H. Marcuse, *One-Dimensional Man*, second edition, Routledge, 1991, p. 57.

27. *Ibid*, p. xlix.

28. P. Hennessy, *Never Again: Britain 1945–51*, Cape, 1992, p. 42.

29. See special issues of the magazine *Arena*, 1951, 1952.

30. F. R. Leavis, *op. cit.*, p. 26.

31. R. Williams, *op. cit.*, p. 75.

32. L. Alloway, ' "Pop Art" since 1949', *Listener*, Vol. 68, No. 1761 (27 December 1962), p. 1087.

33. J. Russell and S. Gablik (eds.), *Pop Art Redefined*, Thames & Hudson, 1969, pp. 31–2.

34. See D. Mellor, *The Sixties Art Scene in London*, Barbican Art Gallery and Phaidon, 1993, p. 14.

35. L. Alloway, *op. cit.*, p. 1086.

36. R. Banham, 'Representations in Protest', reprinted in P. Barker (ed.), *Arts in Society*, Fontana, 1977, p. 64.
37. L. Alloway, 'The Development of British Pop', in L. R. Lippard (ed.), *Pop Art*, Thames & Hudson, third (revised) edition, 1970, p. 27.
38. *Ibid*, p. 38.
39. *Ibid*, p. 32.
40. R. Hamilton, *Collected Words 1953–1982*, Thames & Hudson, 1982, p. 28.
41. *Ibid*.
42. L. Alloway, ' "Pop Art" since 1949', *op. cit.*, p. 1085.
43. L. Alloway, 'The Arts and the Mass Media', *Architectural Design*, Vol. 28, No. 2 (February 1958), p. 84.
44. *Ibid*, p. 85.
45. L. Alloway, 'The Long Front of Culture', reprinted in J. Russell and S. Gablik (eds.), *op. cit.*, p. 41.
46. R. Hamilton, *op. cit.*, p. 43.
47. J. Russell and S. Gablik (eds.), *op. cit.*, p. 22. Richard Hamilton's *Portrait of High Gaitskell as a famous Monster of Filmland* (1964) should, however, be recognised as a satirical, indeed political, work.
48. J. Russell and S. Gablik (eds.), *op. cit.*, p. 39.
49. A. Bowness, *The Conditions of Success: How the Modern Artist Rises to Fame*, Thames & Hudson, 1989, pp. 15–16.
50. 'Pop Goes the Easel', directed by Ken Russell, first transmitted 25 March 1962. I am grateful to Michael Jackson for making a recording of this programme available.
51. H. Read, *The Origins of Form in Art*, Thames & Hudson, 1965, p. 187.
52. E. Lucie-Smith, *Listener*, Vol. 74, No. 1914 (2 December 1962), p. 920.
53. S. Hall and P. Whannell, *The Popular Arts*, Hutchinson Educational, 1964, p. 83.
54. The new charter is reprinted in E. White, *The Arts Council of Great Britain*, Davis Poynter, 1975, pp. 303–7.
55. J. Harris, *Government Patronage of the Arts in Great Britain*, University of Chicago Press, 1970, p. 53.
56. A. Goodman, *Tell Them I'm On My Way: Memoirs*, Chapmans, 1993, p. 6.
57. Arts Council, *Ends and Means, 18th Annual Report, 1962/63*, p. 7.
58. A. Goodman, *op. cit.*, pp. 290–1.
59. *Sunday Times*, 20 February 1966.
60. 'You Can Walk Across It on the Grass', *Time*, 15 April 1966, p. 28.
61. *Ibid*.
62. *Ibid*.
63. G. Steiner, *In Bluebeard's Castle: Some Notes Towards the Re-definition of Culture*, Faber & Faber, 1971, pp. 88–9.
64. A. Sinfield, *Literature, Politics and Culture in Postwar Britain*, Blackwell, 1989, p. 284.

65. P. Anderson, 'The Left in the Fifties', *New Left Review*, No. 29 (Jan–Feb 1965), p. 16.
66. *Ibid*, p. 17.
67. P. Anderson, 'Socialism and Pseudo-Empiricism', *New Left Review*, No. 35 (Jan–Feb 1966), p. 34.
68. P. Anderson, 'The Left in the Fifties', *op. cit.*, p. 17.
69. D. Widgery, *The Left in Britain 1956–76*, Penguin, 1976, p. 513.
70. A. Beckett, 'Popular Music', *New Left Review*, No. 39 (Sept–Oct 1966), pp. 87–90.
71. R. Mertu, 'Comment', *New Left Review*, No. 47 (Jan–Feb 1968), p. 31.
72. P. Anderson, 'The Origins of the Present Crisis', *New Left Review*, No. 23 (Jan–Feb 1964), p. 40.
73. P. Anderson, 'Socialism and Pseudo-Empiricism', *op. cit.*, p. 31.
74. E. P. Thompson, *The Poverty of Theory*, Merlin Press, 1978, p. i.
75. T. Eagleton and B. Wicker (eds.), *From Culture to Revolution*, Sheed and Ward, 1968, p. 3.
76. *Ibid*, p. 15.
77. D. Cooper (ed.), *The Dialectics of Liberation*, Penguin, 1968, p. 190, p. 191.
78. A set of twenty-three long-playing records was issued by Liberation Records, and can be found in the National Sound Archive.
79. See R. Hoggart, *An Imagined Life*, Chatto & Windus, 1992, p. 92 and p. 98.
80. P. Anderson, 'Components of the National Culture', *New Left Review*, No. 50 (July–Aug 1968), p. 57.
81. Quoted in A. Sked and C. Cook, *Post-War Britain: A Political History*, Penguin, 1979, p. 263.
82. Extracts from Lord Goodman's speech were printed in the Arts Council's *A New Charter, 22nd Annual Report 1966–7*, p. 11.
83. Arts Council, 'Report by the Working Party set up by a Conference on the Obscenity Laws', typescript, May 1969, p. 4.
84. *Ibid*, p. 3.
85. Arts Council, *Annual Report 1969/70*, p. 6. In 1971 the Arts Council's experience was replicated at the British Film Institute, when the governors attempted to suppress the activities of the editors and contributors to the revamped and radicalised *Screen* magazine, which they funded.
86. *Ibid*, p. 7.
87. K. Clark, *The Other Half: A Self-Portrait*, John Murray, 1977, p. 178.
88. K. Clark, *Civilisation: A Personal View*, BBC and John Murray, 1969, p. xvii.
89. *Ibid*, p. 346.
90. *Ibid*.
91. *Ibid*, p. 347.
92. G. Steiner, *op. cit.*, p. 14.
93. *Ibid*, p. 64.

94. *Ibid*, p. 85.
95. *Ibid*, p. 66.
96. *Ibid*.
97. J. Russell and S. Gablik (eds.), *op. cit.*, p. 14.
98. *Ibid*, p. 52.
99. *Ibid*, p. 20.
100. *Ibid*, p. 53.
101. T. Hilton, review of 'Art in Britain 1969–70', *Studio International* (July/Aug 1970), p. 58.
102. *New Left Review*, No. 52 (Nov–Dec 1968), p. 7.

VI: The Uses of Subculture

1. A. Sked, *Britain's Decline: Problems and Perspectives*, Oxford, Blackwell, 1987, p. 1.
2. *Ibid*, p. 28.
3. D. Bell, *The Coming of Post-Industrial Society*, Heinemann, 1974, p. 37.
4. J. B. Priestley, *The English*, Heinemann, 1973, p. 12.
5. *Ibid*, p. 243.
6. *Ibid*, p. 22.
7. *Ibid*, pp. 247–8.
8. *Ibid*, p. 248.
9. T. Nairn, *The Break-Up of Britain: Crisis and Neo-Nationalism*, New Left Books, 1977, p. 71.
10. S. Hall, 'The Great Moving Right Show', in *The Hard Road to Renewal: Thatcherism and the Crisis of the Left*, Verso, 1988, p. 40.
11. *Ibid*, p. 39.
12. A. Marwick, *British Society Since 1945*, Allen Lane, 1982, p. 220.
13. P. Gilroy, *There Ain't No Black in the Union Jack: The Cultural Politics of Race and Nation*, Hutchinson, 1987, p. 43.
14. *Ibid*, p. 92.
15. M. Brake, *Comparative Youth Culture: The Sociology of Youth Cultures and Youth Subcultures in America, Britain and Canada*, Routledge, 1985, p. 69.
16. T. Nairn, *op. cit.*, p. 261.
17. *Ibid*, p. 274.
18. See P. Wright, 'The Stain on St George's Flag', *Guardian*, 18 August 1993.
19. Quoted in P. Whitehead, *The Writing on the Wall: Britain in the Seventies*, Michael Joseph, 1985, p. 235.
20. M. Cowling, 'The Sources of the New Right', *Encounter*, Vol. 73, No. 4 (Nov 1989), p. 7.
21. *Ibid* and see p. 11.

22. K. Amis, *Lucky Jim's Politics*, Conservative Political Centre, No. 410 (1968), p. 7.

23. I. Carter, *Ancient Cultures of Conceit: British University Fiction in the Post-War Years*, Routledge, 1990, p. 12.

24. *Ibid*, p. 99.

25. C. B. Cox, *The Great Betrayal*, Chapmans, 1992, p. 150.

26. *Ibid*, p. 35.

27. *Ibid*, p. 92.

28. *Ibid*, p. 106.

29. *Ibid*, pp. 123–4.

30. C. B. Cox, 'The Editing of Critical Quarterly', in D. Weiner and W. Keylor (eds.), *From Parnassus: Essays in Honor of Jacques Barzan*, New York, Harper & Row, 1976, p. 145.

31. C. B. Cox, *The Great Betrayal, op. cit.*, p. 146.

32. B. Martin, *A Sociology of Contemporary Cultural Change*, Oxford, Blackwell, 1981, p. 212.

33. C. B. Cox, *op. cit.*, p. 123.

34. *Ibid*, p. 263.

35. M. Cowling, *op. cit.*, p. 7.

36. C. B. Cox, *op. cit.*, p. 4.

37. J. Pope-Hennessy, *Learning To Look*, Heinemann, 1991, p. 163.

38. A. Goodman, *Tell Them I'm On My Way: Memoirs*, Chapmans, 1993, p. 282.

39. *Ibid*, p. 280.

40. *Ibid*, p. 289.

41. *Ibid*, p. 367.

42. House of Lords, 3 Feb 1971, *Hansard*, 5th Series, Vol. 314, column 1210.

43. C. Osborne, *Giving It Away: The Memoirs of an Uncivil Servant*, Secker & Warburg, 1986, p. 183.

44. Arts Council, *26th Annual Report 1970–71*, p. 9.

45. *Ibid*, p. 7.

46. Arts Council, *29th Annual Report 1973–4*, p. 10.

47. Arts Council, *30th Annual Report 1974–5*, p. 13.

48. Lord Redcliffe-Maud, *Support for the Arts in England and Wales*, Calouste Gulbenkian Foundation, 1976, p. 18.

49. *Ibid*, p. 19.

50. Labour Party, *The Arts and the People: Labour's Policy Towards the Arts* (1977), p. 6.

51. H. Jenkins, *The Culture Gap: An Experience of Government and the Arts*, Marion Boyars, 1979, p. 95.

52. *Ibid*, p. 194.

53. *Ibid*, p. 192.

54. *Ibid*, p. 198.

55. *Ibid*, p. 196.

332 Culture and Consensus

56. R. Williams, 'The Arts Council', reprinted in *Resources of Hope: Culture, Democracy, Socialism*, ed. R. Gable, Verso, 1989, p. 45.
57. *Ibid*, p. 44.
58. *Ibid*.
59. *Ibid*, p. 46.
60. *Ibid*, p. 44.
61. H. Jenkins, *op. cit.*, p. 204.
62. *Ibid*.
63. *Ibid*, p. 198.
64. D. Marquand, *The Progressive Dilemma*, Heinemann, 1991, p. 176.
65. H. Brenton, in *New Theatre Voices of the Seventies*, ed. S. Trussler, Methuen, 1981, pp. 91–2.
66. D. Widgery, *The Left in Britain, 1956–1976*, Penguin, 1976, p. 19.
67. *Ibid*, p. 34.
68. M. Bradbury, *The History Man*, first published Secker & Warburg, 1975, Arena, 1984, p. 24.
69. *Ibid*, p. 48.
70. *Ibid*, p. 50.
71. R. Samuel, *People's History and Socialist Theory*, Routledge, 1981, p. 410.
72. R. Parker and G. Pollock (eds.), *Framing Feminism: Art and the Women's Movement 1970–75*, Pandora, 1987, p. 23.
73. S. Rowbotham, *Women's Consciousness, Man's World*, Penguin, 1973, p. 122.
74. R. Williams, *Marxism and Literature*, Oxford University Press, 1977, p. 5. The essays referred to earlier appear in *New Left Review* Nos. 67 (1971) and 82 (1973).
75. S. Hall (ed.), *Culture, Media, Language: Working Papers in Cultural Studies, 1972–9*, Hutchinson, 1980, p. 26.
76. *Ibid*, p. 9.
77. S. Hall (ed.), University of Birmingham Centre for Contemporary Cultural Studies, *Fifth Report 1968–9* (1969), p. 4.
78. University of Birmingham Centre for Contemporary Cultural Studies Women's Studies Group (eds.), *Woman Take Issue*, Hutchinson, 1978, p. 16.
79. S. Hall, 'Cultural Studies and the Crisis of the Humanities', *October*, No. 53 (Summer 1990), p. 11.
80. S. Hall (ed.), *Culture, Media, Language, op. cit.*, p. 31.
81. *Working Papers in Cultural Studies*, No. 6 (Autumn 1974), p. 3. The joint editors were I. Chambers, J. Ellis, M. Green, S. Lacey, R. Rusher, A. Tolson and J. Winship.
82. *Ibid*, p. 3.
83. *Ibid*, p. 6.
84. *Ibid*.
85. S. Hall, 'Cultural Studies and the Crisis of the Humanities', *October*, No. 53 (Summer 1990), p. 12.

86. S. Hall, C. Critcher, T, Jefferson, J. Clarke, B. Roberts (eds.), *Policing the Crisis: Mugging, the State, and Law and Order*, Macmillan, 1978, p. 320.
87. *Ibid*, p. 321.
88. S. Hall and T. Jefferson (eds.), *Resistance Through Rituals: Youth subcultures in post-war Britain*, (Working papers in Cultural Studies No. 7–8), Hutchinson, 1976, p. 31.
89. *Ibid*, p. 32.
90. *Ibid*, p. 61.
91. *Ibid*, p. 47.
92. Quoted in P. Whitehead, *op. cit.*, p. 336.
93. R. Strong, introduction to P. Cormack, *Heritage in Danger*, second edition, Quartet, 1978, p. 10.
94. *Select Committee on a Health Tax*, House of Commons 696, HMSO, November 1975, Vol. II, p. 384.
95. H. Jenkins, *op. cit.*, p. 143.
96. R. Strong, *The Destruction of the Country House 1875–1975*, Thames & Hudson, 1974, p. 10.
97. T. Nairn, *The Enchanted Glass: Britain and its Monarchy* (first published Radius, 1978), Picador, 1980, p. 110.
98. R. Banham, 'The Style: "Flimsy . . . Effeminate"?', in M. Banham and B. Hillier (eds.), *A Tonic to the Nation: The Festival of Britain 1951*, Thames & Hudson, 1976, p. 196.
99. A. Holden, *Charles: A Biography*, Collins/Fontana, 1989, p. 142.
100. P. Whitehead, *op. cit.*, p. 303.
101. N. Shrapnel, *The Seventies: Britain's Inward March*, Constable, 1980, p. 117.
102. D. Cannadine, 'The Context, Performance and Meaning of Ritual: The British Monarchy and the "Invention of Tradition" ', in *The Invention of Tradition*, ed. E. Hobsbawm and T. Ranger, Cambridge University Press, 1983, p. 160.
103. D. Jarman, *Dancing Ledge*, Quartet, 1984, p. 177.
104. D. Hebdige, *Subculture: The Meaning of Style*, Methuen, 1979, p. 87.
105. J. Savage, *England's Dreaming: Sex Pistols and Punk Rock*, Faber & Faber, 1991, p. 226.
106. Greil Marcus, *Lipstick Traces: A Secret History of the Twentieth Century*, Secker & Warburg, 1989, p. 440.
107. J. Savage, *op. cit.*, p. 235.
108. D. Hebdige, *op. cit.*, p. 87.
109. J. Lydon, quoted in J. Savage, *op. cit.*, p. 348.
110. See J. Savage, *op. cit.*, pp. 364–5.
111. Quoted in P. Gilroy, *op. cit.*, p. 121.
112. D. Widgery, *Beating Time*, Chatto & Windus, 1986, p. 53.
113. P. Gilroy, *op. cit.*, p. 122.
114. D. Widgery, *op. cit.*, p. 120.
115. D. Hebdige, *op. cit.*, p. 94.

116. *Ibid*, p. 100.
117. *Ibid*, p. 139.
118. R. Johnson, 'Histories of Culture/Theories of Ideology: Notes on an Impasse', in *Ideology and Cultural Production*, ed. M. Barrett *et al.*, Croom Helm, 1979, p. 54.
119. *Ibid*, p. 49.
120. E. P. Thompson, *The Poverty of Theory*, Merlin Press, 1978, p. ii.
121. *Ibid*, p. 195.
122. R. Samuel, *op. cit.*, p. 378.
123. S. Hall (ed.), *Culture, Media, Language: Working Papers in Cultural Studies, 1972–9, op. cit.*, p. 30.
124. D. Hebdige, *op. cit.*, p. 139.
125. S. Hall *et al.* (eds.), *Policing the Crisis, op. cit.*, p. 315.
126. R. Johnson, 'What is Cultural Studies Anyway?', Stencilled Occasional Paper, General Series SP No. 74, Birmingham Centre for Contemporary Cultural Studies, 1983, p. 8.
127. Editorial, *New Left Review*, No. 52 (Nov–Dec 1968), p. 7.
128. D. Widgery, *op. cit.*, p. 167.
129. *Ibid*, p. 170.
130. D. Hebdige, *Hiding in the Light: On Images and Things*, Routledge, 1988, p. 8.
131. T. Eagleton, *Criticism and Ideology: A Study in Marxist Literary Theory*, Verso, 1978, pp. 166–7.
132. P. Fuller, *Beyond the Crisis in Art*, Writers' and Readers' Co-operative, 1980, p. 56.
133. *Ibid*, p. 37.
134. R. Johnson, *op. cit.*, p. 25.
135. Quoted in M. Thatcher, *The Downing Street Years*, HarperCollins, 1993, p. 19.
136. *Observer*, 25 February 1979.

VII: The Enterprise Culture

1. M. Thatcher, *The Downing Street Years*, HarperCollins, 1993, p. 15.
2. N. Lawson, *The View from No. 11: Memoirs of a Tory Radical*, Bantam Press, 1992, p. 30.
3. M. Thatcher, *op. cit.*, p. 167.
4. N. Lawson, *op. cit.*, p. 64.
5. *Ibid*.
6. D. Marquand, *The Progressive Dilemma*, Heinemann, 1991, p. 225.
7. *Ibid*, p. 226.
8. *Sunday Times*, 7 May 1988, quoted in P. Heelas and P. Morris (eds.), *The Values of the Enterprise Culture*, Routledge, 1992, p. 7.

9. Lord Young, 'Enterprise Regained', in P. Heelas and P. Morris (eds.), *op. cit.*, p. 29.
10. B. Martin, *A Sociology of Contemporary Cultural Change*, Blackwell, 1981, p. 236.
11. D. Marquand, 'The Enterprise Culture: Old Wine in New Bottles', in P. Heelas and P. Morris (eds.), *op. cit.*, p. 65.
12. *Marxism Today*, 'New Times' special issue, October 1988, p. 3.
13. M. Thatcher, *op. cit.*, p. 14.
14. 'The Thatcher Legacy', *Economist*, 2 October 1993, p. 39.
15. P. Whitehead, *The Writing on the Wall: Britain in the Seventies*, Michael Joseph, 1985, pp. 335–6.
16. Interview with D. Walker for 'Analysis: Off With Their Heads', BBC Radio 4, 22 July 1993.
17. M. Cowling, 'The Sources of the New Right', *Encounter*, Vol. 73, No. 4 (Nov 1989), p. 11.
18. R. Scruton, 'Thinkers of the Left: Raymond Williams', *Salisbury Review*, No. 4 (Summer 1983), p. 25.
19. R. Murdoch, McTaggart Lecture, Edinburgh Television Festival, 1989.
20. D. Marquand, *The Progressive Dilemma, op. cit.*, p. 187.
21. J. Bruce-Gardyne, *Mrs Thatcher's First Administration: The Prophets Confounded*, Macmillan, 1984, p. 59.
22. T. Nairn, *The Break-Up of Britain*, New Left Books, 1977, p. 274.
23. K. Morgan, *The People's Peace: British History 1945–89*, Oxford University Press, 1990, p. 4.
24. A. Barnett, *Iron Britannia*, Allison & Busby, 1992, p. 103.
25. A. Howard, 'Vivat Regina!', *The Times* magazine, 29 May 1993, p. 15.
26. The full text of the speech is reprinted in A. Barnett, *op. cit.*, pp. 149–52. All quotations are taken from there.
27. M. Thatcher, *op. cit.*, p. 627.
28. J. Raban, *God, Man, and Mrs Thatcher*, Chatto & Windus, 1989, pp. 23–4.
29. M. Thatcher, *op. cit.*, p. 306.
30. D. Harvey, *The Condition of Post-modernity: An Enquiry into the Origins of Cultural Change*, Blackwell, 1989, p. vii.
31. F. Jameson, *Postmodernism, or, The Cultural Logic of Late Capitalism*, Verso, 1991, p. 37; and J. Baudrillard, 'The Ecstasy of Communication', in H. Foster (ed.), *Postmodern Culture*, Pluto Press, 1985, p. 126.
32. T. Eagleton, *Ideology: An Introduction*, Verso, 1991, p. 37.
33. F. Jameson, *op. cit.*, pp. 4–5.
34. *Ibid*, p. 3.
35. C. Jencks, *What is Post-Modernism?*, Academy Editions, 1986, p. 14.
36. C. Jencks, *The Prince, The Architects and New Wave Monarchy*, Academy Editions, 1988, p. 30.
37. A. Huyssen, *After the Great Divide: Modernism, Mass Culture, Postmodernism*, Macmillan, 1986, p. 170.
38. J. Baudrillard, *Simulations*, New York, Semiotext(e), 1983, p. 146.

39. *Ibid*, p. 11.
40. J. Baudrillard, 'The Ecstasy of Communication', in H. Foster (ed.), *op. cit.*, p. 127.
41. D. Hebdige, *Hiding in the Light: On Images and Things*, Routledge, 1988, p. 195.
42. *Ibid*, p. 210.
43. B. Taylor, *Modernism, Post-Modernism, Realism: A Critical Perspective for Art*, Winchester School of Art Press, 1987, p. 46.
44. A. McRobbie, 'Moving Cultural Studies on: Post-Marxism and Beyond', *Magazine of Cultural Studies*, No. 4, 1991, p. 20.
45. T. Bennett, *Popular Culture: themes and issues (2)*, Open University Press, 1981, p. 31.
46. A. Easthope, *Literary into Cultural Studies*, Routledge, 1991, p. 5.
47. G. Turner, *British Cultural Studies: An Introduction*, Routledge, 1990, p. 210.
48. T. Eagleton, 'The Crisis of Contemporary Culture', *New Left Review*, No. 196, Nov–Dec 1992, p. 34.
49. R. Hoggart, *An Imagined Life: Life and Times 1959–91*, Chatto & Windus, 1990, pp. 271–2.
50. M. Thatcher, *op. cit.*, p. 638.
51. *Ibid*, p. 634.
52. B. Appleyard, *The Culture Club: Crisis in the Arts*, Faber & Faber, 1984, p. 10.
53. P. Hennessy, 'The Good and the Great', *Listener*, Vol. 113, No. 2895, 7 February 1985, p. 2.
54. *Ibid*.
55. M. Thatcher, *op. cit.*, p. 637.
56. M. Kemp, 'A Loss of Balance: The Trustees and Boards of National Museums and Galleries', *Burlington Magazine*, Vol. 131, No. 1034 (May 1989), p. 356.
57. *Observer*, 1 June 1988.
58. *The Times*, 22 May 1985.
59. Quoted in S. Barnett, 'Broadcasting: Silting up the Channels', in N. Buchan and T. Sumner (eds.), *Glasnost in Britain? Against Censorship and in Defence of the Word*, Macmillan, 1989, p. 39.
60. M. Thatcher, *op. cit.*, p. 636.
61. Quoted in the *Stage*, 9 October 1986.
62. M. Thatcher, *op. cit.*, p. 637.
63. *The Times*, 22 February 1985.
64. Quoted in T. Harrison, *The Durham Phenomenon*, Longman & Todd, 1985, p. 123.
65. K. Thompson, 'Individual and community in religious critiques of the enterprise culture', in P. Heelas and P. Morris (eds.), *op. cit.*, p. 258.
66. Interview with F. Bianchini in Bianchini, 'RIP GLC: Cultural Policies in London', *New Formations*, No. 1 (Spring 1987), p. 105.
67. *Ibid*.

68. T. Banks, GLC Arts and Recreation Committee Discussion Paper, 15 July 1981.
69. D. Widgery, *Beating Time*, Chatto & Windus, 1986, p. 118.
70. *Hansard* (House of Commons Debate on the Arts, 20 May 1988), 6th Series, Vol. 133, column 1266.
71. G. Mulgan and K. Worpole, *Saturday Night or Sunday Morning? From Arts to Industry – New Forms of Cultural Policy*, Comedia, 1986, p. 89.
72. *The Glory of the Garden: The Development of the Arts in England*, Arts Council, 1985, p. 1.
73. *Hansard* (Written Answers, 29 October 1971), 6th Series, Vol. 121, Issue 1425, pp. 356–9.
74. M. Thatcher, *op. cit.*, p. 632.
75. *Ibid.*
76. P. Hall, *Making an Exhibition of Myself*, Sinclair-Stevenson, 1993, p. 298.
77. *Public and Private Funding of the Arts*, 8th Report of the Education, Science and Arts Committee, HMSO, 1982, Annexe 4, p. cxxxiv.
78. N. Lawson, *op. cit.*, p. 122.
79. *The Times*, 1 July 1982.
80. Supplement to *Arts Council Bulletin*, No. 52 (September 1982).
81. N. St John-Stevas, *The Two Cities*, Faber & Faber, 1984, p. 77.
82. C. Osborne, *Giving it Away: The Memoirs of an Uncivil Servant*, Secker & Warburg, 1986, p. 188.
83. N. St John-Stevas, *op. cit.*, p. 75.
84. *The Arts – The Way Forward: A Conservative Discussion Paper*, Conservative Political Centre, 1978, p. 21.
85. A. Feist and R. Hutchison (eds.), *Cultural Trends in the Eighties*, Policy Studies Institute, 1990, p. 9.
86. The precise figures were £993 million out of £244.7 billion.
87. R. Shaw, *The Arts and the People*, Cape, 1987, pp. 42–3.
88. R. Hoggart, *op. cit.*, p. 232.
89. R. Shaw, *op. cit.*, p. 50.
90. *The Times*, 15 July 1993.
91. *Ibid.*
92. W. Rees-Mogg, *The Political Economy of Art: An Arts Council Lecture*, Arts Council, 1985, p. 6.
93. *Independent*, 15 March 1989.
94. *The Times*, 18 October 1989.
95. *Daily Telegraph*, 30 November 1988.
96. P. Hall, *op. cit.*, p. 339.

VIII: Value for Money

1. *Guardian*, 10 November 1979.
2. *Hansard* (House of Lords Debate on the Arts, 6 March 1985), 5th Series, Vol. CDLX, column 1326.
3. *Arts Council Bulletin*, No. 43 (October 1981), p. 3.
4. *Bookseller*, 14 April 1984.
5. *The Times*, 21 September 1981.
6. *Public and Private Funding of the Arts*, 8th Report of the Education, Science and Arts Committee, HMSO, 1982, para. 6.3.
7. *Ibid*, para. 4.1.
8. *Arts Council Bulletin*, No. 53 (October 1982), p. 4.
9. *Arts Council Bulletin*, No. 64 (December 1983/January 1984), p. 2.
10. A. Peacock, *Paying the Piper: Culture, Music and Money*, Edinburgh University Press, 1993, p. 93.
11. Arts Council press release, 14 November 1983.
12. *The Glory of the Garden: The Development of the Arts in England*, Arts Council, 1985, p. iii.
13. Arts Council press release, 2 April 1986.
14. Text of letter to Sir William Rees-Mogg, 28 February 1985, released to the press.
15. *Guardian*, 1 March 1985.
16. P. Hall, *Making an Exhibition of Myself*, Sinclair-Stevenson, 1993, p. 328.
17. *The Times*, 14 February 1985.
18. *Hansard* (House of Commons Debate on the Arts, 15 June 1989), 6th Series, Vol. 154, column 1134.
19. Supplement to *Arts Council Bulletin*, No. 52, 1982.
20. *Stage*, 26 October 1989.
21. Statement at press conference, 11 February 1994.
22. W. Rees-Mogg, *The Political Economy of Art: An Arts Council Lecture*, Arts Council, 1985, p. 3.
23. *Sunday Times*, 15 September 1985.
24. *A Great British Success Story*, Arts Council, 1985, *passim*.
25. *Partnership: Making Arts Money Work Harder*, Arts Council, 1986, p. 6.
26. *Ibid*, pp. 18–19.
27. *The Times*, 5 September 1985.
28. Office of Arts and Libraries press release, 17 September 1985.
29. Office of Arts and Libraries press release, 8 July 1987.
30. *Ibid*.
31. *The Arts: Politics, Power and the Purse*, Arts Council, 1987, p. 4.
32. *Ibid*, p. 61.
33. *Independent*, 18 December 1990.
34. R. Wilding, *Supporting the Arts: A Review of the Structure of Arts Funding*, typescript presented to the Minister for the Arts, 1989, p. 20.
35. *Guardian*, 18 February 1994.

36. St John-Stevas is quoted in A. Jones, *Britain's Heritage: The Creation of the National Heritage Memorial Fund*, Weidenfeld & Nicolson, 1985, p. 192.
37. 'Towards a more consumer-orientated V & A', Victoria and Albert Museum press release, 31 October 1985, p. 2.
38. *Ibid*, p. 4.
39. *Independent*, 22 October 1988.
40. M. Kemp, 'A Loss of Balance: The Trustees and Boards of National Museums and Galleries', *Burlington Magazine*, Vol. 131, No. 1034 (May 1989), p. 356.
41. See H. Rogers, 'Spycatcher: My Country Wright or Armstrong?', in N. Buchan and T. Sumner (eds.), *Glasnost in Britain? Against Censorship and in Defence of the Word*, Macmillan, 1989, p. 133.
42. D. Sutton, 'Illusion and Delusion', *Encounter*, June 1989, p. 67.
43. M. Kemp, *op. cit.*, p. 356.
44. Typescript of Margaret Thatcher's opening speech, Design Museum, 5 July 1989, p. 1.
45. Exhibition placard, and see S. Bayley, *Commerce and Culture: From Pre-Industrial Art to Post-Industrial Value*, Design Museum, 1989, p. 7.
46. S. Bayley, *Commerce and Culture, op. cit.*, p. 7. Two-page advertisement for the Butlers Wharf development, *Blueprint*, No. 61 (October 1989), pp. 42–3.
47. *An Urban Renaissance: The Role of the Arts in Urban Regeneration, The Case for Increased Public and Private Sector Cooperation*, Arts Council, 1988, p. 2.
48. J. Myerscough, *The Economic Importance of the Arts in Britain*, Policy Studies Institute, 1988, p. 6.
49. *Ibid*, p. 2.
50. *Ibid*, p. 164.
51. G. Hughes, 'Measuring the Economic Value of the Arts', *Policy Studies*, Vol. 9, No. 3 (Spring 1989), p. 38. The Policy Studies Institute's *Cultural Trends*, No. 20 (May 1994) estimated employment in the cultural sector to be 175,000.
52. A. Peacock, 'Economics, Cultural Values and Cultural Policies', in R. Towse and A. Khakee (eds.), *Cultural Economics* (papers from the 6th International Conference on Cultural Economics, 1990), Berlin, Springer Verlag, 1992, p. 14.
53. F. Bianchini and M. Parkinson (eds.), *Cultural Policy and Urban Regeneration: The West European Experience*, Manchester University Press, 1993, p. 2.
54. J. Myerscough, *op. cit.*, p. 77.
55. W. Keens *et al.* (eds.), *Arts and the Changing City: An Agenda for Urban Regeneration*, British American Arts Association, 1989, p. 24.
56. S. Damer, *Glasgow: Going for a song*, Lawrence & Wishart, 1990, p. 211.
57. *Ibid*, pp. 12–13.
58. P. Booth and R. Boyle, 'See Glasgow, see culture', in F. Bianchini and M. Parkinson (eds.), *op. cit.*, p. 43.

59. J. Redwood, *Popular Capitalism*, Routledge, 1988, p. 141.

60. *The Times*, 31 October 1989.

61. *Independent*, 13 July 1991.

62. J. Redwood, *op. cit.*, p. 144.

63. B. Vale, 'The Council in the Age of Thatcher', *Connect*, No. 55 (Spring 1991), p. 9.

64. J. Myerscough, *op. cit.*, p. 151.

65. Arts Council, *Annual Report 1988–9*, p. 37.

66. R. Williams, 'Culture is Ordinary' (1958), in *Resources of Hope*, ed. R. Gable, Verso, 1980, p. 11.

67. D. Hebdige, *Hiding in the Light: On Images and Things*, Routledge, 1988, p. 74.

68. D. Hobson, *Crossroads: The Drama of a Soap Opera*, Methuen, 1982, p. 135.

69. P. Willis, *Common Culture: Symbolic work at play in the everyday cultures of the young*, Open University Press, 1990, p. 128.

70. *Ibid*, p. 18.

71. *Ibid*, p. 83.

72. *Ibid*, p. 20.

73. H. Schiller, *Culture Inc: The Corporate Takeover of Public Expression*, Oxford University Press, 1989, p. 153.

74. 'The Thatcher Legacy', *Economist*, 2 October 1993, p. 38. Davies was speaking to the Manchester Business School, 10 March 1994.

75. A. Gamble, *The Free Economy and the Strong State: The Politics of Thatcherism*, Macmillan, 1988, p. 207.

76. P. Heelas and P. Morris (eds.), *op. cit.*, p. 16.

77. *Woman's Own*, 31 October 1987.

IX: The Public Culture

1. *The Best Future For Britain*, Conservative Central Office, 1992, p. iii.

2. Interview with the author, 'State and the Arts', *Sunday Times*, 15 March 1992.

3. *The Best Future For Britain, op. cit.*, p. 44.

4. Lord Gowrie, speech in the House of Lords, 12 June 1996, reprinted in *Arts Council of England Annual Report 1995/96*, p. 7.

5. D. Mellor, 'Gambling on our culture', *Guardian*, 28 November 1996.

6. H. Colver 'Reflections of a departed media manipulator', *Guardian*, 10 November 1995.

7. Department of National Heritage press release, 3 December 1992, para 23.

8. Interview with the author, 'How the arts can avoid disaster', *Sunday Times*, 9 June 1996.

9. Official text of a speech by Stephen Dorrell at a DNH Regional Conference in Nottingham, 7 October 1994, p. 2.

10. D. Horne, *The Public Culture: The Triumph of Industrialism*, Pluto Press, 1986, pp. 183–4.

11. *Ibid.*, p. 59.

12. *Ibid.*, p. 189.

13. M. Fumaroli, *L'État Culturel: Essai sur une Religion Moderne*, Paris, Éditions de Fallois, 1992, p. 32. The translations are the author's.

14. *Ibid.*, p. 23.

15. D. Horne, *op. cit.*, p. 234.

16. I make the case for endowment funding in 'Cultural Policy and the Heritage Business', *European Journal of Cultural Policy*, Vol. 3, No. 1, (Nov 1996), pp. 1–13.

17. R. Williams, *Culture and Society 1780–1950* (first published Chatto & Windus, 1985), Penguin edition, 1961, p. 304.

INDEX